Free Speech and Human Dignity

STEVEN J. HEYMAN

Free Speech and Human Dignity

Yale University Press
New Haven &
London

Published with assistance from the Mary Cady Tew Memorial Fund.
Earlier versions of some of the arguments in this book appeared in the following
law journal articles, and they appear here with the following permissions:
Steven J. Heyman, *Ideological Conflict and the First Amendment*, 78 Chi.-Kent L.
Rev. 531 (2003), by permission of the Chicago-Kent Law Review; Steven J.
Heyman, *Righting the Balance: An Inquiry into the Foundations and Limits of
Freedom of Expression*, 78 B.U.L. Rev. 1275 (1998), by permission of the Boston
University Law Review; Steven J. Heyman, *Spheres of Autonomy: Reforming the
Content Neutrality Doctrine in First Amendment Jurisprudence*, 10 Wm. &
Mary Bill of Rts. J. 647 (2002), by permission, © William & Mary Bill of Rights
Journal.

Set in Sabon by Keystone Typesetting, Inc.
Printed in the United States of America.
Library of Congress Cataloging-in-Publication Data
Heyman, Steven J.
Free speech and human dignity / Steven J. Heyman.
p. cm.
Includes bibliographical references and index.
ISBN-13: 978-0-300-11486-7 (alk. paper)
ISBN-10: 0-300-11486-9
1. Freedom of speech — United States. 2. Civil rights — United States.
3. Hate speech — United States. 4. Dignity. I. Title.
KF4772.H49 2008
342.7308'53 — dc22   2007030931
A catalogue record for this book is available from the British Library.
The paper in this book meets the guidelines for permanence and durability of the
Committee on Production Guidelines for Book Longevity of the Council on
Library Resources.
10 9 8 7 6 5 4 3 2 1

For Kate and Andrew

Without freedom of thought, there can be no such thing as wisdom; and no such thing as publick liberty, without freedom of speech: Which is the right of every man, as far as by it he does not hurt and control the right of another.

— *Cato's Letters No. 15*

Congress shall make no law respecting an establishment of religion, or prohibiting the free exercise thereof; or abridging the freedom of speech, or of the press; or the right of the people peaceably to assemble, and to petition the Government for a redress of grievances.

— *First Amendment to the Constitution of the United States*

Contents

Tables

Acknowledgments

I could not have written this book without the support and encouragement of many friends and colleagues. For insightful comments on earlier versions of this work, I am grateful to Kate Baldwin, Felice Batlan, Vincent Blasi, Susan Brison, Harry Clor, Jacob Corré, Michael Curtis, Richard Delgado, James Fleming, Mark Graber, Carol Greenhouse, Thomas Grey, Daniel Hamilton, Sarah Harding, Hendrik Hartog, Dawn Johnsen, Charles Lawrence, Anna Marshall, Richard McAdams, Sheldon Nahmod, Robert Post, David Rabban, Mark Rosen, Steven Shiffrin, Stephen Siegel, Lawrence Solum, Jeremy Waldron, Robin West, David Williams, Susan Williams, and Adrianne Zahner. I want to thank those who participated in faculty workshops and symposia at Chicago-Kent College of Law, the University of Illinois College of Law, Indiana University School of Law-Bloomington, the University of Minnesota Law School, and Vanderbilt University Law School, as well as those who attended panels at meetings of the Association for the Study of Law, Culture, and the Humanities; the Law and Society Association; and the Midwest Seminar on the History of Early Modern Philosophy. I have also learned a good deal from the students in my seminar on First Amendment Theory.

I received indispensable financial support from the Norman and Edna Freehling Scholars Fund at Chicago-Kent as well as from my deans there, Richard Matasar, Henry Perritt, and Harold Krent. For excellent research assistance, I am indebted to Kerry Bartell, Anna Bednarski, Jack Burnett, Valerie Calhoun, Amanda Couture, Colleen Cullen, Diana Fridman, Elizabeth Katzman, Ted Koshiol, Jennifer O'Neill, Pamela Quigley, Catherine Traugott, Elena Vranas, Lisa Weier, Stephanie Wolfe, Adrianne Zahner, and Sarah Zielinski. Cheryl Simmons helped to proofread the book. I also want to express my appreciation to the research librarians at Chicago-Kent for their tireless and unfailing assistance.

My editor at Yale, Michael O'Malley, believed in this book from the beginning. I am grateful to him and to Lawrence Kenney, my manuscript editor, for improving it in crucial ways.

Over the years, I have been sustained and inspired by my friends Jacob Corré, Richard McAdams, Anna Marshall, David Williams, and Susan Williams. It is impossible to imagine better friends or more generous and stimulating colleagues. It is also a pleasure to acknowledge the influence of three extraordinary teachers: Harry Clor, who introduced me to American political and constitutional theory; the late Jerome Culp, my advisor at Harvard College; and the late Paul Freund, my mentor at Harvard Law School. For me they will always be models of profound and passionate inquiry in law. I owe my parents, Victor and Reba Heyman, more than I can express. Above all, I am grateful for the love and support of my wife, Kate, and my son, Andrew, who was always happy to discuss hypotheticals with me. This book is dedicated to them.

Introduction

The First Amendment right to freedom of expression is a defining feature of American society. Yet the scope and meaning of this right have always been controversial. In recent years, much of the debate has focused on issues like hate speech and pornography. Supporters of regulation argue that such speech causes serious injury to individuals and groups and that it assaults their dignity as human beings and citizens. Civil libertarians respond that our commitment to free expression is measured by our willingness to protect it even when it causes serious harm or offends our deepest values. When the issue is framed in this way, we seem to face a tragic choice, one in which we can protect human dignity only by sacrificing freedom of speech, and vice versa. But both of these values are essential to a liberal democratic society. In this way, hate speech and pornography seem to pose an intractable dilemma for the American constitutional order.

Moreover, the problem is not confined to those forms of speech but extends to First Amendment jurisprudence as a whole. Contemporary disputes often involve conflicts between free expression and other values. Yet we have no coherent framework that would allow us to determine when speech should receive constitutional protection and when it should be subject to regulation. As a result, controversies over freedom of speech often appear to be irresolvable.

To overcome these difficulties, we must transform our understanding of the

First Amendment by developing a theory that is capable of reconciling free speech with other values. That is the goal of this book. Freedom of expression, I shall argue, is founded on respect for the autonomy and dignity of human beings. At the same time, however, this principle also gives rise to other fundamental rights, ranging from personal security and privacy to citizenship and equality. As a general rule, speakers should be required to respect the fundamental rights of others. In this way, the same ideals that justify freedom of speech allow us to determine the limits of that freedom.

As I show in chapter 1, this understanding of the First Amendment has deep roots in American constitutional history. Eighteenth-century Americans held that freedom of speech was one of the natural rights of mankind and was essential to republican government. Like all rights, however, free speech was limited by the rights of others. In this way, the concept of rights provided a standard by which to assess regulations of speech. As chapter 2 explains, however, this traditional view no longer prevails. Instead, modern jurisprudence conceives of First Amendment issues not as conflicts of rights, but as conflicts between the individual right to free speech and "social interests" such as dignity and equality. But there is no clear way to resolve clashes between individual rights and social interests. When First Amendment problems are understood in this way, they seem to involve collisions between incommensurable values. That is one reason these disputes have become so bitter and divisive. The best way to escape this predicament is to return to a rights-based theory of the First Amendment.

Part 2 of the book develops such a theory, drawing both on the natural rights tradition and on modern understandings of rights. According to this theory, which is presented in chapters 3 and 4, rights are rooted in respect for human beings and their capacity for self-determination. Rights represent what it means for people to be free in various areas of life — not only in relation to the external world, but also in their inner lives, in the social and political realm, and in "the sphere of intellect and spirit."[1] These four elements of liberty correspond to the major justifications that have been advanced for freedom of speech: that it is an aspect of external freedom; that it is essential for individual self-realization; that it is indispensable to democratic self-government; and that it promotes the search for truth. But the same principles that support free speech also support other fundamental rights, including external rights to person and property; personality rights such as privacy and reputation; and rights of citizenship and participation in the society. As I shall explain, the people also have some rights as a community, including the rights to engage in political deliberation and to govern themselves through the democratic process.

On this view, freedom of speech must be exercised with due regard for the rights of other individuals and the community as a whole. Speech that infringes these rights should generally be regarded as wrongful and subject to regulation through narrowly drawn laws. In some cases, however, the value of the speech is so great that it should be protected despite the injury it causes. In chapter 5, I develop a general approach to cases of this sort, using the constitutional law of defamation as an illustration.

Chapter 6 contrasts this rights-based theory with the Supreme Court's current jurisprudence, which is based on the doctrine of content neutrality. That doctrine holds that "above all else, the First Amendment means that government has no power to restrict expression because of its message, its ideas, its subject matter, or its content."[2] Although this principle captures our strong commitment to freedom of expression, it is fatally one-sided, for it fails to recognize that some kinds of speech (such as defamation and incitement) inflict serious injury precisely because of their content. For this reason, the Court has carved out a series of exceptions to the content-neutrality doctrine. Yet the Justices have never succeeded in explaining the rationale for these exceptions or in squaring them with the general rule. As a result, the Court's First Amendment opinions often seem arbitrary and unpersuasive.

By contrast, I shall argue that the rights-based theory offers a more coherent and principled account of the First Amendment freedom of speech. Of course, I do not mean to say that this theory is capable of generating easy answers to free speech problems. As I have stressed, these problems typically involve important values on both sides. Individuals and groups will often disagree about the relative importance of these values and about how conflicts between them should be resolved. It follows that there will always be ideological disagreement over the scope of free speech. The goal of First Amendment theory should be not to eradicate such disagreement, but to develop a common language or framework within which we can engage in reasoned debate about controversial issues.

For several reasons, I believe that the rights-based theory is best suited to provide such a framework. First, as I have noted, this theory can find strong support in American constitutional history. Second, a belief in rights is deeply embedded in our contemporary political culture. In many cases, the supporters and opponents of regulation are already inclined to state their positions in the language of rights. By the same token, I believe that the principle that freedom of speech is limited by the rights of others is capable of having strong intuitive appeal, not only to the advocates themselves but also to the public at large. Third, the notion of rights plays a pervasive role in American law. Thus, the theory does not require lawyers and judges to use new or unfamiliar concepts, but instead invites them to determine the boundaries of free speech in part by reference to concepts that have been carefully developed in other areas, such as torts, criminal law, and constitutional law. Finally, the theory of rights that I shall develop is based on the idea of mutual recognition and respect: rights instantiate the respect that individuals owe one another as human beings and citizens. Understood in this manner, the idea of rights may offer a way to overcome the deep divisions and mistrust that mark current debates over freedom of expression.

The final part of the book applies the rights-based theory to a wide range of First Amendment controversies. In accord with the civil libertarian tradition, chapter 7 argues that the Constitution should afford strong protection to revolutionary speech, flag burning, and other forms of expression that criticize the government or the existing political order. By contrast, I believe that the state should have greater authority to regulate speech that is directed against individuals or groups. As I explain in chapter 8, some forms of expression — such as incitement, threats, and fighting words — should be denied constitutional protection because they infringe the fundamental right to personal security or freedom from violence. In chapter 9, I argue that the state should also be allowed to protect the right to privacy against unreasonable intrusion or exposure. I then apply this view to a variety of contemporary problems, including sidewalk counseling at abortion clinics, protests at military funerals, and news reports that reveal the identity of rape victims. Finally, in chapters 10 and 11, I contend that some forms of hate speech and pornography can be regulated on the ground that they violate the most basic right of all — the right to recognition as a human being and a member of the community.

In short, this book argues that freedom of expression should be understood within a broader conception of rights based on human dignity and autonomy. This view recognizes a strong, liberal right to freedom of expression, at the same time that it affords protection against the most serious forms of "assaultive speech."[3] In this way, it seeks to develop some common ground between civil libertarianism and its critics.

The view I present may also be called a liberal humanist theory of the First Amendment. It is liberal in its emphasis on the protection of individual rights; it is humanist in holding that those rights are founded on respect for the intrinsic worth of human beings and are meant to enable them to develop their nature to the fullest extent. I believe that a theory of this sort offers the best hope of reconciling our competing commitments to human dignity and freedom of speech.

PART I

History

Free Speech and the Natural Rights Tradition

In part 1 of the book I explore the natural rights tradition and its impact on the American understanding of freedom of speech. After tracing the rise of Lockean thought in seventeenth- and eighteenth-century England, I show how this view informed the adoption of the First Amendment as well as the first state declarations of rights. I then examine the controversy surrounding the Sedition Act of 1798, the first major debate over the meaning of the First Amendment. Next, I sketch the ideological background of the Fourteenth Amendment, which provides the basis for applying the First Amendment to the states. Finally, in chapter 2, I discuss the fate of natural rights in modern free speech jurisprudence.

Of course, this part of the book does not seek to present a comprehensive history of American thought on freedom of speech.[1] Instead, my goal is to highlight the role that one important idea — the concept of natural rights — has played in our constitutional tradition and to explain why I believe that this idea provides the best starting point for developing an adequate First Amendment theory for our own time.[2]

The English Background

To articulate the nature and scope of freedom of speech, eighteenth-century Americans drew on a variety of sources, including the common law and the civic-republican tradition. But the broadest framework they looked to was provided by the theory of natural rights and the social contract. As developed in the works of John Locke, this theory sought to determine the purpose and the limits of government by tracing its rise from a state of nature. In that state, individuals have an inherent right to liberty, which Locke defines as the power to control one's own person, actions, and possessions without interference by others. The right to liberty is not absolute, however. Instead, it is subject to the constraints of the law of nature, which enjoins individuals to respect the freedom, equality, and rights of others. To secure themselves against aggression, individuals agree to form a society for mutual aid and protection. In so doing, they alienate a portion of their natural liberty to the community, which is empowered to regulate conduct to the extent necessary to protect individual rights and promote the common good.[3]

At the same time, however, Locke insists that some elements of liberty are inalienable and are not surrendered by individuals when they enter society. These forms of liberty are not subject to legislative regulation for the public good, although like other rights they are limited by the duty to respect the rights of others.[4] In addition to religious liberty, the category of inalienable rights includes freedom of thought in general.[5] This right is not only inherent in individuals but lies at the foundation of liberty. According to Locke, human freedom and dignity are ultimately grounded in reason, that is, in our capacity as rational beings to determine our own thoughts and actions. Locke therefore condemns those rulers who seek to "enslave[]" their subjects "in that which should be the freest part of Man, their Understandings."[6]

As this discussion suggests, Locke's account of freedom of thought has an important political dimension. When individuals enter into the social contract, they give up their natural freedom to ascertain and defend their own rights and transfer this power to the community, to be used for the protection of all of its members. It follows that all political authority is originally vested in the community as a whole. In turn, the community generally delegates this power to a particular government. According to Locke, however, the people always retain the right to determine whether the government, as their "Trustee or Deputy," has acted contrary to its trust. In this way, Locke not only justifies a right to revolution, but implicitly lays the foundation for the eighteenth-century libertarian doctrine of political freedom of speech.[7]

These implications of Lockean thought were developed more fully by later writers, especially the radical Whigs John Trenchard and Thomas Gordon. In a work called *Cato's Letters*, first published in the 1720s, Trenchard and Gordon defended and popularized Locke's theory of natural rights, the social contract, and the right to revolution.[8] At the same time, they infused that theory with a strong civic-republican emphasis on the active role of the people in politics.[9] The rhetorical power of this view is evident in Cato's famous essay on freedom of speech. Relying on the Lockean premise that "[t]he administration of government is nothing else, but the attendance of the trustees of the people upon the interest and affairs of the people," Cato argued that the people had a right to oversee public affairs in order to determine whether they were being properly conducted. Drawing on English constitutional history as well as on classical republican writers such as Livy, Plutarch, and Tacitus, Cato declared that freedom of speech was "the great bulwark of liberty," protecting the people against tyranny by preventing and exposing abuses of power.[10]

For Cato, the right to "think what you would, and speak what you thought" was not merely a barrier against government oppression; it was also an essential element of natural liberty. "Government," he argued, "being intended to protect men from the injuries of one another, and not to direct them in their own affairs, in which no one is interested but themselves; it is plain that their thoughts and domestick concerns are exempted entirely from its jurisdiction." The natural right to free speech was limited only by the obligation to respect the rights of others, by "injur[ing] neither the society, nor any of its members." For example, private defamation was wrongful because it violated the individual right to reputation. But Cato expressed strong reservations about the traditional law of seditious libel, which punished even true statements critical of the government or its officials. Although he acknowledged that political libels might foment causeless discontents among the people, he contended that this harm was outweighed by the benefits of having "some check upon [official] behaviour, by . . . warning other people to be upon their guard against oppression." The law of libel had to be carefully confined if it was not to become an instrument of tyranny. In particular, Cato asserted that truthful accusations of public wrongdoing "can never be a libel in the nature of things."[11]

The most powerful conservative response to this view came from Sir William Blackstone, whose *Commentaries on the Law of England* appeared in the late 1760s. Although Blackstone conceded that "[t]he liberty of the press is . . . essential to the nature of a free state," he insisted that this liberty "consists in laying no *previous* restraints upon publications, and not in freedom from censure for criminal matter when published." Thus, the traditional common law, which punished not only private libels but also seditious, blasphemous, and offensive publications, was fully consistent with a free press.[12]

To a modern reader, Blackstone's position appears not merely crabbed but virtually incomprehensible. How can the liberty of the press allow one to publish whatever one pleases, yet afford no protection against subsequent punishment? To understand Blackstone's view, we must briefly explore his political theory.

Following Locke, Blackstone held that "the principal aim of society is to protect individuals in the enjoyment of those absolute rights, which were vested in them by the immutable laws of nature." He identified those rights as personal security (including the right to life), personal liberty, and private property. A major objective of the *Commentaries* was to rationalize the English constitution and the common law by showing the ways in which they protected these natural rights.[13]

Despite holding this common ground with Locke and Cato, however, Blackstone portrayed natural liberty in a less positive light. Although he asserted that such liberty was "a right inherent in us by birth, and one of the gifts of God to man at his creation," Blackstone also subscribed to the traditional Christian doctrine that human nature had become fallen and corrupt. Natural liberty was a "wild and savage" condition which was "infinitely [less] desirable" than the "legal obedience and conformity" that characterized organized society. For Blackstone, the function of society was not merely to protect natural rights but also to civilize human beings. He therefore emphasized the extent to which natural liberty was alienable and subject to regulation by laws made by the community for the public good — a good that embraced not only the rights of individuals, but also social values such as order, morality, and religion.[14]

Blackstone also gave a different account of political authority. Distancing himself from the Lockean doctrine that all power is initially vested in the people, Blackstone contended that when individuals entered into society they agreed to submit to the authority of those they regarded as best capable of governing for the public good. The evidence of this general consent was long-standing tradition. In England, the legislative authority, which was the supreme power in any state, was vested in a Parliament consisting of the king, the aristocracy, and representatives of the people themselves, while the executive power belonged to the king alone.[15]

In contrast to Locke and Cato, Blackstone stressed the hierarchical relationship between rulers and their subjects. Indeed, the very idea of law was that of a "rule of action, which is prescribed by some superior, and which the inferior is bound to obey." A "due subordination of rank" was essential in a well-governed society, so that "the people may know . . . such as are set over them, in order to yield them their due respect and obedience."[16]

In accord with the Whig tradition, Blackstone recognized that the powers of the king as supreme executive were limited by laws declaring the rights of the people, such as the Magna Carta and the Bill of Rights. Moreover, Blackstone defended the English Revolution of 1688, in which the Lords and Commons had declared that King James II's attempts to subvert the constitution amounted to an abdication of the throne. At the same time, however, Blackstone criticized the Lockean theory of revolution, endorsed by "some zealous republicans," which "would have reduced the society almost to a state of nature," leveled all distinctions of property, rank, and authority, overturned all positive laws, and left the people free to establish a new social and political regime.[17] In short, while *Cato's Letters* synthesized natural rights theory with civic republicanism, Blackstone fused that theory with the ideology of the traditional legal, political, and social order.

We are now in a better position to understand Blackstone's views on liberty of the press. For Blackstone, thought and expression were elements of natural liberty. To compel the press to submit to prior censorship would violate that liberty by making the executive "an arbitrary and infallible judge of all controverted points in learning, religion, and government." The press became "properly free" in 1694, when Parliament refused to renew the law authorizing such censorship. The result, however, was merely to place publication on a par with other forms of freedom. For Blackstone, expression was an alienable right which was subject to regulation for the common good. Publications that violated laws against seditious, blasphemous, defamatory, or immoral writings constituted not liberty but licentiousness. Accordingly, Blackstone argued that to subject the authors of such writings to subsequent punishment under the law was "necessary for the preservation of peace and good order, of government and religion, the only solid foundations of civil liberty." This was especially true of libels against public officials: whether true or false, such accusations undermined the respect for authority upon which government depended.[18]

Natural Rights and the Founding of the American Republics

STATE DECLARATIONS OF RIGHTS

As Bernard Bailyn and Gordon S. Wood have shown, the revolutionary ideology of Locke and the radical Whigs had a profound impact on American political thought.[19] In addition to providing the justification for the American Revolution, this ideology was clearly reflected in the bills of rights that accompanied many of the first state constitutions. For example, the Pennsylvania Declaration of Rights opened with an assertion that "all men are born equally free and independent, and have certain natural, inherent and inalienable rights, amongst which are, the enjoying and defending life and liberty, acquiring, possessing and protecting property, and pursuing and obtaining happiness and safety." "[A]ll power," the declaration continued, is "originally inherent in, and consequently derived from, the people; therefore all officers of the government, whether legislative or executive, are their trustees and servants, and at all times accountable to them." In addition to many other personal rights, the declaration maintained that "the people have a right to freedom of speech, and of writing, and publishing their sentiments: therefore the freedom of the press ought not to be restrained."[20]

In this way Pennsylvania placed liberty of speech and press squarely within the framework of natural rights and popular sovereignty. Similarly, the Virginia Declaration of Rights echoed *Cato's Letters* in asserting that "the freedom of the Press is one of the greatest bulwarks of liberty, and can never be restrained but by despotick Governments." At the same time, Americans agreed with Cato that free expression was limited by the rights of others, including the right to reputation. For example, while the Massachusetts declaration provided that the liberty of the press "ought not . . . to be restrained in this Commonwealth," it also declared that "[e]ach individual in the society has a right to be protected by it" and therefore "ought to find a certain remedy, by having recourse to the laws, for all injuries or wrongs which he may receive in his person, property, or *character*."[21]

The same view was expressed in the writings of Thomas Jefferson. In accord with radical Whig ideology, Jefferson regarded freedom of speech as a natural right and freedom of the press as an important barrier against governmental oppression.[22] In his various efforts to draft constitutional protections for those rights, however, Jefferson made clear that they did not extend to false statements injurious to others.[23]

THE ADOPTION OF THE FIRST AMENDMENT

When a new Federal Constitution was proposed in 1787, the most powerful objection leveled against it was that it lacked a bill of rights. In particular, Antifederalists denounced the document's failure to protect liberty of speech and press, which they characterized as inalienable rights of human nature and invaluable bulwarks against tyranny.[24] In response, Federalists contended that a bill of rights was unnecessary. As James Wilson of Pennsylvania explained, when the people adopted state constitutions, they "invested their representatives with every right and authority which they did not in explicit terms reserve." Thus, bills of rights might be required to protect liberty against invasion by state governments. By contrast, under the Federal Constitution, the people would retain all the rights and powers they did not delegate to the government. Among other things, Wilson and his allies insisted that the Constitution granted Congress no power to interfere with the liberty of the press.[25]

Arguments of this sort, however, were unable to overcome the popular desire for a bill of rights. Several state conventions recommended amendments at the same time they ratified the new Constitution, while other states refused to ratify until such amendments were adopted. The amendments were drawn largely from the state declarations of rights and reflected their radical Whig principles. The first state proposal regarding freedom of expression, which came from the Virginia Convention, read, "That the people have a right to freedom of speech, and of writing and publishing their sentiments; that the freedom of the press is one of the greatest bulwarks of liberty, and ought not to be violated." This recommendation, which was to form the basis for James Madison's draft of the First Amendment, combined the Pennsylvania declaration's focus on free speech as a natural right with the Virginia declaration's Catonian description of liberty of the press as a safeguard against abuse of power. At the same time, these freedoms were clearly regarded as limited by the rights of others, such as reputation, for the Virginia amendments included a provision that "every freeman ought to find a certain remedy, by recourse to the laws, for all injuries and wrongs he may receive in his person, property, or character."[26]

In June 1789, Madison introduced his proposal for a bill of rights in the First Congress. In a major speech, he observed that the prevailing American view was that constitutional safeguards were required to secure the liberties of the people. Acting on this belief, "the people of many states have found it necessary to raise barriers against power in all forms and departments of government." Although numerous objections had been raised to the new Constitution, most people who opposed it did so because of the absence of a bill of rights. To satisfy this demand, Madison urged his colleagues to "expressly declare the great rights of mankind secured under this constitution," by adopting guarantees for liberty similar to those contained in the state declarations of rights. Madison observed that those documents protected several different kinds of rights, including (1) the political rights that "are exercised by the people in forming and establishing a plan of government"; (2) the "natural right[s]" that the people "retain[] when particular powers are given up to be exercised by the legislature"; and (3) "positive rights" like trial by jury, which arise from "the social compact which regulates the action of the community, but [which are] as essential to secure the liberty of the people as any one of the pre-existent rights of nature." Madison proposed to incorporate protections for all of these classes of rights in the Federal Constitution.[27]

Adopting the natural rights language of the Virginia Convention, Madison's draft of the First Amendment read: "The people shall not be deprived or abridged of their right to speak, to write, or to publish their sentiments; and the freedom of the press, as one of the great bulwarks of liberty, shall be inviolable." Madison's notes confirm that he regarded free speech as a paradigmatic natural right.[28]

The natural rights basis of the First Amendment emerges most clearly in the version written by Roger Sherman of Connecticut, a member of the House committee that was charged with drawing up a bill of rights. Sherman's draft (which evidently played an important role in the evolution of the text) declared, "The people have certain natural rights which are retained by them when they enter into society, [*sic*] Such are the rights of conscience in matters of religion; of acquiring property, and of pursuing happiness and safety; of Speaking, writing and publishing their Sentiments with decency and freedom; of peaceably Assembling to consult their common good, and of applying to Government by petition or remonstrance for redress of grievances. Of these rights therefore they Shall not be deprived by the government of the united States." Theodore Sedgwick of Massachusetts sounded a similar note during the House debates when he observed that speech and assembly were among the "self-evident unalienable right[s]" of the people.[29]

In short, the First Amendment embodied the same principles as the Revolutionary state declarations of rights: that the freedoms of speech and press were inalienable rights of individuals as well as essential means by which the sovereign people could oversee the conduct of public affairs and check governmental abuse of power. These beliefs were widely held in late eighteenth-century America.

At the same time, however, this consensus concealed an important disagreement over the scope of free expression—a disagreement that reflected the political and ideological struggles of the founding period. As Wood has shown, although the Revolution was animated by radical Whig ideology, during the 1780s social elites increasingly came to believe that, under the state governments, popular liberty and democracy were degenerating into licentiousness. Much of the support for the Federalist movement came from the desire of these elites to establish stronger government and restore respect for property rights, social rank, and political authority.[30] Although conservatives did not reject the Revolutionary conception of free speech, they did not believe that this right extended to unwarranted attacks on public officials. Accordingly, they defended the concept of seditious libel, at least in the case of false accusations. This position put them at odds with libertarians, who supported a broad right to free expression and were sharply critical of the traditional law of seditious libel.

The conflict between these two positions can be illustrated by an exchange in the Pennsylvania Ratifying Convention. The Antifederalist John Smilie had contended that, under the proposed Constitution, Congress would have power to pass laws against libels, thereby endangering the freedom of the press. The Federalist leader James Wilson replied, "I presume it was not in the view of the honorable gentleman to say there is no such thing as a libel, or that the writers of such should not be punished. The idea of the liberty of the press is not carried so far as this in any country. What is meant by the liberty of the press is, that there should be no antecedent restraint upon it; but that every author is responsible when he attacks the security or welfare of the government, or the safety, character, and property of the individual." Wilson insisted, however, that the Constitution would give "the general government no power whatsoever concerning [the press]; and no law, in pursuance of the Constitution, can possibly be enacted to destroy that liberty."[31]

By adopting the First Amendment, the framers expressly declared that the freedoms of speech and press should be protected. But they made no effort to resolve the dispute between libertarians and conservatives over the scope of those freedoms or the issue of seditious libel. Political constraints made it impossible for them to do so.[32] Under Article V of the Constitution, the document could be amended only with the approval of two-thirds of each House of Congress and three-fourths of the state legislatures. To garner such broad support, the Bill of Rights had to be formulated in a way that was acceptable to Federalists and Antifederalists alike. The framers therefore made a conscious decision to draft the Bill of Rights in the form of general principles, while avoiding particular issues that might be divisive. This point was expressed by Madison himself during the House debate over the First Amendment. "[I]f we confine ourselves to an enumeration of simple acknowledged principles," he stated, "the ratification will meet with but little difficulty." By contrast, to pursue amendments of a controversial nature "obliges us to run the risk of losing the whole system." Echoing these sentiments, Sedgwick urged House members to avoid controversial proposals which were "more likely to produce acrimony, than that spirit of harmony which we ought to cultivate."[33]

In this way, Madison and his colleagues were able to obtain the broad agreement they needed to adopt the Bill of Rights. But this consensus could be maintained only at a general level. When the First Amendment came to be applied to particular issues, it would inevitably be subject to conflicting interpretations that were informed by divergent ideological views.

The Sedition Act Controversy

This conflict was not long in coming. During the 1790s, American politics was dominated by increasingly bitter divisions between the governing Federalists and the Republican opposition led by Jefferson and Madison.[34] Alarmed by what they saw as the Federalists' aristocratic and even monarchical tendencies, as well as by the efforts of Treasury Secretary Alexander Hamilton to create a strong, centralized economic system, the Republicans accused their opponents of seeking to undermine democracy and erect a consolidated national government on the ruins of the states. In turn, the Federalists attacked the Jeffersonians as dangerous subversives, both in their domestic politics and in their sympathy with the French Revolution. During the summer of 1798, at the height of fears over incipient war with France, the Federalist-controlled Congress passed the Sedition Act. This statute, which was designed to suppress strident attacks from the Republican press, made it a criminal offense to publish "any false, scandalous and malicious writing" against the government, the Congress, or the President of the United States, "with intent to defame [them] or to bring them . . . into contempt or disrepute; or to excite against them . . . the hatred of the good people of the United States."[35]

The Sedition Act provoked a firestorm of controversy. The Republican-dominated legislatures of Virginia and Kentucky denounced the law as unconstitutional, while their Federalist counterparts in other states supported it. The most powerful Federalist defense of the Act's constitutionality was written by John Marshall on behalf of the Virginia minority. The First Amendment, Marshall observed, barred Congress only from passing laws "ABRIDGING the freedom of speech or of the press." But the liberty of the press had a well-defined and "completely understood" meaning under the common law: "It signifies a liberty to publish, free from previous restraint, any thing and every thing at the discretion of the printer only, but not the liberty of spreading with impunity false and scandalous slanders which may destroy the peace and mangle the reputation of an individual or of a community." In short, "[a] punishment of the licentiousness is not considered as a restriction of the freedom of the press."[36]

At the same time that he invoked Blackstone's conception of the liberty of the press, Marshall (like Wilson before him) attempted to restate that view in terms more acceptable to Americans.[37] For example, while Blackstone defended the common law's proscription of blasphemous as well as defamatory and seditious libels, Marshall confined his argument to defamation and sedition, stressing the ways in which such expression violated the rights of other individuals and the community as a whole. Moreover, he treated sedition as an injury less to the government than to the people themselves, who had established the government to promote their safety and happiness. In these ways, Marshall sought to reconcile the traditional notion of sedition with American concepts of liberty and popular sovereignty.[38]

Responding for the Republicans, Madison contended that the Federalist position was at war with those concepts. According to Madison, Blackstone's narrow view of freedom of the press as the absence of previous restraints "can never be admitted to be the American idea of it," for it "would seem a mockery to say that no laws should be passed preventing publications from being made, but that laws might be passed punishing them in case they should be made." Madison traced the disparity between the two conceptions to the "essential difference between the British Government and the American Constitutions." In Great Britain, the protections of the Magna Carta and the Bill of Rights were aimed only at the king, while the people's representatives in the legislature were regarded as unlimited in their power and as "sufficient guardians of the rights of their constituents." "Under such a government as this," Madison reasoned, "an exemption of the press from previous restraint, by licensors appointed by the king, is all the freedom that can be secured to it." In America, by contrast, the people's rights were secured not merely by laws but by constitutions, and were guarded from invasion by the legislature as well as by the executive. It followed that in America the press was entitled to protection not only from prior restraint by executive officials, but also from subsequent punishment under legislative enactments.[39]

Madison proceeded to address the Federalist claim that, even if press freedom extended beyond protection against prior censorship, its substantive scope must be determined by reference to the English common law. Once more, he argued that the different nature of the two governments required a broader view. In the United States, unlike Great Britain, the people had a right to elect both the legislature and the executive. To exercise this right — which constituted "the essence of free and responsible government" — the people had to be free to discuss the relative merits and demerits of candidates. Moreover, in such a government the people retained the right to judge whether public officials had properly discharged their trust. Echoing the radical Whigs, Madison asserted that, to the extent that officials failed to perform their duties, "it is natural and proper, that . . . they should be brought into contempt or disrepute, and incur the hatred of the people." Although he acknowledged that the Sedition Act had departed from the common law and allowed truth as a defense, Madison denied that this defense provided adequate protection for free speech. Even where facts alone were at issue, it might be difficult to prove them in court. Moreover, sedition prosecutions would often be brought on account of opinions critical of the government, and opinions were not provable before a court in the same way facts were. For all of these reasons, Madison concluded (in the words of the Virginia Resolutions) that the Sedition Act struck at the heart of republican government "because it is levelled against that right of freely examining public characters and measures, and of free communication among the people thereon, which has ever been justly deemed the only effectual guardian of every other right."[40]

In opposing the Sedition Act, the Republicans relied not only on the principle of free expression, but also on the notion of federalism, that is, the proper division of authority between the national government and the states. In particular, the Jeffersonians argued (1) that the original Constitution granted Congress no power over the press; and (2) that the First Amendment was intended to make clear that Congress had absolutely no such power, while reserving any legitimate authority in this area to the states.[41] The first point had strong support in the original understanding: during the ratification debates, Wilson and other Federalists had asserted countless times that Congress could exercise only those powers enumerated in the Constitution, and that those powers did not extend to the press.[42]

By contrast, the Republicans' second point — that the First Amendment "was meant as a positive denial to Congress of any power whatever on the subject"[43] — was more doubtful. Although Wilson's arguments during the ratification debates were ingenious, they failed to persuade the Antifederalists, or the people in general, that their liberties were adequately protected by the structure of the Federal Constitution or that a bill of rights was unnecessary. Following the recommendations of the ratifying conventions, Madison modeled his proposed amendments on the state declarations of rights — documents that were concerned not with allocating power between different levels of government, but with securing substantive rights.[44] In his speech of June 1789, Madison emphasized the parallels between the national Bill of Rights and its state counterparts. His proposal also included an amendment that provided, in similar language, that "[n]o state shall violate the equal rights of conscience, or the freedom of the press," on the ground that "it is proper that every government should be disarmed of powers which trench upon those particular rights."[45] It seems clear, then, that at this point in 1789 Madison regarded his draft of the First Amendment as imposing the same limitations on the federal government that the state declarations imposed on the states. Nothing in the House debates contradicts this understanding. As passed by the House, the speech and press clauses that applied to the national government, as well as the parallel restrictions on the states, were formulated as substantive protections for liberty.[46]

When the Bill of Rights was considered in the Senate, the state restrictions were abandoned, and the federal provision was recast to begin with the words, "Congress shall make no law." This provision was later consolidated with the amendment on religion, which already began with those words.[47] This is the language that provides the strongest basis for the federalism reading of the First Amendment, both in the Sedition Act debates and in the writings of several modern constitutional historians.[48] The language itself, however, does not make clear whether it is an absolute denial of federal power or a protection of substantive rights. Unfortunately, the Senate's reasons for altering the House language are obscure: during this period, the Senate met behind closed doors, and its debates were not published. Although the Senate's changes may have been intended to transform the First Amendment into a federalism provision, it is at least as likely that the Amendment was meant to ensure that, if any of Congress's powers could affect the press, they would be limited by the same principles that applied to the state governments under their own declarations of rights. Certainly it cannot be said that, when the First Amendment was adopted, there was a clear and widely held understanding that the speech and press clauses were federalism provisions rather than substantive protections for rights. For this reason, the Republicans' absolutist, federalism-based reading of the First Amendment was not wholly convincing.

Although the Republicans denied all national power over the press, they did not regard the freedoms of speech and press themselves as absolute. Some Jeffersonians accepted the law of seditious libel, as modified by the defense of truth, while others repudiated that law.[49] Nearly all Republicans, however, believed that freedom of expression was limited by the rights of others. The jurist St. George Tucker expressed the standard Republican position in its broadest form when he wrote, "Liberty of speech and of discussion in all speculative matters, consists in the absolute and uncontrollable right of speaking, writing, and publishing, our opinions concerning any subject, whether religious, philosophical, or political; and of inquiring into and . . . examining the nature of truth, whether moral or metaphysical; the expediency or inexpediency of all public measures, with their tendency and probable effect; the conduct of public men, and generally every other subject, without restraint, *except as to the injury of any other individual, in his person, property, or good name.*"[50] Republicans insisted, however, that the protection of individual rights belonged to the states rather than to the federal government. In Madison's words, individuals were required to seek "a remedy for their injured reputations, under the same laws, and in the same tribunals, which protect their lives, their liberties, and their properties."[51]

Although Federalist judges consistently upheld the Sedition Act, the political controversy it generated played an important role in what Jefferson called the "Revolution of 1800," in which the Republicans won a sweeping electoral victory and took control of the national government. Acting on the belief that the law was unconstitutional, Jefferson pardoned those convicted of violating it.[52] In this way, it may be said that the Sedition Act controversy was resolved in favor of the Republican position.

This was the right result. It is true that, when the framers adopted the First

Amendment, they did not attempt to resolve the specific question of whether the doctrine of seditious libel was consistent with the freedom of speech. In a broader sense, however, the Sedition Act undeniably transgressed the original understanding of the First Amendment. The Amendment was adopted to assure the Antifederalists and the people at large that the great power of the federal government would not be used to suppress dissent or to interfere with the role of the press in canvassing public affairs and criticizing government officials. By endeavoring to crush political opposition through the Sedition Act, the Federalists of 1798 flagrantly violated this pledge. More fundamentally, the Act was incompatible with the principles of natural rights and popular sovereignty on which the American conception of free speech was based. In Madison's words, that conception held that, in a "Republican Government, . . . the censorial power is in the people over the Government, and not in the Government over the people."[53]

Although the libertarian position prevailed during the crisis of 1798–1800, that is by no means the end of the story. The Blackstonian conservative view was deeply engrained in the Anglo-American legal tradition, and it had a strong influence on American law for a long time to come.[54] The liberal revolution in First Amendment jurisprudence did not take place until the twentieth century.[55] The Sedition Act itself was finally laid to rest in *New York Times Co. v. Sullivan* (1964), which declared that "the attack upon its validity has carried the day in the court of history."[56]

While the founding period saw sharp disagreements over liberty of speech and press, there was also a broad area of consensus. Late eighteenth-century Americans believed that freedom of thought, belief, and expression were among the natural rights of mankind. These freedoms were also regarded as inherent in republican citizenship, allowing the people to express their views on public affairs and to guard their liberties against governmental encroachment—a right which extended at least to leveling true allegations against public officials (as the Sedition Act itself recognized). There was also wide agreement that, as natural rights, the freedoms of speech and press were limited by the rights of other individuals. Finally, most Americans believed that those freedoms were also bounded by the rights of the community, such as the right to preserve the public peace.[57]

Free Speech, Natural Rights, and the Fourteenth Amendment

As originally adopted, the Bill of Rights applied solely to the federal government. Only after the adoption of the Fourteenth Amendment did the rights of American citizenship gain national protection against state abridgment.[58] The historical background of this Amendment sheds further light on the meaning of the constitutional guarantees for freedom of expression.

The ideological origins of the Fourteenth Amendment lay in the antislavery movement that intensified in the decades before the Civil War.[59] The opponents of slavery denounced it as a violation of the natural rights proclaimed in the Declaration of Independence. Beginning in the 1830s, antislavery agitation encountered a wave of repression, through mob violence as well as official censorship. In response, antislavery activists strongly defended freedom of expression, which they described as an inalienable right protected by the American constitutions.[60] In accord with the natural rights tradition, antislavery figures acknowledged that this freedom did not authorize violations of the rights of others. This point was expressed most clearly by James G. Birney, a leading abolitionist activist, publisher, and two-time presidential candidate of the antislavery Liberty Party.[61] After declaring that the freedom to publish opinions was an inherent right of "man as a moral, intelligent, and active being," Birney stated that this freedom (like all such rights) was nevertheless subject to "this limitation — that [it] be not exercised, so as to impair the equally precious rights of others. A right pushed to this extremity is no longer a right — it becomes a *wrong*." For example, if you injure another person through "false and slanderous words, . . . you commit a wrong, for which [the law] will compel you . . . to make reparation." Birney added that, even when an act of expression was wrongful, freedom of speech and press required that the wrong "be prevented, precisely as other wrongs in society are prevented" — not by "*previous* restraint," which "amounts to a censorship destructive of the right," but by "punishment for its *abuse*."[62] Like other abolitionists, however, Birney insisted that there was nothing improper about discussing the morality of institutions such as slavery.[63]

The antislavery Republican party came to power in the national elections of 1860.[64] After the Civil War, the Republicans secured the adoption of two constitutional amendments that were intended to more effectually protect natural rights: the Thirteenth, which abolished slavery, and the Fourteenth, which barred the states from abridging the fundamental rights of American citizens. These rights were understood to include those enumerated in the Bill of Rights.[65] In particular, Republicans expressed a strong desire to protect the freedoms of speech and press, which they characterized as natural rights and rights of American citizenship and which they stressed had repeatedly been violated by the southern states before, during, and after the war.[66] The Republicans' discussion of freedom of speech and press during the Reconstruction Amendment debates was confined to general terms and sheds little light on the scope of these freedoms. It seems clear, however, that the Amendment's supporters accepted the principle (which was axiomatic in the natural rights tradition and generally accepted at the time) that these freedoms did not extend to expression that violated the rights of others, such as threats, incitement, and defamation.[67] Mid-nineteenth-century works on constitutional law expressed the same view.[68]

The Transformation of Free Speech Jurisprudence

The natural rights background of the First and Fourteenth Amendments suggests a principle that is capable of providing the basis for a normative theory of freedom of expression. This principle holds that free speech is an inherent right that is limited by the rights of other individuals and the community itself. Although this principle was widely accepted when the Bill of Rights and the Reconstruction Amendments were adopted, it no longer holds a central place in American constitutional theory or doctrine. Instead, modern jurisprudence understands First Amendment problems in terms of an opposition between free speech and "state interests."

In this chapter, I sketch the development of this modern view and contrast it with the classical libertarian position I described in chapter 1. I then argue that the modern approach is irredeemably flawed because it is incapable of resolving conflicts between free speech and other values. The best way to overcome this difficulty is to return to a rights-based understanding of the foundations and limits of freedom of expression.

The Rise of Modern First Amendment Jurisprudence

American legal thought underwent a transformation after the Civil War. During the late nineteenth and early twentieth centuries, the idea of natural rights gave way to a more positivist and utilitarian conception of law. On this view, the function of law was not to protect fundamental rights, but rather to promote social welfare as defined by the community or the state.

One of the leading figures in this development was Oliver Wendell Holmes, Jr. As Morton J. Horwitz has recounted, although Holmes "enlisted in the Civil War 'as a convinced abolitionist,'" his experience of the war's bloodshed and upheaval led him to regard natural rights doctrines as a threat to social order — an attitude that "he shared with much of late-nineteenth-century American culture."[1] In his jurisprudential writings, Holmes rejected Lockean and Kantian notions of the inherent freedom and worth of individuals.[2] In particular, he contended that legal and constitutional interpretation should be divorced from any notion of "the rights of man in a moral sense." Rights had no independent existence but derived their force entirely from positive law, which sought to promote social ends. At bottom, legal disputes involved clashes between different interests, clashes which could be resolved only by "weighing considerations of social advantage."[3]

This interest-oriented approach to law was developed more fully in the sociological jurisprudence of Roscoe Pound, a professor and later dean at Harvard Law School. Like Holmes, Pound rejected traditional natural rights theory and instead contended that "[a]s social institutions, state and law exist for social ends." One way the legal system promoted those ends was by recognizing and protecting certain individual interests, which thereby attained the status of legal rights. Pound insisted, however, that such interests were not entitled to protection for their own sake, but only (in the words of John Dewey) as means to "'the general happiness or the common good.'" For example, while the law's first concern was to prevent violence, it did so not to protect "the so-called natural rights of physical integrity and of personal liberty," but rather to secure "the social interest in preserving the peace."[4]

According to Pound, law was concerned not only with individual interests but also with "public interests," which he defined as "the interests of the state as a juristic person," and with "social interests," or "the interests of the community at large." As a pragmatist, he believed that human interests ought to be satisfied as far as possible. Because interests conflicted with one another, they could not all be fulfilled. The legal system must therefore balance competing interests to determine how far each should be secured. Because law was a social institution, however, it was ultimately concerned only with social interests. Strictly speaking, then, the law took into account not individual interests as such, but rather "the social interest in securing the individual interest."[5]

In criticizing individual-rights theories and emphasizing the social purposes of law, Holmes and Pound articulated themes that were to become central to much early twentieth-century progressive thought. In this way, their views played a critical role in the legal and constitutional revolution that culminated in the New Deal.[6]

The progressive critique of rights was directed primarily against the extreme defense of property symbolized by *Lochner v. New York* (1905), which held that a maximum-hours law that sought to protect workers from exploitation violated an unwritten right to "liberty of contract" enshrined in the Fourteenth Amendment. At the same time, however, the progressive critique also had implications for the status of civil liberties.[7] In particular, Holmesian positivism and sociological jurisprudence had the effect of undermining the traditional American rationale for freedom of expression. Rather than a right of nature or citizenship, free speech on this view merely represented one interest to be weighed against others.[8] There was nothing distinctive about expression that entitled it to special protection or that placed it beyond the authority of the state to regulate like any other activity.

This perspective is evident in *Schenck v. United States* (1919), one of the Supreme Court's earliest efforts to address the meaning of the First Amendment.[9] Writing for a unanimous Court, Justice Holmes upheld the convictions of Socialist Party officials for conspiring to obstruct military recruitment by sending antidraft leaflets to men who had been called for service in the First World War. Although Holmes conceded that individuals ordinarily had a right to express their views, he asserted that this right did not extend to speech that endangered other social interests. "The question in every case," he wrote, "is whether the words used are used in such circumstances and are of such a nature as to create a clear and present danger that they will bring about the substantive evils that Congress has a right to prevent."[10] As *Schenck* and later decisions made clear, this standard was satisfied whenever the legislature determined that speech had a tendency to cause social harm.[11]

In this way, the rejection of natural rights threatened to undermine the constitutional basis for protecting freedom of speech.[12] The central challenge of modern First Amendment theory has been to reconstruct a justification for that freedom within the framework of post-natural-rights jurisprudence. A leading effort in this direction came from Zechariah Chafee, Jr., a Harvard law professor who was to become the era's most influential First Amendment scholar. In an article from 1919 and a book published the following year, Chafee criticized *Schenck* and other Espionage Act decisions for treating free speech "as merely an individual interest, which must readily give way like other personal desires the moment it interferes with the social interest in national security." Instead, Chafee argued that the most important purpose served by free speech was the social interest in "the discovery and spread of truth on subjects of general concern."[13]

This approach was soon adopted by Holmes himself. Dissenting in *Abrams v. United States* (1919), another case involving antiwar speech, Holmes observed that when the expression of opinions threatens important social objectives, suppression appears to be a "perfectly logical" response — essentially the basis of his decision in *Schenck*. Nevertheless, he continued, "when men have realized that time has upset many fighting faiths, they may come to believe even more than they believe the foundations of their own conduct that the ultimate good desired is best reached by free trade in ideas — that the best test of truth is the power of the thought to get itself accepted in the competition of the market, and that truth is the only ground on which their wishes safely can be carried out."[14] In referring to "fighting faiths," Holmes may well have been thinking in part of the abolitionism to which he had been committed in his youth and which he believed was partly responsible for the devastation of the Civil War. In this way, he laid the foundations of modern free speech jurisprudence on the ruins of the natural rights theory which originally supported the First Amendment.

Although Chafee regarded the social interest in truth as extending to all "subjects of general concern," he believed that free speech had special importance in the political realm, "so that the country may not only adopt the wisest course of action, but carry it out in the wisest way."[15] Similarly, in *Whitney v. California* (1927), Justice Louis D. Brandeis argued that free speech was indispensable to the democratic process. This recognition of the social values promoted by speech led Holmes and Brandeis to reinterpret the clear-and-present-danger test to require not merely a tendency to cause social harm, but an imminent danger of serious evil.[16]

As Mark A. Graber and David M. Rabban have shown, these early efforts to reconstruct First Amendment theory accorded with the desire of many progressives to defend freedom of speech without appealing to fundamental rights, which they tended to identify with Lochnerism.[17] In this way, they could support freedom of speech as vital to an open political system, while denying the charge of judicial interference with substantive policy decisions made by the legislature. This process-oriented approach was sketched in *United States v. Carolene Products Co.* (1938), in which Justice Harlan F. Stone (in the most famous footnote in American constitutional history) suggested that laws interfering with freedom of speech and association should be subjected to "more exacting judicial scrutiny" on the ground that they "restrict[] those political processes which ordinarily can be expected to bring about the repeal of undesirable legislation."[18]

Although progressives often criticized the notion of fundamental rights, they recognized that freedom of speech was valuable for individuals as well as for society. For instance, Chafee maintained that the First Amendment protected not only the social interest in truth, but also the need of many individuals to "express their opinions on matters vital to them if life is to be worth living."[19] Of course, as long as this value was understood as "merely an individual interest," it was unlikely to prevail when balanced against important social interests.[20] Yet the notion of fundamental rights was too central to the American constitutional tradition to remain eclipsed for long. Thus, in *Whitney*, Brandeis argued that if (as decisions like *Lochner* had held) the Fourteenth Amendment afforded substantive protection to property rights, it should afford no less protection to "the fundamental personal rights of free speech and assembly." In an eloquent opinion, he argued that the First Amendment was intended to protect those liberties for their own sake as well as for their contribution to democratic self-government.[21] The value of individual liberty also lay at the heart of the Court's decision in *West Virginia State Board of Education v. Barnette* (1943), in which Justice Robert H. Jackson declared that a compulsory flag salute "invade[d] the sphere of intellect and spirit which it was the purpose of the First Amendment . . . to reserve from all official control."[22] This individual-liberty view has gained increased momentum since the 1960s.[23]

Contrasting Modern First Amendment Jurisprudence with Classical Libertarian Thought

These three views—which focus on the value of free speech for the pursuit of truth, democratic self-government, and individual liberty—represent the most influential modern efforts to reconstruct a justification for freedom of speech. Of course, each of these approaches has roots in the classical libertarian tradition of Locke, Cato, Jefferson, and Madison.[24] It may therefore seem that we have come full circle and that modern First Amendment theory simply reproduces the essential features of classical libertarianism. But that impression would be mistaken. To begin with, the classical approach regarded the values of free speech as a relatively unified whole, while the modern justifications are sometimes represented as distinct from or even opposed to one another.[25] In recent years, however, these different rationales have often come to be seen as elements of a more general theory of freedom of expression.[26]

A more fundamental difference relates to the nature of the justifications offered by the classical and modern views. Whereas the classical approach sought to justify free speech primarily on intrinsic grounds, as a right of human nature and republican citizenship, the modern approach is more instrumental, focusing on the individual and social interests promoted by speech. On this view, our constitutional commitment to free expression ultimately rests on an empirical judgment as to the best means of promoting the social good. In the words of Justice Holmes, it is "an experiment . . . based upon imperfect knowledge," which is subject to revision or rejection in the light of experience.[27]

Most important for our purposes, the classical and modern views conceptualize First Amendment issues in fundamentally different ways. On the classical view, many free speech problems involved rights on both sides. As we have seen, progressive jurisprudence recharacterized rights as interests and held that individual interests had value only insofar as they promoted those of society. In this way, individual rights came to be absorbed into the concept of social interests. Initially, First Amendment problems were reconceived as conflicts between two sets of social interests: those that were promoted by speech and those that might be harmed by it. Over time, freedom of expression has once more come to be regarded as a basic right, whether for intrinsic or instrumental reasons or both. But this revival of rights in First Amendment jurisprudence has not extended to the values that may be injured by speech, which continue to be characterized as social interests. In this way, American legal thought has come to a hybrid position which conceives of First Amendment issues as conflicts between *free speech rights* and *social interests*.

These developments have crucial implications for the way one approaches First Amendment problems. On the classical libertarian view, rights had inherent limits, which derived from the nature of a particular right, its place within the larger framework of rights, and the duty to respect the rights of others. Although rights sometimes conflicted with one another, this was the exception rather than the rule. Finally, in determining whether a restriction on free speech was legitimate, the classical view looked to a relatively objective standard — whether it was necessary to protect other rights.

Modern interest jurisprudence differs on each point. Unlike rights, interests are defined in largely subjective terms, as desires, needs, claims, or demands.[28] Understood in this way, interests have no fixed boundaries but extend as far as the desires or demands they represent. As a result, interests necessarily conflict with one another. Moreover, there is no objective standard by which to resolve such conflicts, other than the rather elusive and indeterminate notion of social utility.[29]

Several points follow for the modern understanding of First Amendment problems. First, there is no inherent limit to the interest in free speech, apart from the
desire to engage in it. The same is true when free speech is reconceived as a right
coextensive with that interest. By the same token, there are no inherent limits to
the social interests that may come into competition with speech. It follows that
there is an inescapable conflict between free speech and other interests. Finally,
there is no objective standard by which to resolve such conflicts.

The classical and modern views differ not only on the substantive nature of
free speech problems, but also on their formal structure. On the classical
libertarian view, such problems involved a trilateral relationship between the
speaker, other individuals, and the state. The state had a duty to protect speech
except to the extent that it violated the rights of other individuals or the
community itself. On the modern view, the rights of others are reconceived as
social interests, and the state is regarded as the representative of those interests. Indeed, despite Pound's efforts to distinguish them, the terms "social
interests" and "state interests" are now generally used interchangeably.[30] In
this way, First Amendment problems have come to be viewed in terms of a
bipolar opposition between the state and those who wish to engage in expressive activities — a view that is applied not only to cases involving political
expression or criticism of the government, but also to cases involving speech
that injures private parties. As we shall see, these differences between the
classical and modern views can have crucial implications for the resolution of
particular First Amendment issues.[31]

The Dilemma of Modern First Amendment Jurisprudence

In short, modern First Amendment jurisprudence perceives an inherent
conflict between freedom of speech and the state's efforts to promote other
social values. There are three main approaches one might take to First Amendment problems when they are understood in this way: (1) a statist position,
which would generally defer to the government's authority to regulate for the
common good; (2) a civil libertarian view, which would generally protect
freedom of speech; and (3) a balancing approach, which would weigh the
values on both sides. As I shall now show, however, each of these approaches
suffers from serious difficulties — a fact that should lead us to reexamine the
conceptual framework of modern First Amendment theory.

STATISM

The statist position would allow the government to regulate speech in
much the same way it regulates conduct.[32] Although this approach is sensitive

to the social interests that may be injured by expression, it provides little or no protection to freedom of speech. For this reason, it is clearly inadequate as an interpretation of the First Amendment.

CIVIL LIBERTARIANISM

Of the three modern positions, civil libertarianism comes closest to capturing the spirit of the First Amendment. Over the past century, organizations like the American Civil Liberties Union (ACLU) have been instrumental in defending free speech and other constitutional rights against invasion by the government, particularly during times of national crisis.[33]

Civil libertarianism seeks maximum protection for freedom of expression against the state's efforts to promote other values. As we shall see in chapter 7, this is the appropriate stance to take with regard to speech that is directed against the government itself. As a general approach to the First Amendment, however, the civil libertarian view is more problematic. In particular, while it reflects our strong commitment to free expression, this view makes it very difficult for the law to regulate speech that causes serious injury to other people.

Some civil libertarians would afford absolute protection to speech. The most straightforward argument for this position relies on a literal reading of the First Amendment's command that "Congress shall make no law abridging the freedom of speech, or of the press."[34] Yet the meaning of this language is far from clear. For example, does "the freedom of speech" extend to every exercise of the capacity for speech, or is it limited to speech that falls within some conception of the legitimate bounds of that freedom? Similarly, do all forms of regulation "abridg[e] the freedom of speech," or only those that are illegitimate or unjustified? As these ambiguities indicate, an absolutist interpretation is not mandated by the text itself. Moreover, as we saw in chapter 1, this interpretation has doubtful support in the original understanding. For these reasons, the literalist argument is unconvincing.[35]

The case for First Amendment absolutism has also been made on substantive grounds. First, some writers have advanced what may be called the global balancing argument, which holds that an assessment of the costs and benefits of free speech leads to the conclusion that "freedom is always expedient."[36] Although this contention is plausible, it too is unpersuasive. It is undoubtedly true that, on the whole, the benefits that flow from free speech far exceed the harms, and that a society with absolute freedom of speech would be far better off than one with none. The fallacy lies in the assumption that these are the only alternatives. From an interest-oriented perspective, the goal is to determine the optimal balance between liberty and regulation. On this view, freedom of speech should be protected up to the point where its marginal costs exceed its marginal benefits. Clearly, however, there are many classes of speech whose regulation would promote social utility, from threats and incitement to defamation and false advertising.[37] It follows that First Amendment absolutism cannot be successfully grounded on a balancing of social interests.

Other absolutist arguments eschew balancing and instead assert that freedom of speech has categorical priority over other social interests. For example, Alexander Meiklejohn maintains that our society's most fundamental purpose is its commitment to democratic self-government. Political deliberation orders all other activities and determines their value. For this reason, such deliberation has "an authority over them all which is wholly incongruous with the notion that one of them, or all of them together, might be balanced against it." It is on these grounds that "the absoluteness of the First Amendment rests."[38]

An alternative argument appeals not to democratic self-government but to individual freedom. As Thomas I. Emerson puts it, "[T]he purpose of society, and of its more formal aspect the state, is to promote the welfare of the individual." A person has a "right to express his beliefs and opinions" both as an individual and as a member of the community. "To cut off his search for truth, or his expression of it, is . . . to elevate society and the state to a despotic command and to reduce the individual to the arbitrary control of others." Emerson concludes that, although a "society may seek to achieve other or more inclusive ends," such as justice, equality, or the self-fulfillment of its citizens, it generally may not do so by suppressing individual expression, which must be afforded "full protection" under the First Amendment.[39]

Although Emerson's argument persuasively shows that free speech rights may not be subordinated to social welfare in general, it fails to recognize the possibility that individuals may also have other fundamental rights, the protection of which may justify restrictions on speech. In this respect, Emerson's references to the liberty and welfare of "the individual" are somewhat misleading, for many free speech cases implicate the rights of more than one person. The proposition that one's rights may not be restricted for the sake of social welfare does not entail that they may not be limited to protect other rights.[40]

Emerson's view is also subject to a broader objection, one which applies to Meiklejohn's view as well. Although their arguments may establish the priority of free speech over social welfare in general, they fail to demonstrate its priority over other fundamental rights, because the same sorts of arguments can be made on behalf of those rights. For example, while democratic self-government depends on political free speech, the latter depends on individual liberty of speech and thought. Unless citizens enjoy such liberty, they will be incapable of participating in self-government. It may therefore seem that individual freedom of speech is more fundamental than its political counterpart. In another sense, however, the opposite is true: as Meiklejohn contends, individual liberties may well depend on the existence of political freedom. In this way, it becomes apparent that these two aspects of free speech are interdependent and that neither is more basic than the other. Freedom of speech must be regarded as a unified system that includes both individual and collective elements.[41]

In response to this objection, the absolutist argument may be revised to assert that it is *freedom of speech as a whole* that has precedence over other social interests.[42] Once more, however, the same kinds of arguments can be made for the priority of other rights. For instance, people cannot speak freely unless they are secure against violence. In this way, the right to free speech depends on the right to personal security. Again, it does not necessarily follow that the right to personal security is more fundamental than the right to free speech. Instead, just as individual and political freedom of speech turned out to be interdependent, the same holds true of free speech and other fundamental rights. Only when these rights are taken as a whole, as a system of constitutional liberty, do they have priority over other interests.[43]

Although I cannot explore all of the arguments that have been made for First Amendment absolutism, this discussion should suffice to show some of the problems it faces. Recognizing these difficulties, civil libertarians often defend freedom of expression in less sweeping terms. For example, many follow Chafee in endorsing a form of balancing that assigns a strong value to free speech, while leaving open the possibility that this value could be outweighed by interests of overriding importance.[44] As we shall see in chapter 6, in recent decades the Supreme Court has adopted a similar position. Despite its attractions, however, this approach only compounds the problem: the nearer it comes to absolutism, the more it is liable to the same objections, while as a form of balancing it also suffers from the difficulties of that approach.[45]

In short, while the civil libertarian view provides strong protection for free speech, it is unable to identify the appropriate limits of that freedom. This point might be of little concern if it simply meant that free speech would be overprotected at the expense of social welfare in general. As Justice Potter Stewart once observed, this may be regarded as "the price to be paid for constitutional freedom."[46] For three reasons, however, the inability to identify limits should be of serious concern to those (like myself) who are committed to strong protection of civil liberties. First, if one is unable to persuasively distinguish between legitimate and illegitimate restrictions on speech, it is more difficult to successfully oppose the latter. Second, what modern First Amendment jurisprudence labels social welfare includes the rights of others. For this reason, a maximalist approach to free speech has the unintended effect of sacrificing other individual rights — rights which, in other situations, civil libertarians themselves would defend against infringement by government.[47] Finally, by protecting speech even when it wrongfully invades the rights of others, a quasi-absolutist approach tends to undermine the normativity of free speech, that is, its character as a *right*. In this way, an excessive defense of First Amendment freedoms may weaken the legitimacy — and thus the public acceptance — of the very rights it means to defend.[48]

BALANCING

The third approach, balancing, seeks to avoid the pitfalls of statism and libertarianism. In recognizing that both free speech and competing interests have important value and that neither should be unreasonably sacrificed to the other, this approach is appealing from a commonsense standpoint. From a theoretical perspective, however, balancing is perhaps the least coherent of the three views, for it is difficult to see how free speech and state interests are to be compared with each other. As originally conceived by Pound and others, a major purpose of interest jurisprudence was to reduce competing values to common terms — those of social welfare — so they could be weighed on the same scale. On this view, which Chafee applied to the First Amendment, free speech and other interests should be measured in order to determine what result would most promote the common good.[49] Yet this good provided only an indeterminate standard for deciding between competing interests.[50] Moreover, the balancing of social interests is often thought to be an essentially legislative function.[51] Thus, this approach, which may be called quantitative balancing, fails to ensure strong protection for speech — a point that emerged most dramatically in *Dennis v. United States* (1951), which employed a generalized balancing test to uphold the convictions of leaders of the American Communist Party.[52]

For this reason, the thrust of most modern First Amendment theory has been to reverse the efforts of Pound and Chafee and to show that freedom of speech is *qualitatively different* from other social interests.[53] When First Amendment problems are viewed in this way, however, it is difficult to see what it would mean to balance free speech against other social interests, for this would involve comparing claims of an entirely different character. And this is even more true when free speech is reconceived as an individual right. In short, while a quantitative approach to balancing fails to adequately protect free expression, a qualitative approach appears to be impossible.

Conclusion

Modern jurisprudence conceives of First Amendment disputes as conflicts between free speech and state interests, a term within which the rights of others have been absorbed. When the problem is understood in this way, strong protection for freedom of speech results — unintentionally but necessarily — in sacrificing the rights of others, while upholding state interests results in sacrificing freedom of speech. Modern First Amendment theory offers no coherent solution to this dilemma.

This problem — which goes to the heart of the modern framework — stems from its failure to recognize other rights as an independent element in First Amendment cases. The inadequacy of this view should lead us to give renewed consideration to a rights-based approach to free expression. Of course, this does not mean we should simply return to the eighteenth-century understanding, even if that were possible. While a contemporary theory of the First Amendment must be rooted in the American constitutional tradition, it must ultimately reflect our own best understanding of free expression and other rights.[54] The remainder of this book seeks to develop such a theory.

PART II

A Rights-Based Theory of the First Amendment

3

The Basic Approach

In this part of the book I develop a rights-based or liberal humanist theory of the First Amendment. On this view, the Constitution does not protect freedom of speech merely for instrumental reasons or because of its tendency to promote various individual or social interests. Instead, free speech is an inherent right which is rooted in human dignity and autonomy. But those values also give rise to other fundamental rights, including personal security, privacy, reputation, citizenship, and equality. As a general rule, speakers have an obligation to respect those rights. Speech that violates them is wrongful and subject to regulation through narrowly drawn laws, except in cases where the value of the speech is sufficient to justify the injury it causes. In this way, the same principles that support freedom of expression allow us to identify the appropriate boundaries of that freedom.

In this chapter I lay the groundwork for the theory. I begin by exploring the basis of individual rights in respect for personhood. I then show that, contrary to what is often thought, the liberal tradition views people as having rights not only as individuals but also as a community. Next, I discuss the sources one can look to in identifying fundamental rights. In addition to the natural rights tradition, those sources include traditional and modern American law, the law of other liberal democratic nations, the international law of human rights, and contemporary political philosophy. I conclude by sketching a basic model of the scope and limits of the First Amendment freedom of speech.

The two chapters that follow present the core of the theory. In chapter 4, I explore the foundations of our constitutional commitment to freedom of expression as well as its place within a broader framework of rights. In chapter 5, I explain how conflicts between free speech and other rights can be resolved. Finally, in chapter 6, I use the theory to criticize the Supreme Court's current jurisprudence, which focuses on the idea of content neutrality.

The Basis of Individual Rights

There are many ways to argue that human beings have fundamental rights — rights that do not derive merely from positive law and that are entitled to recognition by the legal order.[1] My approach will draw on the liberal natural rights tradition associated with Locke and Immanuel Kant.[2] As we saw in part 1, this tradition profoundly shaped the understanding of free speech and other civil liberties throughout much of American history, particularly during the periods when the Bill of Rights and the Fourteenth Amendment were adopted. Despite the impact of legal positivism and utilitarianism, this tradition continues to represent a deep current in American thought, as reflected in the contemporary revival of fundamental rights adjudication and contractarian political philosophy.[3] This tradition has also had a powerful influence on the law of other liberal democratic countries as well as on the international law of human rights.

In the natural rights tradition, rights are founded on respect for the inherent freedom and dignity of human beings. The core meaning of freedom is self-determination: a free person is the author of her own thoughts and actions. On this account, freedom has two aspects. In a negative sense, it means independence from determination by external forces and from interference by other persons. In a positive sense, it means the capacity to actively direct one's own thoughts and actions through the use of reason.[4]

At the same time that reason enables human beings to freely determine their actions, it also sets limits to that freedom. Reason compels me to acknowledge that other individuals have the same capacity for self-determination that I do. Thus, my claim to freedom entails an obligation to respect the freedom of others.[5] To put the point another way, the concept of liberty includes immunity from interference. If liberty is to exist, therefore, it must be bounded by a duty to refrain from interfering with the equal liberty of others.[6]

These ideas lie at the heart of the liberal conception of right. Right in general may be understood as freedom insofar as it is consistent with the equal freedom of others.[7] Specific rights such as those to life, liberty, and property are instances of this freedom.[8]

In the liberal tradition, rights also flow from respect for human dignity.[9] A classic account of dignity appears in the writings of Kant. As a natural being, man has a merely finite, extrinsic value, which is based on his usefulness for particular purposes and which is commensurate with the value of other commodities. As an autonomous being, on the other hand, man "is not to be valued merely as a means to the ends of others or even to his own ends, but as an end in himself, that is, he possesses a *dignity* (an absolute inner worth)." In addition to grounding his own self-esteem, this dignity allows him to "exact[] *respect* for himself from all other rational beings in the world."[10]

This duty of respect applies both in the moral and in the legal realm, where it takes the form of an obligation to respect the legal rights of others. To intentionally violate another's rights is to deny her status as a person who is entitled to respect.[11] It follows that all basic rights have a dignitary dimension. This is certainly true of freedom of expression. As John Milton puts it, to subject a speaker or writer to unwarranted censorship "is the greatest displeasure and indignity to a free and knowing spirit that can be put upon him."[12]

Other rights have a dignitary dimension as well. This is true not only of rights like privacy and reputation, which focus on injuries to personality, but also of rights that are concerned with more material kinds of harm. The right to bodily security is a good example. Of course, this right can be invaded by acts of physical violence or "harmful batteries," which subject the actor to liability under both tort and criminal law. But the law also forbids "offensive batteries," such as spitting in a person's face or subjecting him to sexual contact without his consent. Acts of this sort treat an individual's body not as the embodiment of a free being of intrinsic worth, but as a mere object that can be treated however one pleases. In this way, they infringe the personal dignity that underlies the right to bodily security.[13]

As this discussion suggests, rights such as bodily security have both a substantive and a formal dimension. A person has a right to be free from substantive bodily harm, a right that is violated by harmful battery. But she also has a right to the formal *integrity or inviolability* of her body — a claim to be free from contact that invades her sphere of personal autonomy. This right is violated by offensive battery, the deliberate infliction of contact that "offends a reasonable sense of personal dignity."[14] As we shall see, this notion of inviolability is essential to many other rights as well.[15]

Thus, the concepts of liberty and dignity both have an essential place in a jurisprudence of rights. In the liberal tradition, these two concepts are inseparably related: human dignity is rooted in the capacity for autonomy or self-determination, while individuals must respect the liberty of others because they are beings of intrinsic worth.

At the same time, legal systems differ in the relative emphasis they place on these two concepts.[16] International human rights law accords crucial importance to the value of dignity. Thus, the Universal Declaration of Human Rights opens with a recognition of "the inherent dignity and . . . the equal and inalienable rights of all members of the human family."[17] The idea of dignity is also central to the law of many liberal democratic nations.[18]

By contrast, American law tends to conceive of rights in terms of liberty.[19] At the same time, however, dignity is an important theme in the Supreme Court's jurisprudence.[20] For example, in *Cohen v. California* (1971), Justice John Marshall Harlan observes that the First Amendment right to free expression is designed to place "the decision as to what views shall be voiced largely into the hands of each of us, in the hope that use of such freedom will ultimately produce a more capable citizenry and more perfect polity and in the belief that no other approach would comport with the premise of individual dignity and choice upon which our political system rests."[21] The Justices have also described dignity as lying at the core of many other constitutional protections, including the Fourth Amendment freedom from unreasonable searches and seizures,[22] the Fifth Amendment privilege against self-incrimination,[23] the Eighth Amendment ban on cruel and unusual punishments,[24] the Fifth and Fourteenth Amendment guarantees of equal protection,[25] and the liberty and privacy protected under the doctrine of substantive due process.[26] Thus, both freedom and dignity play a vital role in the American legal order.

Liberalism and Community Rights

On the view I shall present, rights are capable of belonging to communities as well as to individuals. At first glance, this idea may seem contrary to the liberal tradition, with its strong emphasis on individual freedom. But the liberal tradition has a communitarian dimension that is often overlooked. Thus, while Locke describes individuals in a state of nature as "free, equal and independent," he also holds that they are naturally "sociable" and destined to live together.[27] By nature, all human beings constitute *"one Community"* — what Locke calls the "great and natural Community" of *"Mankind."*[28] Individuals possess freedom, dignity, and rights by virtue of their membership in this community. Conversely, an act of violence directed against one person constitutes a wrong against all, for it undermines the very possibility of peaceful coexistence. Because their rights are not secure in a state of nature, individuals agree to unite into a particular society for mutual preservation. Under the social contract, they give up a portion of their natural liberty and transfer it to the political community they have established. Thus the powers that the community has are simply the rights that individuals have transferred to it.[29] Locke emphasizes that, through the social contract, the parties become "one Body, *One Community*," which has both the authority and the duty to protect its members and to promote the common good. In this way, the people come to have rights and liberties not only as individuals, but also as a political society or state.[30]

To restate this point in the terms I used earlier, human beings exercise their capacity for self-determination not only individually but also collectively, when they engage in decision making on matters regarding their common life. It follows that they possess some collective rights. For example, under international human rights law, "[a]ll peoples have the right of self-determination," by virtue of which they are entitled to "freely determine their political status and freely pursue their economic, social and cultural development."[31] Similarly, in a modern constitutional state, the people have a right to govern themselves through the democratic process.[32] As these examples show, there is an important sense in which individual and collective freedoms are complementary: individuals have a right to participate in the institutions that make collective self-determination possible, while it is only through such institutions that they are capable of exercising some control over their common life.[33]

In these ways, the idea that human beings possess both individual and collective rights is consistent with the liberal tradition. This idea also has deep roots in Anglo-American law, where it provides the basis for the distinction between tort and criminal law. Torts are wrongs against individuals, while crimes are wrongs against the community.[34] For instance, battery is a crime as well as a tort because it violates the community's right to freedom from violence.[35] In other cases, such as perjury and tax evasion, conduct may violate the rights of the public even though it does not result in injury to particular individuals.

In this book, I shall employ the idea of community rights in two ways. First, this idea constitutes a vital part of the justification for freedom of expression. As we saw in chapter 1, Americans have traditionally understood free speech both as an individual right and as a right that the people as a whole must possess if they are to engage in self-government.[36]

Second, I shall use the idea of community rights to explain why the law can properly restrict some forms of expression, such as speech that endangers the public peace.[37] This use of the idea is likely to be controversial: some people will feel that the notion of community rights should have no place in a liberal theory of the First Amendment. In my view, however, this position is mistaken. Apart from absolutist doctrines, all First Amendment theories recognize that speech may sometimes be restricted to safeguard important public values, such as preserving the peace and protecting the nation from attack. As we saw in chapter 2, modern free speech jurisprudence characterizes such values as state interests and holds that when they are strong enough they can justify restrictions on speech. But there are two problems with this conventional approach. First, interests like national security often seem very powerful, especially in times of war and public danger. Second, there is no clear way to resolve First Amendment problems when they are framed as conflicts between individual liberties and state interests.[38] For these reasons, the government's invocation of national security will frequently be allowed to overwhelm other values, as it so often has since the terrorist attacks of September 11, 2001. By contrast, as I shall argue in chapter 7, when interests such as national security are recharacterized as rights of the community, the effect is *to cabin those interests* by situating them within a larger framework of rights — a framework that is based on principles of individual liberty and democratic self-government. Thus, the rights-based approach provides a powerful basis for arguing that speech that is directed against the government should be protected unless it threatens to cause grave and immediate injury.[39] As later chapters will show, the idea of community rights can also cast light on other First Amendment issues, from fighting words and threats against abortion providers to hate speech and pornography.

The Dynamic Nature of Rights

Although it is deeply informed by the natural rights tradition, the conception of rights that I shall develop is a dynamic one. Rights are founded on respect for persons. As our understanding of human personality evolves, so do the rights that flow from it. For this reason, I shall approach the theory of rights not as a fixed set of principles but as an evolving body of thought, from early writers like Locke, Blackstone, and Jefferson through later philosophers like Jean-Jacques Rousseau, Kant, and G. W. F. Hegel to contemporary thinkers like John Rawls and Jürgen Habermas.

For rights to be effective, they must be realized within a concrete social order.[40] It follows that, in formulating an account of rights, we should look not merely to general theory but also to the prevailing understanding of rights within American law and culture.[41] This understanding has also developed substantially over time. For example, while classical law focused on the external rights to life, liberty, and property, modern jurisprudence emphasizes rights of autonomy and personality — a development that is reflected in the contrast between *Lochner v. New York* (1905), which used the doctrine of substantive due process to protect "liberty of contract," and recent decisions like *Planned*

Parenthood v. Casey (1992) and *Lawrence v. Texas* (2003), which employ that doctrine to protect personal dignity and autonomy.[42]

In several recent cases, the Supreme Court has referred to the law of other nations, as well as to the international law of human rights, in interpreting the freedoms protected by the United States Constitution.[43] This practice has come under sharp attack from many conservatives, who maintain that it conflicts with a proper approach to constitutional interpretation. For example, in his confirmation hearings before the Senate Judiciary Committee in 2006, Justice Samuel A. Alito, Jr., suggested that "the Framers would be stunned" by this development. "The purpose of the Bill of Rights," he asserted, "was to give Americans rights that were recognized practically nowhere else in the world at the time. The Framers did not want Americans to have the rights of people in . . . other countries . . . ; they wanted them to have the rights of Americans."[44]

This view, which is shared by Justices Antonin Scalia and Clarence Thomas,[45] reflects a fundamental misunderstanding of the Bill of Rights. As we saw in chapter 1, that document did not reflect a parochial conception of rights. Instead, as Madison explained, a central purpose of the Bill of Rights was to protect "natural right[s]" or "the great rights of mankind."[46] Although the framers believed that these rights were more fully recognized in America than anywhere else in the world, that does not mean they intended to secure rights that were peculiar to Americans. On the contrary, they sought to protect rights that all human beings were entitled to.[47] In interpreting these rights, one may reasonably consider not only American sources, but also the experience of other liberal democratic countries and the principles of human rights that are accepted by the international community.[48]

In sum, in developing an understanding of fundamental rights, one can look to a variety of sources, including the natural rights tradition, classical and modern American law, the civil liberties jurisprudence of other nations, the international law of human rights, and contemporary legal and political theory. Taken together, these sources provide the basis for a rich, dynamic conception of rights.

The approach I shall take is dynamic in another sense as well. As we saw in chapter 1, the First Amendment was enacted against the background of strong ideological disagreement. The framers reaffirmed the principle of free speech, but they made no effort to resolve disputes over the scope of that freedom. As a result, the meaning of the First Amendment has always been controversial. It follows that—contrary to a widely accepted view of constitutional interpretation—free speech doctrine cannot be determined through the elaboration and interpretation of a single, coherent set of principles.[49] Instead, constitutional meaning emerges dialectically, through debate and conflict between opposing views.[50] Thus, the theory I shall present is not intended to resolve all ideological debates over the First Amendment. But it does seek to establish a common framework within which those debates can take place.

The Scope and Limits of Freedom of Speech

At the core of the rights-based theory are two principles which emerged from my account of the natural rights background of the First and Fourteenth Amendments. First, freedom of speech is an inherent right that belongs to individuals both as human beings and as citizens in a democratic society. Second, like all rights, free speech may be regulated to protect the rights of others.[51]

As we saw in part 1, although these two principles were once widely accepted, they fell into disfavor in the late nineteenth and early twentieth centuries. In recent times, the idea that individuals have an inherent right to free speech has once more gained currency. By contrast, the idea that this freedom is limited by the rights of others no longer plays a major role in First Amendment jurisprudence. Nevertheless, one can still find traces of this idea in the Supreme Court's opinions. This is true even of the dissent in *Abrams v. United States* (1919), which helped give birth to the modern view. In that case, Justices Holmes and Brandeis argued that the First Amendment should protect political expression except in the most extraordinary circumstances. At the same time, they implied that a different standard should apply "where private rights are . . . concerned." Similarly, in *West Virginia State Board of Education v. Barnette* (1943), which held that public school children could not be compelled to salute the flag, Justice Jackson observed that "[t]he freedom asserted by these [individuals] does not bring them into collision with rights asserted by any other individual. It is such conflicts which most frequently require intervention of the State to determine where the rights of one end and those of another begin."[52] In recent decades, the Justices have occasionally described particular issues as conflicts between free speech and other rights such as reputation, privacy, and the constitutional guarantee of a fair trial.[53] In some cases, they have even perceived conflicts between different First Amendment values.[54] Moreover, even when the Justices use the language of competing interests, they may analyze issues in a way that resembles a balancing of rights.[55]

Although these cases do not represent the dominant position in contemporary First Amendment jurisprudence, they do offer some doctrinal support for the principle I wish to establish: that freedom of speech must be exercised with due regard for the rights of others. This principle is also accepted within the broader human rights tradition.[56] For example, it appears in such documents as the International Covenant on Civil and Political Rights and the European Convention on Human Rights, both of which hold that expression is a fundamental freedom which is subject to restriction on certain grounds, including where necessary to protect the rights or reputations of others.[57]

Against this background, we can now formulate a basic model of the scope and limits of the First Amendment freedom of speech. On the liberal humanist view, free speech generally should be considered a fundamental right. At the same time, that right is bounded by the rights of other individuals and the community. More specifically, an act of expression should be regarded as presumptively wrongful and subject to legal regulation when it (1) causes or is otherwise responsible for[58] (2) an infringement of a fundamental right belonging to another, and (3) the actor has a level of fault that should make her responsible for that result. Speech can cause injury to other rights either directly (as when *A* threatens *B*) or indirectly (as when *A* incites *B* to attack *C*). To ensure broad protection for free speech, an act of expression should not be deemed to cause the infringement of another right unless it has a concrete and substantial impact on that right.[59] The precise scope of responsibility will vary, however, depending on such factors as the nature and value of the competing rights and the type of sanctions at issue (for example, criminal punishment or civil liability).[60] Similar factors are relevant in determining the appropriate standard of fault. In many cases, individuals should be held responsible only when they intentionally violate the rights of others.[61] Other situations may call for a different standard, such as recklessness or negligence.[62]

The principle that free speech is limited by the rights of others is subject to several important qualifications. First, as I shall explain in chapter 5, there are situations in which the value of the expression is so great that it should be protected despite its impact on other rights. A classic example is *New York Times Co. v. Sullivan* (1964), in which the Supreme Court held that the right to criticize the conduct of public officials is so important for democratic self-governance that the speech should generally be protected, even if it turns out to be false and damaging to an official's reputation.[63]

Second, in its effort to do justice, the law must take account not only of what is right in itself, but also of the law's own nature and limitations.[64] For instance, the state cannot properly regulate speech (or any other form of activity) unless it is able to draw the line between lawful and unlawful action in reasonably clear terms that are capable of being understood by those who must administer or comply with the law. This is the basis of the constitutional doctrines of vagueness and overbreadth, which play an especially prominent role in First Amendment jurisprudence. Regulation is also inappropriate if it is likely to do more harm than good from the standpoint of constitutional liberty.[65] Again, government should have less authority to regulate in contexts where it is likely to be biased in favor of restriction.[66] I shall refer to considerations of this sort as those of institutional right. In some cases, those concerns will justify according speech more (or less) protection than it is entitled to as a matter of substantive right. This course should be followed, however, only where necessary to make the law more consistent with right as a whole.

Third, in arguing that freedom of speech is limited by other rights, I do not mean to deny that some speech is properly subject to broader regulation. As we saw in chapter 1, classical natural rights theory held that some aspects of liberty were inalienable while others were alienable. Inalienable rights were limited solely by the rights of others, while alienable rights were also subject to regulation for the public good. Similarly, modern constitutional law distinguishes between fundamental rights, which can be restricted only for compelling reasons, and nonfundamental rights, which are subject to reasonable regulation to promote social welfare. Although freedom of speech generally should be regarded as a fundamental right, that is not true of all sorts of speech. For example, I am inclined to think that commercial advertising, like other forms of business activity, should be considered a nonfundamental right subject to reasonable regulation.[67] For the most part, however, I shall not pursue such issues in this book but shall focus instead on the limits that arise from the rights of others and that apply to all forms of expression.

Finally, my claim that free speech may be restricted solely to protect the rights of others is meant to apply only to regulations that are based on the content or "communicative impact" of expression—that is, on what the speaker was saying or the effect it might have on others. The extent to which the government may impose other kinds of regulations (such as those that are limited to the time, place, and manner of speech) is a separate issue.[68] Although I believe that the rights-based theory is capable of shedding light on this question, I shall not explore the subject here.

4

Free Speech in a Framework of Rights

In the previous chapter, I outlined some of the main ideas of a rights-based or liberal humanist approach to the First Amendment. My goal in the next two chapters is to develop those ideas into a general theory of the foundations and limits of freedom of expression. On this view, rights reflect what it means for human beings to be free in different areas of life, including (1) the external world; (2) the internal domain of thought and feeling; (3) the political, social, and cultural life of the community; and (4) the intellectual and spiritual realm. These four elements correspond to the major justifications that have been advanced for freedom of speech and thought: that they are instances of external freedom in general; that they are essential for individual self-realization; that they are central to democratic self-government; and that they are necessary for the pursuit of truth. At the same time, these four elements give rise to other individual and collective rights that are also entitled to protection under the law. In this way, we can view freedom of speech and thought as existing within a broader framework of rights based on respect for human dignity and autonomy — a framework that not only justifies the liberties protected by the First Amendment, but also enables us to identify their limits.[1]

Free Speech and External Rights

Our ideas of freedom and dignity begin with what it means to be a free person in the external world. This leads to the first category of fundamental rights. Individuals have a right to life and, more broadly, to personal security, or the right to control one's own mind and body, free from violence or interference by others. This power over oneself includes the freedom to direct one's outward actions and movements without constraint. Finally, to live and act in the world, individuals must have some control over external things. In this way, we arrive at the traditional rights to life, liberty, and property.[2]

Freedom of speech and thought clearly fall within the scope of these classical rights. The right to personal security applies to all of one's faculties and thus includes freedom of thought, belief, and emotion.[3] Freedom of speech may be understood as a form of personal liberty, or the power to direct one's actions without constraint.[4]

Of course, the right to liberty is not absolute. It is bounded by the rights of other individuals to their own life, liberty, and property. An act that violates these rights is wrongful and may be restricted by law.

Acts of expression can clearly violate rights in this way. An extremist like Timothy McVeigh who blows up a government building to protest against oppression deprives the people inside of their right to life. Likewise, when demonstrators blockade an abortion clinic, they interfere with the patients' liberty of movement as well as the clinic's right to property.[5]

In both of these cases, the injury results from what First Amendment jurisprudence calls the *noncommunicative impact* of expression — the effect that it would have regardless of whether the actor intended to communicate a message or the message was understood by others. But expression can also infringe rights because of its *communicative impact*.[6] To see this point, we need to explore the right to personal security in more depth.

THE INDIVIDUAL RIGHT TO PERSONAL SECURITY

As I have said, the concept of personal security includes a right over one's body.[7] From one perspective, body and self are not separate but form a natural whole: I exist only in and through my body. Thus, "violence done to *my body* by others is violence done to me."[8] As a free person, such an act is an infringement of my personal security, understood here as a passive or negative right to be free from interference by others.

The relationship between body and self is not merely given by nature, however, but is also constituted by the self. Because a person can exist and act only through her body, one of her most basic acts of self-determination must be to

Table 4.1. The Structure of the Right to Personal Security Against Violence

---

I. Objective: right to be free from violence or interference by others
    A. Substantive: right to be free from bodily injury (violated by harmful battery)
    B. Formal: right to bodily integrity and inviolability (violated by offensive battery)
II. Subjective: right to feel secure from violence or interference by others (violated by assaults and threats)

---

assert sovereignty over her body.[9] From this perspective, personal security is an active, positive right to possess and control one's own body.[10]

Because it is rooted in the relationship between the body and the self, the right to personal security has both an objective and a subjective dimension. The objective dimension protects the individual's body—the object over which he has a right—while the subjective dimension protects his consciousness in relation to his body, that is, his awareness of his safety and immunity from attack. To put it another way, the objective element consists of the right to *be* safe from violence, while the subjective element consists of the right to reasonably *believe* oneself to be safe. Corresponding to these two elements are two different types of wrongs: assaults and threats violate the subjective side of personal security, while battery violates the objective side. Finally, as we saw in chapter 3, the category of battery includes both harmful battery, which inflicts substantive bodily injury, and offensive battery, which consists in touching another person in a way that "offends a reasonable sense of personal dignity."[11] (See table 4.1.)

We are now in a position to specify the ways in which the right to personal security can be violated by the communicative impact of expression. By definition, this impact is the effect that expression has not on the material world but on the minds of those who hear it. Thus, it is impossible for communicative impact to directly cause substantive bodily injury.[12] But speech is capable of violating the subjective side of personal security by causing a person to fear for her safety. A speaker is liable for assault when he threatens another in a way that (taken together with other acts and circumstances) intentionally causes her to apprehend an imminent attack.[13] Threats of future violence can also be prohibited in cases in which the speaker means to communicate a serious intention to commit unlawful violence against others.[14]

Although it may seem obvious that assaults and threats are wrongful, we should briefly explore why this is so, as the answer will have important implications for more controversial issues. Individuals are concerned for their personal safety in two ways. First, as living beings, they have an innate desire for self-preservation and feel threatened by anything that endangers it now or in the future. Second, as autonomous beings, individuals assert a right over their lives and bodies at all times. Assaults and threats convey an image or representation of violence to be inflicted on the victim,[15] and thereby cause him to *experience this violence in his own mind*. In this way, they invade his right to personal security. At the same time, they may also restrict his personal liberty, by compelling him to forego his own lawful activities out of fear.

The Supreme Court's jurisprudence makes clear that assaults and threats are unprotected by the First Amendment.[16] In addition to invading individual rights, speech of this sort violates the public peace.

THE COMMUNITY'S RIGHT TO THE PUBLIC PEACE

The ideal of peace plays a central role in the natural rights tradition. As we saw in chapter 3, Locke holds that by nature all human beings constitute a single community. This community is governed by the law of nature, which wills "the Peace and *Preservation of all Mankind*." Acts of violence constitute wrongs not only against the particular individuals who are injured, but also against "the Peace and Safety" of "the whole Species." The problem is that, in a state of nature, there are no effective means of preventing and punishing such wrongs. Although individuals have a right to defend themselves as well as others, they are vulnerable to attack by anyone who is stronger than they are. For this reason, they would agree "to joyn and unite into a [particular society] for their comfortable, safe, and peaceable living one amongst another." Through the social contract, the community comes to have a right, as well as a duty, to keep the peace and protect its citizens from injury. This collective right to the peace is parallel to the individual rights to personal security and self-defense against wrongful violence.[17]

However, the public peace is not simply a condition of external or negative freedom from violence. Instead, it also has an inward, positive dimension. In Locke's words, it is a condition of "Peace, Good Will, Mutual Assistance, and Preservation," in which people show a disposition to recognize and respect the rights of others.[18] Each individual trusts that the community will protect her, and this attitude reflects the shared sense of security that prevails within the society.[19] Conversely, acts of violence have an impact on the whole community. When one person is assaulted, others sympathize with her and the injury she suffers.[20] At the same time, their own sense of security and inviolability is diminished. Thus, an attack on one person is experienced as an attack on all.[21] In legal terms, such acts are regarded not only as torts, or wrongs against individuals, but also as crimes, or wrongs against the community. It follows that an individual who assaults or threatens another may be subjected to criminal punishment as well as civil liability to the injured person.

The community's right to protect the peace extends beyond this, however. For example, incitement to riot can be treated as a crime because of its impact on the security of the community and its members, regardless of whether it violates the rights of any particular person. Likewise, the act of blowing up a government building violates the peace even if no individuals are harmed.

Free Speech and Rights of Personality

As I showed in the previous section, the right to personal security protects against injuries ranging from harmful battery to offensive battery to assaults and threats. As one moves along this continuum, the objective or external dimension of the wrong becomes less important, while the subjective or internal dimension — the injury to the victim's mind and feelings — moves to the foreground. In the case of threats, it becomes clear that the harm to be prevented is not merely the danger that violence will occur, but also the serious distress that they cause.[22] If that is so, however, then there seems to be no principled reason to draw the line at threats. For instance, in the classic English case of *Wilkinson v. Downton* (1897), the defendant falsely told the plaintiff that her husband had been "smashed up in an accident," causing her to suffer intense anguish. Recognizing that acts of this sort constitute serious wrongs, *Wilkinson* and later cases fashioned the tort of intentional infliction of emotional distress.[23] In this way, the development of external rights against violence naturally leads to a recognition of rights that protect the inner lives of individuals.

This movement from external to internal rights was an important theme in Samuel Warren's and Louis Brandeis's famous article, *The Right to Privacy*. Early law, the authors explained, was largely concerned with the prevention of violence and other tangible forms of harm. As civilization progressed, people increasingly came to find their well-being not only in material things, but also in an "intense intellectual and emotional life." It was inevitable that the law should respond to this development by protecting individuals in their thoughts, emotions, and sensations. Warren and Brandeis characterized the right involved as that of "an inviolate personality."[24]

This discussion points to a second set of rights, which I shall call rights of personality. Like the traditional triad of life, liberty, and property, these rights derive from our nature as autonomous beings. The focus of self-determination has shifted, however: rather than acting in the external world, the self now turns inward to shape its own mental and emotional life. Rights of personality reflect what it means to be a free person in this sphere.

Table 4.2. The Structure of External Rights and Rights of Personality

External Rights	Rights of Personality
I. Right to personal security	I. Right to personality
II. Right to personal liberty	II. Right to self-expression through speech and conduct
III. Right to property	III. Right to image or reputation

In many ways, the structure of this second category of rights resembles that of the first. (See table 4.2.) Just as the first category began with the right to one's body, the second begins with the right to one's personality — the capacity to autonomously determine one's inner life without wrongful interference by others. Second, one has a right to express oneself through one's actions, including speech as well as conduct. This right is parallel to that of liberty in the external realm. The difference is that, while both rights relate to action, the latter regards action as outward movement, whereas the former views it as an expression of the self. Finally, through one's actions, one affects others and makes impressions upon them. These impressions, taken as a whole, constitute one's image or reputation. While reputation belongs to the self, in another sense it is external to the self, existing within the minds of others.[25] In this way, it resembles the right to property, which also is external to the individual.[26]

In this section, I first discuss the ways in which freedom of speech and thought can be understood as personality rights. I then explore the other rights that flow from personality and show how they give rise to normative limits on speech in the same way that the external rights of life, liberty, and property did.

SPEECH AND THOUGHT AS RIGHTS OF PERSONALITY

At the core of personality is the right to self-determination. Speech and thought play an essential role in this process. By forming and expressing her own thoughts, beliefs, values, and emotions, a person realizes her nature as a human being and defines her particular identity as an individual.[27] Because self-realization is not a single event but a continuing process, it may also be described in terms of self-development.[28] Finally, if one regards self-realization as an important or even ultimate end for human beings, it may also be said to promote self-fulfillment.[29]

For these reasons, speech and thought are fundamental rights. To be free in a full sense, a person must possess internal as well as external freedom. It follows that unwarranted censorship is wrongful not merely because of the restrictions it imposes on outward liberty, but also in a deeper way, because it obstructs the individual's freedom to autonomously develop and express his personality.[30]

This account leads to several additional points. First, the purpose of the First Amendment is not merely to protect speech, but also to protect the inner life that is expressed through speech. For this reason, freedom of thought, belief, and feeling, although not mentioned in the constitutional text, should receive no less protection than freedom of speech and press.[31] Second, the means by which individuals express their ideas and emotions are not limited to oral and written language but include symbolic conduct as well. Such conduct should also be protected by the First Amendment.

While both of these positions are generally accepted, a third is somewhat more controversial. Courts and theorists often equate "speech" for First Amendment purposes with communication to others.[32] However, if a basic aim of the Amendment is to protect self-expression, then this protection should also extend to solitary forms of expression, such as recording one's thoughts in a diary or lighting a candle in memory of a loved one. Expression of this sort is an exercise of the freedom to shape one's mental and emotional life and may be no less important than communication as a form of self-realization.[33]

The concept of self-realization also helps to explain two other rights that are recognized in contemporary First Amendment jurisprudence. The first is the right to refrain from expression. Because individuals are entitled to control their inner lives, the state may not compel them to speak or to affirm beliefs or attitudes they do not hold.[34]

Second, just as self-realization includes the freedom to express oneself in the external world, it also includes a right that is the mirror image of this: the right to receive images and ideas from the external world and to use them to shape the self.[35] As in the case of self-expression, this right should not be restricted to interaction with others. If the right to receive images and ideas includes the freedom to view an artistic depiction of a landscape or to read a book on plant biology, it should also include the freedom to watch a sunset or to examine plants in a laboratory. It follows that the First Amendment should be understood to secure a general freedom of inquiry and observation as well as a right to receive communications from others. Conversely, the right to form the self should include at least some freedom to decide what one does not wish to be exposed to.[36]

In addition to the intrinsic value of First Amendment activities for developing and expressing the self, they may have instrumental value in promoting the purposes of individuals, groups, and the society at large. For instance, commercial advertising may enable individuals to make more informed choices about goods and services, while instructional manuals may facilitate a variety of other activities. Speech that has merely instrumental value also has a claim to First Amendment protection. Of course, that does not mean it may not be regulated insofar as it affects the rights of others.[37]

FREE SPEECH AND THE RIGHTS OF OTHERS

Although it includes solitary activities, the concept of self-expression would clearly be incomplete if it did not extend to communication with others. Why should this be the case, however? Self-realization theories of free speech have not always explored this question or recognized its crucial importance for an adequate view of the First Amendment.

The answer to the question would seem to lie in the basic notion of self-realization.[38] Human beings cannot be content with being merely potential. Instead, they have a drive to realize themselves, to give their subjectivity an existence in the world. One way they do so is by asserting themselves in relation to the physical environment, for example, by acquiring and possessing property. Because property is a mere thing, however, it is inadequate as an expression of the self. To fully realize themselves, individuals must do so in a medium that is adequate to the selves they are trying to express. And this can only be other selves. Thus, individuals have a need to express themselves to other people.

In this way, individuals realize themselves not only on their own, but also in and through the consciousness of others. But this raises the possibility that an individual will use others as mere instruments for her own self-fulfillment, contrary to the Kantian injunction to treat persons as ends in themselves.[39] If this is not to occur, the right to self-expression must be exercised in a way that is consistent with respect for other persons and their own rights to self-realization. Speech transgresses this principle when it constitutes intentional infliction of emotional distress, invasion of privacy, or defamation. (See table 4.3.)

Substantive injury to personality: intentional infliction of emotional distress. Just as the right to personal security includes freedom from violence, the right to personality includes freedom from unwarranted assaults on one's mental and emotional well-being. Attacks of this sort inflict substantive injury to personality, a wrong that is analogous to harmful battery in the realm of external rights. Under the formulation adopted by the *Second Restatement of Torts,* an individual can be required to pay damages for intentional infliction when she engages in "extreme and outrageous conduct" that intentionally or recklessly causes another person to suffer severe emotional distress.[40]

Intentional infliction can take the form of conduct, such as a life insurance

Table 4.3. The Structure of Personality Rights and Corresponding Wrongs

---

  I. The right to personality
   A. Substantive: the right to mental and emotional well-being (violated by
      intentional infliction of emotional distress)
   B. Formal: the right to "an inviolate personality"
     1. The right to privacy (violated by unreasonable intrusion or exposure)
     2. The right to personal dignity (violated by insulting words, see pp. 144–
       46)
 II. The right to self-expression through speech and conduct (violated by improper
    regulation)
III. The right to image or reputation (violated by defamation and related torts)

---

company's bad-faith refusal to honor a valid claim by beneficiaries who are emotionally distraught and financially desperate. Because intentional infliction is essentially an injury to the mind and feelings, however, it often takes the form of expression. This brings it into potential conflict with the First Amendment.

In the liberal tradition, rights are ultimately grounded in reason, which is the capacity that makes self-determination possible.[41] As reasonable beings, people have a fundamental interest in the discovery of truth, a process that requires the exploration of conflicting views.[42] It follows that an individual has no right to be shielded from controversial ideas simply because they may result in emotional distress. In addition to being inherent in the right against emotional distress itself, this limitation is necessary to reconcile that right with freedom of speech and thought.

That does not mean, however, that the right to emotional tranquillity can never be violated by speech, as the case of *Wilkinson v. Downton* makes clear.[43] Instead, the law should draw a distinction between ideas, which are protected by the First Amendment, and personal abuse and other attacks on personality, which should not be. In many cases this distinction will be clear, while in others it will be more difficult to draw. I shall return to this problem in chapters 8 and 10, which discuss whether insults and hate speech should be protected by the First Amendment.

Formal injury to personality: invasion of privacy. Like the right to personal security, the right to personality is not limited to freedom from substantive harm, but also includes a right to the formal integrity or inviolability of the self.[44] Many infringements of this right fall under the rubric of invasion of privacy.[45] Privacy may be understood as the right to maintain the integrity of one's personality and inner life by preserving the boundary that separates them from other persons.[46]

The philosophical basis of privacy may be described as follows.[47] In the sphere of external right, the individual is oriented toward the outside world. In the realm of personality, on the other hand, the self turns inward, withdrawing from the external world into its own internal life. In this respect, privacy is rooted in negative freedom.

Privacy is not merely negative, however. By withdrawing into itself, the self frees itself from external constraints and thereby attains the capacity for active self-determination. This includes the freedom to direct one's own thoughts and actions within the boundary that separates oneself from others. Thus, privacy creates an inviolable realm of subjectivity within which a person can develop a rich inner life. This is the positive dimension of privacy and its connection with positive freedom.

For these reasons, privacy should be regarded as a fundamental right.[48] Indeed, a minimum of privacy may be necessary to the very existence of human personality.[49] Persons differ from things in being not merely external, but in having an inward dimension as well. It is this distinction between internal and external that makes it possible for human beings to be self-determining. Without inwardness, individuals would be mere objects vulnerable to determination by external forces or to manipulation or domination by other people. In this way, privacy is essential to individual dignity and autonomy.[50]

Privacy has two facets. The first is the right to be free from unauthorized *intrusion* into one's private life. This right is safeguarded by section 652B of the *Second Restatement of Torts,* which imposes liability on one who "intentionally intrudes, physically or otherwise, upon the solitude or seclusion of another or his private affairs or concerns, . . . if the intrusion would be highly offensive to a reasonable person."[51] Acts of this sort (such as obscene or harassing telephone calls) wrongfully interfere with the plaintiff's inner life in much the same way that acts of offensive battery interfere with his body.

In addition to intrusion, the right to privacy protects individuals against the unwarranted *exposure* of their private lives to others. This is the subject of section 652D of the *Restatement,* which imposes liability on one who "gives publicity to a matter concerning the private life of another," if the matter "is of a kind that would be highly offensive to a reasonable person" and "is not of legitimate concern to the public."[52]

For a dramatic illustration of this tort, consider the Texas case of *Kerr v. Boyles*. After concealing a video camera in his closet and focusing it on the bed, Dan Boyles took his girlfriend Susan Kerr back to his room and had sex with her. He later screened the videotape for his college fraternity brothers, and word of the video spread across campus. Kerr then brought a lawsuit against Boyles and the fraternity.[53]

Kerr is a classic example of invasion of privacy through exposure. The injury in this case consists in wrongfully transforming a person into a mere object for others. This injury can be understood on two levels. First, the videotape was shown to people who had no interest in or concern for Kerr as a person. In this way, she was stripped of the dignity of personality and reduced to the status of a mere body.

On a second and deeper level, one can see the wrong in *Kerr* as the exposure not of the body but of the self. Those who watched the videotape were given access to Kerr's most intimate feelings and sensations without her consent. Again, the result was to transform her into an object for the enjoyment of others. Of course, both of these wrongs were greatly intensified when she discovered what had been done.

One can understand the wrongfulness of exposure not only in terms of privacy, but also in terms of self-expression. To have value for self-realization, speech must be freely chosen by the self.[54] Far from promoting this value, involuntary or coerced expression does violence to the self. Thus, the right against unreasonable exposure can be understood as a right to decide for oneself whether, and to what extent, to reveal one's private thoughts and feelings to others.[55]

Defamation and injury to social personality. Leading commentators in the natural rights tradition, such as Blackstone and Chancellor James Kent, held reputation to be a fundamental right.[56] Yet they had some difficulty in explaining the nature of this right. They classified reputation as an element of personal security, although it seems quite different from the other rights in this category (life, limb, body, and health). Moreover, the only justification they offered for this right was an instrumental one. As Blackstone put it, "reason and natural justice" dictate that reputation be protected, "since without [this protection] it is impossible to have the perfect enjoyment of any other advantage or right." To accuse an individual of a crime may subject him to prosecution; to assert that he has a loathsome disease may "exclude him from society"; to impugn his professional skill or integrity may endanger his livelihood.[57] On this view, reputation deserves protection less for its own sake than because of its relationship to other rights or interests.

This difficulty in accounting for the right to reputation can be traced to the basic assumptions of classical natural rights theory. As we have seen, that theory conceived of rights largely in external terms. Moreover, it focused on what Blackstone and Kent called "absolute rights" — those that belonged to individuals as separate, independent beings rather than as members of society.[58] It is hardly surprising, then, that the classical theory would have difficulty with reputation, a right that is rooted in personality and that has an important social dimension.

By the early nineteenth century, some legal writers were characterizing reputation in less instrumentalist terms. As St. George Tucker wrote, injuries to reputation were, "to a man of sensibility, and of conscious integrity, . . . the most grievous that can be inflicted."[59] On one hand, this view harkened back to an older conception of reputation as honor,[60] while on the other hand it anticipated a growing recognition of the value of individual personality. Modern thought also stresses the social dimension of individual rights. Against this background, we may be able to sketch a deeper and more satisfying account of the right to reputation, one that regards it as having intrinsic as well as instrumental value.

The starting point is to recognize that human beings relate to one another only through the *images* they have of each other. We have no direct or immediate access to other selves: our knowledge of them depends on the way they appear to us. That is not to say that we are incapable of knowing others as they really are; it is merely to say that any such knowledge must be derived from our perceptions of them.[61]

A person's image includes not only her name and appearance, but also her reputation, that is, what others say and think about her. In turn, reputation is a function of both (1) an individual's own character and activity and (2) the way these are viewed by others. A person's actions implicitly or explicitly express her self, revealing her thoughts, feelings, and character. These actions make an impression on others. Other people interpret these actions as reflecting back on the self; they attribute the actions, as well as the thoughts and feelings they appear to express, to the actor. The sum of what is imputed to an individual in this way constitutes her reputation.[62]

Image or reputation is not a mere representation of the self, however. Because people interact only on the basis of their perceptions of one another, an individual's image may be said to constitute his social personality, or his self in relation to others. Indeed, this is the root meaning of *persona* — a Latin term that originally referred to the mask worn by an actor and hence came to mean the character in which an individual appears to other people.[63]

It follows that the duty to respect others as persons extends to their image or reputation.[64] The right to reputation has two aspects. Negatively, it consists in a right not to have actions or characteristics falsely imputed to oneself.[65] Positively, it is a right not to be deprived of the image one has legitimately acquired through one's interaction with others.[66]

Defamatory speech injures an individual's reputation by falsely representing her character or actions in a way that lowers her in the esteem of others. Defamation constitutes an intrinsic wrong to personality and may cause instrumental harm in the ways that Blackstone discusses. Defamation is wrongful only if it is false, however, because one has a right to reputation only to the extent that it accurately reflects the self.[67]

In addition to causing substantive harm to reputation, defamation infringes the victim's dignity. There is a fundamental distinction between the images we form of persons and those we form of things: things are mere passive objects that we are free to visualize as we please, while persons are autonomous subjects with some claim to shape the way in which they are viewed.[68] To falsely represent an individual's character or actions for our own purposes is to treat him as a mere object, contrary to his right to dignity.

This account of reputation recalls our earlier discussion of privacy. Both rights serve to protect the self from improper forms of objectification. Within the bounds of the right to privacy, an individual is free to develop her personality without intrusion from or exposure to the outside world. By contrast, reputation is concerned with the social dimension of personality. In this context, a person has no right to be free from the observation or judgment of others. The right to reputation does not preclude this, but rather seeks to protect individuals from being reduced to the status of *mere* objects as opposed to autonomous subjects. In short, the right to privacy creates an inner realm within which the self may not be viewed as an object at all, whereas the right to reputation regulates the *manner* in which the image of the self is constructed in the social realm.[69]

SPEECH AND CHARACTER

Thus far, I have been discussing the rights that flow from a conception of the person as a free being of intrinsic worth. But one can also approach personality by asking what constitutes a good person. In several insightful essays, Vincent Blasi has sketched a theory of free speech that focuses on the idea of good character.[70] Drawing on writers like Milton and Brandeis, Blasi argues that "a culture that prizes and protects expressive liberty nurtures in its members certain character traits such as inquisitiveness, independence of judgment, distrust of authority, willingness to take initiative, perseverance, and the courage to confront evil." Blasi considers such traits to be valuable "not for their intrinsic virtue but for their instrumental contribution to collective well-being, social as well as political."[71] But we can also regard these traits as good in themselves, that is, as part of our conception of a good person. A conception of this sort can play an important role within a rights-based view. For example, Kant holds that self-development is an essential end for human beings. For this reason, individuals have a moral duty to develop their natural capacities as well as their moral characters.[72] But whatever individuals have a duty to do, they also have a right to do, within the bounds of the rights of others.[73] In this way, a conception of good character can provide support for an intrinsic as well as an instrumental justification for rights.

Blasi persuasively argues that freedom of speech tends to promote courage, independence, and the other virtues set forth above, as well as other valuable traits such as "aversion to simplistic accounts and solutions, capacity to act on one's convictions even in the face of doubt and criticism, self-awareness, imagination, intellectual and cultural empathy, resilience, temperamental receptivity to change, tendency to view problems and events in a broad perspective, and respect for evidence."[74] As broad as this list is, however, it fails to include at least one crucial trait: respect for other people. Surely this is essential to our idea of good character. Moreover, respect for others is inextricably connected with self-respect, a virtue that would seem to lie at the root of many of the qualities Blasi celebrates.[75]

In this way, the idea of good character not only justifies a strong right to expressive freedom, but also points to limitations on that right. Like the qualities that Blasi discusses, respect for others involves an internal attitude and thus cannot be coerced by law. But the law can legitimately require individuals to refrain from violating the rights of others.[76] Although this is merely an external form of respect, it tends to promote an internal disposition to show consideration for other people and their rights. A broad right to free speech that is qualified in this way may well promote good character more fully than such a right standing by itself.

To put the point another way, the idea of good character supports rights in addition to free speech. For example, the law must protect individuals against violence if they are to enjoy "independence of judgment." Similarly, the right to privacy is important for nurturing "self-awareness." In general, human personality is likely to flourish to the greatest extent if the law protects the full range of rights explored in this chapter.

Blasi acknowledges the possibility that good character may be promoted by imposing some limitations on speech. But he argues that "corrective dynamics" are already present within the society: "The spectacle of a person or cause or profession losing all sense of balance and decency tends to bring home to others the need to reinvigorate the moral and social order." It is better to rely on "informal limits" than to invoke "the heavy, slow-moving, clumsy artillery of the law." For instance, "[r]eporters who take liberties with the truth will be corrected far more by demanding editors and readers than by libel judgments," while "[p]rotesters who assault the sensibilities of the public will be reined in when their tactics cause audiences to recoil and their opponents to succeed in discrediting them."[77]

Blasi is right to stress that some of the most important limitations on action derive from social norms rather than from legal rules. But these two kinds of restraints are not mutually exclusive. It seems likely that a combination of legal and social limits would be most effective in controlling improper action while at the same time respecting individual liberty. Blasi responds that, while this may be true in theory, as a practical matter the existence of legal regulation tends to undermine rather than to reinforce social restraints.[78] This is highly debatable, however. For instance, it is difficult to believe that the media would be *more* respectful of individual privacy and reputation if they were freed from all possibility of lawsuits.

More fundamentally, however persuasive Blasi's notion of "corrective dynamics" may be in the context of his own instrumentalist approach — an approach that emphasizes the impact of legal principles on character and culture in general — it is much less convincing in the context of a theory that focuses on the protection of individual rights. Even if it is true that excesses by reporters or protesters will ultimately provoke a backlash, a rights-based view would still recognize a need to protect those individuals who are wrongfully injured at the present time by irresponsible journalism or by protests that violate rights (such as blockades that shut down abortion clinics). As I noted in chapter 3, there are situations in which it would be inappropriate for the law to intervene, because legal regulation would be ineffective or would do more harm than good.[79] But this judgment should be made in particular contexts rather than on an across-the-board basis. Surely Blasi would not say that the law should refuse to protect personal security against threats and other violent forms of expression. Similarly, there is no reason personality rights should be categorically excluded from legal protection.

Free Speech and Community

In the previous section, I explored rights of personality, a category which includes rights to (1) emotional tranquillity and privacy, (2) self-expression through speech and conduct, and (3) image or reputation. These rights can be viewed as a continuum, from those that focus on an individual's inner life to those that focus on her interaction with others. In this way, the development of personality rights leads to the next category of rights — those that people have as members of society.

What does liberty mean in this sphere? Society may seem antithetical to freedom because of the constraints it imposes on individuals. A central insight of the social contract tradition, however, is that those constraints can be reconciled with the idea of self-determination if, and insofar as, they can be regarded as limitations that people freely impose on themselves.[80] In particular, laws made by the political community are consonant with freedom (1) in a formal sense, insofar as they result from a process of collective self-determination in which all citizens have a voice; and (2) in a substantive sense, insofar as they are necessary to protect individual rights or advance the common good — that is, those ends that people have in common and would authorize the community to pursue through collective action. According to this view, the purpose of society is not to restrict but to promote freedom. Society does this not only by protecting natural liberty, but also by creating new opportunities for the realization of individual capacities through social interaction, as well as by enabling people to pursue ends collectively that they could not achieve as well (or at all) on their own.[81]

Against this background, I want to sketch what it means to be a free person in the social realm. First, and most fundamentally, it means *to be a citizen or member of the community* and to be treated as such by others and by the community as a whole. In addition to the tangible rights and benefits that it confers, citizenship has an important dignitary dimension. As Kant puts it, "[N]o man in a state can be without any dignity, since he at least has the dignity of a citizen."[82] I shall return to this point in discussing the problem of hate speech in chapter 10.

Second, in a free society individuals are entitled to *civil liberty,* which includes the two forms of freedom I have already discussed — external rights and personality rights — subject to such regulation as is necessary to protect the rights of others and the common good.[83] Third, individuals are entitled to *political liberty,* or the right to full and equal participation in the process by which the society governs itself.[84] Finally, they have a claim to *social liberty,* or the right to form relationships with others and to take part in community life.[85]

Taken together, these four elements — citizenship and the civil, political, and social rights that flow from it — define what it means to be free within the sphere of community.[86] Only in this way can it be said that individuals remain autonomous even though they are subject to social constraint.

Just as liberty provided justifications for freedom of expression in the first two spheres, so it does in this realm. First, free speech is entitled to constitutional protection as a form of civil liberty — a rationale that applies to private as well as public forms of expression. Second, free speech is a form of political liberty. From a negative standpoint, the First Amendment protects the expression of dissent and allows the people and the press to check abuse of governmental power.[87] From a positive perspective, freedom of speech plays a vital role in democratic self-government. As Justice Brandeis argues in *Whitney v. California* (1927), the First Amendment seeks to promote "the discovery and spread of political truth" by enabling citizens to engage in "free and fearless reasoning" about the common good.[88]

This Brandeisian theme is developed more fully by Alexander Meiklejohn in a classic series of lectures first published in 1948.[89] The American form of government, Meiklejohn maintains, is founded on a "social compact" that we

have made as free and equal individuals to constitute a self-governing community. The First Amendment protects freedom of speech because it is necessary
to democratic deliberation. Meiklejohn elaborates this view by discussing the
traditional town meeting, in which citizens gather to debate and act on matters
of public concern. In this meeting, every individual "has a right and a duty to
think his own thoughts, to express them, and to listen to the arguments of
others." Free speech must be protected so that the community can reach the
wisest and most fully informed decisions on the issues that come before it. This
means that no view "shall be denied a hearing because it is on one side of the
issue rather than another" or because others think it false or dangerous.[90]

Although Meiklejohn's theory is often described as an instrumentalist one, it
has an important dignitary dimension as well. "Whether it be in the field of
individual or of social activity," he asserts, "men are not recognizable as men
unless, in any given situation, they are using their minds to give direction to
their behavior." Echoing Kant, Meiklejohn holds that citizens have dignity
insofar as they participate in making the laws by which they themselves are
governed. Freedom of thought and expression are essential in political matters
as well as in art, literature, philosophy, science, and education, in order "to so
inform and cultivate the mind and will of a citizen that he shall have the
wisdom, the independence, and, therefore, the dignity of a governing citizen."[91]

In the nature and requirements of a self-governing community, Meiklejohn
finds not only the basis but also the limits of political freedom of speech.
Again, he makes the point in the context of the town meeting. That forum
cannot function unless its members observe certain rules of order — rules that,
for example, forbid interrupting a person who has the floor or making abusive
personal attacks on other members. Speech of this sort obstructs the delibera-
tive process and thereby "threatens to defeat the purpose of the meeting." For
this reason, it is not protected by the principle of political free speech.[92]

This highlights a crucial point about freedom of speech as political liberty.
Many of the rights we have explored may be described as inherently individual
rights, that is, rights that individuals can exercise without any necessary interaction with others. By contrast, political free speech is best understood as a
relational right — a right to interact with others in a particular way or to take
part in a shared activity.[93] As Brandeis and Meiklejohn describe it, it is a right
to engage in discourse with others who have the same rights of citizenship and
participation and who are engaged in the "common enterprise" of democratic
self-governance.[94] The right to participate in public deliberation therefore
carries with it a duty to respect the corresponding rights of other citizens and
of the community itself.

Like the previous justifications, then, the concept of political liberty both supports a right to free speech and at the same time points to limitations on that right. In the case of political freedom of speech, these limits are internal to the right itself. Like other liberties, political free speech is also subject to external constraints arising from other rights, such as personal security and reputation. Because of its great value, however, political speech sometimes should be protected at the expense of other rights, as in the *New York Times* case.

Thus far, I have been treating political free speech as an individual right. At the same time, this freedom is also one that belongs to the community as a whole. In Lockean terms, free speech allows the people to oversee the conduct of public affairs. In Meiklejohn's language, First Amendment liberties play an integral part in the "activities . . . by which we govern." It follows that unjustified restraints on political discourse invade the rights not only of individual citizens but also of the community itself.[95]

Finally, free speech is an element of social liberty. Communication plays a vital role in establishing and maintaining social relationships. Individuals also have a right to participate in and contribute to the culture of the community.[96] Once again, when free speech is viewed in this way, it is best understood as a relational right to take part in shared activity.[97]

Free Speech and the Search for Truth

Another justification for the liberties protected by the First Amendment is that they are essential to the search for truth.[98] For the liberal tradition, this activity has intrinsic as well as instrumental value. As Milton, Locke, and John Stuart Mill stress, in pursuing truth, individuals exercise and develop their intellectual capacities. In this way, they realize their nature as rational beings, the source of human freedom and dignity.[99] It follows that there is a fundamental right to engage in this activity.

The search for truth takes place not in the abstract, but rather within the different spheres I have identified. Thus, it includes efforts to attain knowledge of the external world, of the self, of the social and political realm, and of "the sphere of intellect and spirit."[100] In each of these settings, the search for truth depends on freedom of speech.

Let us begin with the external world. As I have suggested, people can attain knowledge of external things only through their appearances.[101] Yet it is difficult to know how far one's perceptions are accurate and how far they are distorted by one's own biases and limitations. To attain accurate knowledge in this sphere, individuals need to correlate their perceptions with those of others. In addition to its importance in everyday life, this process is central to judicial fact-finding, scientific investigation, and other modes of inquiry.

The search for truth takes a very different form in the personal realm. There, instead of seeking an objective perception of the external world, the individual turns inward in search of self-knowledge. To a large extent, such knowledge can be attained only through introspection. Even in this sphere, however, expression and communication can play an important role in clarifying one's thoughts and feelings; in enabling one to understand how one's actions affect other people and how one is viewed by them; and in reflecting on the aspects of one's identity that one shares with others.[102] Moreover, individuals derive much of their identity from the various communities to which they belong.[103] To know oneself, one must explore what it means to be a member of these communities as well as what it means to be a human being in general.[104] In these ways, self-knowledge has a social as well as a normative dimension.

This brings us to the social and political realm. In this domain, the search for truth takes the form of an effort by the members of society to develop shared understandings of such matters as justice and the common good, which constitute the object of truth in this realm, just as the external world and the self did in the first two spheres.

The search for social and political truth can be understood in several ways. Perhaps the most familiar is Justice Holmes's image of the marketplace of ideas. According to laissez-faire economic theory, the pursuit of individual self-interest leads, through the workings of the market, to the greatest aggregate welfare of the society. In addition, market competition results in the success of those products that best satisfy the needs and desires of consumers. Similarly, in his famous dissenting opinion in *Abrams v. United States* (1919), Holmes suggests that "the best test of truth is the power of the thought to get itself accepted in the competition of the market," and that the truth that emerges in this way is most likely to bring about "the ultimate good" that people desire.[105]

Despite its powerful impact on American thought, Holmes's marketplace metaphor is unpersuasive as an account of the search for social and political truth. As market actors, individuals pursue their own private goods. Thus, the participants in a marketplace of ideas would opt for those ideas that best promoted their subjective interests and beliefs, and the ideas that prevailed would be those that satisfied the interests and beliefs of the greatest number of people. The outcome of this process, however, would be not an objective truth but merely an aggregate subjective belief. Although this belief might accord with the interests and views of a majority, there is no necessary reason it should be consistent with those of other members of the community. Holmes's account therefore fails to explain how the subjective perspectives of individuals and groups can be transformed into truths that are shared by the society as a whole.[106]

In contrast to Holmes's economic metaphor, Brandeis and Meiklejohn articulate a civic model of the search for truth.[107] According to this view, public discourse is best understood as a forum within which free and equal citizens articulate competing views on justice and the public good, in a common effort to advance those ends. Only in this way can we arrive at political truth. This view does not necessarily assume that discussion will lead to consensus. Indeed, diversity of opinion is valuable so that issues may be illuminated from every point of view.[108] For the civic conception, the most important truth is not any particular outcome of the process, but rather a commitment to the process itself.

This civic conception is superior to Holmes's marketplace of ideas in showing how people can arrive at common understandings through free discussion. Yet if the marketplace model conceives of individuals in an overly private way, the civic conception errs in the opposite direction. According to Meiklejohn, individuals possess two "radically different" capacities — their role as citizens and their role as private persons. Likewise, he draws a fundamental distinction between public speech, which concerns the common good, and speech that is directed toward private interests. As Meiklejohn himself recognizes, however, in a liberal society "the public interest is not another different interest superimposed upon our individual desires and intentions," but rather "is made up out of the separate purposes of the citizens."[109] If this is so, then the quest for political truth requires that citizens give a hearing not only to competing conceptions of the common good, but also to the particular interests of which it is composed. For this reason, political speech should not be thought of as occurring solely on a public level. Instead, such speech also mediates between the private and public realms by showing how the interests of particular individuals and groups should be understood as forming part of the community's good. On this revised civic conception, the search for social and political truth involves an effort to arrive at mutual understanding through the transformation of subjective views that reflect particular interests, as well as through debate over more general conceptions of justice and the common good. This view incorporates elements of both the civic and the marketplace models, with their respective views of individuals as public and private actors.

In pursuing knowledge of the external world, of the self, and of the social and political realm, human beings often come to raise more ultimate questions. What is the relationship between these spheres? Can they be understood to form a larger whole? What are the nature and origins of this whole? What place do human beings have within it? This is the deepest level on which the search for truth takes place, a realm that is explored in much art, literature, religion, philosophy, and science.

It is on this level that many of the great controversies over freedom of expression have taken place. A traditional justification for censorship was that it was required in order to prevent the spread of ideas that would undermine the fundamental truths upon which a particular social order was based. Advocates of free expression like Milton, Locke, and Mill responded in several ways. First, they argued that this justification failed to recognize the subjective dimension of truth. Even if a belief is objectively true, it will lack vitality unless it is actually held by those who profess it. Second, these writers asserted that proponents of censorship were mistaken in identifying their own views or the dominant beliefs of the society with objective truth. Truth is not directly accessible to human beings but can be arrived at only through a clash of diverse perspectives. Finally, they implied, one of the most important truths about human beings is that they are rational beings whose self-fulfillment requires that they actively pursue truth. For all of these reasons, freedom of thought and expression are necessary for the search for truth regarding ultimate meaning and value.[110]

In exploring external liberty, personality rights, and rights of citizenship, I contended that the same values that supported freedom of expression also pointed to certain limitations on that freedom. The same may be said of the right to pursue truth. First, this right is rooted in a conception of a person as a free subject endowed with consciousness. But the same is true of other human beings as well. It follows that when individuals view others as mere objects, rather than as subjects in their own right, they contradict the very basis on which the search for truth rests. While such a belief may reflect the subjective consciousness of particular individuals, it is necessarily contrary to the truth about human beings. That is not to say that such beliefs have no value at all in connection with the search for truth.[111] It is merely to say that any value they have cannot derive from the possibility that they may turn out to be true. Second, we have seen that in many different ways the pursuit of truth requires interaction with others.[112] Insofar as this is true, the search for truth is a relational right which should be exercised with due respect for other participants.[113] In short, the truth rationale points to two limitations on the proper use of free speech: (1) the negative constraint that individuals should not view other human beings as mere objects; and (2) the positive constraint that they should recognize others as participants in a common enterprise of searching for truth.

I should emphasize the limited role of these constraints. They do not provide an affirmative justification for restricting free expression. In the liberal tradition, the coercive powers of government do not extend to matters of thought or belief as such; government may never restrict expression simply because of disagreement with it or fear that it will undermine the truth.[114] Nevertheless, these constraints do serve to make an important point: that expression has less value in the search for truth when it represents others as mere objects or refuses to acknowledge their own capacity to participate in this activity. In some contexts, this attenuated value may mean that, where the expression violates the rights of others, it should not be protected because of its value in relation to truth.[115]

Free Speech and Equality

In this chapter, I have explored a wide range of substantive rights, including (1) external rights to life, liberty, and property; (2) rights to individual self-realization; (3) rights to participate in the political, social, and cultural life of the community; and (4) rights to intellectual and spiritual freedom. All of these rights flow from one's status as a free person. But persons are not only free but equal. This brings us to a final right — the right to equality.

In contrast to modern thought, which often sees liberty and equality as antithetical to one another, the natural rights tradition views the two concepts as inseparably related.[116] Because all individuals are equal, no one may interfere with the legitimate freedom of another. Similarly, because all are free, no one has a right to dominate another. Equality can be defined in two ways: in negative terms, it means the right to be free from subordination by others, while in positive terms it means an equal claim to one's liberty or rights.[117] In addition, all persons have a right to equal protection under the law without unjust discrimination.[118]

Equality is also closely related to dignity.[119] To treat other persons as inferior or subordinate constitutes a denial of their worth as human beings. Of course, the right to equality is among the most fundamental principles of modern law. It is recognized not only by the Fourteenth Amendment but also by state constitutions, by federal, state, and local civil rights legislation, by the law of other liberal democratic nations, and by the international law of human rights.[120]

In this chapter, I have argued that the substantive values that underlie freedom of speech also enable us to identify the appropriate limits of that freedom. The same is true of the right to equality. As we shall see in chapter 6, much of contemporary First Amendment doctrine is based on the principle that every individual has an equal right to engage in expression and that the state may not improperly discriminate between different speakers or ideas. On the other hand, some kinds of speech should be regarded as wrongful because they violate their targets' right to equality — a point that will play an important role in the discussion of hate speech and pornography in chapters 10 and 11.

5

Conflicts of Rights

On the view I am developing, the liberties protected by the First Amendment exist within a broader framework of rights based on human dignity and autonomy. As a rule, speakers should have a duty to respect the rights of others. Some cases, however, pose difficult conflicts between free speech and other rights. In this chapter, I first discuss how such conflicts should be resolved in general. I then consider the roles that legislatures and courts should play in this area. Finally, I address two important objections to this theory of the First Amendment.

Resolving Conflicts of Rights

A THREEFOLD INQUIRY

Although free speech must be exercised with due regard for other rights, that does not mean it must always give way to those rights. Rights may be clearly defined at the core, but their outer bounds are not fixed.[1] In some cases, what appears to be a conflict can be resolved by adjusting the boundaries of the competing rights. Even when this is not possible, there is only a prima facie justification for regulating speech that infringes other rights, for the value of the speech may be so substantial that it should be regarded as privileged under the First Amendment.

Whether one conceives of the problem in terms of adjustment or privilege depends in part on the nature of the right that is affected by the speech. If the right is one that is injured solely, or at least typically, by speech, it is natural to view the issue as one of determining the boundary between the two rights (such as the right to informational privacy on one hand and the public's right to know on the other). By contrast, rights that can be injured both by speech and by conduct are often defined most easily without reference to speech. In such cases, the issue is best formulated as whether speech should be privileged to override the other right.[2] Regardless of how the problem is framed, a similar analysis should apply. Under the rights-based theory, there are three closely related ways to approach conflicts between freedom of speech and other rights.

Balancing of rights. The first method, balancing, seeks to determine which right has more weight. This determination should be made at the margin — that is, instead of asking whether freedom of speech or, say, the right to privacy has greater value in general, one should ask (1) how much the value of privacy would be affected by the speech at issue, and (2) how much the value of free speech would be impaired by regulations to protect privacy. In this analysis, the availability of alternatives has great importance. The state is not warranted in regulating speech if there is a less restrictive alternative that would afford the same protection to other rights. By the same token, a speaker is not justified in infringing other rights if the values underlying freedom of speech would be promoted just as well without the infringement.

Of course, to assess the value of competing rights, one needs a common standard by which to measure them. In the liberal humanist approach, that standard may be found in the same principles that justify these rights in the first place. Rights have value as aspects of (1) external freedom, (2) freedom to develop and express one's personality, (3) freedom to participate in the social, cultural, and political life of the community, and (4) intellectual and spiritual freedom. Ultimately, the value of a right reflects its importance as an aspect of human freedom and dignity.

The value of rights is subject to a crucial constraint, however: an asserted right can derive no value from its negation of another right. For example, an individual who threatens another with violence might contend that the speech has value as a form of self-realization. From a rights-based perspective, however, the speaker's self-realization cannot count as a value insofar as it depends on causing another to fear injury. If the right to personal security has positive value, then the negation of that right cannot also have such value. That is not to say that the speech has no value at all: it may have value as an exercise of external freedom or even as a form of individual self-realization, insofar as this derives from something other than the infliction of fear. Of course, these values are unlikely to justify serious invasions of personal security.

In short, when an act of expression comes into conflict with another right, the balancing approach seeks to determine whether regulation is warranted by weighing (1) the value of the speech and (2) the extent of the restriction against (3) the value of the other right and (4) the impact of unregulated speech on that right. The aim of this approach is to harmonize the competing rights by protecting both as far as possible and, to the extent they conflict, by protecting the right that at the margin constitutes the most important form of liberty.[3]

It is vital to observe that, while this method involves balancing, it is fundamentally different from a generalized weighing of social interests. Such an approach regards speech, like other interests, as valuable insofar as it promotes social welfare. By contrast, the method I propose would allow speech to be restricted only when necessary to protect another right that, under the circumstances, is more valuable as an aspect of human freedom.[4] Unlike interest balancing, this approach is consistent with what Rawls calls "the priority of liberty."[5]

Finally, let us consider the level of generality at which the characterization and balancing of rights should occur. On one hand, it would be neither meaningful nor useful to ask whether, in the abstract, freedom of speech has more value than rights like privacy or personal security. All of these rights are fundamental and have their basis in human dignity and autonomy. Moreover, rights are not abstractions but have meaning and force only insofar as they are realized in the world. Thus, the question is not the value of the competing rights in the abstract, but their relative value in actual situations.

On the other hand, an ad hoc balancing of rights in each case would be equally unsatisfactory. Rights are not mere claims to act in specific ways (or to be free from such action) in particular contexts. Instead, they reflect more general principles of liberty. Ad hoc balancing risks overlooking this deeper dimension of rights and deciding cases on the basis of accidental factors or subjective predilections.

Thus, in resolving conflicts of rights, one should not proceed on a level of either abstract generality or ad hoc particularity. Instead, one should seek to identify certain *kinds* of speech and other rights and then weigh them against each other.[6] In other words, rights should be balanced at what has been called the "definitional" rather than the ad hoc level.[7]

Internal relationships between rights. In contrast to balancing, which involves an external comparison of the competing claims, the second approach to resolving conflicts of rights explores whether there is any internal relationship between them.[8] In some instances, one right is partly defined in relation to another. As we have seen, for example, the right to reputation presupposes that other people have a right to make accurate judgments about one's character and conduct. It follows that the right to reputation cannot be violated by true statements, regardless of how damaging they may be.[9]

In other cases, it may be argued that one right should prevail over another because it is more fundamental. For example, individuals cannot freely engage in speech (or any other activity) unless they feel safe from violence. In this sense, personal security is the most basic of rights. It follows that speech is not entitled to protection when it is used to seriously threaten the safety of others.

As we have seen, however, relationships between rights do not necessarily run only in one direction.[10] Thus, while personal security is necessary for freedom of speech, the reverse is also true: free speech is essential to political freedom, the ultimate safeguard of all other rights.[11] For this reason, political speech should be restricted only when it amounts to a serious infringement of other rights.

The system of constitutional liberty. This discussion of the interrelationship between rights suggests that they form a larger whole. This leads to a third way of resolving conflicts, which is to ask which right, under the circumstances, is most important to the system of constitutional liberty. To recur to the previous example, if individuals were allowed to assault or threaten others, the result would be to greatly weaken the overall system of liberty. On the other hand, the system would also be undermined if speech could be restricted because of distant or speculative fears of violence.[12] Thus, interpretations of the First Amendment that would lead to either result should be rejected.

Elaborating the approach. The three methods of resolving conflicts between freedom of speech and other rights are closely related to one another. Each one seeks to identify what the rights have in common and to use that as a criterion for determining which one should prevail. The first method locates this common ground in the principles that underlie the competing rights; the second, in the internal relationship between them; and the third, in the role that each plays in the system of constitutional liberty. Rather than being mutually exclusive, the three approaches overlap with and reinforce one another. Constitutional arguments and decisions frequently rely on more than one.

Up to this point, the discussion has focused on conflicts between freedom of speech and other rights. But conflicts can also take place within free expression itself. For example, hecklers who seek to drown out a speech at a political rally interfere with the First Amendment rights of the speaker and the audience. The same is true of crowd members who threaten the speaker with violence. In cases of this sort, expressive values are at stake on both sides. Such cases can be analyzed through the same threefold approach outlined above. First, loud noises and threats of violence clearly have less value, in terms of the four elements of liberty, than does the right to engage in political discourse. Second, personal security and the ability to be heard are necessary conditions for all freedom of speech. Speech that negates these conditions therefore undermines its own normative basis. Finally, it is clear that political expression holds a higher place in the system of constitutional liberty than the two forms of speech with which it here conflicts. In cases like this, speech may properly be restricted for the sake of free expression itself.

For purposes of clarity, my discussion has also assumed that only two competing rights are involved. First Amendment problems often are more complex than this, however, involving multiple rights of individuals and the community. For example, suppose that an extremist speaker at a political rally urges her followers to attack opponents who are staging a counterdemonstration nearby. To determine whether this speech should be protected, one would have to consider not only the speaker's right to free expression and the opponents' right to personal security, but also the rights of the audience and the public to hear the speech, as well as the community's right to preserve the peace.

It follows that resolving conflicts of rights is a multifaceted process. Sometimes the answer is intuitively obvious: few people would hold threats of imminent violence to be protected speech. Other problems call for more complex and difficult analysis. In such cases, while the rights-based approach does not yield clear, uncontroversial results, it does serve to focus our attention on the critical issue — the relative value and importance of different forms of liberty.

AN ILLUSTRATION: DEFAMATION AND THE FIRST AMENDMENT

Public officials. To illustrate this approach to conflicts of rights, I want to briefly explore a central issue in modern constitutional law — how defamation should be treated under the First Amendment. The common law imposed a form of strict liability for false statements that injured an individual's reputation. The Supreme Court first addressed the validity of this regime in the landmark case of *New York Times Co. v. Sullivan* (1964). The *Times* had published an advertisement which denounced acts of violence and repression directed against the Reverend Dr. Martin Luther King, Jr., and other civil rights activists in the South. Although the statements in the ad were largely true, they were inaccurate in several respects. Alleging that the ad had defamed him, the police commissioner of Montgomery, Alabama, L. B. Sullivan, brought suit against the newspaper in state court and was awarded half a million dollars in damages. On appeal, the Supreme Court overturned the award under the First Amendment. Writing for the Court, Justice William J. Brennan, Jr., held that a public official could recover for defamation related to his official conduct only if he could show by clear and convincing evidence that the defendant acted with "actual malice," that is, that the statement was either knowingly or recklessly false.[13]

From a rights-based perspective, the Court was correct to resolve the conflict strongly in favor of speech. Although the right to reputation is an important one, in cases involving government officials the values served by free speech are even more important. As Brennan emphasized in *Garrison v. Louisiana* (1964), the right to debate public issues and to evaluate the conduct of public officials is "the essence of self-government." Speech of this sort is vital to political freedom as well as to the protection of civil liberty against governmental oppression (which was a central theme of the allegedly defamatory speech in the *Times* case). Moreover, restrictions on good-faith criticism may have a substantial impact on the willingness of citizens to criticize government officials, while immunizing such speech may have much less impact on reputation, since officials often can effectively respond to attacks through counterspeech.[14]

Thus, a balancing of rights dictates that free speech should receive strong protection in this context. This conclusion is greatly reinforced by the second approach, which explores the internal relationship between the two rights. An individual's reputation consists in what other people say and think about her. The very concept of reputation presupposes that others will assess a person and her actions. It follows that reputation may be understood as a relational right, that is, as a right to interact with other people in a particular way. Such rights are inherently limited by the corresponding rights of others — in this case, their right to freely discuss an individual's character and conduct.[15]

This free speech right is a mirror image of the right to reputation; it represents the same relationship between observers and observed, now viewed from the observers' standpoint. It too is relational in nature: it is a right to assess the character and conduct of another person and thereby affect her reputation. As a relational right, it is limited by the rights of the other person. As we have seen, reputation is, or should be, a reflection of an individual's actions as well as the way these are viewed by others. To misrepresent an individual is to treat her as a mere object rather than as an autonomous subject.

In short, both (1) the right to reputation and (2) the right to shape the reputation of others through speech may be understood as relational rights. These rights represent two different aspects of the same relationship between observers and observed. This relationship does not exist merely in the abstract, however. Instead, it takes different forms in different contexts. The form that the relationship takes will have a crucial bearing on the force of the respective rights.

In some contexts, observers and observed relate to one another as equals. In cases like *New York Times,* however, the relationship is very different. In a democratic society, government officials are regarded as representatives of the people, who as the ultimate sovereign have a right to oversee their conduct. The relationship between the people and their officials is therefore one of principal and agent, superior and subordinate.[16] Because this relationship is an asymmetrical one, so are the rights that inhere in it. It follows that the people's right to judge the character and conduct of government officials is more fundamental than the latter's right to reputation.

In discussing the relationship between free speech and official reputation, we have been led to explore where each fits within the overall structure of constitutional liberty. This inquiry — the third way of approaching conflicts — clearly supports the same result, for this form of speech is the cornerstone of constitutional democracy.

Thus, *New York Times* was right to establish a high level of constitutional protection for criticism of government officials. The standard of knowing or reckless falsity that the Court announced is a reasonable way to afford this protection.[17]

Public and private figures. A rights-based analysis also suggests that the Court was justified in extending the *New York Times* rule to cases involving public figures.[18] Some prominent persons exert an influence on political affairs comparable to that of public officials. Others play an important role in shaping the society and its culture. Although they may not be elected, their status and influence derive from public recognition. A strong right to discuss the character and conduct of public figures therefore is supported by considerations similar to those in *New York Times.*

In *Rosenbloom v. Metromedia, Inc.* (1971), a plurality of the Court asserted that the First Amendment should afford the same high level of protection to all communications on matters of public concern, regardless of whether they involve government officials or public figures. Accordingly, the plurality held that private individuals who were falsely accused in the media could recover only if they could meet the demanding standard of knowing or reckless falsity. Three years later, however, in *Gertz v. Robert Welch, Inc.* (1974), the Court overruled *Rosenbloom,* concluding that the decision unduly restricted the states' authority to protect private reputation.[19] A liberal humanist analysis suggests that this conclusion was sound.

As the social aspect of personality, reputation is central to individual dignity and self-realization. Moreover, in contrast to individuals who seek public office or other forms of social prominence, those who remain in the private sphere have done nothing to surrender their right to reputation, nor do they generally have effective means of responding to defamatory reports in the media.[20]

On the other hand, as Brennan contended for the plurality in *Rosenbloom,* the conduct of private individuals is often a matter of public concern.[21] To assess the strength of this interest, one should begin by recognizing that *public* has more than one meaning. In one sense, it refers to the people collectively, that is, to the polity or community as a whole. In another sense, it refers to the people regarded as an aggregate of private individuals.[22]

A person's conduct can be a matter of public concern in both senses. First, private individuals often show a strong desire to know about the lives of others. As businesses, media organizations have an interest in meeting the demand for such information. This activity is entirely legitimate, so long as it respects the rights of its subjects.

It should be clear, however, that the relationship between free speech and reputation is quite different in this context from what it was in *New York Times.* In that setting, the individuals who were subject to observation were the agents and subordinates of those who desired to monitor their conduct — the people in their capacity as citizens. For this reason, the right to free speech was more fundamental than the right to reputation. But no such inequality exists between nonpublic figures and other private individuals who wish to report upon or learn about their lives. To be sure, people have a right to make judgments about the character and conduct of others. In the present context, however, the observers and observed are on a level of equality. The right of the former to judge is no stronger than the right of the latter to be represented in a fair and accurate way.

To the extent that a person's conduct affects the community as a whole, it may also be of public concern in the collective sense. For example, the public has a legitimate interest in knowing about criminal conduct as well as other behavior that violates the norms of the community and that is not shielded by the right to privacy. Again, however, individuals are not subordinate to the community in the same way that public officials and figures are. Although the community has a right to make judgments about its members' conduct, individuals equally have a right that such judgments be as accurate as possible. Just as there is a right to due process in legal proceedings, there should be an analogous right to fairness when a person is tried in the court of public opinion.

This analysis of the relationship between free speech and private reputation suggests that neither of these rights is more fundamental than the other. An exploration of their role in the system of constitutional liberty leads to the same conclusion. The *New York Times* decision was based on the Madisonian view that the " 'right of freely examining public characters and measures . . . [is] the only effectual guardian of every other right.' " The right of *private* reputation, on the other hand, is among the fundamental rights that society exists to protect. As Justice Stewart once observed, that right "reflects no more than our basic concept of the essential dignity and worth of every human being — a concept at the root of any decent system of ordered liberty."[23]

It follows that free speech confers no general right to violate private reputation. Because these rights are of the same order of value, it was appropriate for the Court in *Gertz* to conclude that speakers may be held responsible for causing injury to reputation when they are at fault, that is, when they fail to use reasonable care to determine whether the defamatory statements are actually true.[24]

The Role of Legislatures and Courts

Thus far, I have been discussing how the boundaries between free speech and other rights should be determined in general. Now I want to briefly consider which institutions should exercise decision-making authority in this area.

On the view I have presented, the fundamental right to freedom of speech is subject to regulation only through narrowly drawn legal rules that are justified to protect the rights of others. These rules can take the form either of statutes enacted by the legislature (such as criminal laws against threats and incitement) or of doctrines adopted by the courts through the common law process (such as the tort standards that impose liability for defamation and invasion of privacy). In adopting such rules, the legislature or the common law court makes several judgments. First, it decides that a particular right should be recognized and protected by law. Second, it defines the scope of that right. And finally, it draws a boundary between that right and freedom of expression.

In assessing the constitutionality of such a rule, a court exercising the power of judicial review must evaluate each of these determinations: it must decide whether the lawmaking body was correct to determine that individuals have the right in question; whether the rule defines the scope of the right in an appropriate way; and above all, whether the rule unduly infringes the freedom of speech and press. At the same time, the constitutional court should bear in mind that the goal is not to maximize free speech at all costs, but rather to harmonize it with other basic rights. The judges should also recognize that there may be more than one reasonable way for the law to achieve this goal. If, after a serious and searching review, the court determines that the law represents an appropriate effort to reconcile the competing rights and that it does not unjustifiably restrict free expression, the court should uphold the regulation under the First Amendment.[25]

A Response to Some Objections

In this part of the book, I have outlined a liberal humanist theory of the First Amendment. According to this view, the same aspects of human dignity and autonomy that justify freedom of speech and thought also give rise to other fundamental rights, including rights of personal security, personality, and full and equal membership in the community. In general, speakers have a duty to respect these rights. Conflicts between rights should be resolved in light of their relative value, the relationship that exists between them, and their place within the system of constitutional liberty. In concluding this overview, I would like to consider two objections to this theory.

MAY FREE SPEECH BE RESTRICTED TO PROTECT NONCONSTITUTIONAL RIGHTS?

First, a critic might object that even if freedom of speech can properly be restricted for the sake of other rights, such restrictions can be imposed only to protect rights that themselves enjoy constitutional status (such as the Sixth Amendment guarantee of a fair trial), not to protect rights like reputation that derive from state law. Although this objection is plausible, a little reflection shows that it would lead to unacceptable results. For example, few people would deny that the law may punish threats of imminent violence. Yet the right to be free from private violence, like the right to reputation, is protected not by the Constitution but merely by state law.

To respond more fully to the objection, one should begin by observing that it reflects the assumptions of modern legal positivism. According to that view, rights have no independent existence, but derive their force from positive law.[26] It may seem to follow that the rights that are guaranteed by the Federal Constitution necessarily have greater authority than those that are secured merely by statutory or common law. In cases of conflict, then, the latter rights must yield to the former.

As we saw in chapter 1, however, the Bill of Rights and the Fourteenth Amendment were predicated on a very different understanding of rights. On that view, individuals derive their rights not from positive law but from the law of nature. Society and government are formed to protect those rights against invasion by other individuals. Once government is established, it also becomes necessary to safeguard those rights against the power of government itself. The object of a bill of rights is not to *create* fundamental rights, but merely to *secure* those rights against the government.

Thus, from a nonpositivist perspective, rights that are safeguarded by ordinary civil and criminal law may be no less fundamental than those protected by the Constitution itself. The importance of a right ultimately depends on its relationship to human freedom and dignity, not on the particular form in which the right is protected by positive law. The rights explored in chapter 4 are rooted in the same principles as free speech itself. For this reason, they have the same fundamental status and value, even if they are not themselves constitutional rights.

Of course, this is not to say that the Constitution should not prevail in cases where it conflicts with ordinary law. It is merely to say that, in interpreting the *scope* of the First Amendment, one should not readily assume that it abrogates fundamental rights protected by other bodies of law. To put the point another way, the Constitution not only secures rights, but also grants certain powers to the federal government, while reserving others to the states. Those powers include the authority to make and enforce laws for the protection of rights. Strictly speaking, then, the rights-based theory does not hold that constitutional rights may be limited to protect nonconstitutional rights. Instead, it merely holds that First Amendment liberties must be interpreted in the context of the Constitution as a whole, including those provisions that grant or recognize the government's authority to protect other fundamental rights. Thus, the rights-based theory is fully consistent with the status of the Constitution as supreme law.[27]

Moreover, in an important sense it would be incorrect to say that the Constitution does not recognize the rights discussed in chapter 4. Although it generally does not protect those rights against private parties,[28] it does safeguard many of them against the government itself. The rights to life, liberty, and property are protected by the Fifth and Fourteenth Amendments. Along with the Fourth Amendment, those provisions have also been held to protect certain rights of privacy.[29] The right to autonomy or self-determination is an important theme in the Court's substantive due process decisions.[30] The right to citizenship is secured by the first sentence of the Fourteenth Amendment, and rights of political participation have been held protected by that Amendment as well as by other provisions of the Constitution.[31] The right to intellectual and spiritual freedom lies at the core of the First Amendment, while the right to equality is enshrined in the Fourteenth. Finally, the Ninth Amendment reminds us that the people retain other basic rights which should not be "den[ied] or disparage[d]" on the ground that they are not specifically mentioned in the Constitution.[32] All of these rights, which are shielded by constitutional law against the power of the government, should be regarded as equally fundamental when protected by civil and criminal law against invasion by private parties.

In sum, the rights discussed in this part of the book should not be discounted on the ground that they lack constitutional status. This point was expressed most forcefully by Justice Stewart in *Rosenblatt v. Baer* (1966). After observing that the right to reputation is essential to individual dignity, he added, "The protection of private personality, like the protection of life itself, is left primarily to the individual States under the Ninth and Tenth Amendments. But this does not mean that the right is entitled to any less recognition . . . as a basic of our constitutional system."[33]

DOES A RIGHTS-BASED APPROACH UNDERMINE FREEDOM OF EXPRESSION?

It may be objected further that, while the liberal humanist theory affords protection to other fundamental rights, it does so at too high a cost to free speech. Far from undermining freedom of expression, however, the theory actually strengthens the normative basis of that right in two ways. First, the more that free speech is regarded as authorizing the violation of other important rights, the more difficult it becomes to perceive a difference between speech as a right and speech as a wrongful invasion of the rights of others. The result is to undermine the *rightfulness* of free speech. Thus, an excessive defense of free speech ironically may have the effect of weakening the normative basis of that right as well as public support for it. By contrast, free speech may enjoy the strongest status as a right when it must be exercised with due regard for the rights of others.

A second point relates to the teleology of free expression. Americans have traditionally thought of freedom of speech as promoting the good of the society and its members.[34] As we have seen, however, rights like personal security, privacy, and reputation reflect the same fundamental values as free speech itself and are also essential to individual and social well-being. Yet it is impossible for a society to attain all goods to an unlimited degree. Where different goods compete, achieving one will inevitably result in some sacrifice of another. When speech that has relatively little value for human liberty and dignity infringes rights that have substantial value, protecting the speech has the result of diminishing rather than promoting the good. Thus, free speech furthers the well-being of individuals and the society most effectively when speakers are required to respect the rights of others.

6

Content Neutrality and the First Amendment

The preceding chapters formulated a rights-based or liberal humanist theory of the First Amendment. In this chapter, I use the theory to evaluate the Supreme Court's current jurisprudence, which is based on the doctrine of content neutrality.

The origins of this doctrine may be found in *Police Department v. Mosley* (1972). For some months, a postal worker named Earl Mosley conducted a lonely vigil on the sidewalk outside a Chicago public school, protesting against racial discrimination. After the city council banned picketing in front of schools, Mosley challenged the constitutionality of this ordinance, urging the Court to hold that all peaceful, nondisruptive picketing was entitled to protection under the First Amendment. Declining to reach this broad issue, Justice Thurgood Marshall observed that the Chicago ordinance did not forbid all demonstrations near schools, but made an exception for "the peaceful picketing of any school involved in a labor dispute." Because the city was unable to offer a persuasive reason for this discrimination between labor and nonlabor picketing, Marshall concluded that the ordinance denied protesters like Mosley the equal protection of the laws guaranteed by the Fourteenth Amendment.[1]

At first glance, *Mosley* appeared to be a routine case which was disposed of on narrow grounds. This appearance was deceptive, however, for Marshall used the occasion to articulate a broad vision of the First Amendment. "The central problem with Chicago's ordinance," he declared, "is that it describes permissible picketing in terms of its subject matter. . . . But, above all else, the First Amendment means that government has no power to restrict expression because of its message, its ideas, its subject matter, or its content. . . . To permit the continued building of our politics and culture, and to assure self-fulfillment for each individual, our people are guaranteed the right to express any thought, free from government censorship. The essence of this forbidden censorship is content control. Any restriction on expressive activity because of its content would completely undercut the 'profound national commitment to the principle that debate on public issues should be uninhibited, robust, and wide-open.'"[2]

Although the decision attracted little notice at the time, *Mosley*'s doctrine of content neutrality has become the cornerstone of the Supreme Court's First Amendment jurisprudence.[3] The doctrine has two facets. The first is the rule against *content regulation*: government may not restrict speech because of its content. The second is the rule against *content discrimination*: government may not use content as a basis for treating some speech more favorably than other speech. Laws that contravene these principles are said to be "presumptively invalid" under the First Amendment. In addition, the Court has repeatedly rejected the notion that expression may be restricted "to shield the sensibilities of listeners" or to prevent "an adverse emotional impact on the audience."[4] These doctrines lie at the heart of many important decisions, including *American Booksellers Association v. Hudnut* (1985), which struck down a feminist antipornography ordinance; *Simon & Schuster, Inc. v. Members of New York State Crime Victims Board* (1991), which invalidated the state's Son-of-Sam law; *Texas v. Johnson* (1989) and *United States v. Eichman* (1990), which held flag burning protected under the First Amendment; *Collin v. Smith* (1978), which permitted a neo-Nazi group to march in Skokie, Illinois; and *R.A.V. v. City of St. Paul* (1992), which overturned a ban on cross burning and other forms of hate speech.[5]

As the mere recitation of these cases indicates, the content neutrality doctrine remains deeply controversial both on and off the Court.[6] The problem stems from the fact that some speech causes harm precisely because of its content. For example, threats may instill fear, incitement may provoke violence, defamation may injure reputation, and so on. This poses a dilemma for First Amendment jurisprudence. According to *Mosley*, speech may "never" be regulated on account of its content, for that is "[t]he essence of . . . censorship."[7] If this absolutist position were taken literally, however, it would disable the government from regulating speech even when necessary to prevent serious injury to individuals or the community.

In response to this concern, the Court has carved out two major exceptions to the neutrality doctrine. First, the Justices have adhered to the traditional view that some categories of speech (such as fighting words and obscenity) are entitled to little or no protection under the First Amendment.[8] Second, the Court has held in principle — though almost never in practice — that even fully protected speech may be regulated on the basis of content if the government is able to meet the requirements of "strict scrutiny," that is, if it can demonstrate that the regulation is necessary to achieve a compelling government interest.[9]

Unfortunately, however, the Court has never succeeded in explaining how these exceptions can be reconciled with the general principle of content neutrality. Instead, First Amendment jurisprudence has been marked by a deep and unresolved conflict between a strong commitment to that principle and an uneasy recognition of its limits. This tension is clearly reflected in the Justices' rhetoric, in which sweeping statements of content neutrality often appear side by side with ad hoc exceptions and qualifications.[10] In many cases, there appears to be no principled way for judges to choose between following the general rule and recognizing an exception. For this reason, the Court's free speech decisions often seem arbitrary. Far from illuminating the problem, the doctrine of content neutrality, when taken as the central concern of the First Amendment, only makes it more obscure.

In this chapter, I argue that content neutrality is an important element of free speech jurisprudence, but that it should not be regarded as "the first principle of the First Amendment."[11] Instead, it should be understood within a broader normative framework based on the idea of autonomy or self-determination. When individuals act within the scope of their own autonomy, government may not intrude into this realm by regulating the content of thought or expression. Nor may government interfere with the collective autonomy of citizens by imposing unjustified restrictions on public debate. As previous chapters have shown, however, some types of speech, such as defamation and incitement, should be regarded as infringing the autonomy or rights of other people. In such cases, the rationale for content neutrality no longer holds: in regulating speech, the government is not invading the province of the speaker or the community but is protecting the rightful freedom of others. In this way, we can harmonize the rule of content neutrality with the exceptions and formulate a principled basis for determining which should prevail in particular cases.

After discussing the meaning of *content,* the following section outlines the justifications for the neutrality doctrine. Next, I explore the limits of that doctrine. Finally, I discuss how the doctrine should be reformed in order to reconcile it with a liberal humanist approach to freedom of expression.

The Justifications for Content Neutrality

THE MEANING OF CONTENT

Although content is often identified with what a speaker is saying,[12] this understanding fails to capture the full range of the concept. We need to develop a richer account in order to see why content should be protected under the First Amendment and what the limits of this protection should be.

The content at issue is that of speech and other activity that falls within the scope of the First Amendment. The Amendment protects both *inward thought* and *outward expression or communication*. In turn, communication comprises the following elements: (1) an act of expression by the speaker; (2) the speech itself; and (3) its reception by the listener, which may have an impact not only on the listener herself but also on others (such as individuals who are defamed by the speech). Moreover, while these elements can be distinguished, they can also be regarded as an integrated whole. Thus, the First Amendment is also concerned with (4) the relationship that is formed through communication between the speaker and listener, or within which this communication takes place.

Content can be understood in parallel terms. One can speak of the content of inward thought as well as the content of outward expression or communication. The content of communication includes (1) its meaning for the speaker, that is, the thoughts and emotions that he intends to express; (2) the speech itself; and (3) the meaning of the speech for those who hear it or who are otherwise affected by it.[13] Finally, content can refer to (4) a shared meaning or understanding that arises through communication. In the remainder of this section, I show how each of these aspects of thought and communication supports the principle of content neutrality by establishing a sphere of autonomy that is generally entitled to protection against governmental interference.

CONTENT NEUTRALITY AND FREEDOM OF THOUGHT

Although the First Amendment does not expressly mention freedom of thought, it is generally agreed that this freedom lies at the heart of what the provision was meant to protect.[14] As Justice Marshall declared in *Stanley v. Georgia* (1969), the state may not seek to "control the moral content of a person's thoughts": "Our whole constitutional heritage rebels at the thought of giving government the power to control men's minds."[15]

As we have seen, this view has deep roots in the liberal tradition. For Locke, the freedom to think for oneself is a natural and inalienable right. Although government has authority to regulate the external affairs of individuals, it may not intrude into the internal realm of thought and belief. Kant draws a similar distinction, holding that the force of law applies only to outward actions, not to internal ones, such as thoughts. Likewise, in *On Liberty,* Mill argues that the rightful power of society is limited to "the external relations of the individual" and does not extend to those matters that concern only himself. At the core of this personal sphere is "the inward domain of consciousness," including "liberty of conscience, . . . thought and feeling."[16]

This liberal perspective provides one of the foundations of the First Amendment doctrine of content neutrality. On this view, while the state may regulate external interaction between individuals, it may not seek to control their thoughts and feelings — the content of the inner realm. As Justice Jackson wrote in the *Flag Salute Case* (1943), state action of this sort "invades the sphere of intellect and spirit" which the First Amendment was intended to protect.[17]

CONTENT NEUTRALITY AND FREEDOM OF COMMUNICATION

The four aspects of communication that I have identified also provide strong support for content neutrality. Communication begins with an act of expression by the speaker. In *Mosley,* Justice Marshall endorses Emerson's view that freedom of expression is necessary "to assure self-fulfillment for each individual." He also cites Justice Harlan's assertion that the First Amendment rests in part on our belief in "individual dignity and choice." Relying on these principles, the Court has held that "a speaker has the autonomy to choose the content of his own message."[18] This autonomy is impaired when the government restricts speech because it disapproves of the fact that an individual holds certain thoughts or attitudes or because it disapproves of his decision to express them. For example, flag burning may not be banned on the ground that it reflects a disloyal attitude toward the state.[19]

The second element of communication is the speech itself. In the liberal tradition, the government has no jurisdiction over meaning as such, but only over actions. It follows that the state has no power to restrict ideas simply because it disapproves of them or believes them to be false.[20]

The third element is the reception of the speech by others. The listener's liberty is a mirror image of the speaker's: just as the speaker is entitled to express her views, the listener should be free to hear them. This right is also rooted in respect for individual dignity and self-determination. The expression to which one is exposed plays a powerful role in shaping the self and its inner life. It follows that individuals should have broad freedom to decide for themselves what they wish to see and hear.[21] Access to information is also crucial to the exercise of practical choice by individuals.[22] For these reasons, *Stanley v. Georgia* and other cases hold that the First Amendment protects a "right to receive information and ideas."[23] Once more, the government invades a sphere of personal autonomy when it unjustifiably restricts expression out of concern for the effect it may have on willing listeners or viewers. For example, the state should not be allowed to restrict pornography on the ground that it causes moral harm to adults who choose to watch it.[24]

To fully understand communication, one must view it not only in terms of these separate elements, but also as a unified whole — an idea that has recently been explored by the philosopher Charles Taylor. In a series of illuminating essays, Taylor argues that the function of communication is not merely to transmit information from one person to another. Instead, speech transforms what initially was a subject of individual awareness into a subject of common awareness. In this way, the matter being discussed "is no longer just a matter for me, or for you, or for both of us severally, but is now *for us,* that is for us together." In other words, the goal of communication is not simply to convey ideas, but to develop a shared understanding. At the same time, communication establishes a relationship between the participants, a common ground or perspective "from which we survey the world together." Thus, in addition to its importance to separate individuals, speech has an intersubjective or social dimension.[25]

This insight leads to a further justification for the content neutrality rule. Just as the inner lives of individuals constitute spheres of autonomy, so do the relationships that arise through communication. Government intrudes into these relationships when it attempts, without adequate justification, to restrict communication between willing participants. This is true of speech that occurs in private conversations as well as within personal relationships like the family. And it is also true of speech that takes place in public discourse.[26] In particular, the First Amendment sharply restricts the government's power to regulate the content of speech within the sphere of democratic deliberation. As Meiklejohn explains, "When men govern themselves, it is they — and no one else — who must pass judgment" on the merits of competing views. It follows that the government may not restrict speech simply "because it is on one side of the issue rather than another." In this sense there is "an equality of status in the field of ideas." In *Mosley,* Marshall quotes Meiklejohn's view, which represents another key source of the content neutrality doctrine.[27]

This discussion of Meiklejohn points to a final basis for content neutrality, one that focuses on the ideal of equality. This ideal is implicit in the justifications I have already discussed.[28] The right to self-fulfillment through thought and expression is one that is shared by all. Likewise, everyone has a right to participate in public discourse. It follows that, when the government improperly denies these freedoms to particular individuals, it violates their right to equality as well as their substantive rights.

In this way, expressive liberty and equality are closely related, and the two can often be understood as two sides of the same coin. That does not mean, however, that the equality rationale is merely redundant. Even when the state has authority to regulate speech (say, by imposing reasonable time, place, and manner restrictions), it may not single out particular speakers or sorts of expression without sufficient justification. That would violate the right to equality and constitute impermissible content discrimination. *Mosley* itself is a classic example. Because the City of Chicago had no good reason for allowing labor picketing near schools while prohibiting all other forms of picketing, the ordinance infringed the right to equality, regardless of whether a ban on all picketing would have violated the First Amendment.[29]

Thus, the equality rationale has some independent force. Ultimately, however, this rationale depends on the substantive justifications developed above. It is only because thought and communication constitute spheres of autonomy that the government generally may not discriminate between different forms of speech and thought. To put the point another way, the neutrality doctrine finds its ultimate basis in the First Amendment rather than in the Equal Protection Clause.

THE SCOPE OF THE CONTENT NEUTRALITY DOCTRINE

The idea of autonomy also helps to explain the scope of the neutrality doctrine. Within the general category of content-based regulations, a distinction is commonly drawn between those based on *subject matter,* which restrict speech on an entire issue, and those based on *viewpoint,* which restrict speech on one side of an issue. For example, a ban on all demonstrations related to the war in Iraq would be a subject-matter regulation, whereas a ban on demonstrations that oppose the administration's policy would be a viewpoint-based restriction.[30]

Some Justices and scholars have asserted that the content neutrality rule is principally, or even exclusively, concerned with viewpoint regulation.[31] This assertion might be persuasive if the doctrine were based solely on a concern that the government might abuse its power by suppressing dissent. For the most part, however, the Court has taken a broader view, holding that the doctrine applies not only to viewpoint-based regulations, but also to those based on subject matter—a rule which was laid down in *Mosley* itself and which has been reaffirmed in many subsequent cases.[32] In my view, this rule does not rest merely on the notion that subject-matter regulations may serve as a cloak for viewpoint discrimination. Instead, the basic problem with such regulations is that they restrict expressive freedom.

The Limits of Content Neutrality

The account developed in the previous section allows us to identify not only the justifications but also the limits of content neutrality. *Mosley* protects the autonomy of speakers, listeners, and the community as a whole to determine the content of their own expression. Content regulation invades this autonomy and thereby violates the First Amendment. But this doctrine loses much of its force in cases where speech goes beyond the bounds of a sphere of autonomy and infringes the autonomy of others. When the law regulates such speech, it does not abridge the speaker's liberty but rather performs its core function of protecting the rights of others from violation. To put the point another way, expression can never properly be regulated on the basis of content in senses (1) or (2) — that is, because the government disapproves of an individual's holding or expressing a particular idea or disapproves of the idea itself. As I shall show, however, speech may sometimes be regulated on the basis of content in sense (3) — that is, because of its impact on those who hear it or on others who are affected by it.

THE COMMUNICATIVE IMPACT APPROACH TO FREE SPEECH

Of course, I recognize that this claim goes against the current of contemporary First Amendment jurisprudence. According to the dominant view, the content of speech may be identified with its communicative impact — that is, with the effect it has on its audience. And the regulation of speech based on communicative impact is precisely what the First Amendment forbids.

The seeds of this view may be found in the well-known case of *United States v. O'Brien* (1968). After burning his draft card to dramatize his opposition to the war in Vietnam, David Paul O'Brien was convicted of violating a federal law that prohibited the willful destruction of such documents. On appeal, Chief Justice Earl Warren emphasized that O'Brien had been prosecuted only for "the independent noncommunicative impact of [his] conduct" — interference with the efficient operation of the selective service system — and not because of any harm that might be thought to arise from "the alleged communicative element" in his conduct. Finding that the government had a substantial justification for ensuring the preservation of draft cards, Warren upheld O'Brien's conviction.[33]

Warren's distinction between the communicative and noncommunicative aspects of expression proved to be highly influential. In his classic essay on flag desecration, John Hart Ely argued that the distinction provided the key to First Amendment analysis. "The critical question," he wrote, was "whether the harm that the state is seeking to avert is one that grows out of the fact that the defendant is communicating, and more particularly out of the way people can be expected to react to his message, or rather would arise even if the defendant's conduct had no communicative significance whatever." Although regulations of the latter kind were sometimes acceptable under the First Amendment, those of the former kind rarely were.[34]

For Ely, one of the virtues of the communicative/noncommunicative distinction was that it offered a way to harmonize two First Amendment approaches, absolutism and balancing, which had long been at war.[35] Regulations based on noncommunicative impact were appropriately reviewed by balancing the government interests they served against their effects on speech. By contrast, a ban on restrictions based on communicative impact was rooted in the absolutist approach to the First Amendment that had been championed by Justices Hugo L. Black and William O. Douglas. Although Ely himself was sympathetic to this approach, he acknowledged that it had never commanded a majority on the Supreme Court.[36] Moreover, in his later work, Ely came to recognize that a pure form of absolutism was untenable even in principle: "[O]ne simply cannot be granted a constitutional right to stand on the steps of an inadequately guarded jail and urge a mob to lynch the prisoner within." For these reasons, Ely advocated the adoption of "[a]nother, more viable, form of 'absolutism' ": the view that the First Amendment proscribes all regulation of communicative impact except where the speech "*falls within a few clearly and narrowly defined categories*," such as incitement and libel.[37] Unfortunately, however, he offered no explanation of how these categories were to be identified or defined.

Ely's approach was soon adopted by Laurence H. Tribe, who used it to structure the account of First Amendment jurisprudence in his leading treatise, *American Constitutional Law*. According to Tribe, the First Amendment generally barred regulation based either on what the speaker was saying or on its effects on other people. He described regulation of this sort as "*aimed at communicative impact*" and equated it with *Mosley*'s concept of regulation based on content. For Tribe, as for Ely, this view reflected an "essentially" absolutist view of the First Amendment, qualified only by some narrowly drawn exceptions.[38]

The Ely-Tribe approach has garnered widespread acceptance among scholars as well as by the Supreme Court itself. For example, in two landmark flag-burning cases, *Texas v. Johnson* (1989) and *United States v. Eichman* (1990), the Court equated the "content" of expression with its "communicative impact" and declared that the "fundamental flaw" of flag desecration laws was that they "suppress[ed] expression out of concern for its likely communicative impact."[39] Similarly, in *Hustler Magazine v. Falwell* (1988) and many other cases, the Court has asserted that speech may not be restricted "because [it] may have an adverse emotional impact on the audience."[40] At the same time, the Court has followed the "categorical approach" urged by Ely and Tribe and has "permitted restrictions upon the content of speech in a few limited areas," such as obscenity, defamation, and fighting words.[41]

Yet the basis for this categorical approach remains obscure. How are these exceptions to be determined, and how can they be reconciled with the First Amendment rule against content regulation? At times, the Justices have been content to invoke long-standing tradition.[42] But of course the mere fact that rules are traditional does not make them right. In recent decades, the Supreme Court has dramatically expanded the scope of First Amendment protections, while steadily narrowing the traditional exceptions. Thus, the question of whether a particular kind of speech should receive constitutional protection cannot be resolved merely by reference to history, but calls for a normative standard.

To identify such a standard, the Justices have sometimes looked to the seminal case of *Chaplinsky v. New Hampshire* (1942), which first formulated the categorical approach. In that case, the Court unanimously declared that "[t]here are certain well-defined and narrowly limited classes of speech, the prevention and punishment of which have never been thought to raise any Constitutional problem. These include the lewd and obscene, the profane, the libelous, and the insulting or 'fighting' words — those which by their very utterance inflict injury or tend to incite an immediate breach of the peace. It has been well observed that such utterances are no essential part of any exposition of ideas, and are of such slight social value as a step to truth that any benefit that may be derived from them is clearly outweighed by the social interest in order and morality."[43]

Implicit in *Chaplinsky* is the notion that categorical judgments about First Amendment protection should be made by weighing the social value of the speech against the harm it causes to other social interests.[44] In some cases, the Court has made this balancing approach explicit. For example, in *New York v. Ferber* (1982), the majority asserted that "a content-based classification has been accepted [when] it may be appropriately generalized that within the confines of the given classification, the evil to be restricted so overwhelmingly outweighs the expressive interests, if any," that the speech should be denied

constitutional protection.[45] This approach, which has been labeled "definitional balancing," has also been advocated by scholars such as Tribe and
Melville Nimmer.[46]

Whatever the merits of this approach, it is difficult to see how it can be
harmonized with the doctrine of content neutrality. As we have seen, that
doctrine is rooted in the absolutist position taken by Justices Black and Douglas as well as by theorists like Emerson and Meiklejohn.[47] Moreover, on the
Mosley view, speech is protected not merely for instrumental reasons but also
because of its intrinsic value. An interest-balancing approach rests on entirely
different premises. Speech is protected only to the extent that it promotes
social welfare. Under that approach, a class of speech should not be protected
if its social value is outweighed by the social harm it causes. It is reasonable to
believe, however, that there are many kinds of speech that on balance cause
more harm than good.[48] If balancing is taken seriously, then, it is unlikely to be
consistent with a rule that speech may rarely, if ever, be regulated because of its
communicative impact. In short, far from resolving the question of how exceptions are to be justified, the appeal to balancing only makes the problem
seem more intractable.

For Ely, an important advantage of the categorization approach was that it
would obviate the need for ad hoc balancing in particular cases — an approach
that he, like many others, regarded as inadequate to protect freedom of
speech, particularly in times of national crisis. Departing from Ely's view, the
Court in *Simon & Schuster* declared that even fully protected speech may be
subjected to content-based regulation if the requirements of strict scrutiny are
met. Although this position was strongly criticized by Justice Anthony Kennedy, the majority offered no reasoned explanation for its view.[49]

In summary, the communicative impact approach has become the prevailing view both on and off the Court. This view identifies content-based restrictions with restrictions based on communicative impact and holds that they are
forbidden by the First Amendment. Yet in some situations regulation is clearly
called for. Accordingly, the dominant approach would permit restrictions in
some cases. But neither courts nor scholars have been able to offer a satisfac-
tory account of how these exceptions are to be determined or how they can be
harmonized with the general rule. In all of these ways, First Amendment
jurisprudence finds itself in a quandary.

RECONSIDERING THE ROLE OF COMMUNICATIVE IMPACT

To escape this predicament, we must return once more to the notion of
content. As we have seen, Ely holds that the "critical question" is "whether the
harm that the state is seeking to avert is one that grows out of the fact that the

defendant is communicating, and more particularly out of the way people can be expected to react to his message."[50] In light of our earlier discussion, we can see that this formulation contains two distinct parts. The first part, "the fact that the defendant is communicating," corresponds to what I have called the first element of communication (the speaker's act of expression), while the second part, "the way people can be expected to react to his message," corresponds to the third element (the reception of speech by its audience). Earlier in the same passage, Ely states that the key issue is whether "the danger was created by what the defendant was saying," which corresponds to what I have called the second element (the speech itself). In this way, Ely conflates several different elements of communication.

Of course, these elements are closely related to one another. But the distinctions between them take on crucial importance when one is trying to understand the basis and limits of content neutrality. The government, I have argued, may never regulate speech simply because it disapproves of the fact that the speaker holds particular views, for that would violate the speaker's autonomy. Nor may speech be regulated merely because of the ideas themselves, because the government has no jurisdiction over the realm of thought as such. But whether speech may be regulated to protect listeners is a more complex question.

As I have explained, both speakers and listeners have rights to autonomy. Just as speakers are entitled to determine the content of their own expression, other individuals have a right to decide what they wish to hear. It follows that government may not regulate the content of speech to protect willing listeners.

At first glance, this view might also seem to imply that individuals have a right to be free from all unwanted communication. But that conclusion would be far too sweeping. For instance, citizens have a right to engage in expression on matters of public interest—a right that is especially strong in public places. Furthermore, this right is not limited to politics but extends to culture, morality, religion, science, and other matters of common concern.[51] When expression of this sort is addressed to the public at large, it does not lose First Amendment protection simply because some (or even all) other individuals object to it. Instead, as Justice Harlan declared in *Cohen v. California* (1971), "The ability of government, consonant with the Constitution, to shut off discourse solely to protect others from hearing it is . . . dependent upon a showing that substantial privacy interests are being invaded in an essentially intolerable manner."[52]

These principles derive, in part, from the social dimension of expression. Speech is not merely individual but social in nature.[53] For this reason, speech that is properly directed toward the community as a whole and that does not

violate the rights of individuals may not be restricted for purely private reasons. Moreover, speakers should have some latitude to attempt to communicate directly, on matters of public concern, even with those who initially may
be unwilling to speak with them. Citizens should have a right to presume that
others are interested in communicating on such matters, until particular listeners make clear that they are not.

Ultimately, however, speakers cannot have an unlimited right to force communication on unwilling individuals if the idea of listener's autonomy is to have
any meaning. Speech of this sort can violate the listener's rights in two ways.
First, in some situations a person should have a right to decline all unwanted
communication. As the Supreme Court observed in *Hill v. Colorado* (2000),
this is an aspect of the right to privacy, or what Justice Brandeis called the
" 'right to be let alone.' "[54] Speech that invades this right is wrongful because it
disregards the recipient's capacity for free choice and disrespects the boundary
that separates the self from others. I shall call this sort of injury *formal*. Such
injury does not necessarily depend on the content of the speech: an individual
should have a right to be free from unwanted telephone calls at three o'clock in
the morning regardless of what message the speaker wants to convey.[55]

In other situations, speech is capable of inflicting *substantive* injury on the
listener. In such cases, speech causes harm precisely because of its content or
communicative impact. Thus, an individual can be placed in terror by threats
of present or future violence. Likewise, he may suffer severe distress upon
being told (falsely) that a loved one has been gravely injured or killed.[56] In
cases like these, the injury flows directly (in Ely's words) from "what the
defendant was saying," and "more particularly [from] the way people can be
expected to react" to it.[57]

Opponents of regulation might respond in several ways. First, they might
deny that mere words can cause injuries to others, or at any rate that speakers
should be regarded as responsible for those injuries. As C. Edwin Baker argues, individuals can control their own speech, but they cannot control how
others respond to it. Respect for the autonomy of both speakers and listeners
dictates that "[a]ny consequences involved in the listener's reaction . . . must be
attributed, in the end, to the listener" herself. Similarly, in *American Booksellers Association v. Hudnut* (1985), Judge Frank H. Easterbrook contends
that speech is only "as powerful as the audience allows it to be." It follows that
injuries that depend on "mental intermediation" cannot justify regulation of
speech.[58]

There is no doubt that where free speech is at stake, notions of causation
and responsibility must be carefully confined. Thus, for the most part, modern
First Amendment doctrine allows regulation only where there is a close rela-

tionship between speech and harm.[59] Nevertheless, the assertion that speech should never be deemed responsible for causing injury is far too broad. Speech that is directed toward another person is generally meant to have an effect. It is true that this effect will be a function not only of the speaker's intentions but also of the listener's state of mind, that is, his thoughts, beliefs, attitudes, and emotions. But that does not mean that his reaction should be attributed only to himself and not to the speaker. For example, it is natural for a person to experience fear when he is threatened with imminent violence. It is no answer to say that if he were very courageous, he could steel himself against this fear. Like other rights, personal security should be defined with reference to the ordinary or reasonable person. Moreover, even if the victim does not suffer fear, he will at least perceive an intentional threat to his safety, and this in itself constitutes a violation of his right to personal security.[60]

In some instances, then, the attitudes that determine the listener's reaction to speech are innate or instinctive, such as a fear of bodily harm or death. In other cases, those attitudes reflect conscious thought. It does not follow, however, that they should be regarded as arbitrary and hence attributable solely to the listener herself. As I argued in chapter 4, some attitudes are inextricably connected with personhood. These include an affirmation of one's life and personal security, one's personality, one's relationships with other persons and the community, and one's intellectual and spiritual integrity. Individuals do not simply choose to adopt such attitudes: they are part of what it means to be an autonomous, self-respecting person. For example, while it is true that an individual who is subjected to degrading racial epithets feels insulted because they violate her sense of personal dignity, the speaker cannot escape responsibility for this reaction on the ground that the listener can freely choose whether to have a sense of dignity or not.

Instead, in cases where the speaker intentionally (or in some cases recklessly or negligently) produces an effect on the listener, and where the speech would have the same effect on a reasonable person, the speaker should be considered responsible for causing that effect.[61] One can hold otherwise only by focusing on some elements of speech (the speaker's self-expression or the speech itself) in isolation from others (the speech's impact on the listener and the intersubjective nature of communication). But viewing the elements in this way overlooks the fact that they also constitute an integral whole. A person who directs speech toward another typically intends to produce some effect.[62] Communicative impact is not an accidental but an essential feature of communication. Indeed, that is one reason the First Amendment generally protects communicative impact. But just as speech can have beneficial effects on listeners, it can also have harmful effects. When a speaker is at fault for imposing those effects on an unwilling listener, she should be held responsible for causing them.[63]

Alternatively, opponents of regulation might concede that speech can cause mental or emotional injuries but deny that such injuries are serious ones. This response runs contrary to common sense — most people would suffer fear upon receiving a threat of violence or intense grief upon being told that a loved one had died, and would regard these as serious injuries. The response also runs contrary to the view taken by tort and criminal law, which often treat such statements as unlawful and subject them to liability under the heading of assaults, threats, or intentional infliction of emotional distress.[64] Finally, this response is inconsistent with the premises of First Amendment theory itself. That theory rests in part on the notion that the thoughts and feelings of individuals have important value. If that is true of speakers, then it is true of listeners as well. But just as speech is capable of expressing the speaker's thoughts and feelings, it is capable of injuring those of others. Moreover, as I argued in chapter 4, these injuries are not mere harms or setbacks to welfare, but constitute injuries in the strict sense — that is, infringements of rights.[65] My contention is that, under the First Amendment, speech may be regulated on the basis of communicative impact when it violates the rights of others.

Up to this point, I have focused on the injuries that speech may cause to unwilling listeners. As we have seen, however, speech can also cause injury to third parties, by invading their privacy, damaging their reputations, inciting violence against them, and so on. The targets of such speech have even less ability to protect themselves from it, while the injuries they suffer are no less serious. It is true that these injuries come about through "mental intermediation," that is, through the response listeners have to the speech.[66] But that does not mean that the listeners should be seen as solely responsible for those injuries. In the case of invasion of privacy, once highly personal information has been made public, the damage has been done. Likewise, in many cases it is reasonable for listeners to believe defamatory statements to be true, even though the speaker himself knew or should have known they were false. Finally, as I shall argue in chapter 8, both speakers and listeners should be held responsible for violence that results from acts of incitement.[67]

Reforming the Content Neutrality Doctrine

REVIEWING CONTENT-BASED REGULATIONS UNDER THE FIRST AMENDMENT

I now turn to the doctrinal question of how courts should review regulations of speech that are based on content.[68] Although *Mosley* declared that such regulations are "never permitted," the Court has recognized two exceptions to this rule. First, the law can restrict expression that falls within an unprotected or less protected category, such as fighting words, incitement, or obscenity. Second, even fully protected speech is subject to content-based regulation when necessary to promote a compelling government interest.[69]

Unfortunately, these exceptions have done little to mitigate the rigidity of the *Mosley* doctrine. The Court has been quite reluctant to recognize new categories of unprotected speech. Indeed, it has done so only once, by holding in *New York v. Ferber* that child pornography is outside the protection of the First Amendment.[70] In two other contexts, commercial advertising and "adult" expression, the Court has granted a category some protection, but less than that enjoyed by fully protected speech.[71]

To be sure, the courts should be extremely careful not to unduly expand the bounds of regulable expression. New categories should be recognized only when they are clearly justified. But there is no reason to assume that the categories established in previous cases are the only valid ones. As one would expect from a process of case-by-case adjudication, the categories of unprotected speech have been determined in piecemeal fashion and have never been worked out in a logical or systematic way.[72] Thus, the Court should not refuse to recognize a category simply because it has not done so in the past.

The second exception to *Mosley* has also done little to safeguard other rights. In the vast majority of cases in which judges determine that a law is based on content and that the speech does not fall within an unprotected category, they invalidate the law under strict scrutiny. That is hardly surprising, for this form of review is designed to sharply limit governmental power in the areas to which it applies.

Even if strict scrutiny were not applied in such an inflexible manner, there are two reasons it would be difficult to use the doctrine to uphold laws that seek to protect other rights from infringement by speech. First, strict scrutiny allows regulation only for the sake of an extraordinary or "compelling" government interest. Second, the regulation must be shown to be "necessary" in a strong sense — that is, it must be the least restrictive means of promoting that interest. These two facets of the doctrine are meant to erect a very high barrier against regulation. That may be entirely proper when First Amendment problems are viewed as the strict-scrutiny doctrine views them — as conflicts between the right to free speech and "government interests."[73] As we have seen, however, many First Amendment problems are better understood as conflicts between free speech and other fundamental rights. In such cases, strict scrutiny is inappropriate.[74] Instead, courts should carefully consider the strength of the rights on both sides.

Rather than apply a compelling-interest analysis or merely inquire whether the speech at issue falls within a traditionally unprotected category, courts should first ask whether the speech infringes basic rights that belong to other individuals or the community. If so, the court should determine whether the value of the speech justifies the injury it causes. If it does, then the speech should be held privileged under the First Amendment; if not, the speech improperly invades the rights of others and should not be protected by the rule against content regulation. Finally, the court should consider whether the law at issue violates the rule against content discrimination by treating the regulated speech less favorably than other speech that has the same value and that causes the same sort of injury.[75]

STATE-SUPPORTED SPEECH

In this chapter I have focused on how the principle of content neutrality should apply to laws that impose restrictions on speech. But the issue of neutrality also arises when the government takes a more affirmative approach to expression. When the government itself speaks, either directly or through private surrogates, there is general agreement that the content neutrality doctrine does not apply and that the government may determine the content of its own speech.[76] The problem is much more complex, however, when the government provides funding for private expression while imposing content-based restrictions on that funding. In struggling with this problem, the Supreme Court has oscillated between two diametrically opposite views. Some opinions apply the content neutrality doctrine to funding decisions in much the same way it applies to traditional restrictions on speech.[77] Other opinions reject this view and maintain that the First Amendment imposes few if any constraints on funding decisions.[78]

Both of these positions are unsatisfactory. Under the First Amendment, the government cannot have arbitrary power to determine what speech to support. But the problem cannot be adequately understood on the model of traditional censorship. In relation to individual autonomy of thought and expression, government represents an external force. The government may restrict this autonomy only when necessary to protect the autonomy or rights of others. But the situation is quite different in the funding context. In this setting, the relationship between the government and expression is more internal. When the government establishes a program to support speech, it does so to further some public good. If the program is to be effective, the government must be able to determine what forms of expression will best promote this good. For example, if a state creates a program to support the arts, it will provide funding for artistic expression but not for scientific inquiry. In addition, the state may decide to award grants based on artistic excellence or to give preference to works that relate to the state's history and culture. Of course, such distinctions are content-based and would be impermissible if used to regulate private expression. Under the First Amendment, the state may not punish people who choose to pursue careers in science rather than art, or who produce art that falls short of excellence or that does not relate to the history or culture of the state. Yet distinctions of this kind may be perfectly appropriate in the context of funding programs, whose aim is not to restrict liberty, but rather to provide benefits both for individuals and for the community at large. In the context of private expression, the ideal of autonomy means that individuals should generally be free to make their own decisions. By contrast, in the funding context, autonomy is not merely individual but also communal: while individuals should have a right to seek to participate in public programs, the community should also have a right to shape such programs in a way that best advances its conception of the public good.

These considerations lead to a centrist position on state-supported speech. On one hand, the government should have substantial authority to determine the contours of funding programs. On the other hand, it must be prevented from using this power to penalize private expression. Moreover, the benefits of public programs should be distributed in a way that is fair in light of the purposes they are intended to serve. To satisfy these concerns, laws that impose restrictions on funding should be reviewed as follows. First, as a threshold matter, the court should ask whether the law denies support to applicants because of speech that takes place *outside the context of the public program*. If so, the law should be treated in the same way as a traditional regulation of expression. Absent adequate justification, the law should be struck down as an unconstitutional condition or penalty on protected speech.[79]

When a law restricts funding for expression only within the context of the program itself, the problem should not be viewed as one of unconstitutional conditions.[80] Instead, the statute should undergo a form of intermediate scrutiny. Under this approach, criteria for funding should be upheld if several requirements are met. First, the criteria must be substantially related to the purposes of the program. Second, those purposes must be constitutionally legitimate. Third, the criteria must treat the program's beneficiaries (and others) in a way that accords with constitutional norms of respect for individual liberty and equality. Finally, the program must not have the purpose or effect of undermining other aspects of the constitutional order. Under this analysis, a state arts program could award funds on the basis of artistic excellence. But it could not provide funding only for Democratic artists, for this would not be substantially related to any legitimate purpose served by the program. Nor could funding be conditioned on an artist's agreement to submit her completed work to government officials and to make any changes they demanded, for this would be inconsistent with the autonomy of thought and expression protected by the First Amendment.

In short, while funding decisions should not be free from constitutional constraints, those constraints do not apply in the same way in all areas. Under the First Amendment, the state's authority to restrict expression on the basis of content is rather limited. By contrast, when the state establishes a program to support expression, it may take content into account to the extent necessary to advance the public purposes of the program, so long as other constitutional principles are respected.[81]

PART **III**

Contemporary Controversies

7

Subversive Speech

In part 2 I developed a general theory of the First Amendment. According to this view, freedom of speech is an inherent right. But the same principles that justify free speech also support other fundamental rights, including personal security, liberty, privacy, reputation, citizenship, and equality. The law can require speakers to respect these rights, except in situations where the value of speech is sufficient to justify the injury it causes. This is the way in which the legal order can best promote human freedom and dignity as a whole.

In part 3, I apply this approach to a wide range of contemporary disputes, from revolutionary speech to antiabortion protests to hate speech and pornography. Of course, any effort to resolve such profound issues is bound to be controversial. Although I shall make the strongest case I can for the results I would reach, my overriding goal is to show that the rights-based theory provides a useful framework for debating difficult issues of this sort.

In this chapter, I explore the problem of subversive speech, or expression that is directed against the government itself. I begin with a question that the Supreme Court has grappled with for nearly a century: whether the First Amendment protects speech that advocates revolution or other forms of unlawful action. Next, I consider whether journalists may be prosecuted for disclosing classified information about secret programs in the war on terror.

Finally, I address the continuing controversy over whether the government should be permitted to ban desecration of the American flag.

Advocacy of Revolution and Unlawful Action

FROM *SCHENCK* TO *BRANDENBURG*

The Supreme Court's first major effort to address the problem of subversive speech came in response to the wave of prosecutions that were directed against radical opponents of American involvement in the First World War.[1] In *Schenck v. United States* (1919), Socialist Party officials had mailed antiwar leaflets to fifteen thousand men who had been drafted for military service. In "impassioned language," the circulars denounced the war effort as "a monstrous wrong against humanity in the interest of Wall Street's chosen few," "denied the [government's] power to send our citizens away to shoot up the people of foreign lands," and argued that conscription violated the principle embodied in the Thirteenth Amendment, which outlawed slavery and involuntary servitude. The leaflets strongly encouraged opposition to the draft but did not explicitly advocate illegal action. Instead, readers were invited to join the Socialist Party, to contact their congressmen, and to petition for a repeal of the Conscription Act.[2]

In an opinion by Justice Holmes, the Supreme Court affirmed the Socialists' convictions for conspiracy to violate the Espionage Act of 1917 by attempting to obstruct military recruitment and to cause insubordination in the armed forces. Although Holmes admitted that in ordinary times the defendants would have a First Amendment right to speak as they did, he asserted that "the character of every act depends upon the circumstances in which it is done." "The question in every case," he wrote, "is whether the words used are used in such circumstances and are of such a nature as to create a clear and present danger that they will bring about the substantive evils that Congress has a right to prevent."[3]

At first glance, the requirement of "clear and present danger" appears to offer strong protection for speech. In fact, however, Holmes made little effort to determine whether the leaflets were likely to bring about unlawful action. Instead, it was enough that a reasonable jury could conclude that they had a "tendency" to "influence" others to resist the draft and that the defendants intended them to have this effect. In subsequent cases, the Court sustained several other convictions for antiwar agitation, including a series of newspaper articles expressing sympathy with Germany, as well as a speech by the Socialist leader Eugene V. Debs that extolled the virtues of socialism, praised opponents of the draft, and told workers that they were "fit for something better than slavery and cannon fodder." In none of these cases did the Court make a serious inquiry into the nature of the speech or its impact on conduct, let alone consider any value it might have had under the First Amendment. Instead, these decisions reflected the view that, in Holmes's words, "[w]hen a nation is at war many things that might be said in time of peace are such a hindrance to its effort that their utterance will not be endured so long as men fight."[4]

Although these early decisions were unanimous, the Court's consensus proved to be short-lived. In *Abrams v. United States* (1919), the defendants were anarchists and revolutionaries who believed that the American government planned to send a military force to defeat the Russian Revolution. In response, they wrote two leaflets, which were distributed by being thrown from the window of a building onto the street below. The leaflets criticized President Woodrow Wilson, denounced the United States and other capitalist nations, and called for a general strike to shut down American munitions factories, which were "making bullets not only for the Germans, but also for the Workers Soviets of Russia." The leaflets declared that only an "open challenge" would "let the Government know that not only the Russian Worker fights for freedom, but also here in America lives the spirit of Revolution." Concluding that the defendants had not only urged curtailment of things necessary for the war against Germany, but had also called for a revolution to "put down by force the Government of the United States," Justice John H. Clarke upheld their convictions under the Espionage Act. Their First Amendment challenge was summarily rejected on the authority of *Schenck*.[5]

Remarkably, in this case Holmes dissented in an opinion joined by Justice Brandeis. Although much of the discussion was devoted to a technical argument that the defendants' conduct did not violate the statute, the heart of the opinion was a powerful defense of freedom of speech. Tacitly acknowledging his earlier views, Holmes observed that "[p]ersecution for the expression of opinions seems to me perfectly logical": if you strongly desire to achieve a certain result, "you naturally express your wishes in law and sweep away all opposition." However, Holmes continued, "when men have realized that time has upset many fighting faiths, they may come to believe even more than they believe the very foundations of their own conduct that the ultimate good desired is better reached by free trade in ideas." For this reason, the First Amendment should bar all efforts to ban the expression of views thought to be dangerous, "unless they so imminently threaten immediate interference with the lawful and pressing purposes of the law that an immediate check is required to save the country." This, Holmes insisted, was the true meaning of the clear-and-present-danger standard he had announced in *Schenck*.[6]

This judicial debate over the meaning of the First Amendment continued throughout the 1920s. In *Gitlow v. New York* (1925), the defendant had arranged for publication of the manifesto of the Left Wing Section of the Socialist Party. The document advocated widespread industrial strikes, which were to culminate in "revolutionary mass action" to destroy "the bourgeois, democratic parliamentary state" and replace it with "a revolutionary dictatorship of the proletariat." In *Whitney v. California* (1927), the defendant had assisted in organizing the Communist Labor Party of California, which stood on a similar platform. Like Benjamin Gitlow, Charlotte Anita Whitney was convicted of criminal syndicalism, which the California statute defined as "any doctrine . . . advocating, teaching or aiding and abetting the commission of crime, sabotage . . . or unlawful acts of force and violence or unlawful methods of terrorism as a means of accomplishing a change in industrial ownership or control, or effecting any political change." In both cases the Supreme Court upheld the convictions under the First Amendment. As Justice Edward T. Sanford explained in *Gitlow,* the state had a "primary and essential right" to ensure its own preservation by punishing "utterances endangering the foundations of organized government and threatening its overthrow by unlawful means." Moreover, there was no need for the Court to apply the clear-and-present-danger test to cases like this, for the legislature itself had determined that utterances of this sort were "so inimical to the general welfare and involve such danger of substantive evil that they may be penalized in the exercise of its police power." So long as this determination was a reasonable one, the Court was bound to uphold it.[7]

In *Whitney,* Brandeis responded with the most powerful and eloquent defense of free speech in the nation's history. In an opinion joined by Holmes, he wrote,

> Those who won our independence believed that the final end of the State was to make men free to develop their faculties; and that in its government the deliberative forces should prevail over the arbitrary. They valued liberty both as an end and as a means. . . . They believed that freedom to think as you will and to speak as you think are means indispensable to the discovery and spread of political truth; that without free speech and assembly discussion would be futile; that with them, discussion affords ordinarily adequate protection against the dissemination of noxious doctrine; that the greatest menace to freedom is an inert people; that public discussion is a political duty; and that this should be a fundamental principle of the American government. They recognized the risks to which all human institutions are subject. But they knew that order cannot be secured merely through fear of punishment for its infraction; that it is hazardous to discourage thought, hope and imagination;

that fear breeds repression; that repression breeds hate; that hate menaces stable government; that the path of safety lies in the opportunity to discuss freely supposed grievances and proposed remedies; and that the fitting remedy for evil counsels is good ones. Believing in the power of reason as applied through public discussion, they eschewed silence coerced by law — the argument of force in its worst form.

Brandeis concluded that the First Amendment permits the government to censor expression only when it clearly threatens to cause a "serious injury to the State" that "is so imminent that it may befall before there is opportunity for full discussion." In all other cases, "the remedy to be applied is more speech, not enforced silence."[8]

Although this position began to prevail during the 1930s, it was unable to withstand the intense pressures on civil liberties that arose during the Second World War and the early years of the Cold War. In *Dennis v. United States* (1951), the leaders of the Communist Party had been convicted of violating the Smith Act of 1940 by conspiring "to advocate and teach the duty . . . of overthrowing and destroying the Government of the United States by force and violence." The convictions clearly could not stand under the Holmes-Brandeis view, for any such revolution necessarily would have had to take place at some point in the indefinite future. In response to this difficulty, Chief Justice Fred Vinson adopted a modified, and much watered-down, version of the clear-and-present-danger test. As formulated by Judge Learned Hand in the court below, the test asked simply "whether the gravity of the 'evil,' discounted by its improbability, justifies such invasion of free speech as is necessary to avoid the danger." Convinced that the defendants had formed "a highly organized conspiracy, with rigidly disciplined members" who were committed to an effort to overthrow the government when the time was ripe, Vinson rejected their First Amendment defense and upheld the convictions. In dissent, Justices Black and Douglas pointed out that the defendants had not been prosecuted for attempting to overthrow the government or even for conspiring to do so, but merely for conspiring to organize a political party to teach the doctrine of violent overthrow "with the hope that some day it would be acted upon." At least in the absence of any immediate danger, the dissenters argued, such a prosecution was flatly inconsistent with the First Amendment.[9]

During the 1960s, the pendulum swung back toward a more expansive interpretation of freedom of speech. In *Brandenburg v. Ohio* (1969), a dozen members of the Ku Klux Klan held a rally which was filmed at their invitation by a local television crew. After the hooded figures burned a large wooden cross, their leader, Clarence Brandenburg, made speeches in which he declared that "the nigger should be returned to Africa, the Jew returned to Israel."

Brandenburg added that "if our President, our Congress, our Supreme Court, continues to suppress the white, Caucasian race, it's possible that there might have to be some revengeance taken." Brandenburg was convicted of violating a criminal syndicalism law like the one upheld in *Whitney*. On appeal, the Supreme Court overruled that decision and adopted a position much like the one advocated by Holmes and Brandeis. Under the Court's new test, "the constitutional guarantees of free speech and free press do not permit a State to forbid or proscribe advocacy of the use of force or of law violation except where such advocacy is directed to inciting or producing imminent lawless action and is likely to incite or produce such action." Unfortunately, the Court's brief per curiam opinion offered virtually no justification for this doctrine, and what it did offer was strikingly unpersuasive, for it attributed the new rule to earlier decisions such as *Dennis,* which had *upheld* convictions for advocating revolution in the indefinite future.[10]

SHOULD ADVOCACY OF REVOLUTION OR UNLAWFUL ACTION RECEIVE ANY PROTECTION UNDER THE FIRST AMENDMENT?

Since 1969, the Supreme Court has treated *Brandenburg* as settled law. At the same time, the doctrine has generated a good deal of controversy in the academic literature, where it has come under fire from two directions. Some conservatives argue that advocacy of revolution or unlawful action should receive no protection at all under the First Amendment. On the other side, some civil libertarians contend that the state should virtually never be permitted to restrict such speech. In contrast to both views, I believe that the *Brandenburg* incitement doctrine is largely correct. In this section, I defend the doctrine against conservative objections. Because the libertarian argument is best addressed in connection with speech that promotes violence against individuals, I postpone a discussion of that argument to chapter 8.[11]

The most prominent conservative critic of *Brandenburg* is Robert H. Bork, a former Yale law professor and federal judge whose nomination to the Supreme Court was rejected by the Senate in 1987.[12] Articulating a deeply positivist view of the Constitution, Bork contends that our political system rests on the premise that "in wide areas of life majorities are entitled to rule for no better reason than that they are majorities." Although majority rule is not unlimited, the Supreme Court is justified in enforcing only those constraints that are expressly stated in the Constitution or clearly implied by its text, history, or structure. The language of "fundamental human right[s]" has no place in constitutional law, for there is no principled way to determine that one right is more important than another.[13] In particular, Bork argues that the First Amendment does not protect freedom of speech for its own sake or for the sake of values such as individual self-fulfillment. Instead, free speech should be understood as a "[s]econdary or derivative" right that is conferred on individuals in order to promote the processes of democratic government.[14]

For Bork, the only principled reason for protecting freedom of speech is that it contributes to "the 'discovery and spread of political truth.' "[15] In turn, "political truth" should be understood as "a term of art, a concept defined entirely from a consideration of the system of government." The values that are protected in the Constitution are one set of political truths. For the most part, those truths are "procedural" in character, such as the rules that govern the democratic process. A second set of political truths consists of the results that the majority reaches through this process. "Truth is what the majority thinks it is at any given moment precisely because the majority is permitted to govern and to redefine its values constantly." By contrast, Bork rejects any notion of a higher truth that "exist[s] independently of Constitution or statute," for in our system "there is no absolute set of truths, to which the term 'political truth' can refer."[16]

On these grounds, Bork contends that the First Amendment should protect only "explicitly political speech," that is, speech that is directly concerned with government officials, policies, or behavior. This category does not embrace literary, artistic, scientific, or educational speech as such. Although these forms of expression may have an indirect effect on political attitudes, the same thing is true of all human activity, and the First Amendment should not be viewed as "a broad denial of the power of government to regulate conduct."[17] Moreover, Bork argues that, even within the category of explicitly political speech, no protection should be afforded to "speech advocating forcible overthrow of the government or violation of law." Revolutionary speech undermines First Amendment values "because it violates constitutional truths about processes and because it is not aimed at a new definition of political truth by a legislative majority." Likewise, advocacy of unlawful action violates the premises of the democratic system by urging its hearers "to set aside the results that political speech has produced." It follows that the Constitution should not protect either form of expression.[18]

It is important to note that this argument is not limited to speech that poses a clear and present danger of lawlessness or revolution. Bork's claim is that these forms of expression categorically lack value under the First Amendment and may be banned whenever the legislature determines that they pose a danger, regardless of how remote or improbable the danger might be.[19] In responding to this claim, I first explore the problem of revolutionary speech and then turn to speech that advocates the violation of particular laws.

Revolutionary speech. In contrast to Bork's positivist vision, my approach begins with the natural rights theory that informed the American Revolution, the Constitution, and the Bill of Rights. According to that view, the people establish government to protect their inherent rights and to promote the common good. At the same time, they retain the authority to oversee the conduct of public officials and even to overthrow the government if they determine that it has abused its trust.[20] Indeed, even individuals and groups have a right to use force if that is the only way to defend their rights against invasion by the government.[21] As we saw in chapter 1, freedom of speech holds a central place in this model. It is through speech that the people are able to monitor official conduct, to protest against mistreatment, to expose abuse of power, and to rally resistance to an oppressive or tyrannical government.

This radical understanding of free speech played a crucial part in the American Revolution. During the 1760s and 1770s, pamphlets and articles poured from the colonial presses, addressing the crisis with Great Britain and advocating the revolutionary cause. Speeches and sermons stirred opposition to the authorities. Committees of correspondence coordinated plans of resistance.[22] As Madison later observed, if liberty of speech and press had been subjected to rigorous control during this period, the Revolution might have been stifled at birth. When the newly independent states began to adopt declarations of rights, they extolled freedom of the press as "one of the great bulwarks of liberty" against governmental oppression. These themes were central to Antifederalist demands for a bill of rights as well as to the proposed amendments submitted by the state ratifying conventions — proposals that ultimately led to the adoption of the First Amendment.[23] In all of these ways, the right to free speech and the right to revolution were closely linked in late eighteenth-century America. Thus, Bork is wrong to suggest that revolutionary speech is antithetical to the American constitutional tradition.

A conservative might respond that even if the people have a right to overthrow an authoritarian government, that right has no application within a modern constitutional state, in which civil liberties are protected, majorities rule through the democratic process, and "the existing structure of the government provides for peaceful and orderly change."[24] This response has considerable force, but it is not conclusive. Although the existing order affords a good deal of protection to individual rights, that does not mean it adequately secures the freedom, dignity, and equality of all those subject to its jurisdiction. Nor is the current order entirely democratic. Instead, it includes many impediments to majority rule, such as the equal representation of each state in the Senate, a bicameral legislature, and the electoral college, as well as many formal and informal obstacles to suffrage and the pervasive influence of wealth in the political process.[25] Moreover, by providing that amendments could be adopted only by a two-thirds vote of each House of Congress, followed by the ratification of three-quarters of the state legislatures, the framers intentionally made the constitutional order quite difficult to change. For all of these reasons, while "the existing structure of the government" does "provide[] for peaceful and orderly change," it does not necessarily ensure that a majority of the people could accomplish such change if they came to believe that the government was oppressive or that it no longer adequately served the purposes for which it was instituted. Yet both the Revolution and the adoption of the Constitution were predicated on the view that the people had an inherent right to change the form of government in such circumstances.[26]

Thus, one cannot conclude that, although the people once possessed a right to revolution, that right no longer exists in the modern state. Of course, the possibility that such a revolution will occur in the contemporary United States is remote. Nor am I suggesting that one would be justified. However much our political system may fall short of its ideals, it does secure a large measure of liberty and democracy, and it enjoys a high level of popular acceptance and consent. The point is that one cannot conclusively presume that these conditions exist at present and that they will continue to exist in the future. According to the classical theory, only the people themselves can judge whether or not a revolution is justified or desirable. It follows that they must be free to discuss the question.

In this way, the Jeffersonian idea of a right to revolution provides one basis for the view that revolutionary speech is entitled to First Amendment protection. However, a modern defense of this view does not rely solely on the theoretical possibility that the people would be justified in overthrowing the government. Instead, that defense focuses on the role of reason in a free and democratic society.

In the liberal tradition, freedom is rooted in reason, which is the capacity that makes self-determination possible. Accordingly, individuals must be free to think as they like and to speak as they think. As Justice Brandeis stressed in *Whitney*, these rights are also essential to democratic self-government, which depends upon "the power of reason as applied through public discussion."[27]

Speech and reason are applied to public affairs on several levels. (1) The first is ordinary political discourse, in which citizens and government officials debate issues related to legislation, policymaking, and other matters of public concern. (2) Another level of discourse concerns the meaning of the Constitution. Speech of this sort takes place not only among lawyers and judges in the course of constitutional adjudication, but also within other branches of government, the academic community, and the public at large.[28] (3) A third level of discourse occurs in debates over what the Constitution *ought* to say. This category embraces the speech of those who framed and ratified the original Constitution and the amendments to it, as well as discussion of current proposals to amend the Constitution.

Each of these forms of speech takes place within the existing constitutional order or plays a role in establishing it. But the role of reason in public affairs goes beyond this and extends to (4) speech that evaluates the legitimacy of the current order.[29] Because this speech takes place on a level that transcends the existing regime, it need not be based on principles that are accepted by that regime. Thus, while one can assess the Constitution's legitimacy from a liberal democratic perspective, one can also do so from the standpoint of anarchism, communism, fascism, Christian nationalism, or Islamic radicalism. Although these views conflict with liberal political theory, that theory is no more entitled to immunity from criticism than any other set of beliefs. For these reasons, the First Amendment's protection of radical speech should extend not only to advocacy of Jeffersonian revolution but also to arguments for nonliberal forms of revolution.

In response, it might be said that while individuals have a right to advocate political *ideas,* they have no right to advocate illegal *actions* such as violent overthrow of government. But this response misapprehends the nature of political speech, which is not a form of abstract theory or speculation, but a form of practical activity. All political advocacy seeks to accomplish particular results in the world, whether they are expressed or merely implied.[30] As I explain below, when revolutionary speech unjustifiably poses a serious danger of unlawful action, it violates the rights of others and may be prohibited. By contrast, in cases where it does not pose such a danger, it is entitled to protection under the First Amendment.

Although Bork recognizes the first three levels of discourse I have identified, he rejects the fourth on the ground that the idea of "political truth" has no meaning outside of an existing constitutional order. I believe this is a serious mistake for three reasons. First, speech that assesses the existing order is one of the most fundamental ways in which reason is applied to public affairs. Speech of this sort is essential not only to evaluate the legitimacy of the regime, but also *to generate that legitimacy.* Individuals cannot consent to the constitutional order unless they are free to debate its merits. For this reason, a ban on subversive speech would backfire by undermining the very legitimacy it was meant to defend.[31] In addition, radical dissent can lead to reforms that enhance the legitimacy of the existing order.[32]

Second, the various levels of public discourse are not separate and independent but are integrally connected with one another. For example, when citizens and legislators debate the merits of proposed legislation, they often consider not simply whether it would make good policy, but also whether it would comport with constitutional values and with broader notions of justice and the common good. Similarly, when the Supreme Court confronts issues like segregation and capital punishment, it often takes into account, implicitly or explicitly, the impact that a particular decision would have on the actual and perceived legitimacy of the American constitutional order, both at home and abroad.[33] Because the different levels of discourse interact with one another, allowing the state to ban speech that relates to legitimacy would also have the effect of undermining the forms of speech that Bork regards as vital to democratic government.[34]

Finally, citizens cannot engage in political deliberation unless they are free to think for themselves. Thus, the right to political free speech necessarily presupposes a more fundamental right to intellectual autonomy or freedom of thought. And this right cannot be confined to issues that arise within a particular political order but extends to art, literature, philosophy, religion, science, and the whole range of human thought and expression, including the radical speech that Bork would hold outside the First Amendment.

Advocacy of unlawful action. Similar considerations support First Amendment protection for speech that advocates unlawful action. First, just as the people may have a right to revolution, so they may have a right to disobey specific laws. This principle is recognized by the legal system itself, which holds that laws that contravene the Constitution are null and void. Moreover, even if a particular law is considered valid within the existing legal order, it may conflict with fundamental human rights or principles of justice. In such cases, the liberal tradition holds that individuals may have a moral right to violate the law.[35] For example, blacks had no moral duty to submit to slavery or segregation but were entitled to resist if they could.[36] Likewise, gay and lesbian people had no moral duty to obey the laws that made sodomy a crime, for those laws were inconsistent with their liberty and dignity, as the Supreme Court ultimately held in *Lawrence v. Texas* (2003).[37] Because there are circumstances in which people have a right to disobey the law, they must also have a right to discuss whether those circumstances exist.

This leads to a second argument for a right to advocate unlawful action, which is based on the role of reason in public discourse. Just as individuals must be free to question the legitimacy of the constitutional order and to advocate its overthrow, so they must be free to debate the legitimacy of particular laws and to advocate conduct that violates them. To ban such discussions would also undermine ordinary political and constitutional discourse with regard to such laws. Finally, the freedom to criticize the law falls within the rights to intellectual autonomy and self-expression.

THE SCOPE OF FIRST AMENDMENT PROTECTION

Revolutionary speech. As a rule, then, the protections of the First Amendment should extend to radical speech, including speech that advocates overthrow of the government. At the same time, however, this speech may have an impact on other rights. In particular, the people have a right to govern themselves through the representative institutions they have established in the Constitution, as well as a right to live under laws that are democratically adopted and that secure their fundamental rights. Although the American political system is far from perfect in its implementation of these ideals, it does enjoy a substantial measure of legitimacy. In principle, if the people should decide that the system has become oppressive or no longer promotes the ends for which it was adopted, they have a right to alter or abolish the Constitution, either peacefully or by force, by means of a Jeffersonian revolution — that is, a revolution that is made by a majority and that is intended to protect the rights of all. From the standpoint of liberal democratic theory, however, other forms of revolution — such as those intended to establish a Stalinist dictatorship or a Christian or Islamic theocracy — are illegitimate, either because they would be imposed by a minority on the rest of the community or because they would deprive individuals of their basic rights. A revolution of this sort would violate the people's rights to democratic self-government and individual liberty under the rule of law. And the same is true of speech that advocates such a revolution, if there is a close enough connection between the speech and the danger that revolution will take place.[38]

It follows that the problem of revolutionary speech requires us to reconcile two sets of rights: (1) rights to freedom of expression and (2) rights to democratic self-government and individual liberty under the rule of law. There is no question that the second set of rights is of vital importance. As we have seen, however, liberal democracy itself depends on the free use of reason in public discourse, and this includes speech that criticizes the existing order. Indeed, the very legitimacy of the state depends on people's ability to engage in such speech. Moreover, the right to political free speech is rooted in an even more basic claim to intellectual autonomy. Because of the fundamental nature of these rights, the government should be allowed to restrict speech on the ground that it is subversive only when the restriction is necessary "to protect the State from destruction or from serious injury."[39] For the most part, however, subversive speech poses relatively little danger to the state, precisely because of the broad popular acceptance and support it enjoys, together with the overwhelming force it commands and the availability of other lawful means of protecting itself.[40] For all of these reasons, revolutionary speech should be subject to restriction only when it comes very close to causing serious injury to the state. That is the thrust of the *Brandenburg* standard, which allows such speech to be punished only when it is both intended and likely to bring about "imminent lawless action."[41]

Advocacy of law violation. The same sort of reasoning applies to speech that advocates the violation of particular laws. As I have said, individuals have no obligation to obey laws that are invalid or fundamentally unjust. Our legal system seeks to protect citizens against the enforcement of such laws insofar as it authorizes the courts to review the constitutionality of legislation, and insofar as it empowers them to interpret the Constitution broadly enough to protect basic human rights, whether or not those rights are expressly set forth in the document. If a law is not unconstitutional on these grounds, then (at least from the perspective of the legal system itself) individuals have no right to disobey the law, for such conduct would be inconsistent with the rights to democratic self-government and the rule of law. However, because individuals have a fundamental right to think for themselves and to evaluate the legitimacy and morality of laws, speech that advocates the violation of valid laws should be denied First Amendment protection only when there is a very close connection between the speech and the unlawful action.[42] Once again, this is the basic meaning of *Brandenburg*.

That is not to say that the *Brandenburg* formulation is perfect or that it provides a comprehensive solution to the problem of advocacy of unlawful action. Instead, the doctrine should be refined in several ways. First, as several scholars have argued, the term "imminent" should not be read literally, that is, to mean that the unlawful action is likely to come about *immediately.*[43] For example, speech that advocates the bombing of a federal building may pose a grave danger even if the crime would not take place for days or even weeks.

Second, as Kent Greenawalt explains in his book *Speech, Crime, and the Uses of Language,* the level of constitutional protection should vary with the nature of the speech and the context in which it occurs. The justification for the *Brandenburg* rule is strongest as applied to the type of case in which it was formulated, namely, public communications that are ideological in nature. By contrast, there is no good reason to apply this demanding rule to ordinary criminal solicitation, or what Greenawalt calls private nonideological communication. For instance, suppose that one person urges another to rob a liquor store so that they will have money to go to the racetrack that weekend. Because the "expressive value of such utterances is slight in comparison with their dangerous tendencies," they should receive little or no protection under the First Amendment — a position that the courts have uniformly endorsed.[44]

As Greenawalt observes, private ideological speech poses a more difficult problem. Suppose that, at a meeting of a small white supremacist group, the group's leader denounces the influence of blacks in the local community and urges his followers to blow up a statue of Martin Luther King, Jr., that stands in the town square. Although speech of this sort has substantial value under the First Amendment, it also poses a greater danger than communication that takes place in public. The leader's speech may well have a more powerful impact on its audience. In addition, because outsiders do not know about the speech, it is less likely to be counteracted by more speech, and the government will not be able to take effective measures to prevent the commission of the crime. Balancing these considerations, Greenawalt persuasively argues that speech of this sort should receive some First Amendment protection, but less than that accorded to public ideological expression. In particular, imminence should not be required; instead, the speech should be unprotected if it presents a "significant danger of criminal harm."[45]

A final difficulty with the Court's approach is that it fails to distinguish between speech that is directed against the government itself (the sort of speech that was involved in the whole line of cases from *Schenck* through *Brandenburg*) and speech that advocates violence against individuals (such as the killing of abortion providers). As I shall explain in chapter 8, although expression that targets individuals may be ideological in character, it has less First Amendment value and at the same time poses a greater danger. For these reasons, I shall argue that a less stringent standard should apply: the speech should be unprotected if it poses a serious danger of violence, even if that danger is not imminent.[46]

Publication of Confidential Information

In contrast to earlier conflicts from the First World War to Vietnam, the war on terror, which began after the destruction of the World Trade Center on September 11, 2001, has seen few direct efforts to suppress dissent through the use of criminal law.[47] That such efforts would be widely viewed as unconstitutional is a testament to the strength of the contemporary understanding of the First Amendment represented by *Brandenburg v. Ohio*. At the same time, however, the government sought to restrict civil liberties in many other ways.[48] One of the most dramatic of these efforts was the threat by the Republican administration of George W. Bush to use the espionage laws to prosecute the press for revealing classified information.

This threat came in response to a cascade of news stories about the administration's covert antiterrorism initiatives. In November 2005, the *Washington Post* reported that the Central Intelligence Agency (CIA) had established a system of secret overseas prisons or "black sites," in which more than a hundred alleged terrorists were being subjected to interrogation techniques that were impermissible under American military law as well as international human rights treaties. The following month, the *New York Times* disclosed that shortly after the attacks of September 11 President Bush had secretly authorized the National Security Agency (NSA) to engage in warrantless electronic surveillance of communications between individuals inside the United States and those in other countries who were suspected of having direct or indirect ties to al Qaeda. The *Post* and *Times* stories won Pulitzer Prizes for investigative journalism. In May 2006, *USA Today* revealed that the NSA had obtained, without judicial authorization, the domestic telephone records of tens of millions of Americans in an effort to discover patterns associated with terrorism. In June 2006, four newspapers — the *New York Times,* the *Los Angeles Times,* the *Wall Street Journal,* and the *Washington Post* — reported that, beginning in 2001, the Treasury Department had secretly, and without judicial approval, gained access to the financial records contained in a vast international database known as SWIFT and was using them to monitor the banking transactions of individuals suspected of having terrorist connections.[49]

These disclosures led to a political uproar. Many Democrats and other critics contended that the government's actions constituted grave abuses of power. In response, the administration vigorously defended the legality and constitutionality of the programs and asserted that they were essential weapons in the war on terror. Far from acknowledging wrongdoing, the White House and its supporters attacked the news organizations, especially the *New York Times,* for revealing sensitive information about national security. President Bush called the disclosures "shameful" and "disgraceful." The Republican-controlled House of Representatives passed a resolution condemning the disclosure of the SWIFT financial tracking program for compromising the government's antiterrorism efforts and thereby endangering the lives of Americans around the world. Some legislators, including Peter J. King, the chairman of the House Homeland Security Committee, went further and accused the *Times* of treason. In public statements and congressional testimony, Justice Department officials contended that the newspapers could legitimately be prosecuted under the Espionage Act of 1917 for revealing classified information.[50]

The argument for this position is straightforward. Under the Constitution, the government has the power to protect national security. One way it does so is by classifying information whose disclosure would be harmful. Several provisions of the Espionage Act make it a crime to reveal such information to anyone who is not entitled to receive it. That is what newspapers do when they publish accounts of secret government programs. Under the First Amendment, journalists are free to report on the activities of government, but they are not free to violate generally applicable laws. It follows that they are subject to prosecution when they publish classified information. In the words of Attorney General Alberto R. Gonzales, Congress made a "policy judgment" to this effect when it passed the espionage laws, and the Justice Department has "an obligation to enforce those laws" by "prosecut[ing] those who engage in criminal activity."[51]

Although this argument is powerful, it suffers from two major flaws. First, the scope and meaning of the espionage laws are far from clear.[52] One of the most pertinent statutes is 18 U.S.C. § 793(e), which reads as follows: "Whoever having unauthorized possession of, access to, or control over any document, writing, . . . [or] information relating to the national defense[,] which information the possessor has reason to believe could be used to the injury of the United States or to the advantage of any foreign nation, willfully communicates, delivers, [or] transmits . . . the same to any person not entitled to receive it [shall be fined or imprisoned for up to ten years]." Although this provision is plainly directed against ordinary acts of espionage, at first glance it seems broad enough to encompass the publication of information in a newspaper. On closer examination, however, one discovers that although the word *publishes* is used in several other provisions of the Espionage Act, it does not appear in § 793(e). The legislative history suggests that this was no accident. When Congress was considering the Act in 1917, President Wilson strongly urged the adoption of a version of § 793 that would have authorized the President, in time of war, to declare a national emergency and "prohibit the publishing or communicating of . . . any information relating to the national defense which, in his judgment, is of such character that it is or might be useful to the enemy." Congress rejected this proposal after a heated debate in which opponents asserted that it would trample on the First Amendment. This history suggests that when Congress passed the Espionage Act, it made a "policy judgment" *against* subjecting the press to criminal punishment in such cases.[53]

Another provision, 18 U.S.C. § 798, offers stronger support for the administration's position. This section, which was added in 1950 at the height of the Cold War, applies to anyone who "knowingly and willfully communicates, furnishes, transmits, or otherwise makes available to an unauthorized person, or *publishes,* or uses in any manner prejudicial to the safety or interest of the United States . . . any classified information" that concerns any code or cryptographic system or "the communication intelligence activities of the United States." The language of this statute does seem to apply to publication of information by the press. One can reasonably argue, however, that the statute should be construed to protect only lawful programs, not those that are illegal or unconstitutional.[54] Moreover, even if the statute does cover recent news accounts regarding the NSA's "communication intelligence activities," it does not apply to the other articles at issue—those relating to the CIA's secret prisons and the SWIFT financial tracking program.

A second and deeper problem with the administration's position is that it overlooks the critical role of the press in our constitutional system. As we have seen, a central purpose of the First Amendment was to enable the people to oversee public affairs and to check abuses of power. These are precisely the functions served by the press's recent stories on the administration's antiterrorism initiatives. Moreover, no other actor or institution is fully capable of performing these functions. Although Congress has enacted "whistleblower" laws which encourage employees to report illegal government conduct, those laws do not adequately protect against retaliation and do not apply at all to employees in the intelligence community.[55] Congress has a constitutional duty to oversee the activities of the executive branch, but it may lack the political will to do so (especially when the two branches are controlled by the same political party), and the executive often refuses to provide Congress with the confidential information it requires to carry out this function. Finally, although the courts can provide some protection against unlawful action, there are institutional limits to their ability to monitor the executive branch.

Once again, therefore, this dispute should be understood in terms of a conflict between two sets of rights. On one hand, the community has a right to defend itself and its members against attack. This is the basis of the government's constitutional power to protect national security.[56] On the other hand, in a democratic society, the people are the ultimate sovereign and have a right to supervise the activities of the government, which they can do only by means of a free and unrestrained press. The goal is to reconcile these two values in a way that best promotes the system of constitutional liberty as a whole.

In analyzing this problem, one should begin by distinguishing between two categories of cases in which the press might reveal classified information. The first involves disclosures that serve a substantial public interest, either because they expose governmental incompetence, corruption, or wrongdoing or because they raise issues of policy that the people are entitled to debate in a democratic society. The second category consists of disclosures that do not serve a substantial public interest in these ways. A classic instance is a news report that reveals technical details about the government's efforts to break an enemy code—information that does not raise issues of policy or abuse of power and that might well be useful to the enemy.[57]

Even the first kind of disclosure can adversely affect national security. Nevertheless, this is an inescapable cost of our commitment to liberal democracy.

As Justice Black once observed, "The guarding of military and diplomatic secrets at the expense of informed representative government provides no real security for our Republic."[58] Such an approach is self-defeating because it undermines the very values of freedom and democracy that it seeks to protect. Except in extraordinary circumstances, then, national security must be pursued within the normal constraints imposed by a democratic constitutional order, including liberty of speech and press.

It follows that the First Amendment generally should protect the media's right to publish classified information in situations where this serves a substantial public interest. Although it is difficult to specify the boundaries of this right, I suggest that the following four principles should apply. First, the government should rarely, if ever, be allowed to subject the publication of such information to prior censorship. That is the teaching of the Pentagon Papers case, *New York Times Co. v. United States* (1971). In that case, Daniel Ellsberg and Anthony Russo unlawfully provided the *Times* and the *Washington Post* with a secret, highly classified history of the Vietnam War that had been prepared by the Defense Department. The government went to court to enjoin the publication of this material on the ground that it would cause "grave and irreparable" harm to national security, including " 'the death of soldiers, the destruction of alliances, [and] the greatly increased difficulty of negotiation with our enemies.' " Nevertheless, in a six to three decision, the Supreme Court ruled that the government had failed to meet the "heavy burden" required to justify a prior restraint on expression.[59] Although the majority did not speak with one voice, several of the Justices indicated that prior censorship was permissible only when a disclosure would "surely result in direct, immediate, and irreparable damage to our Nation or its people" (at least in the absence of specific legislation authorizing such censorship).[60]

The second principle concerns the First Amendment standards that should apply to government efforts to subject the press to criminal liability for publishing classified information of substantial public interest. In the Pentagon Papers case, several Justices suggested that they would uphold criminal convictions in such cases.[61] These statements were mere dicta, however, and the Justices devoted little attention to the First Amendment values at stake. As I have explained, those values should lead us to protect publication except in extraordinary circumstances. More specifically, an actor who discloses such information should be immune from criminal prosecution unless the government is able to prove that the defendant knew, or clearly should have known, that the disclosure would create a substantial danger of grave harm to national security in the near future (or that the defendant actually intended to create such a danger).[62]

The third principle is one of clear statement. The press should never be subject to criminal prosecution in this area except under a statute that defines the offense in a clear, narrowly drawn way and that expressly indicates that the offense is one that can be committed by the publication of news stories. A rule like this would ensure that Congress has in fact considered the competing values at stake and has made an informed judgment that the dangers posed by such articles outweigh the public's right to know. Such a rule is also essential to provide adequate notice to journalists and news organizations and to avoid the *in terrorem* effect of vague laws such as the existing provisions of the Espionage Act. Similarly, as in the Pentagon Papers case, the courts should be extremely reluctant to impose prior restraints on publication in the absence of clear congressional authorization.

Fourth, when high-ranking officials, or those acting with their approval, have already revealed classified information about a particular program to the press, the government should be barred from prosecuting others for disclosing other information about the same program. Any other rule would allow the administration to distort public debate through selective leaks that portray its policies in a favorable light.[63]

These four principles should apply in all situations where the press publishes classified information, except in those cases where the defendant knew or clearly should have known that the publication served no substantial public interest. In this second category of cases, there should be no First Amendment protection for knowing publication of classified information, so long as the court determines, on an independent review, that the information was properly classified because its disclosure would pose some danger to national security. Similarly, if a court has statutory authority to grant an injunction in such a case, it may do so under less stringent standards than those applied in *New York Times Co. v. United States.*

Under this approach, the press clearly should be immune from criminal prosecution for the news stories I have described. As a threshold matter, the current provisions of the Espionage Act do not expressly state that they apply to the press. Even if they did, the articles should be protected under the First Amendment. All of the articles revealed government activities that may very well have been unlawful or unconstitutional at the times they took place.[64] The disclosure of these activities sparked intense public criticism, congressional hearings, legal challenges, and even some talk of impeachment. Thus, the articles served the classic function of exposing and checking abuse of power. At a minimum, they raised serious issues of public policy, such as the balance that ought to be struck between civil liberties and national security. In these ways, the stories served substantial public interests. Moreover, it is highly unlikely that the government could prove that the articles posed any serious danger to national security or that the newspapers intentionally, knowingly, or recklessly created such a danger. For instance, one can hardly believe that members of al Qaeda would be surprised to learn that the American government was monitoring their electronic communications or financial transactions. And while the secret prison story may have led some of our allies to shut down the "black sites" they operated in conjunction with the CIA, this should not be regarded as an injury to the legitimate security interests of the United States, for those sites were established for the very purpose of evading American law and were operated in violation of international human rights conventions as well as the law of the host nations.[65] Finally, in the case of the SWIFT program, President Bush and other administration officials had already spoken publicly and proudly of their efforts to block the flow of money to terrorist groups, and therefore should not be permitted to punish journalists for disclosing additional information regarding the same program.

In cases of this sort, then, the First Amendment should immunize the press from liability. That is not to say that the government should be powerless to prevent the publication of classified information. Instead, the executive can seek to control leaks at the source by disciplining and even prosecuting employees who unlawfully divulge such information.[66] Even this power has its limits, however: the government should not be allowed to punish employees for disclosing illegal activities,[67] nor should it be allowed to selectively leak information while punishing those who leak less favorable accounts. Finally, in situations where the press has a First Amendment right to publish confidential information, the government should not be permitted to defeat this right in an indirect way by prosecuting journalists for inchoate crimes such as receiving or retaining classified information or conspiring with employees to reveal such information.[68] While these rules are not perfect, I believe that they strike a reasonable balance between the government's responsibility to protect national security and the right of the people to be informed about governmental activities that are conducted in their name.

Flag Desecration

THE ONGOING CONTROVERSY

In August 1984, Gregory Lee Johnson burned an American flag during a political demonstration outside the Republican National Convention in Dallas. He was charged with violating a Texas law that made it a crime to intentionally damage a state or national flag "in a way that the actor knows will seriously offend one or more persons likely to observe or discover his action." Johnson was convicted and sentenced to one year in prison and a two-thousand-dollar fine.[69]

In 1989, the Supreme Court reversed Johnson's conviction by a vote of five to four. Writing for the majority, Justice Brennan declared that the government could not ban flag desecration that was intended as a form of political protest, for that would violate the "bedrock [First Amendment] principle . . . that the government may not prohibit the expression of an idea simply because society finds the idea itself offensive or disagreeable." In a vigorous dissent, four Justices argued that in the course of American history the flag had come to hold "a unique position" that merited legal protection.[70]

Texas v. Johnson sparked intense controversy. Although some defended the Court's decision, others denounced it for permitting desecration of the nation's most cherished symbol. President George H. W. Bush urged Congress to approve a constitutional amendment to overturn the decision. After considerable debate, Congress chose instead to enact the Flag Protection Act of 1989. The statute was carefully drafted to cover all "conduct (other than disposal) that damages or mistreats a flag, without regard to the actor's motive, his intended message, or the likely effects of his conduct on onlookers." In this way, Congress hoped to satisfy the objections expressed in *Johnson.* One year later, however, in *Eichman v. United States* (1990), an identical five to four majority declared that the federal statute suffered from "the same fundamental flaw" as the Texas statute, namely, that it restricted expression because of its "communicative impact" on others.[71]

The Court's decision in *Eichman* led to renewed calls for a constitutional amendment authorizing the government to ban flag desecration. This proposal passed the House of Representatives on a number of occasions. During a Senate debate in June 2006, the amendment fell one vote short of the two-thirds majority required to send it to the states, where it almost certainly would have been ratified.[72]

THE VALUES AT STAKE

Those who support desecration laws argue that the flag serves several important values. First, it constitutes "the visible symbol embodying our Nation." In addition, the flag "embodies the spirit of our national commitment" to such ideals as "liberty, equality, and tolerance." Finally, by encouraging individuals to identify with the nation and its ideals, the flag helps to unify a diverse and often fractious society.[73] As Brennan acknowledged in *Eichman,* these values justify government efforts to "create national symbols, promote them, and encourage their respectful treatment."[74] But they do not show that the government should have the power to ban conduct that disrespects the flag.

Promoting national unity. First, while the government may encourage individuals to identify with the nation, it may not compel them to do so. This principle lies at the heart of the Supreme Court's decision in *West Virginia State Board of Education v. Barnette* (1943), which held that individuals cannot constitutionally be forced to salute the flag.[75] To state the point in contractarian terms, individuals must be free to decide for themselves whether to consent to the regime, and flag burning is a dramatic way to deny one's consent. Far from strengthening the political order, a ban on flag desecration would undermine its legitimacy by punishing expressions of dissent.[76]

The symbol of our nation. Defenders of the flag also point to its value as "the symbol of our Nation."[77] This statement conceals a crucial ambiguity, however, for "the Nation" is a term that can mean several different things. In one sense, it refers to the American people, that is, to the people who live in this country and who have a common history and culture. In a second sense, "the Nation" refers to America as an independent political society.[78] In a third sense, the term refers to this political society under a particular form of government, that is, the form of government established by the Constitution of the United States. Finally, the term refers to the United States as a sovereign power in the international arena.

The American flag is "the symbol of our Nation" in each of these senses. But it especially represents the nation in the last three, political meanings of the term. The flag is also closely associated with the government of the United States, which displays the banner in all three branches, in the armed forces, and in a wide variety of official settings.

In light of these distinctions, it is clearly inadequate to say (as Chief Justice William H. Rehnquist did in his *Johnson* dissent) that flag burning simply conveys a "bitter dislike of [one's] country."[79] When Americans burn the flag, they rarely do so to express their hatred of the American people in general or their opposition to the existence of the United States as an independent political society. Instead, flag burning is commonly intended as a protest against the leaders and policies of the government of the United States or against its conduct in relation to other nations and peoples. In some cases, flag burning may also be intended to challenge the very legitimacy of the government or the constitutional order. It follows that flag desecration constitutes a classic form of antigovernment speech and that laws banning such expression are a species of sedition law. Indeed, one of the earliest congressional efforts to protect the flag came in the Sedition Act of 1918, which made it a crime, when the United States was at war, to utter or publish "any disloyal, profane, scurrilous, or abusive language about the form of government of the United States, or the Constitution of the United States, or the military or naval forces of the United States, *or the flag of the United States,"* or to utter or publish "any language intended to bring [them] into contempt."[80] Laws that prohibit flag desecration as a form of political protest should therefore be held unconstitutional for the same reasons as the laws against radical speech discussed earlier in this chapter.[81]

National identity. Many Americans would say that the flag represents not only our nation but also the ideals on which it is founded. For this reason, they naturally experience flag desecration as an assault on our collective identity. Under the First Amendment, however, individuals must be free to challenge our values and our sense of identity. Moreover, in some cases, flag burning is intended not to disparage those values but to criticize the nation for failing to live up to them.[82] A classic example is *Street v. United States* (1969). An African American man named Sidney Street was listening to the radio in his apartment when he "heard a news report that the civil rights leader James Meredith had been shot by a sniper in Mississippi." "Saying to himself, 'They didn't protect him,'" Street took a flag that he had displayed on national holidays and burned it on the street corner, shouting, "If they let that happen to Meredith we don't need an American flag." In cases like this, the actor burns the flag not to repudiate ideals like liberty and equality, but precisely to affirm them and to accuse the nation or the government of failing to secure them.[83] For all of these reasons, the majority in *Johnson* was correct to hold that flag desecration is a form of expression that lies at the core of the First Amendment.

In response, the dissenting Justices asserted that Johnson's conduct "conveyed nothing that could not have been conveyed . . . just as forcefully in a dozen different ways." As in *Chaplinsky v. New Hampshire* (1942), therefore, his act was "'no essential part of any exposition of ideas,'" and could properly be banned to protect other important interests.[84] But this argument misapprehends the power of flag burning as a form of expression—a power it derives from the flag itself. The meaning of the flag is not merely cognitive: it does not simply stand for certain ideas such as national unity.[85] Instead, the flag is a symbol that is performative in nature: in expressing national values, it also tends to realize those values. The flag inspires individuals to identify with their country; it promotes the unity of the nation; it affirms ideals such as liberty and equality. This is what gives the flag its power as a symbol. At the same time, however, this explains why protests like those of Street and Johnson need to take the form they do. The most effective way to counteract a symbol of this kind is through a direct attack on the symbol itself.[86] This is one reason flag burning has a strong claim to constitutional protection.

However, flag burning should not be understood merely as a negation of the values embodied in the flag. Instead, both the display and the desecration of the flag can be regarded as part of a broader process of expression, one in which individuals determine the extent to which they will identify with the nation and in which they collectively shape their values and their sense of national identity.[87] Government should not be permitted to truncate or distort this process by permitting what it regards as patriotic forms of expression while punishing acts of dissent.

As the Court's opinions in *Johnson* and *Eichman* make clear, this does not mean the government has no legitimate interest in the flag. The government has the authority to encourage respectful treatment of that symbol, for example, by adopting nonbinding guidelines regarding its proper use. In addition, the Court has left open the question whether the law may ban some forms of conduct regarding the flag, including its use for commercial purposes, nonexpressive conduct that mistreats the flag (such as the conduct of a tired person who drags a flag through the mud), and desecration of a flag that is public property.[88] But the First Amendment protects — and should continue to protect — flag desecration as a form of political protest.

Conclusion

This chapter has explored three First Amendment problems involving speech that attacks or criticizes the government. In each case, I argued that the problem is best understood as a clash between the right to free speech and other rights that belong to the community, such as the power to protect national security. It might seem that any recognition of community rights would lead to unacceptable limits on freedom of expression. As I have shown, however, precisely the opposite is true: the best way to cabin interests like national security is to view them within a broader framework of rights based on individual liberty and democratic self-government. If we adopt this perspective, we will be extremely reluctant to limit free speech except when it poses an imminent danger of serious injury to individuals or the state. This is the rule we should apply to revolutionary speech, to advocacy of unlawful action, and to publication of classified information on matters of substantial public concern. Finally, we can resolve the issue of flag burning by recognizing that, while the community has a right to create and promote symbols of our national identity, individuals must be free to decide whether they wish to embrace those symbols or to repudiate them in an effort to challenge or revise that identity. In these ways, we can acknowledge the legitimate claims of the community without undermining the freedoms on which it is based.

8

Speech and Violence

In chapter 7, I began to explore the problem of speech that promotes violence and other forms of unlawful action.[1] Here I want to discuss that problem in depth. I begin with incitement, an issue that lies at the heart of modern free speech jurisprudence. Next, I address two closely related issues: how the First Amendment should apply to threats of violence, and how it should apply to speech that facilitates the commission of crimes. These issues are posed by two of the most hotly contested cases in recent years: *Planned Parenthood v. American Coalition of Life Activists* (2002), which upheld a large damages award against an activist group that targeted abortion providers by declaring them guilty of "crimes against humanity," and *Rice v. Paladin Enterprises* (1997), which upheld a lawsuit against the publisher of *Hit Man*, an instruction manual for contract killers. Finally, I discuss whether the law should be allowed to ban "fighting words" on the grounds that they inflict injury or are likely to provoke a violent response.

Incitement

In *Brandenburg v. Ohio* (1969), the Supreme Court declared that, under the First Amendment, the government "may not forbid or proscribe advocacy of the use of force or of law violation except where such advocacy is directed to inciting or producing imminent lawless action and is likely to incite or produce such action."[2] In the preceding chapter, I defended this doctrine against the conservative view that advocacy of unlawful action should receive no constitutional protection. In this section, I respond to the libertarian argument that *Brandenburg* does not go far enough and that the state should have little or no authority to restrict such speech.

This position has been advanced by several leading First Amendment theorists. For example, in a provocative article entitled *Harm, Liberty, and Free Speech*, Edwin Baker contends that every individual should be free to express herself and "to act in and . . . affect the world . . . by trying to persuade . . . others" through speech. This is true even when the speaker urges the listener to harm a third party. Banning such expression would violate the autonomy not only of the speaker but also of the listener, by denying her status as "an agent presumptively capable of responsible choice" and by "interfer[ing] with her decision whether to follow the law." For Baker, this analysis has important implications for the allocation of responsibility between the parties: "[W]hen a person 'offers' a view to another, the person only presents herself, exercises her autonomy. Any consequences involved in the listener's reaction or response, if the speaker's autonomy is protected and the listener's recognized, must be attributed, in the end, to the listener." Baker concludes that the speaker has "a right . . . to present her viewpoint even if its assimilation by the listener leads to . . . serious harm" to others.[3]

The difficulty with this analysis is that it focuses almost entirely on the speaker and the listener, while the victim largely disappears from view. From a rights-based perspective, the question is whether the speaker has a right to intentionally persuade the listener to harm another person. To put it another way, the issue is whether she can properly be held responsible for the resulting injury.

To address this issue, I need to sketch a conception of action and responsibility.[4] I take action to be the process by which an individual seeks to realize her ends and intentions in the world. An actor is responsible, at a minimum, for all the consequences she intends to bring about through her act.[5]

To take a concrete example of incitement, suppose that a speaker successfully urges a crowd to lynch a prisoner inside a jail. Clearly the crowd members are responsible for the prisoner's death, for it results from their own intentional action. But the same thing is true of the speaker herself. As Baker recognizes, speaking is a form of action which seeks to change the world in accord with the speaker's intentions.[6] In this case, the very purpose of the speech is to induce the crowd to kill the prisoner. Speech can induce action in several ways. The most obvious is by inflaming the hearers' passions, for example, by stirring up their hatred and desire for revenge. But speech can also provide its listeners with reasons for action — for example, by persuading them that the legal system will not punish the prisoner as much as he deserves and that justice can be achieved only through direct action. Even if the listeners are already inclined to attack the prisoner, the speech can nevertheless have an impact by encouraging them to do so, by assuring them that others support them, by overcoming their hesitations, and by making the action appear to be legitimate. Finally, the speech can serve as a catalyst that leads the listeners to transform their relatively inchoate thoughts and feelings into a definite intention to act.

By inciting others to act, the speaker is able to realize her ends and intentions in the world. The speaker uses her audience to accomplish her own purpose, the lynching of the prisoner.[7] Again, that does not mean that the audience members should escape responsibility. From the speaker's perspective, the listeners are means to an end. When we focus on the listeners, on the other hand, we can see that they too are autonomous individuals who are responsible for their own actions, which reflect their own ends and intentions. It follows that in this case both the speaker and the crowd members should be held responsible for the prisoner's death.[8]

Up to this point, I have followed Baker and other theorists by analyzing incitement in individualist terms — that is, in terms of the separate actions of the speaker and the listeners. But incitement is not only a form of individual action; it is also a form of social action.[9] A speaker who incites others rarely says, in effect, "*You* should lynch the prisoner." Such an appeal would almost surely backfire, for it would imply that the speaker stood apart from the action and took no responsibility for it. Instead, the speaker effectively says, "*We* should lynch the prisoner." In other words, the speaker addresses the listeners not as unrelated individuals but as a group with shared interests, values, and beliefs, and urges them to engage in collective action in pursuit of a common goal. In this way, the speech gives social meaning and value to the crowd members' conduct: instead of viewing themselves as committing lawless acts of violence, they regard themselves as vigilantes who are acting courageously to ensure that justice is done. In many cases, the speaker can also be viewed as directing and coordinating the common action. When the crowd members storm the jail, they act in accord with intentions and ends that are shared by all. It follows that each person, including the speaker herself, shares responsibility for the death. Of course, all of this is even more clear if the group existed prior to the events in question and the speaker was an acknowledged leader of the group.

For these reasons, speakers can properly be held responsible when they incite listeners to attack third parties. Contrary to the libertarian view, this position does not violate individual autonomy. Although individuals have a right to express themselves and to act in the world, they have no right to do so in a way that intentionally brings about an invasion of the autonomy or rights of others — in this case, the prisoner's right to life and personal security as well as the community's right to the public peace. It follows that the incitement doctrine is consistent with a rights-based approach to the First Amendment.

The view I have sketched also accords with existing American law. Criminal law imposes responsibility not only on those who directly participate in the commission of a crime, but also on those who intentionally assist or encourage others to commit a crime.[10] This traditional doctrine of complicity or aiding and abetting may be understood as resting on the principle that one who intentionally helps or encourages another to commit a wrongful act voluntarily identifies himself with, and thereby assumes responsibility for, that act.[11] For similar reasons, tort law imposes liability on one who orders or induces another to commit an act that the speaker should know is a tort, or who knowingly provides substantial assistance or encouragement to another to commit a tort.[12] Thus, in the lynching case, both the speaker and those whom she successfully incites would be subject to criminal prosecution for murder as well as to civil liability for wrongful death.

Of course, incitement is not always successful. Suppose that, just as the crowd is about to attack the prisoner, the police arrive and quell the disturbance. What position should the law take in this situation? Here the speech does not result in actual violence. Nevertheless, because the speech constitutes a grave threat to the peace, it violates the rights of the community and can reasonably be treated as a crime in itself. In many American jurisdictions, the speaker in this case would be subject to prosecution for criminal solicitation, incitement, or similar offenses.[13]

Thus far, my discussion has focused on speech that advocates violence against individuals. Similar reasoning applies to speech that urges other forms of unlawful action, such as tax evasion or violent overthrow of the government. Although these forms of expression do not violate the rights of individuals, they may violate other rights, such as the community's right to govern itself and to implement the laws adopted through the democratic process. As we saw in chapter 7, the *Brandenburg* rule of imminent incitement generally represents the appropriate standard to use in determining whether advocacy of unlawful action should be protected.[14] In my view, however, a less stringent standard should apply to speech that advocates violence against individuals. This point can best be seen in connection with a related problem: how the First Amendment should apply to threats of violence.

Threatening Speech: The Nuremberg Files Case

At a press conference in January 1995 during the annual March for Life in Washington, D.C., the American Coalition of Life Activists (ACLA) unveiled a poster called The Deadly Dozen. Under the heading GUILTY OF CRIMES AGAINST HUMANITY, the poster displayed the photographs of thirteen doctors who performed abortions, together with their names and addresses. Over the following year, ACLA released posters featuring other doctors and announced the creation of a Web site called the Nuremberg Files, which listed personal information on two hundred abortion doctors and clinic owners and employees, as well as many politicians, judges, law enforcement officials, spouses, and supporters of abortion rights.

In *Planned Parenthood v. American Coalition of Life Activists,* several of the doctors and clinics filed a federal lawsuit in Oregon against ACLA, an affiliated organization called Advocates for Life Ministries (ALM), and the activists who composed the two groups.[15] The case was brought under the Freedom of Access to Clinic Entrances Act of 1994 (FACE), a federal statute that makes it unlawful to intentionally intimidate others by "force or threat of force" to prevent them from providing or obtaining reproductive health services.[16]

The plaintiffs in *ACLA* conceded that the guilty posters and the Nuremberg Files contained no explicit threats of force. But they asserted that in this case context was crucial. Three doctors who had previously appeared on such posters — David Gunn, George Patterson, and John Bayard Britton — had subsequently been murdered by abortion opponents. Those killings were part of a broader wave of violence directed against abortion providers and clinics. ACLA and its members (who had broken away from the mainstream of the prolife movement over this very issue) consistently advocated and endorsed such violence and declared that the killing of abortionists was a form of "justifiable homicide" that was necessary to protect the unborn. Against this background, the Federal Bureau of Investigation took the Deadly Dozen poster so seriously that it offered the doctors round-the-clock protection. The plaintiffs testified that they were terrified when they learned of the new poster, which they understood to mean that they "would be assassinated, as the other doctors have been assassinated." Moreover, the defendants knew that the posters would cause such fear. For example, in an article in September 1993, ALM asserted that the murder of Gunn six months before had "sent shock waves of fear through the ranks of abortion providers across the country. As a result, many more doctors [have] quit out of fear for their lives, and the ones who are left are scared stiff." The same article reported that a wanted poster was being prepared for Britton; ten months later, he too was murdered. Like the posters, the Nuremberg Files site contained no overt threats of violence, but it listed the names and addresses of "abortionists" and asserted that they were guilty of crimes against humanity. When a doctor on the list was murdered, a line was drawn through his name — sometimes on the same day — while the names of those wounded were printed in gray.

After a two-week trial in federal district court, the jury and the judge ruled that the posters and the Web site constituted "true threats," that is, statements that communicated a serious intention to commit acts of unlawful violence against the plaintiffs. Under Supreme Court decisions like *Watts v. United States* (1969), such threats are outside the protection of the First Amendment. Finding that the defendants had acted in reckless disregard of the plaintiffs' rights, the jury ordered them to pay the doctors and the clinics more than $500,000 in compensatory damages and more than $108 million in punitive damages.[17] The judge also issued an injunction barring the defendants from threatening the plaintiffs in the future. The defendants then appealed to the U.S. Court of Appeals for the Ninth Circuit.

The Nuremberg Files case led to a heated debate which divided the civil liberties community. The Oregon chapter of the ACLU joined several feminist, abortion rights, and civil rights groups in support of the plaintiffs, while the Thomas Jefferson Center for the Protection of Free Expression filed an amicus brief on the other side. In 2001, a three-judge panel reversed the district court decision, but the following year the full court of appeals ruled for the plaintiffs by a vote of six to five. The Supreme Court declined review, allowing this ruling to stand.

ACLA is one of the most difficult First Amendment cases in recent years. Nevertheless, I believe the Ninth Circuit's decision was correct. As the trial judge and jury found, by targeting the doctors through the posters and the Nuremberg Files, the defendants intentionally caused them to suffer grave fear of bodily harm or death. In this way, the defendants invaded their right to personal security as well as the community's right to the public peace. As we saw in chapter 4, the peace may be understood not merely as an absence of violence, but as a condition of mutual trust in which individuals expect others to respect their personal safety. In *ACLA,* the defendants violated the peace by issuing what amounted to a "hit list" against particular individuals.[18]

The judges who dissented in the court of appeals argued that even if the defendants' acts intentionally caused fear, they did not amount to true threats. As Judge Alex Kozinski put it, "In order for [a] statement to be a threat, it must send the message that *the speakers themselves* — or individuals acting in concert with them — will engage in physical violence." In this case, the speech caused the doctors to fear that they would be attacked not by the defendants or by persons under their control, but rather by "unrelated terrorists" like John C. Salvi III (who murdered two abortion clinic employees during a shooting rampage in 1994). According to Kozinski, it followed that the posters and the Web site were not threats; at most, they advocated violence by persons not associated with the defendants. Under *Brandenburg*, such advocacy may not be restricted unless it is both intended and likely to result in *imminent* violence, which was not the case here. For these reasons, Kozinski concluded that ACLA's speech was protected by the First Amendment.[19]

Although this analysis is plausible, it is ultimately unconvincing.[20] Threats and incitement should not be regarded as mutually exclusive categories. In this case, the posters and the Web site did encourage unlawful action, but they also made threats of violence. Kozinski fails to recognize this point because he treats those involved as unrelated individuals and thus overlooks the social dimension of the expression. In *ACLA*, the defendants purported to speak not merely as individuals but as the leaders of a movement. Their speech can reasonably be understood to mean, "If you continue to perform abortions, we will kill you," where "we" means "we and our followers" or "those committed to our cause." The terror that this speech instills in its targets does not depend on who would fire the fatal shot — indeed, it may well be greater when they do not know who will assault them.[21]

The speech in *ACLA* falls within the concept of a threat as developed in chapter 4 — a representation of violence against an individual that causes her to experience that violence in her own mind.[22] In this case, the speech constituted a representation in two ways: (1) the defendants claimed to represent, or to speak on behalf of, their movement, and (2) they implicitly represented that they or their followers would kill the doctors if they did not stop performing abortions. In this situation, the key issue is not whether the defendants had the power to control potential assailants, but whether the representations they made were — and were meant to be — convincing. The district court found that the posters and the Nuremberg Files caused the doctors to live in constant fear of death or bodily harm, wearing bulletproof vests, "borrowing cars and varying routes to avoid detection," and even ceasing to practice medicine, and that the defendants specifically intended the speech to cause such fear.[23] In this way, the speech seriously infringed the doctors' rights to personal security.

Yet personal security is not the only right at stake here. As Judge Marsha S. Berzon observed in dissent, what makes *ACLA* such a hard case is that the posters and the Web site "were, on their face, 'expressions of grievance and protest on one of the major public issues of our time,'" and thus would constitute "quintessentially" protected speech if they were not held to be threats.[24] Thus, the central problem in *ACLA* is how to strike a balance between the right to political or ideological expression and the right to freedom from violence.

Of course, people must be free to contend that abortion is murder, that it should be outlawed, and even that the killing of abortion providers should be regarded as justifiable homicide. Ideological speech of this sort lies at the heart of the First Amendment. Moreover, such speech should not be denied protection merely because it contains vague threats against abortion providers in general. But the First Amendment should not protect concrete threats of violence, even when they are made in public discourse.[25] This is particularly true of threats that are directed against identifiable individuals. On one hand, such threats have a grave impact on the targets' personal security, while on the other hand, the ability to make such threats adds little to the speakers' freedom to express their ideological views. Indeed, I would argue that public discourse is enhanced rather than diminished by excluding such threats.[26]

As the dissenters emphasized, however, speech should not lose constitutional protection merely because it forcefully condemns the conduct of others. There is a real danger that judges and juries will determine that unpopular acts of expression are threats when they are merely the kind of rhetorical attacks that fall within our nation's commitment to robust public debate. For this reason, the courts should enforce particularly demanding standards in cases involving speech that publicly addresses political or ideological issues. Speech of this sort should be held to constitute a threat only when it is "unambiguous, given the context," as shown by clear and convincing evidence. Moreover, speakers should not be subject to civil or criminal liability in such cases unless they intended their statements to be understood as threats. In a subsequent decision, *Virginia v. Black* (2003), the Supreme Court appeared to endorse such a standard when it observed that the category of true threats "encompass[es] those statements where the speaker means to communicate a serious expression of an intent to commit an act of unlawful violence to a particular individual or group of individuals."[27] In *ACLA*, the district court found that these strict standards were met, although the dissenters disagreed.

For all of these reasons, the Ninth Circuit was correct to hold the posters and Web site unprotected under the true threat doctrine. The dissenters were concerned that applying the doctrine in this way would undermine the protections of *Brandenburg*. On one level, the two doctrines do not conflict. As I have noted, incitement and threats are not mutually exclusive: a statement can be unprotected as a threat even though it does not meet the constitutional standard for incitement. It is true that in the case of incitement the danger of violence must be imminent, while no such requirement applies to threats. But this disparity flows from the different nature of the injuries that result from the two kinds of speech. Threats inflict injury in a direct, immediate way by causing the victim to suffer fear. By contrast, incitement causes injury only if it persuades others to commit violence in the future. As a general matter, then, it makes sense to impose an imminence requirement for incitement but not for threats.[28]

Although these considerations explain why the two categories are governed by different standards in general, they do not fully resolve the problem that arises in a case like *ACLA,* which may be described as a mixed case of threats and incitement. Under *Brandenburg,* the defendants' speech could not be punished as incitement absent a danger of imminent violence, yet the Ninth Circuit held the same speech unprotected as a threat. Moreover, the speech in this case was threatening partly *because* it urged others to attack the plaintiffs.

In a situation like this, there is undeniably some tension between *Brandenburg* and the true threat doctrine. It does not follow, however, that this tension should be resolved by curtailing the law's ability to protect against threats. Instead, the most reasonable solution is to hold that *Brandenburg*'s imminence requirement does not apply to speech that intentionally advocates violence against individuals, in situations where there is a substantial danger that the violence will come about. As we saw in chapter 7, *Brandenburg* is the culmination of a long line of cases that focused on speech directed against the government itself. Speech of this sort has great value under the First Amendment, while in our society the government is so strong that the danger posed by the speech is relatively small, so long as the speaker stops short of imminent incitement. By contrast, individuals are far more vulnerable to attack and far less able to protect themselves. Thus, speech that advocates future violence against individuals poses more objective danger to them than the danger posed by subversive speech. Speech that targets individuals also has more subjective impact, causing fear in much the same way that threats do. It is true that denying protection to such speech would impose some limit on the ability of speakers to promote their ideological views, but this limit would be relatively slight in comparison to the injury that the speech causes to personal security and the public peace. Therefore, while the First Amendment should protect the right to advocate future unlawful action against the government itself, that protection should not extend to speech that urges future violence against individuals, in situations where there is a significant likelihood that the violence will occur.[29]

This approach would resolve the anomaly that the dissenters perceived in *ACLA,* for it would hold the defendants' speech unprotected not only as threats but also as incitement. The posters and the Web site had a powerful tendency to incite violence—a tendency that largely derived from the performative nature of the speech. The posters announced that the leadership of one wing of the antiabortion movement had determined that the doctors were "guilty of crimes against humanity." In effect, the posters declared the doctors to be outlaws who could and should be killed to protect the unborn. Similarly, as the majority recognized, the listing of abortion providers on the Nuremberg Files constituted a virtual hit list that targeted them for attack. Speech of this sort was highly likely to incite violence in the context of the bitter conflict over abortion. From the evidence in the case, it also appears highly probable that the defendants intended to incite such violence.

For these reasons, *ACLA* correctly held that the posters and Web site violated FACE and that they constituted true threats unprotected by the First Amendment. Nevertheless, one may be troubled by the fact that the defendants were ordered not merely to compensate the plaintiffs for the harm they suffered, but also to pay more than one hundred million dollars in punitive damages. Punitive damages are designed to punish defendants for engaging in wrongful conduct that intentionally or recklessly disregards the rights of others.[30] Although this is a rule of ordinary law, it should also be regarded as a requirement of the First Amendment.[31] In *ACLA,* the defendants may well have believed that their speech was constitutionally protected and that it therefore did not violate the doctors' legal rights. If the defendants did believe this, their belief undeniably was a reasonable one, because *ACLA* was in many ways a case of first impression, and five of the eleven judges on the appeals court made strong arguments for holding the speech protected. Under these circumstances, an award of punitive damages should be regarded as inconsistent with the First Amendment as well as with the ordinary law governing punitive damages. On the other hand, it was appropriate to require the defendants to compensate the plaintiffs for intentionally injuring them and to enjoin the defendants from threatening them in the future.

Speech That Facilitates Crime: The Hit Man Case

On March 3, 1993, James Perry brutally murdered Mildred Horn, her eight-year-old quadriplegic son Trevor, and Trevor's nurse, Janice Saunders. Perry had been hired by Mildred's ex-husband, Lawrence Horn, to kill the family so that he could receive a two-million-dollar trust fund that had been set up for Trevor's care under a medical malpractice settlement. In committing the murders, Perry followed the detailed instructions set forth in a book published by Paladin Press called *Hit Man: A Manual for Independent Contractors.* Perry and Horn were convicted of first-degree murder. The victims' families then brought a tort suit against Paladin for wrongful death, alleging that the publisher had aided and abetted Perry in the commission of the murders. Paladin responded that, even if the book did contribute to the crimes, it was protected by the First Amendment.[32]

Like the Nuremberg Files case, *Rice v. Paladin Enterprises* provoked a vigorous debate over the scope of free speech. Several chapters of the ACLU joined with media organizations and writers' associations in filing an amicus brief that contended that *Hit Man* was entitled to constitutional protection. Other civil libertarians, victims' groups, and the Department of Justice took the opposite view.[33] Ruling that *Hit Man* was protected by the First Amendment, the district court granted Paladin's motion for summary judgment. In 1997, the U.S. Court of Appeals for the Fourth Circuit reversed this decision and remanded the case for trial. In an opinion by Judge J. Michael Luttig, the court held that the plaintiffs would have a valid claim if they could prove that Paladin intended to aid murderers like Perry, and that in such a case the First Amendment would be no bar to liability. After the Supreme Court declined review, Paladin agreed to settle the claim for five million dollars rather than face trial before a jury.[34]

The Fourth Circuit reached the correct result. From a rights-based perspective, the first question is whether Paladin played a substantial part in depriving the victims of their right to life. Of course, Horn and Perry were primarily responsible for the three murders. The issue is whether Paladin also bears some responsibility. Tort law holds an actor liable when he "knowingly gives substantial aid to another who, as he knows, intends to do a tortious act."[35] As Luttig recognized, however, while this standard may be appropriate in ordinary tort cases, the First Amendment requires that a different rule should apply in cases where a publisher is sued for allegedly providing assistance to criminals. The publishers of news reports and mystery novels, not to mention chemistry textbooks, may know that some people will use their work to commit crimes, yet no one believes that this is enough to make them responsible for those crimes.[36] Thus, if liability can be imposed at all in cases like *Rice,* it can only be on the basis of a more demanding standard — for example, that the defendant intentionally (and not merely knowingly) aided in the commission of a crime.

There is no doubt that Paladin's book provided substantial assistance to Perry. As Luttig's opinion made clear, Perry "meticulously followed countless of *Hit Man*'s detailed factual instructions" on how to solicit, prepare for, and commit the murders and then escape from the scene. Indeed, *Hit Man* was so integral to the commission of the crimes that it played a key role in solving them and in obtaining the convictions of Perry and Horn.[37]

The plaintiffs could also make out a strong case of intent. In connection with its motion for summary judgment, Paladin made some extraordinary concessions: that it had "engaged in a marketing strategy intended to attract . . . criminals and would-be criminals who desire information and instructions on how to commit crimes"; that the publisher not only knew but intended that *Hit Man* "would be used, upon receipt, by criminals . . . to plan and execute the crime of murder for hire"; and even that Paladin had assisted Perry in perpetrating the three murders in this case.[38] In making these stipulations, Paladin's attorneys evidently hoped to establish the strongest possible defense to lawsuits of this kind, by obtaining a ruling that even if these facts were true, the publication would be constitutionally protected. As it turned out, this strategy backfired dramatically, leading the court to write a powerful opinion rejecting a First Amendment defense in such circumstances.

Paladin made these concessions solely for purposes of its summary judgment motion; if the case had gone to trial, the plaintiffs would have been required to prove their allegations. As the court observed, however, the jury could have relied on several kinds of evidence to find that Paladin specifically intended to assist criminals like Perry: (1) *Hit Man* expressly claimed to be "an instruction book on murder"; (2) it contained many passages that encouraged readers to pursue careers as professional killers; (3) Paladin marketed the book in a way that targeted criminals and would-be criminals; and (4) the book had little if any use other than to instruct them in the art of contract killing. Thus, the plaintiffs had a good chance of proving at trial that Paladin intentionally helped readers like Perry to commit murder.[39]

Lurking in this analysis, however, is a serious problem the court did not address. In the usual case where a defendant assists another person to commit a wrongful act, the defendant desires that the wrongful act take place. But that is not true in *Rice:* it would be difficult to show that Paladin wanted the victims dead in this or any other case. Instead, the publisher's goal was simply to sell as many books as it could. On this basis, it could be argued that a court cannot rely on Paladin's intent to hold *Hit Man* unprotected by the First Amendment.[40]

This argument is unpersuasive, however. It is true that when Paladin published *Hit Man,* it did not have *an intent that individuals commit murder.* But it did have *an intent to assist them to commit murder,* by providing them with detailed instructions on how to do so. Nor does it matter that Paladin's ultimate motivation was profit. Of course, it is true that when an individual provides a good or service to another in exchange for money, he intends to promote his own purposes. At the same time, however, he knows that in order to do so he must promote the purposes of the other.[41] From the seller's perspective, aiding the other may be simply a means to his own end, but if he wills the end, he must also will the means necessary to achieve it. It follows that the seller does intend to promote the buyer's purposes, even though he does this in return for money. The real question is *what* purposes he intends to promote. When the good or service is one that can be used for various purposes, some of which are lawful, the seller should not necessarily be held to intend to promote an unlawful purpose. But when the good or service is specifically designed for an unlawful use and when the seller intentionally provides it to another knowing that she intends to use it in that way, it is reasonable to say that the seller intends to promote the other's unlawful purpose.

In *Rice,* Paladin sold *Hit Man* not only to individuals who desired to commit unlawful acts, but also to many other people who wanted to read the book for entertainment or other lawful purposes. It could be argued that, in this situation, one cannot properly attribute to Paladin an intent to assist unlawful acts.[42] As I shall argue below, the principal purpose of *Hit Man* was to assist in the commission of murder, while other purposes were secondary and derivative. In any event, when a work is specifically designed for unlawful purposes and when it is provided to persons some of whom the seller knows will use it for those purposes, it is reasonable to say that *one purpose* of the seller is to facilitate unlawful acts, even if she had other aims as well.

In sum, while Paladin may not have desired its readers to commit murder, the Fourth Circuit was right to conclude that the publisher intended to assist in the commission of murder. In some jurisdictions, that would be sufficient to establish criminal liability for aiding and abetting.[43] It is certainly sufficient for civil liability, which ordinarily requires only knowing assistance.[44] Moreover, this form of intent should satisfy the requirements of the First Amendment.[45] In contrast to the publishers of news stories, mystery novels, and chemistry textbooks, Paladin published a work that was intended to assist readers in committing crimes and that was specifically adapted to that end. That is enough to clearly distinguish *Hit Man* from forms of expression that are constitutionally protected.

For these reasons, Paladin should be regarded as partly responsible for the three murders in this case. Under the rights-based approach, the next question is whether the publisher's conduct is nevertheless entitled to protection under the First Amendment. Paladin and its amici argued that the case should be governed by *Brandenburg v. Ohio.* As we have seen, that decision holds that the government may not ban advocacy of unlawful action except where the advocacy is both intended and likely to incite "imminent lawless action."[46] In *Rice,* Paladin contended that the imminence requirement was not satisfied and that the book was therefore protected by the First Amendment. As the Fourth Circuit explained, however, there are two related reasons why *Brandenburg* should not apply to a case like this. First, the vast bulk of *Hit Man* consisted not of advocacy but of instructions on how to commit crimes. Second, the plaintiffs sought to hold Paladin liable not because it *advocated* the commission of murder, but rather because it *assisted* criminals in the commission of murder. When speakers publicly urge others to violate the law, their views can be counteracted by more speech, unless the violation is imminent. That is not true of speech that provides concrete assistance like the instructions contained in *Hit Man*. Indeed, information of this sort may well be more valuable when it is provided in advance and can be used to plan a crime than when it is provided immediately before the offense is to be committed. It follows that cases like this are not subject to the *Brandenburg* imminence standard.[47] Instead, one must strike a fresh balance between the values at stake.

Hit Man's primary value was instrumental. The book was just what it claimed to be—a "technical manual" that offered instructions on how to perform a certain activity. It is sometimes said that the First Amendment should not protect speech that has merely instrumental value.[48] But this view is mistaken: when people have a right to engage in an activity, they should also have a right to receive information related to that activity. Thus, the First Amendment protects sex manuals, information on the availability of contraception and abortion, guides for political and community organizing, rubrics for performing religious rituals, and so on. Because all of these activities are constitutionally protected, so is speech that is instrumental to them. At least to some extent, the First Amendment should also protect speech that is instrumental to activities that are permitted under existing law, even though they are not protected by the Constitution (such as brewing beer). On the other hand, speech has no instrumental value for First Amendment purposes when the activity that it promotes is itself wrongful and unlawful, such as murder.[49] That was the case with *Hit Man*.

According to Paladin, *Hit Man* served a variety of purposes other than the promotion of criminal conduct.[50] For example, the publisher asserted that the book was useful to mystery and "true crime" writers, to law enforcement officers, and to criminologists, all of whom are interested in the methods and mentality of crime. But such uses were merely secondary to and derivative of *Hit Man*'s principal purpose, which was a wrongful one. Although writers, scholars, and police officers may learn a good deal from studying a manual designed for contract killers, that hardly excuses Paladin's publication of such a manual, any more than researchers would be justified in bringing about real crimes in order to study them. The other purposes asserted by Paladin also had little weight. Although some people may have read *Hit Man* "for purposes of entertainment," those purposes can be served almost as well by literature that is not specifically designed for use by criminals. In any event, mere entertainment has little value in comparison to human life. The same is true of the book's value for "persons who fantasize about committing crimes but do not thereafter commit them." Finally, whatever minimal ideological content the book contained could have been presented without giving detailed instructions on how to commit murder.[51] In short, *Hit Man*'s value clearly was not substantial enough to justify the grave wrong it helped to bring about. Thus, the Fourth Circuit was right to hold the work unprotected by the First Amendment.

Reflecting on cases like *Rice*, Eugene Volokh, a leading civil libertarian scholar, argues that we should protect speech even when it promotes murder. "The First Amendment," he writes, "requires us to run certain risks to get the benefits that free speech provides, such as open discussion and criticism of government action, and a culture of artistic and expressive freedom. These risks may include even a mildly elevated risk of homicide — for instance, when speech advocates homicide, praises it, weakens social norms against it, leads to copycat homicides, or [as in *Rice*] facilitates homicides. Each such crime is of course a tragedy, but a slightly increased risk even of death — a few extra lives lost on top of the current level of over 17,000 homicides per year — is part of the price we pay for the First Amendment."[52]

On one level, Volokh is correct: the law should not impose liability for works like *Hit Man* if that would endanger the overall system of freedom of expression. In this case, however, no such threat existed. As I have argued, the law is capable of drawing a clear distinction between murder manuals and speech that the First Amendment exists to protect.

On another level, Volokh's discussion serves to bring out, in the sharpest possible relief, the difference between the prevailing approach to free speech and the approach developed in this book. Volokh characterizes life itself as a mere social interest that can justify restrictions on free speech only in extraordinary circumstances. By contrast, I have argued that the First Amendment should be understood within a broader framework of rights that defines the legitimate scope of free expression — a freedom that should not extend to speech that intentionally invades the right to life or personal security.[53]

From Preserving the Peace to Protecting Personality: The Fighting Words Doctrine

THE *CHAPLINSKY* CASE

In *Chaplinsky v. New Hampshire* (1942), the Supreme Court reviewed a conviction under a statute that made it unlawful to "address any offensive, derisive, or annoying word to any other person who is lawfully in any street or other public place, [or] call him by any offensive or derisive name." Walter Chaplinsky had called the city marshal "a God damned racketeer" and "a damned Fascist." Affirming the conviction, Justice Frank Murphy declared that the First Amendment did not protect "insulting or 'fighting' words," which he defined as "those which by their very utterance inflict injury or tend to incite an immediate breach of the peace." Such words, he wrote, "are no essential part of any exposition of ideas, and are of such slight social value as a step to truth that any benefit that may be derived from them is clearly outweighed by the social interest in order and morality."[54]

Chaplinsky is a paradigm case of the modern tendency to conceptualize First Amendment problems as conflicts between free speech and social interests — in this case the "interest in order and morality."[55] This understanding of the issue has led to a spirited debate. On one hand, *Chaplinsky* has come under fire from many civil libertarians, who believe it imposes an unwarranted limitation on free speech.[56] On the other hand, it has found defenders on both the right and the left, who argue that the fighting words doctrine is necessary to preserve civility or to protect disadvantaged groups from psychological injury and social subordination.[57] When the problem is posed in this way, it appears to present a "tragic conflict" in which we can protect freedom of expression only by sacrificing civility, dignity, and equality, and can protect these values only by doing violence to the ideal of free expression.[58]

FIGHTING WORDS, PERSONAL SECURITY, AND THE PUBLIC PEACE

How would this problem look if it were recast in terms of opposing rights? Traditionally, the law regarded insults as wrongful because of their tendency to incite a breach of the peace. At first blush, this rationale seems inconsistent with a rights-based view, for it seems to allow the state to restrict free speech merely because others may respond lawlessly. Rather than punishing the speaker, would it not be preferable for the law to simply hold people responsible for their own violent acts?[59]

This objection has a great deal of force when applied to a broad notion of fighting words that would make the lawfulness of speech turn simply on the reaction of others. One who is properly exercising her First Amendment rights should not be restrained simply because others may act wrongfully.[60] The objection itself is too sweeping, however, because it fails to distinguish between rightful and wrongful acts of speech. From a rights-based perspective, speech may properly be restricted when it is likely to provoke violence *because of its wrongful character.*

Speech is wrongful when it constitutes a form of aggression against others. As Alexander M. Bickel puts it, "There is such a thing as verbal violence, a kind of cursing, assaultive speech that amounts to almost physical aggression, bullying that is no less punishing because it is simulated."[61] A dramatic example may be found in the case of *Gomez v. Hug* (1982). In that case, the defendant allegedly shouted, "You are a fucking spic. . . . A fucking Mexican greaser like you, that is all you are. You are nothing but a fucking Mexican greaser, nothing but a pile of shit."[62] In a situation like this, it is natural for the victim to experience a combination of fear and anger as well as a strong urge to respond with force.[63] Indeed, one of the very purposes of the speech may be to provoke or challenge the target to fight. Thus, in the course of his tirade, Hug repeatedly called Gomez a coward and demanded to know what he was "going to do about it."[64]

In addition to their tendency to provoke others to violence, fighting words may be regarded as a breach of the peace in and of themselves. A speaker who uses language like that in *Gomez* indicates that he cannot be trusted to respect the target's safety. In this way, the speech undermines the peace that exists between members of the society.[65] To put the point another way, an important function of speech is to indicate what sort of social space the parties are in and to establish the terms of interaction between them. Some forms of discourse are used to indicate that the participants are friends, neighbors, or members of a particular group, while others are used to show mere civility. Fighting words signal a condition of mutual hostility and animosity, a condition in which the parties intend to treat one another as enemies. In the imagery of traditional social contract theory, fighting words conjure up a Hobbesian or Kantian state of nature, in which there is no law or social order to impose restraints on aggression. In these ways, fighting words have a direct impact on personal security and the public peace, as well as increase the likelihood that actual violence will break out.

Insults also tend to provoke violence because of their impact on personal dignity, a point that is best captured in the writings of Thomas Hobbes. As Hobbes explains, demeaning remarks attack the targets' sense of dignity as well as their standing in the community. Individuals who are subjected to insults have a powerful inclination to strike back in order to reassert their self-worth. Because "all signes of hatred, or contempt, provoke to fight," they violate the law of nature, whose fundamental aim is to establish a condition of peace. Although the law should take no notice of trivial insults, it should forbid those that pose a serious danger to the peace.[66]

In both of these ways — by degrading others and by undermining their personal security — fighting words are wrongful and tend to provoke a violent response.[67] At the same time, it is important to emphasize that *Chaplinsky* does not imply that individuals may *rightfully* respond to insults with violence. The law permits the use of force only when necessary to defend persons or property from imminent attack.[68] In some situations, fighting words do create a reasonable apprehension of immediate danger. In all other cases, people who respond to insults with force are themselves guilty of breaching the peace. In short, the fighting words doctrine does not imply that individuals will not be held responsible for their own conduct. It simply means that a speaker who deliberately uses words likely to provoke violence should also bear some responsibility for the resulting confrontation.

This defense of the fighting words doctrine may be summarized as follows. It is precisely *because* fighting words "inflict injury" that they "tend to incite an immediate breach of the peace." Fighting words injure others through aggression as well as through assaults on their dignity. These two aspects are intertwined: a person who shows utter contempt for another is unlikely to respect her right to safety, while there is no greater form of disrespect than to threaten another with violence. Individuals who are treated in these ways have a strong tendency to fight back, even though that response may itself be wrongful. Properly understood, then, the fighting words doctrine does not permit an individual's legitimate exercise of free speech to be restricted merely because of the wrongful conduct of others. Instead, it is because fighting words are wrongful that they have a tendency to provoke violence.

WORDS THAT INFLICT INJURY BY THEIR VERY UTTERANCE

In *Chaplinsky,* Justice Murphy defined the category of "insulting or 'fighting words' " to include not only words which "tend to incite an immediate breach of the peace," but also "those which by their very utterance inflict injury."[69] In recent decades, the Court has sometimes focused on the first half of this definition to the apparent exclusion of the second.[70] In *R.A.V. v. City of St. Paul* (1992), the defendant urged the Justices to narrow the category in this way, but they chose to decide the case on other grounds.[71] Thus, it remains an open question whether the "inflict injury" branch of *Chaplinsky* is still good law.

Many civil libertarians have argued that this branch of the doctrine should be rejected.[72] As several scholars have pointed out, however, the result would be that abusive speech could be used with impunity so long as it was directed toward people who were unlikely to fight back, for example, because they were very young, old, disabled, opposed to violence, or dependent on the speaker.[73] In *Gomez v. Hug,* for example, the defendant was a county commissioner, while the plaintiff was a county employee who was hardly in a position to respond with force. If the sole purpose of *Chaplinsky* were to prevent violence, it would make perfect sense to hold insulting speech protected in such cases. It seems clear, however, that a relatively defenseless person should be entitled to at least as much protection from abuse as one who is able to defend herself. As I have suggested, insults tend to provoke violence precisely because of the injury they inflict. This injury may be a serious one even when violence is not likely to result.

Insulting speech can cause injury in several ways. First, as we have seen, it can constitute a form of aggression against others. One's right to be free from aggression should not depend on whether one is likely to strike back. Instead, it should be regarded as an aspect of personal security.

Abusive speech may also constitute an attack on personality. In some cases, the emotional injury may be severe enough to warrant recovery for intentional infliction of emotional distress. In *Gomez*, for example, the court allowed the plaintiff to proceed with such a claim.[74] Suppose, however, that Hug's invective did not cause Gomez to suffer *severe* distress, either because he had great strength of character or because he had become inured to repeated abuse. In that case, he would be unable to satisfy the requirements for intentional infliction.[75] Yet it seems clear he would have suffered a serious injury to personality.

How can we understand the nature of this injury? In chapter 4, I argued that the right to personality includes not only freedom from substantive injury (that is, infliction of emotional distress), but also a formal right to the inviolability of personality. That right was violated by invasion of privacy.[76] Profoundly abusive speech can be understood in similar terms. Regardless of whether it causes severe distress, the kind of speech used in *Gomez* infringes the right to "an inviolate personality"[77] in the same way that offensive battery infringes the right to bodily integrity. When the speech degrades an individual in front of others, it also constitutes an attack on social personality that is analogous to defamation.

The notion that insults are wrongful has deep roots in the natural rights tradition. As we have seen, Hobbes emphasizes the tendency of insults to provoke violence. Other theorists regard them as intrinsically wrongful. For example, Adam Smith holds that an individual has a natural right to his character or reputation. Insults and other "verball injuries" violate this right by dishonoring him before others. The law would be deficient if it failed to protect against such affronts, which cause injury far beyond any tangible harm that might result. Kant's account also focuses on the concept of honor. "*Rightful honor,*" he explains, "consists in asserting one's worth as a man in relation to others," a notion that lies at the foundation of law and justice. Insults or "verbal injur[ies]" should be banned because of the "outrage" they inflict on the victim's sense of honor, which derives from his inherent dignity as a human being. Likewise, for Hegel, abusive speech and other "injuries to the honour of individuals" are wrongful because they violate the fundamental imperative to "*respect human beings . . . as persons.*"[78]

It follows that insults should be unlawful not only when they create a danger of responsive violence, but also when they inflict emotional or dignitary injury.[79] Of course, this is not to say that individuals have a right to be free from all offense. Like other rights, personal dignity is founded on a conception of people as rational and autonomous beings. As I have said, individuals cannot reasonably complain of offense caused by the expression of ideas contrary to their own.[80] Moreover, in everyday life, people are inevitably exposed to much that they find offensive or disagreeable. If the law is to protect a right to personal dignity, it should be concerned only with the most serious invasions of that right. In defining the subcategory of words "which by their very utterance inflict injury," we might draw on the law of privacy and hold that speech is wrongful only if it intentionally attacks the dignity of another in a way that is "highly offensive to a reasonable person."[81]

FIGHTING WORDS AND FREEDOM OF SPEECH

Insulting or fighting words are wrongful because of their impact on individual security, personal dignity, and the public peace. Before we can determine whether *Chaplinsky* was right to hold such speech unprotected by the First Amendment, however, we must consider whether the value of this speech is sufficient to justify the injuries it causes.

It is sometimes said that insults are a form of self-expression.[82] However, any value they have for the speaker's self-realization clearly derives from their negation of the personality and rights of the target. For this reason, that value cannot serve to justify the speech under a rights-based theory.[83]

Some civil libertarians have argued that freedom of speech includes the right to express "disrespect or dislike" for others, a right that extends to the use of "personal invective" and "racial and religious slurs."[84] As we have seen, however, the natural rights tradition points in a different direction. In Kant's words, the concept of human dignity means that "[e]very man has a legitimate claim to respect from his fellow men and *in turn* is bound to respect every other."[85] In addition to infringing the dignity of others, abusive speech undermines the possibility of reasoned communication between people.[86] For these reasons, freedom of speech should not include the right to express profound contempt or disrespect for other human beings.

This principle is subject to some crucial limitations, however. First, as I have explained, it applies only to personal abuse, not to the expression of *ideas* that are offensive to others. Second, in a democratic society, citizens do and should have the right to express disrespect for the government and its officials. It follows that, while the general doctrine articulated in *Chaplinsky* may be sound, the Court was wrong to uphold the conviction in that case.

Indeed, on its facts, *Chaplinsky* is a First Amendment horror story. As the New Hampshire court summarized the record, the defendant was lawfully distributing Jehovah's Witness literature when he was violently assaulted by some members of the crowd who were offended by his religious views. Instead of arresting the assailants, the police led Chaplinsky away toward the police station (although he was not then told he was under arrest). As the court conceded, Chaplinsky's resentment over these events "might well have extended to the police if [as he testified] they had failed to take any step reasonably within their power to control the crowd, or if they had failed to prosecute anybody who they had reasonable ground to believe assailed him."[87] In this context, the words Chaplinsky uttered clearly did not constitute personal abuse so much as a forceful protest against what he regarded as gross mistreatment and abuse of power by the city marshal and the police.[88] For this political expression, Chaplinsky was sentenced to six months in prison, and his conviction was unanimously upheld by the U.S. Supreme Court, which was unable to see "any Constitutional problem" in this situation.[89]

More recent decisions have effectively overruled this aspect of *Chaplinsky*. In *New York Times Co. v. Sullivan* (1964), the Court held that the First Amendment right to discuss public affairs extends to "vehement, caustic, and sometimes unpleasantly sharp attacks on government and officials." In a later case, *City of Houston v. Hill* (1987), the Court declared that "the freedom of individuals verbally to oppose or challenge police action without thereby risking arrest is one of the principal characteristics by which we distinguish a free nation from a police state."[90] It seems clear, then, that the Court would no longer apply the fighting words doctrine to expression like Chaplinsky's.

More broadly, there are serious problems in applying the doctrine to any speech that is directed toward police officers. As Justice Lewis F. Powell, Jr., once observed, "[A] properly trained officer may reasonably be expected to exercise a higher degree of restraint than the average citizen, and thus be less likely to respond belligerently to 'fighting words.'" Moreover, there is a substantial "possibility of abuse" when a defendant is convicted merely on the officer's testimony.[91] These considerations, combined with those articulated in *New York Times,* ought to preclude the application of the fighting words doctrine to speech directed against police officers.[92] Changing the doctrine in this way would satisfy one of the major concerns expressed by its critics.[93]

The *Chaplinsky* doctrine should be modified in two other ways as well. First, a speaker should not be held responsible for using fighting words unless she had a wrongful intent. *Chaplinsky* itself is silent on this point. To be sure, the state should not have to show that the defendant intended to provoke violence, for such a rule would allow an abusive speaker to escape responsibility whenever she did not expect the target to fight back. Nevertheless, the defendant should have to intend to violate the rights of others in a way that the doctrine is meant to prevent. Second, the speaker should have a good defense if her actions were reasonable (say, because she was provoked).

On this view, a speaker can be held responsible for using insulting or fighting words when he intentionally and unreasonably (1) insults, threatens, or aggresses against another, or challenges her to fight, under circumstances where there is a substantial likelihood that this will result in a breach of the peace; (2) uses words that threaten another in a way that causes her substantial apprehension for her personal safety; or (3) violates another's personality rights by inflicting severe emotional distress or by attacking her dignity in a way that a reasonable person would find highly offensive. Speech that falls into the first and second categories violates the community's right to the peace, while speech that falls into the second and third categories violates the individual rights to personal security, dignity, and emotional well-being. In all of these cases, the speech should be held unprotected by the First Amendment.

Conclusion

At the core of liberalism is the idea that human affairs should be governed by "Reason" rather than by "Force and Violence."[94] This idea also lies at the heart of the First Amendment, which reflects a belief "in the power of reason as applied through public discussion" and which therefore rejects "silence coerced by law — the argument of force in its worst form."[95] At the same time, even political speech may be denied constitutional protection when it wrongfully incites, threatens, or facilitates violence against others. When the law regulates speech of this sort, it not only protects the rights to personal security and the public peace, but also promotes the values that underlie the First Amendment itself, by insisting that people resolve their differences through reason and not through force.

By requiring respect for the rights of others, this body of law also protects individual dignity. This is especially true of the *Chaplinsky* fighting words doctrine, which is concerned with emotional and dignitary injury as well as with breach of the peace. In this way, the doctrine provides a bridge between external rights and rights of personality — a category I explore in the next chapter.

9

Speech and Privacy

While there is broad agreement that the Constitution should not protect speech that threatens or incites violence, the problem of dignitary or emotional harm is far more controversial. Many people would assert that, under the First Amendment, speech may never be restricted merely because it offends the sensibilities of others. I have argued, on the contrary, that freedom of expression is limited by other rights and that those rights are founded on respect for the autonomy and worth of human beings. It follows that the law should be allowed to safeguard not only external rights to life, liberty, and property, but also those rights that flow from the idea of "an inviolate personality."[1] Earlier chapters applied this principle to defamation, which invades the right to reputation, and insulting speech, which invades the right to personal dignity.[2] In this chapter, I explore the conflict between free speech and privacy, or the right to shield one's personal life from unwarranted intrusion by or exposure to others.[3]

Freedom of Expression and Freedom from Intrusion

PRIVATE SPEECH IN THE PUBLIC FORUM:
SIDEWALK COUNSELING AT ABORTION CLINICS

Conflicts between free speech and freedom from intrusion have arisen in a broad range of situations. In this area, the Supreme Court has sought to achieve a reasonable accommodation between the two values, in much the same way it has in the defamation area. The most interesting and controversial of these cases is *Hill v. Colorado* (2000).[4]

Like *Planned Parenthood v. ACLA, Hill* involved antiabortion speech. After hearing testimony that "demonstrations in front of abortion clinics impeded access to those clinics and were often confrontational" and that "sidewalk counselors" who sought to dissuade women from having abortions "sometimes used strong and abusive language in face-to-face encounters," the Colorado legislature enacted a statute that made it unlawful to "knowingly approach" within eight feet of another person, without her consent, for the purpose of "engaging in oral protest, education, or counseling" with her. This restriction applied to all encounters within one hundred feet of the entrance to a health care facility.[5]

In a six to three decision, the Supreme Court rejected a First Amendment challenge to the law. Justice John Paul Stevens's majority opinion began by recognizing that both sides had "legitimate and important concerns." On one hand, the statute restricted the freedom of sidewalk counselors to engage in constitutionally protected speech in public places. On the other hand, the law sought to protect the health and safety of patients by ensuring "unimpeded access to health care facilities and the avoidance of potential trauma . . . associated with confrontational protests." The law also protected "[t]he unwilling listener's interest in avoiding unwanted communication," which Stevens described as an aspect of the broader right to privacy. The statute's restrictions on speech were relatively slight: it imposed no limitation on the messages that protesters could communicate; it permitted them to speak from a distance of eight feet and to approach anyone who was willing to talk with them; and it even allowed them to stand at a fixed point in front of the clinic and to offer leaflets to passersby without regard to the eight-foot limit. At the same time, the measure served to protect an individual "from the harassment, the nuisance, . . . and the implied threat of physical touching that can accompany an unwelcome approach . . . by a person wishing to argue vociferously face-to-face and perhaps thrust an undesired handbill upon her." For these reasons, Stevens concluded that the statute reflected "an acceptable balance between the constitutionally protected rights of law-abiding speakers and the interests of unwilling listeners."[6]

In dissent, Justice Scalia ridiculed the idea that a person is entitled *"to be let alone from unwanted speech."* Under the Constitution, he wrote, that simply is "not an interest that may be legitimately weighed against the speakers' . . . rights." To hold otherwise would be "patently incompatible with the guarantees of the First Amendment" and would render it "a dead letter."[7]

These assertions were too sweeping, however, for in some situations the Supreme Court *has* recognized a right to be free from unwanted speech. For example, in *Rowan v. Post Office* (1970), the Justices unanimously upheld a federal law that authorized householders to bar advertisers from sending them sexual materials they found offensive. While freedom of expression is of vital importance, wrote Chief Justice Warren E. Burger, "the right of every person 'to be let alone' must be placed in the scales with the right of others to communicate." Similarly, in *Frisby v. Schultz* (1988) — another case involving anti-abortion protests — the Court upheld a ban on picketing in front of a person's residence. Observing that "[t]he State's interest in protecting the well-being, tranquillity, and privacy of the home is . . . of the highest order in a free and civilized society," Justice Sandra Day O'Connor declared that "[t]here simply is no right to force speech into the home of an unwilling listener."[8]

Acknowledging decisions like *Frisby* (a ruling he himself had joined), Scalia narrowed his argument to focus on speech *in the public forum*. Under modern First Amendment doctrine, public places such as sidewalks, streets, and parks are regarded as forums for expression — areas that (in the words of *Hague v. CIO* (1939)) have been used "time out of mind . . . for purposes of assembly, communicating thoughts between citizens, and discussing public questions." Absent a compelling justification, the government may not impose content-based restrictions on expression in a public forum, although it may adopt reasonable regulations of time, place, and manner.[9] Moreover, the Court has indicated that, in public places, citizens generally "must tolerate insulting, and even outrageous, speech in order to provide adequate breathing space to the freedoms protected by the First Amendment."[10]

Relying on these principles, Scalia argued that individuals simply have no right to be free from unwanted speech in a public forum. The Court, he asserted, would apply strict scrutiny and invalidate a law like this *"in an instant* if the case . . . involved antiwar protesters, or union members seeking to 'educate' the public about the reasons for their strike." The fact that the majority in *Hill* was willing to rule otherwise could be explained only by its determination to protect abortion at all costs. In short, Scalia contended, *Hill* was yet another product of the "ad hoc nullification machine that the Court has set in motion to push aside whatever doctrines of constitutional law stand in the way of that highly favored practice."[11]

Although Scalia's rhetoric is powerful, it is ultimately unconvincing, for it overlooks a critical distinction between antiwar and labor speech on one hand and sidewalk counseling on the other. In an eloquent passage, Scalia described the conduct at issue in *Hill* as follows: The sidewalk counselor "hopes to forge, in the last moments before another of her sex is to have an abortion, a bond of concern and intimacy that might enable her to persuade the woman to change her mind and heart. The counselor may wish to walk alongside and to say, sympathetically and as softly as the circumstances allow, something like: 'My dear, I know what you are going through. I've been through it myself. You're not alone and you do not have to do this. There are other alternatives. Will you let me help you? May I show you a picture of what your child looks like at this stage of her human development?' "[12]

In this passage, Scalia portrays sidewalk counseling in its best light (the speech is often more confrontational than this). At the same time, however, the passage inadvertently shows how this speech differs from antiwar and labor speech: they address what *Hague v. CIO* called "public questions," whereas sidewalk counseling is intensely personal speech. This is true in at least three respects. First, sidewalk counseling does not deal with abortion as a general moral or political issue; instead, it seeks to influence a particular individual's decision about whether to terminate a pregnancy. Second, this decision is a deeply personal one. In the words of *Planned Parenthood v. Casey* (1992), it is one of "the most intimate and personal choices a person may make in a lifetime, [a choice that is] central to personal dignity and autonomy."[13] Finally, to achieve her goals, the sidewalk counselor tries to get very close to the addressee, in both a physical and an emotional sense.

The question in *Hill* is whether one should be free to force such highly personal speech on another individual against her will. In my view, such conduct disrespects the dignity and autonomy of the unwilling listener and constitutes a serious intrusion into her personal life. In these ways it violates her right to privacy.

Of course, that is not to say that prolife demonstrators have no right to urge women to choose childbirth over abortion. Under the Colorado statute, counselors were permitted to approach any woman who agreed to speak with them, as well as to address anyone from outside the eight-foot zone; they simply could not approach unwilling listeners. This restriction did not violate the speakers' First Amendment rights, for no one has a right to impose what Scalia calls a "bond of concern and intimacy" on another person without her consent. And it seems even more clear that there is no right to accost others for the purpose of engaging in abusive or confrontational speech with regard to such private matters.

In response, it might be said that the Colorado statute was too sweeping because it was not limited to deeply personal expression, but extended to such classic forms of public speech as the distribution of leaflets and the discussion of abortion as a political or moral issue. This objection is unpersuasive for three reasons. First, as the dissenting Justices emphasized, a core purpose of sidewalk counseling is to influence the personal choices of women entering the clinic.[14] In this setting, even speech that purports to discuss abortion in general is likely to be understood by both speakers and listeners as directed toward individual choice. Second, as a practical matter, it would be quite difficult to administer a rule that allowed speakers to approach for the purpose of general discussion but not personal counseling. Finally, to the extent that speakers truly desire to express their views about abortion in general, they can do so in a fairly effective way while maintaining a distance of eight feet from unwilling listeners. In short, the Colorado statute did little to interfere with the protesters' ability to articulate a general or public message, while they had no right to press an intimate personal message on unwilling listeners at close range.

It follows that *Hill* does not depart from established First Amendment jurisprudence in a way that can be explained only by the majority's commitment to abortion rights. Instead, the decision may be understood to stand for a perfectly defensible principle: the state may adopt reasonable time, place, and manner regulations to protect unwilling listeners from the invasion of privacy that results from being subjected to highly personal speech in a public forum. Although the Justices may have had no previous occasion to apply this principle, it cannot be said to conflict with their precedents. For example, in the leading case of *Cohen v. California* (1971), Justice Harlan held that the government had little power to protect unwilling listeners from offensive speech in public places, such as a jacket emblazoned with the slogan "Fuck the Draft." At the same time, however, Harlan observed that regulation would be justified "upon a showing that substantial privacy interests are being invaded in an essentially intolerable manner."[15] The speech in *Hill* falls squarely within this exception. In other words, *Hill* is in line with a more or less coherent body of decisions, ranging from *Rowan v. Post Office* to *Cohen v. California,* in which the Justices have attempted to strike a balance between freedom of speech and the right to privacy.

Finally, this analysis of *Hill* provides a response to the objection, raised by the dissenting Justices as well as by many scholars, that the Colorado law discriminated on the basis of content or viewpoint.[16] Although the regulation applied to all health care facilities in the state, there is no doubt that it was enacted in response to the actions of antiabortion demonstrators. However, as Justice David H. Souter observed in a concurring opinion, a law should not be regarded as viewpoint- or content-based simply because it regulates wrongful conduct that has become associated with one side of a controversy.[17] To be sure, it would be troubling if the principle I have attributed to *Hill* were applicable only to antiabortion demonstrators. But it is not difficult to imagine other situations in which that principle would come into play. For example, it would apply if bigots began to accost members of wedding parties in order to persuade them not to take part in interracial, interfaith, or same-sex ceremonies; if proselytizers were to besiege persons entering churches, mosques, or synagogues in an effort to convert them to a different faith; or if atheists were to deliberately interrupt individuals engaged in prayer or meditation in public parks. But there is no reason to suppose that Coloradans suffered from these forms of intrusive personal speech, while they did suffer from intrusions by sidewalk counselors. The rule against content discrimination should not prevent communities from legislating against real problems unless they are able to envision all situations that might be regarded as comparable.

PUBLIC SPEECH THAT INTRUDES INTO PRIVATE LIFE:
FUNERAL PROTESTS

As decisions like *Cohen* make clear, individuals generally have no right to be free from unwanted speech on matters of public concern. But even public speech can infringe the right to privacy when it intrudes into private life. This point is best illustrated by the recent wave of protests directed against military funerals.

During the summer of 2005, members of the Westboro Baptist Church, a small fundamentalist group based in Topeka, Kansas, began to hold demonstrations throughout the country at the funerals of soldiers killed in Iraq and Afghanistan. The purpose of the protests was to demonstrate the church's belief that God was punishing the United States for its "perversions" in tolerating homosexuality and other immoral conduct. The group's leader, the Reverend Fred Phelps, declared that "God almighty has killed these soldiers" because they "chose to fight for a sodomite nation" that had called down upon itself "a severe stroke of divine judgment, retribution and vengeance." The protesters displayed signs with statements like THANK GOD FOR DEAD SOLDIERS and GOD HATES FAGS and shouted at mourners that the dead were "rotting in hell." In 2006, Congress enacted a bill to restrict such demonstrations. The statute makes it a crime to willfully disturb "the peace or good order" of a funeral by means of a demonstration that takes place within 150 feet of a road that provides access to a national cemetery, for a period of one hour before to one hour after the funeral. Congress urged the states to adopt similar laws within their own jurisdictions, and most states have followed suit.[18]

Under a liberal humanist approach to the First Amendment, these laws should be upheld so long as they are narrowly drawn. It is difficult to imagine a deeper intrusion into private life—or a more outrageous infliction of emotional distress—than a demonstration that intentionally interferes with the ability of family members to mourn a loved one in peace.[19] To the extent that the protest disrupts a funeral, it also interferes with the mourners' right to religious or spiritual freedom. These injuries are not justified by the value of the speech, for the protesters have many other avenues of expression that do not have such a serious impact on the rights of others.[20] In addition, laws like the federal statute are drafted to apply only within strictly defined limits of space and time. Finally, such laws draw no distinction based on the content or viewpoint of the speech—they apply to all demonstrations that intentionally disrupt a funeral, regardless of whether they support or oppose homosexuality or the war, or indeed whether they relate to other subjects altogether.[21] As I have said, the ultimate touchstone for resolving First Amendment controversies should be the extent to which each of the competing rights promotes the values of human freedom and dignity. In the present context, those values clearly are better served by upholding narrowly drawn restrictions on funeral protests than by striking them down as violations of free expression.[22]

RECONCILING THE COMPETING VALUES

Although there is no straightforward formula for resolving conflicts between free speech and freedom from intrusion, our discussion has pointed to several factors that lawmakers and courts ought to consider. The first is the extent to which the speech occurs in or near a private place—a category that should be understood to include not only homes, as in *Rowan* and *Frisby,* but also medical facilities, places of worship, and cemeteries, as in *Hill* and the Westboro protests. A second factor is the extent to which the speech intrudes into the private thoughts, feelings, or activities of others. This factor is present both in the funeral cases and in the sidewalk counseling context, for patients who are approaching a reproductive health facility are likely already to be focused on the intensely personal decisions or procedures they are to face. A third factor is the extent to which the speech itself is personal, in the sense that it relates to the private affairs of the listener or involves an attempt at intimate conversation. This was the decisive factor in *Hill.* By contrast, the case for affording constitutional protection to speech is strengthened to the extent that it relates to a matter of public concern, occurs in a public place, or does not intrude into the private thoughts or activities of others. These factors support decisions like *Cohen,* which hold that, in the absence of serious invasions of privacy, individuals generally have no right to be free from offensive speech in public places.

Free Speech and Informational Privacy

THE COURT'S DECISIONS

Although the Supreme Court has struck a sensitive balance between expressive liberty and freedom from intrusion, it has taken a very different approach to cases involving freedom from exposure. In this context, the Justices have paid lip service to the notion that both "press freedom and privacy rights are . . . plainly rooted in the traditions and significant concerns of our society."[23] Nevertheless, in every decision the Court has handed down, it has rejected governmental efforts to protect individuals from unwarranted publicity.[24]

The most striking of these cases is *Florida Star v. B.J.F.* (1989). After being raped and robbed at knifepoint by an unknown assailant, B.J.F. notified the county sheriff's department. A crime report that was posted in the department's pressroom inadvertently failed to delete her name. A reporter for the *Florida Star* took down all the information in the report, although she knew from a sign in the pressroom that the names of sexual assault victims were not matters of public record and could not be published under state law. The *Star* then published an account of the rape, identifying B.J.F. by name. In addition to hearing comments from coworkers and acquaintances, B.J.F. and her family received several telephone calls from a man who threatened to rape her again. These events forced her to move, to change her telephone number, and to seek police protection as well as psychological counseling. B.J.F. brought a civil suit against the *Star* for violating a Florida law that barred the publication of the name of a sexual assault victim in any instrument of mass communication. Finding that the newspaper had "acted with reckless indifference to the rights of others," the jury awarded her seventy-five thousand dollars in compensatory damages as well as twenty-five thousand dollars in punitive damages.[25]

On appeal, the Supreme Court reversed the judgment by a vote of six to three. In an opinion that reflected the assumptions of modern First Amendment jurisprudence discussed in chapter 2, Justice Marshall framed the issue as a clash between the freedom of the press and the "state interest" in protecting rape victims. To justify restrictions on publication, Marshall held, the state had to satisfy the requirements of strict scrutiny under the rule set forth in an earlier case: " '[I]f a newspaper lawfully obtains truthful information about a matter of public significance then state officials may not constitutionally punish publication of the information, absent a need to further a state interest of the highest order.' "[26] In this case, B.J.F. argued that the statute furthered the state's interests in protecting the privacy and safety of rape victims as well as in encouraging them to report assaults. Although the majority acknowledged that these were "highly significant interests," it held that, under the circumstances of the case, the statute was not necessary to protect them, for the government could have prevented the harm simply by not disclosing the information in the first place. Moreover, the law was underinclusive because it applied only to the media, not to individuals, a fact that raised serious doubts about whether it was effective in promoting the state's interests. Thus, these interests could not survive strict scrutiny.[27]

How would *Florida Star* look from a rights-based perspective? On this view, it becomes clear that the statute's aim was not to promote the interests of the state but rather to protect the rights of the victim. The government's inadvertent failure to comply with the law should not have the effect of waiving B.J.F.'s rights or absolving the newspaper of its own responsibility to respect them. As to the statute's scope, the legislature could reasonably believe that mass publication causes more serious injury than mere private discussion and that a ban on such discussion would be impractical as well as intrusive. Moreover, even if the Florida law could be faulted for underprotecting privacy, it is difficult to see why that should lead a court to deny protection in a case that falls within the statute's ambit.

Although Marshall stated that the "sensitivity" of clashes between free speech and privacy rights should lead the Court to rely on "limited principles that sweep no more broadly" than necessary to resolve the case, the strict scrutiny standard he endorsed would make it difficult for the law to protect privacy in any situation. Rather than applying a standard that is heavily weighted toward one side of the balance, the liberal humanist approach would assess the competing rights in an evenhanded manner. In a case like *Florida Star,* the rights of the victim have a great deal of force. As Justice Byron R. White observed in dissent, "Short of homicide, rape is the ultimate violation of self."[28] In addition to physical harm, rape inflicts severe emotional trauma and humiliation — injuries that may well be magnified when the attack is disclosed to large numbers of people. A report that identifies a sexual assault victim may also subject her to further threats and harassment, as it did in *Florida Star.* In these ways, the article infringed B.J.F.'s rights to privacy, dignity, emotional tranquillity, and personal security.

How strong is the First Amendment interest in this situation? As Marshall pointed out, "[T]he article generally, as opposed to the specific identity contained within it, involved a matter of paramount public import: the commission, and investigation, of a violent crime which had been reported to authorities."[29] But this begs the critical question in *Florida Star,* which is whether "the specific identity" of the victim *is* a matter of public import. From one point of view, everything that occurs within the society is a matter of common concern. As I shall explain below, however, this view is inconsistent with the very existence of a right to privacy—a right that is essential to protect the inner lives of individuals.[30] Thus, in drawing the line between the public and private spheres, one must assess the values on both sides. In a case like *Florida Star*, the victim has a strong claim to privacy, while, as Marshall implicitly conceded, the public has little need to know her name. It follows that the law should be allowed to protect privacy in cases of this sort.

In response, it might be said that rape should not be regarded as a mere private injury suffered by the victim. The right to be free from sexual violence is one that is shared by all women and members of the community. This right can be vindicated only if assailants are brought to justice within the legal system, a system that is inherently public. For this reason, the identity of victims should not be treated as private information. Although this argument has some force, it is not conclusive. Respect for the autonomy and dignity of rape victims dictates that they should be free to decide for themselves whether to pursue accusations through the criminal justice system. Once an accusation has been made, it triggers a process of investigation. If and when an individual is arrested and brought to trial for the crime, the proceedings take place in public view.[31] At that point, the identity of the accuser should no longer be protected by law, and the media should have a First Amendment right to publish her name if they believe there is good reason to do so.[32] Unfortunately, however, only a small proportion of sexual assaults lead to the arrest and prosecution of an offender. In other cases, the values served by publicity are clearly outweighed by the victim's right to privacy.[33] Thus, the Court reached the wrong result in *Florida Star*.[34]

In *Bartnicki v. Vopper* (2001), the Supreme Court erected a further obstacle to the protection of informational privacy. In that case an unknown person illegally intercepted and recorded a cell phone conversation between two officials of a local teachers' union. During the conversation, one speaker appeared to threaten violence against school board members if they took a hard line in ongoing, contentious negotiations with the union. A tape recording of the call appeared in the mailbox of one of the union's opponents, who passed it along to Fred Vopper, a radio talk show host who was strongly critical of the union. After Vopper broadcast the tape, the union officials sued him for damages under federal and state wiretapping statutes that make it unlawful to intentionally disclose the contents of wire, oral, or electronic communications that one knows or has reason to know were illegally intercepted. Writing for a six to three majority, Justice Stevens held these laws unconstitutional as applied to the facts of the case. Although he acknowledged that individual privacy was an "interest[] of the highest order" and that "the disclosure of the contents of a private conversation can be an even greater intrusion on privacy than the interception itself," Stevens ruled that the statutes could not be enforced in this situation without contravening "the core purposes of the First Amendment" by "impos[ing] sanctions on the publication of truthful information of public concern."[35]

Bartnicki goes even further than *Florida Star* in curtailing legal protection for privacy. In *Florida Star,* the Court emphasized that the information at issue had been lawfully obtained from the government itself.[36] By contrast, *Bartnicki* upholds the media's right to publish information that was obtained *unlawfully* by a source in violation of another individual's privacy rights. For example, under *Bartnicki,* if someone had illegally intercepted a telephone conversation in which B.J.F. had told her mother about the rape, the newspaper would have been free to publish this information so long as its own reporters had taken no part in the interception. Such a result is inconsistent with any serious regard for privacy.

In addition to its refusal to allow protection for highly personal information of this sort, *Bartnicki* is liable to another objection: the majority fails to appreciate that private conversations generally should be entitled to protection regardless of their content. Individuals should be free not only to form their own thoughts and feelings, but also to decide whether and how to communicate them to others. From one point of view this is an aspect of the right to privacy, while from another it is an aspect of freedom of expression, which includes the right to choose whether or not to speak.[37] In addition to their intrinsic importance as aspects of individual and social liberty, these rights are essential to democratic deliberation, which depends on the ability of individuals to think for themselves, to communicate and associate with like-minded people, and to decide how best to participate in public discourse. These rights also make it possible for citizens to develop and articulate views that dissent from the existing order.[38] For all of these reasons, individuals should generally be free to engage in private discussions, a right that extends to matters of public as well as private concern. As Stevens recognized, outsiders have no right to intrude on such discussions by unlawfully intercepting or recording them, and this intrusion is compounded when the discussions are made public.[39] It follows that the majority was wrong to hold that the First Amendment affords the media a blanket privilege to publish the contents of illegally intercepted conversations whenever they relate to matters of public concern.

Fortunately, *Bartnicki* can be read in a less sweeping way than the Stevens opinion suggests. In a separate opinion, Justice Stephen G. Breyer, joined by Justice O'Connor, concurred on substantially narrower grounds. Because their votes were necessary to constitute the majority, one may reasonably treat their views as limiting the holding of the case.

Although Breyer uses the language of interests rather than of rights, his opinion may be regarded as a model of how the rights-based approach would apply to a case like *Bartnicki*. Breyer begins by observing that the case "implicates competing constitutional concerns." While the statutes at issue "directly interfere with free expression in that they prevent the media from publishing information," they also "help to protect personal privacy — an interest here that includes not only the 'right to be let alone,' but also the interest . . . in fostering private speech" by assuring individuals that their conversations will not be made public against their will. In cases like this, Breyer argues, "[w]hat this Court has called 'strict scrutiny' — with its strong presumption against constitutionality — is normally out of place." Instead, the Court should determine "whether the statutes strike a reasonable balance" between the competing values, or whether they "instead impose restrictions on speech that are disproportionate when measured against their corresponding privacy and speech-related benefits, taking into account the kind, the importance, and the extent of these benefits, as well as the need for the restrictions in order to secure those benefits."[40]

Applying this approach, Breyer contends that the statutes at issue should generally be upheld under the First Amendment. As applied to the present case, however, they fail to provide sufficient protection to free speech. This conclusion is based on several considerations. First, the broadcasters played no role in the unlawful interception of the conversations. Second, by voluntarily participating in the public controversy over the teachers' contract, the union officials became " 'limited public figures' " and "thereby subjected themselves to somewhat greater public scrutiny and had a lesser interest in privacy than an individual engaged in purely private affairs." Moreover, "the subject matter of the conversation at issue here is far removed from that in situations where the media publicizes truly private matters" such as sexual relations. Finally, and most important, because the speakers appeared to threaten violence against others, they "had little or no *legitimate* interest in maintaining the privacy of the particular conversation." In short, the First Amendment should protect publication under the "special circumstances" of this case, in which "the speakers' legitimate privacy expectations are unusually low," while "the information publicized involved a matter of unusual public concern, namely a threat of potential physical harm to others." At the same time, Breyer stresses that the Court's decision should not be read to "create a 'public interest' exception that swallows up the statutes' privacy-protecting general rule." Breyer's opinion was far more successful in reconciling the competing rights at stake than was the Stevens opinion, which would have created such an exception, or the dissent by Chief Justice Rehnquist, which would have subordinated free expression to privacy in all cases of this sort.[41]

DOES THE FIRST AMENDMENT PERMIT THE STATE TO PROTECT INDIVIDUALS FROM UNREASONABLE PUBLICITY?

Decisions like *Florida Star* and *Bartnicki* impose sharp limits on the government's ability to protect individuals from unwarranted exposure, not only through statutes but also through the common law tort of giving unreasonable publicity to private facts.[42] Several leading scholars endorse this trend, and indeed urge the Court to go further and hold that all such laws violate the First Amendment.[43] This position is based on several grounds. First, these scholars question whether there is a philosophical basis for the right to privacy and suggest that the harms caused by exposure generally are trivial ones.[44] As I have tried to show, however, the right to privacy is rooted in the belief that individuals have a duty to respect the autonomy, dignity, and personality of others — a duty that is violated by unjustifiably intruding into their inner lives or personal affairs or by unreasonably exposing those matters without their consent. As cases like *Florida Star* show, invasion of privacy can cause intense anguish, humiliation, and indignity — injuries that can hardly be considered trivial.[45]

The critics also contend that laws against unwarranted exposure simply "cannot coexist with constitutional protections for freedom of speech and press." For example, it is said that "[t]he Court's decisions in *New York Times Co. v. Sullivan* and its progeny leave little doubt that truth should be considered a constitutionally mandated defense, at least in the context of common law tort actions for harmful speech." Because privacy law imposes sanctions on the publication of truthful information, it violates the First Amendment.[46] But the *New York Times* line of cases involved lawsuits for defamation. A person who sues for this tort does not claim that her character and conduct lie beyond the proper bounds of public discussion. Instead, she objects to the *way* in which she was characterized by the defendant's speech, which she alleges has wrongfully injured her reputation. But an individual has a claim to reputation only to the extent that it is an accurate representation of herself. In defamation cases, then, truth must be a defense, for the right to reputation cannot be violated by true statements, while the public has a right to pursue the truth about matters of public concern. By contrast, privacy laws rest on the belief that some matters are so intimate and personal that individuals have a right to shield them from public view altogether.[47] If one accepts this premise, then truth should not be a defense in privacy cases.

Of course, the critics are inclined to reject this premise. For example, Volokh persuasively argues that courts have sometimes failed to recognize the ways in which putatively private information (such as an individual's "long past" criminal history) actually is of legitimate concern to others, who may reasonably want to use this information in deciding whether and how to interact with him. Diane L. Zimmerman goes further, arguing that "[a]ll information is potentially useful in some way to the public in forming attitudes and values," and thus "every communication is arguably privileged" under the First Amendment.[48] From one point of view, Zimmerman is clearly right. Detailed knowledge about the medical condition of individuals would have enormous value for the study and promotion of public health. The same is true of the things that people tell their counselors, psychotherapists, and pastors. Research into human sexuality would benefit greatly from information on what people do behind closed doors, and the reliability of this information would undoubtedly be greatly enhanced if researchers did not have to depend on self-reporting by subjects. Knowing what goes on in people's homes would shed great light on family life as well as on topics like education, the economy, and domestic violence. In these ways, it is true that all information about private life has a bearing on matters of public concern. It seems clear, however, that most Americans would find it intolerable to live in a society that did not protect the privacy of medical records, counseling sessions, sexual activity, and family life. This attitude is not a mere matter of "embarrassment" or "a dislike of being talked about by the general public"[49] but flows from a sense of personal dignity and self-respect. For these reasons, the sphere of public discourse should not be regarded as unbounded. Instead, the law should be allowed to impose some limits to protect individual privacy.[50]

As Emerson has argued, the best way to accomplish this goal is to focus not on the scope of "matters of public concern," but rather on a core area of personal privacy. This area "would include sexual relations, the performance of bodily functions, family relations," and other "intimate details of a person's life," that is, "those activities, ideas or emotions which one does not share with others or shares only with those who are closest." Emerson adds that the right to privacy should not protect information that is revealed in the course of criminal trials or other public proceedings, or information that is relevant to evaluating the character or conduct of persons who have "voluntarily injected [themselves] into public affairs" and thus assumed the status of public figures.[51] As I have suggested, the right to privacy should also extend to information that was initially obtained by means of wrongful intrusion (for example, by illegal wiretapping or interception). Information that falls within the sphere of privacy should be protected except in situations that involve some overriding public concern (such as the threats of violence in *Bartnicki*). Although many difficult cases would remain, principles such as these would go a long way toward safeguarding privacy while ensuring adequate protection for freedom of speech.

Conclusion

The law of privacy seeks to shield the personal lives of individuals from unwarranted intrusion as well as unreasonable exposure. These are not two unrelated ideas, but two complementary aspects of a more general right to privacy. Although the Supreme Court has sought a reasonable accommodation between First Amendment liberties and freedom from intrusion, it has consistently blocked legal efforts to protect informational privacy. It is not difficult to understand why the Court has taken this approach, for such laws appear to regulate speech on the basis of its content. But the same is true of the law of defamation, an area in which the Justices have engaged in a careful weighing of interests. It is true that defamation law aims to restrict only false speech — speech that the Court has said has "no constitutional value."[52] But it does not follow that the public is entitled to know everything about a person's life so long as it is true. Instead, respect for autonomy dictates that individuals should generally be free to decide for themselves whether to reveal their thoughts, feelings, and personal affairs to others.[53] Like reputation and freedom from intrusion, this aspect of privacy "reflects no more than our basic concept of the essential dignity and worth of every human being"[54] — a concept that lies at the foundation not only of personality rights, but also of the First Amendment itself.

## IO

Hate Speech

In recent decades, no aspect of First Amendment jurisprudence has generated more controversy than the problem of hate speech — expression that abuses or degrades others on the basis of such characteristics as race, religion, and gender.[1] Some states and localities, as well as many colleges and universities, have sought to regulate such speech on the ground that it causes serious injury to its targets and to the community itself. Critics respond that, while the society should do everything it can to combat bigotry and prejudice, it may not do so by curtailing freedom of expression.

In struggling with this problem, the courts have drawn a rough distinction between hate speech that is directed toward particular individuals and that which is communicated to the public at large. The courts have allowed the government to regulate the first kind of hate speech so long as it does so pursuant to general laws that restrict categories of speech that have been held outside the protection of the First Amendment. For example, if a state has a general law banning the use of fighting words, there is no constitutional problem with applying this law to the use of fighting words that are based on group hatred. However, in *R.A.V. v. City of St. Paul* (1992), the Supreme Court ruled five to four that the state may not make distinctions *within* an unprotected category by subjecting speech based on group hatred to more stringent regulation than other speech that falls in the same category. According to Justice Scalia, selective restrictions of this sort — such as laws that ban fighting words

164

only when based on race, religion, or gender — amount to a form of content or viewpoint discrimination forbidden by the First Amendment.[2] The courts have also rejected efforts to regulate hate speech that does not fall within an existing category of unprotected speech. In particular, they have held that when group hatred takes the form of political expression, as in the Nazi march in Skokie, it should be seen as a form of "lawful political speech at the core of what the First Amendment is designed to protect."[3]

In this chapter I explore the problem of hate speech from a liberal humanist perspective. As I show in the first section, when hate speech is directed toward particular individuals, it often violates their rights of personal security, personality, and equality. For this reason, the courts are correct to hold that expression of this sort (which I shall call private hate speech) may be restricted when it falls within an unprotected category. But the Supreme Court was wrong to hold in *R.A.V.* that the government may regulate hate speech only pursuant to general laws that regulate entire categories of unprotected speech. Hate speech inflicts more severe injury on its targets and the community as a whole and therefore merits a stronger response. In the second section, I argue that the courts are also wrong to hold that political hate speech such as the Nazi march should be protected by the First Amendment. Finally, I say a word about whether colleges and universities should be permitted to regulate hate speech on campus.

Private Hate Speech

SHOULD PRIVATE HATE SPEECH BE PROTECTED BY THE FIRST AMENDMENT?

I begin with hate speech that is directed toward particular individuals. In many cases, speech of this sort violates the target's right to personal security, the community's right to the public peace, or both. Thus, white men who say, "Now you're going to die, nigger," as they prepare to douse a black man with gasoline, have committed an assault.[4] Threats of future harm may also constitute a crime, and may result in civil liability for intentional infliction of emotional distress.[5] Slurs and epithets constitute one of the most common forms of insulting or fighting words.[6] And expressions of hatred can be punished as criminal incitement[7] when they are intended and likely to provoke others to imminent violence.[8]

Hate speech that is directed toward particular individuals may also violate their personality rights. As we saw in chapter 8, expressions of group hatred can cause severe psychological injury, giving rise to a tort claim for intentional infliction of emotional distress.[9] Speech of this sort can also infringe the right to privacy, as in the case of anonymous threatening or offensive messages.[10] Finally, by injuring others on invidious grounds such as race, hate speech violates the right to equality.[11]

In all of these ways, private hate speech can infringe the rights of individuals and the community. Under the liberal humanist approach, speech of this sort should be held unprotected unless it has sufficient value to justify the injuries it causes.

As an illustration, consider the classic form of hate speech in the United States — the burning of a cross to express hostility toward racial, ethnic, and religious minorities. Suppose the Ku Klux Klan burns a cross in front of the home of an African American family that has recently moved to a white neighborhood, in order to terrorize them and force them to leave. One can hardly imagine a more serious invasion of personal security. The act may constitute an assault if the family members observe it and fear an imminent attack. The act may also violate laws that forbid threats of future violence. If the cross burning occurs inside the family's yard, it infringes their property rights as well.

The Klan's conduct also violates the family members' rights of personality. The act is a flagrant and deeply offensive intrusion into their private lives and thus can be considered an invasion of privacy. Moreover, it is hard to think of a clearer case of intentional infliction of emotional distress through "extreme and outrageous conduct." Finally, the cross burning violates the targets' rights to equality — rights which are protected by antidiscrimination laws that secure the freedom to purchase and hold real property and to live wherever one chooses, without regard to race.[12]

Does cross burning, when directed against specific individuals, have sufficient value to justify the injuries it causes? Undoubtedly it constitutes a form of self-expression. But an act of expression cannot be privileged on account of the very aspect that makes it wrongful in the first place.[13] Individuals have no right to pursue their own self-realization when that is defined in terms of denying the legitimate self-realization of others. Moreover, as I argue below, targeted cross burning should not be protected as a form of political speech or because of its contribution to the search for truth.[14] Instead, like other acts of private hate speech, this conduct should be held outside the protection of the First Amendment.

IS ALL WRONGFUL SPEECH EQUAL?
HATE SPEECH AND THE *R.A.V.* DECISION

Up to this point, I have been treating hate speech in the same way as any other speech that violates general laws for the protection of rights. The next question is whether there is anything distinctive about hate speech that might justify greater regulation. This was the central issue in *R.A.V. v. City of St. Paul.*[15]

Late one night in June 1990, R.A.V. and several other white teenagers burned a crude wooden cross inside the yard of an African American family who lived across the street from him. R.A.V. was arrested and charged with violating a St. Paul ordinance that made it a misdemeanor to "place[] on public or private property a symbol . . . including, but not limited to, a burning cross or Nazi swastika, which one knows or has reasonable grounds to know arouses anger, alarm or resentment in others on the basis of race, color, creed, religion or gender."[16] On its face, the ordinance was clearly overbroad, for speech does not lose First Amendment protection merely because it provokes "anger" or "resentment" in others.[17] Relying on an earlier Minnesota decision, however, the state supreme court held that the St. Paul ordinance was confined to what *Chaplinsky v. New Hampshire* (1942) called "insulting or 'fighting' words—those which by their very utterance inflict injury or tend to incite an immediate breach of the peace." The court concluded that, when the ordinance was construed in this manner, it was constitutional because it applied only to speech that was outside the protection of the First Amendment.[18]

A deeply divided U.S. Supreme Court reversed. Writing for the five-member majority, Justice Scalia accepted the state court's construction of the ordinance as authoritative and assumed that it covered only unprotected fighting words. Nevertheless, he held that the ordinance was unconstitutional because, instead of prohibiting fighting words in general, it banned only a subset of that category—words "that insult, or provoke violence, 'on the basis of race, color, creed, religion or gender.'" Asserting that "[s]electivity of this sort creates the possibility that the city is seeking to handicap the expression of particular ideas," Scalia ruled that the ordinance was inconsistent with the First Amendment doctrine of content neutrality.[19]

At the same time, however, Scalia conceded that some instances of speech that fall within an unprotected category may cause greater injury than others. In such cases, the government may choose to regulate only the most harmful acts of speech without violating the rule against content discrimination. For example, "the Federal Government can criminalize only those threats of violence that are directed against the President, . . . since the reasons why threats . . . are outside the protection of the First Amendment . . . have special force when applied to the person of the President."[20] But this raises the obvious question of whether the St. Paul ordinance could be justified on the same ground: that it sought to regulate only the most harmful forms of fighting words.

There are several reasons for believing that insults based on race, gender, or religion cause greater harm than insults in general. First, unlike those that express merely personal dislike, group-based insults often deny the very humanity of their targets. In this way, they inflict a deeper injury.[21] Second, in an important sense, group-based insults are directed not only against specific individuals, but also against the group in general. For this reason, they may injure more people and may provoke violence on a broader scale. By exacerbating tensions between groups, such insults also have a greater impact on the community as a whole. And all of these injuries are heightened when the insults are directed against members of groups that historically have been subjected to discrimination and oppression.[22] Thus, the reasons for restricting fighting words and other unprotected categories "have special force" when applied to hate speech, and the state should be allowed to subject it to greater regulation.[23]

The Supreme Court recognized the force of these considerations only one year later in *Wisconsin v. Mitchell* (1993). After Todd Mitchell and some friends watched *Mississippi Burning*—a movie that contains scenes of violence against blacks during the civil rights movement—he incited the group to severely beat a white boy who happened to pass by. Upon conviction for aggravated battery, Mitchell was sentenced under a state hate crimes law that imposed a higher penalty for intentionally selecting a victim on the basis of "race, religion, color, disability, sexual orientation, natural origin or ancestry." Relying on *R.A.V.*, the Wisconsin Supreme Court struck down the statute on the ground that it punished defendants for the "ideological content of [their] thought[s]." In an opinion by Chief Justice Rehnquist, the U.S. Supreme Court unanimously reversed, observing that there was reason to believe that "bias-motivated crimes are more likely [than other crimes] to provoke retaliatory crimes, inflict distinct emotional harms on their victims, and incite community unrest." "The State's desire to redress these perceived harms," Rehnquist contended, "provides an adequate explanation for its penalty-enhancement provision over and above mere disagreement with offenders' beliefs or biases." Yet if this is true of laws against hate crimes, why is it not equally true of laws against hate speech, where that speech falls within an unprotected category such as fighting words? In both instances, the state seeks to impose greater regulation on bias-motivated acts because they are "thought to inflict greater individual and societal harm" than other unprotected acts.[24]

The doctrine and reasoning of *R.A.V.* were further eroded in *Virginia v. Black* (2003). In that case, the defendants were convicted under a state law that banned cross burning when done with "an intent to intimidate a person or group of persons." This statute clearly appeared to violate the content discrimination rule of *R.A.V.*: although the legislature may ban acts of intimidation (which the state courts equated with threats of bodily harm), the Virginia legislature did not ban all such acts, but only those accomplished by means of a particular symbol—a symbol that was closely associated with a specific ideology. The state supreme court held the statute unconstitutional under *R.A.V.*, but once again the U.S. Supreme Court reversed. After reviewing the long history of violence associated with cross burning by the Ku Klux Klan, Justice O'Connor concluded that this form of conduct was "a particularly virulent form of intimidation." Accordingly, she ruled that the statute fell within the exception in *R.A.V.* that allows a state to ban only the most harmful instances of an unprotected category of speech.[25]

Although it purported to distinguish *R.A.V.*, *Black* goes a long way toward undermining the logical foundations of that decision. If a state may reasonably determine that cross burning is "a particularly virulent form of intimidation," why may it not reach a similar conclusion about other forms of hate speech? For example, why should it be precluded from finding that *nigger* is a "particularly virulent form" of fighting words? Moreover, if the state is allowed to make such determinations on an ad hoc basis, it certainly should be permitted to make them with regard to general classes of speech, such as racial epithets, for general rules of this sort pose far less danger of improper content or viewpoint discrimination than statutes like the one in *Black,* which singled out a particular ideological symbol.

For all of these reasons, *R.A.V.* should be overruled. Hate speech inflicts deeper injuries on its targets and the community than do other instances of unprotected speech and therefore calls for a stronger response.[26]

Public Hate Speech

Of course, Justice Scalia's ultimate concern in *R.A.V.* is that hate speech regulations may be directed at the political message conveyed by the speech. This brings us to the most difficult and controversial problem—that of public or political hate speech.

Suppose that, as in the *Skokie* case, a group of neo-Nazis or Klansmen decides to march in full regalia through a Jewish or African American neighborhood in order to express their view that the group should be subjected to segregation, deportation, genocide, or other extreme forms of discrimination or oppression.[27] Should this expression be protected under the First Amendment? The freedom to engage in political discourse is a fundamental right in a democratic society. As we have seen, however, this right is not absolute. For example, the First Amendment does not protect political speech when it amounts to a true threat of violence, when it incites its audience to imminent lawbreaking, when it recklessly defames a public figure, or when it negligently defames a private person. These forms of speech may be restricted to protect the rights of others.[28] The question is whether the same is true of public hate speech such as a Nazi or Klan demonstration. Under the liberal humanist approach, we should first ask whether the march would infringe the rights of other individuals or the community and then consider whether it should nevertheless be protected because of its political character.

THE IMPACT OF PUBLIC HATE SPEECH ON OTHER RIGHTS

Personal security. In view of the history of violence by Nazis and the Klan, the march is likely — and may very well be intended — to undermine the personal security of the groups against whom it is directed. However, unless the speech clearly amounts to a threat of or incitement to violence, its impact on personal security should not be regarded as sufficient to justify regulation.

Rights of personality. The march does, however, constitute a serious infringement of the personality rights of its targets. By treating them not as persons but as inferior beings who may be oppressed or murdered, the march may inflict severe distress or even lasting trauma on many members of the group. Whether or not it does so, it constitutes a fundamental attack on their right to personal dignity.[29]

In response, it may be said that the targets can avoid this attack simply by staying away from the march.[30] This objection might be persuasive if the speech took place out of public view. By contrast, speech that is political and that occurs in a public place is intended and must be deemed to be communicated to the public at large, not merely to those who happen to be present at the time. As citizens, minority-group members have a responsibility to attend to the political speech of others, while as the targets of such expression they have a compelling reason to do so. Thus, even if they were to stay away from the march, they could hardly avoid its impact.

It is true, as Justice Harlan observes in *Cohen v. California* (1971), that in public we are "often . . . subject to objectionable speech" and that public discourse may not be restricted merely because it offends others.[31] It would be a serious mistake, however, to hold that personality is entitled to no protection in the public realm. Individuals do not cease to be persons when they participate in the public life of the community, and they should not be required to wholly sacrifice their personality rights to do so.[32] One can hardly imagine a form of public discourse that injures those rights more deeply than does hate speech.

The right to recognition. Above all, hate speech violates what I shall call the right to recognition. Rights are rooted in respect for personhood. It follows that an individual cannot enjoy rights in relation to others unless they recognize him as a person.[33] Recognition is the most fundamental right that individuals have, a right that lies at the basis of all their other rights. At the same time, mutual recognition is the bond that constitutes the political community. For these reasons, individuals have a duty to recognize one another as human beings and citizens. Hate speech violates this duty in a way that profoundly affects both the targets themselves and the society as a whole.

The concept of recognition has deep roots in the natural rights tradition. An early version may be found in the writings of Hobbes. According to Hobbes, the law of nature dictates that individuals should establish peaceful relations with one another in order to escape from the state of nature, which he represents as a condition of universal hostility, a war of all against all. From this basic principle, he derives a variety of more specific obligations, including a duty to recognize the equality of others. As he explains, "If Nature . . . have made men equall; that equalitie is to be acknowledged: or if Nature have made men unequall; yet because men that think themselves equall, will not enter into conditions of Peace, but upon Equall termes, such equalitie must be admitted. And therefore [it is a law of Nature,] *That every man acknowledge other for his Equall by Nature.*"[34] From this proposition, Hobbes develops the further rule that individuals must not arrogantly claim for themselves greater rights than they are willing to allow others. Finally, in a passage that bears most directly on the problem of hate speech, he holds that it constitutes a violation of natural law for any person by word or deed to "*declare Hatred, or Contempt of another,*" because "all signs of hatred, or contempt, provoke to fight." This evil, he notes, may be caused not only by insults against individuals themselves, but also by expressions of contempt for the various groups to which they belong.[35]

Locke also condemns speech that denies the equal rights of others. According to Locke, the freedom and dignity of human beings derive from their nature as "rational creatures" who are capable of directing their own actions.[36] Reason is also the basis of the law of nature, which teaches that, because all are free and equal, no one should wrongfully harm another. In this way, reason forms a natural bond of community between human beings. Locke describes the social contract in similar terms, as a "mutual agreement" among persons who regard one another as free and equal, without any "Subordination or Subjection" between them. Through the social contract, individuals establish a community for the mutual preservation of their rights—a community that necessarily supposes that its members recognize one another as human beings and citizens.[37]

In contrast to Hobbes, Locke was a strong advocate of freedom of thought and belief.[38] In *A Letter Concerning Toleration,* he explores the scope of this freedom in connection with one of the most controversial issues of his time, the problem of conflict and coexistence between religious groups. Locke maintains that individuals have an inalienable right to hold and express their beliefs. At the same time, he argues that this liberty does not extend to speech that refuses to acknowledge the duty to tolerate others, or that asserts a claim to superiority or dominion over them within civil society—a claim that the speakers presumably intend to make good whenever they have the power to do so. Locke argues that speech of this sort "undermine[s] the Foundations of Society" and should not receive legal protection.[39]

The concept of recognition finds its fullest development in the philosophy of Hegel. Hegel depicts human beings in a state of nature as separate and independent individuals, each of whom regards himself in an egoistic way as the sole, absolute value. When one of these individuals comes face to face with another, he finds his selfhood threatened. This gives rise to a struggle for recognition, in which each party seeks to demonstrate his superiority by subjugating or destroying the other. According to Hegel, this conflict can be resolved only through mutual recognition, a condition of reciprocity in which each individual comes to know himself in the other. Mutual recognition is the basis of personhood, rights, and the state. Within the state, "man is recognized and treated as a *free* and *rational* being, a *person*." Conversely, "the individual . . . makes himself worthy of this recognition" by obeying the law and "acknowledging each as the recognizedly free person he wishes to be himself." In this way, reciprocal recognition lies at the foundation of a society based on "rational freedom and genuine civic respect." Although Hegel does not explicitly address the problem of speech that denies recognition to others, his account sheds a good deal of light on this phenomenon. In particular, we can understand hate speech as reflecting the stage of consciousness in which individuals find themselves deeply threatened by the selfhood of others and respond by trying to dominate or destroy them. Thus, hate speech clearly conflicts with what Hegel regards as the basic principle underlying the system of rights: the duty to *"respect others as persons."*[40]

In these ways, the concept of recognition plays a central role in natural rights theory. On this view, the most basic function of speech is to assert one's status and to demand recognition from others as a person and a member of the community.[41] Conversely, one has a duty to accord such recognition to others. This duty is violated by public hate speech, such as a Nazi march through a Jewish neighborhood. By denying recognition to others, the speech also attacks their rights to personal security, dignity, equality, and emotional tranquillity.

SHOULD PUBLIC HATE SPEECH BE PROTECTED BECAUSE OF ITS POLITICAL CHARACTER?

For all of these reasons, public hate speech should be regarded as presumptively wrongful. Under the liberal humanist approach, the next question is whether the value of this speech outweighs its impact on the rights of others. In particular, should the speech be protected on the ground that it is intended as a contribution to public discourse?

The way one answers this question will be strongly influenced by one's conception of political speech. According to two of the leading theories in this area — Justice Holmes's vision of the marketplace of ideas and Robert C. Post's theory of public discourse — no principled distinction can be drawn between public hate speech and other forms of political expression. I shall criticize these two theories and propose an alternative view of public discourse as speech that takes place within a community that is based on mutual recognition. From this perspective, public hate speech is not entitled to constitutional protection because it violates the principles that should govern democratic debate.

Holmes's theory of the marketplace of ideas. In *Abrams v. United States* (1919), Holmes declared that "the best test of truth is the power of the thought to get itself accepted in the competition of the market."[42] On this view, the ideas contained in hate speech are no less worthy of consideration than any other beliefs. Whether or not those ideas prevail should be determined by the marketplace itself.[43]

As I argued in chapter 4, however, this view is unpersuasive as a model of the search for political truth. Individuals regarded as market participants pursue their own private good. Thus, the consumers in a marketplace of ideas would tend to "buy" those ideas that accorded with their own interests, and the ideas that prevailed in the marketplace would be those that reflected the interests of the greatest number of people. But the result would merely be the self-interested belief of the majority, rather than an objective truth or one that was capable of being shared by the society as a whole. Indeed, since interests tend to be opposed to one another, the ideas that triumph in the marketplace may well conflict with the most basic interests of some members of the society. There is no justification for regarding this process as "the best test of truth."

These objections to Holmes's view are especially serious in the case of hate speech. To take an extreme example, consider the idea that genocide should be committed against a relatively small and powerless group within the society. Nothing in the marketplace model precludes the possibility that this idea could prevail if a majority of citizens found that it accorded with their interests and beliefs.[44] Plainly, however, this idea would merely represent the subjective views of the majority, not a truth that in principle could be accepted by all reasonable persons within the society, including members of the target group itself. For these reasons, Holmes's view is unconvincing. An adequate understanding of political speech must be found elsewhere.

Post's theory of public discourse. In recent years, no one has developed a richer or more illuminating theory of free speech than Robert Post. According to this theory, constitutional principles apply in different ways within different areas of social life. Post identifies three distinct "domains" or "forms of social order" that "are especially relevant to understanding [American] constitutional law" in general and First Amendment jurisprudence in particular. The first domain, which he calls community, is a form of social life that is governed by "shared mores and norms." The second domain, management, "organizes social life instrumentally to achieve specific objectives." The third domain is democracy, which embodies the value of collective self-determination. As Post explains, "[C]ollective self-determination occurs when through participation or potential participation in public discourse, the citizens of a state come to identify with the actions and decisions of their government." More broadly, public discourse is the medium through which independent citizens come together to shape their common identity and to "choose the forms of their communal life." In these ways, public discourse functions "to reconcile, to the extent possible, the will of individuals with the general will." In a formulation that Post adopts from Jean Piaget, " 'The essence of democracy resides in its attitude towards law as a product of the collective will, and not as something emanating from a transcendent will or from the authority established by divine right. It is therefore the essence of democracy to replace the unilateral respect of authority by the mutual respect of autonomous wills.' "[45]

For Post, a central purpose of the First Amendment is to protect speech that is relevant to democratic self-governance. Although the state should often be allowed to regulate speech within other domains, the contemporary American understanding of free speech requires that public discourse "be as free from legal constraint as is feasible to sustain" so that citizens can fully engage in collective self-determination.[46]

This theory of the First Amendment leads Post to adopt a complex and nuanced approach to the problem of hate speech. The state, he suggests, may forbid "certain kinds of racist communications in *nonpublic* speech," on the ground that they conflict with the community's standards of civility and respect or on the ground that they interfere with the accomplishment of legitimate objectives within managerial domains. For example, he would permit some restrictions on hate speech within the workplace as well as within organizations such as state universities.[47]

By contrast, Post contends that "racist speech is and ought to be immune from regulation within public discourse." "[T]he value of self-determination," he writes, "requires that public discourse be open to the opinions of all." "If the state were to forbid the expression of a particular idea, the government would become, with respect to individuals holding that idea, heteronomous and nondemocratic." This would violate the fundamental principle that (in Rawls's words) citizens should be treated " 'in ways consistent with their being viewed as free and equal persons.' "[48] It follows that, under the First Amendment, the state has no power to restrict public forms of hate speech like the Nazi march in Skokie.[49]

The problem with Post's argument is that it fails to come to terms with the distinctive nature of hate speech. Because hate speech denies recognition to other citizens, it is plainly incompatible with Piaget's description of democracy as founded on "the mutual respect of autonomous wills," as well as with Post's "image of independent citizens deliberating together to form public opinion."[50] Hate speech disrespects the autonomy of others and refuses to deliberate with them. In these ways, it tends to undermine rather than to promote the formation of a genuinely common will.

This discussion suggests that Post's account of the preconditions of public discourse is incomplete. Although individuals have a right to take part in public discourse, they also have a duty to respect other citizens as equal participants in that discourse. In other words, it is not enough that the *state* should view individuals as free and equal; citizens must also view *one another* in this light. Only in this way can public discourse serve the functions that Post attributes to it: to reconcile individual and collective autonomy by promoting the development of a shared identity and a common will.[51]

According to Post, any effort to mandate respect for others within public discourse would subordinate democracy to the demands of a very different realm, that of community. In Post's terms, a community is "a social formation that inculcates norms into the very identities of its members." These norms or "civility rules" prescribe the forms of respect that individuals are obligated to show one another. In ordinary social life, the law enforces these norms by regulating speech as well as conduct—for example, by means of "such communicative torts as defamation, invasion of privacy, and infliction of emotional distress." "Through these torts, the common law not only protects the integrity of the personality of individual community members, but also serves authoritatively to articulate a community's norms and hence to define a community's identity." As Post explains, however, while the domain of community regards individual identity as the product of social norms, the domain of democracy conceives of individuals as autonomous actors who are capable of collectively defining their identity and shaping their common life. For this reason, he holds that the legal enforcement of civility rules must be suspended within public discourse, so that citizens can freely engage in collective self-determination. Public discourse must be as free from legal restriction as possible, so as not to constrain "the boundless possibility of social self-constitution."[52]

But this argument does not justify Post's view that the state should have no power to regulate racist speech in public discourse. First, as I argue below, a law regulating political hate speech need not be understood as imposing the norms of community on democratic deliberation. On the contrary, the duty to respect others can be understood as an integral feature of public discourse itself. Second, and more fundamentally, I believe that Post is mistaken when he asserts that norms of dignity and respect represent merely the conventional rules of a particular community — rules whose enforcement must be suspended so that citizens can freely determine how they wish to live. Instead, while specific forms of respect differ from one community to another, the requirement that individuals recognize one another as human beings and community members is not simply a contingent or conventional one but is inherent in the very idea of a community. A collection of individuals who did not regard one another in this way would not be a community at all. It follows that restrictions on recognition-denying speech do not limit our freedom to collectively "choose the forms of our communal life" by compelling us to adhere to the conventions of a particular society. To put the point another way, Post overstates the case when he describes our ability to shape our common life as "boundless." For example, no society can legitimately adopt extreme racist measures such as forced segregation, deportation, or genocide, for such measures would violate the most basic duties a society has to those subject to its jurisdiction. Thus, a ban on hate speech should not be regarded as restricting the legitimate scope of democratic self-governance merely because it precludes a society from considering or adopting policies of this sort.[53]

Although Post believes that democratic debate must be protected from the imposition of civility rules, he recognizes that in some ways democracy depends on the observance of those rules: "[B]ecause the identity of democratic citizens will have been formed by reference to community norms, speech in violation of civility rules will characteristically be perceived as both irrational and coercive." This leads to what he calls the "paradox of public discourse": "the First Amendment, in the name of democracy, suspends legal enforcement of the very civility rules that make rational deliberation possible." It follows that democracy "depends in some measure on the spontaneous persistence of civility." "In the absence of such persistence, the use of legal regulation to enforce community standards of civility may be required as an unfortunate but necessary option of last resort."[54]

In this way, Post qualifies his broad view that norms of dignity and respect may not be enforced within public discourse. For two reasons, however, this qualification fails to adequately reconcile the demands of free speech and human dignity. First, Post makes clear that limits of this sort are exceptional and that they can be applied only at the "periphery" of the realm of public discourse, not at its "core." For example, while he would allow the state to ban fighting words in a face-to-face setting, he would reject legal restrictions on the use of racial epithets in public discourse.[55] Second, Post represents the duty to respect others as an external limitation on public discourse, one that is imported from the domain of community and that is at odds with the principles that govern democracy. I want to argue, on the contrary, that this duty is internal to the realm of public discourse itself.[56]

Public discourse and mutual recognition. In contrast to both Holmes and Post, I believe that political speech is best understood as discourse among individuals who recognize one another as free and equal persons and members of the community. In addition to classical natural rights theorists such as Locke (whose views I discussed above), this view can find support in the work of contemporary theorists such as Meiklejohn and Habermas.

As we saw in chapter 4, Meiklejohn understands political debate on the model of the traditional town meeting. Everyone has a right to participate in this forum and to deliberate about the public good. At the same time, Meiklejohn stresses that speakers can be required to observe certain rules of order. These rules do not abridge freedom of speech, but rather make reasoned deliberation possible. In particular, Meiklejohn observes that "[i]f a speaker . . . is abusive or in other ways threatens to defeat the purpose of the meeting, he may be and should be declared 'out of order.'"[57]

This position reflects Meiklejohn's conception of the nature of a democratic community. "[U]nder our form of government," he asserts, "every citizen has . . . a right to . . . dignity—the dignity of men who govern themselves." Self-government is possible only on the basis of mutual respect among persons who regard one another as free and equal citizens engaged in "a common enterprise." These ideas lie at the heart of Meiklejohn's account of political freedom of speech.[58]

The relationship between speech and mutual recognition also plays an important role in the work of Habermas, perhaps the leading contemporary theorist of public discourse. "[T]he democratic constitutional state," Habermas observes, "understands itself as an association of free and equal persons." "Such an association is structured by relations of mutual recognition in which each person can expect to be respected by all as free and equal. Each and every person should receive a threefold recognition: they should receive equal protection and equal respect in their integrity as irreplaceable individuals, as members of ethnic or cultural groups, and as citizens, that is, as members of the political community."[59]

For Habermas, these relations of mutual recognition are the foundation of rights: "[A]ll rights ultimately stem from the system of rights that free and equal legal subjects would mutually accord to one another." People are entitled to a wide range of basic rights, from individual rights such as life, liberty, bodily integrity, and personal dignity, to political rights such as freedom of expression, which allow everyone to "participate in the processes of opinion- and will-formation in which citizens exercise their *political autonomy*." Habermas characterizes these political rights as forms of "communicative freedom" — a term he applies to activities that seek to achieve mutual understanding through reasoned discourse. These activities are essential in order to generate legitimate law in accord with what he calls the "discourse principle," which holds that laws and other norms are valid insofar as "all possibly affected persons could agree [to them] as participants in rational discourses."[60]

Habermas maintains that political communication instantiates the discourse principle in two ways. From a cognitive perspective, public discourse operates to "filter[] reasons and information, topics and contributions in such a way that the outcome of a discourse enjoys a presumption of rational acceptability." At the same time, public discourse "has the *practical sense* of establishing relations of mutual understanding that are 'violence-free,' " in the sense that participants seek uncoerced agreement rather than dominating or manipulating others. Accordingly, Habermas describes the forms of communication that constitute political discourse as "structures of mutual recognition."[61]

In these ways, Meiklejohn and Habermas provide support for the view that political speech should be understood as discourse between individuals who recognize one another as free and equal persons and members of the community.[62] This view dovetails with the general theory of rights I have presented, which holds that rights are founded on the duty to respect the autonomy and dignity of human beings — a duty that applies not merely to the state but also to individuals.[63]

From this perspective, the Supreme Court was mistaken in *Virginia v. Black* when it declared that cross burning and other forms of public hate speech should be regarded as "lawful political speech at the core of what the First Amendment is designed to protect." Instead, hate speech transgresses the most basic ground rules of public discourse. To use Meiklejohn's language, hate speech may be regarded as a form of abuse that violates the rules of order that make democratic deliberation possible. In Habermasian terms, one can argue that hate speech is not an instance of "communicative freedom" oriented toward mutual understanding. Rather, the aim of hate speech is to dominate and subordinate others. In this way it is inconsistent with those "relations of mutual recognition in which each person can expect to be respected by all as free and equal."[64]

It follows that, in principle, public hate speech does not fall within the First Amendment right to political freedom of speech. Instead, as I suggested in chapter 4, that right should be understood as a *relational* one, that is, as a right to participate in a certain kind of interaction with others. Political free speech is a right to interact with others as free and equal citizens who are engaged in discourse on matters of common concern. Because this is a right to take part in a cooperative activity, it carries with it a duty to respect the rights of other participants.[65] Thus, the duty to refrain from speech that denies recognition to others is not one that is imposed on public discourse from the outside, but one that is inherent in the concept of political freedom of speech.

REFINING THE RIGHTS-BASED ACCOUNT OF PUBLIC HATE SPEECH

American courts generally hold that public hate speech must be protected because there is no principled way to distinguish it from other forms of political discourse, a category of speech that lies at the heart of the First Amendment.[66] I have argued that this view is incorrect for two reasons. First, public hate speech violates the rights of its targets in a variety of ways: by undermining their sense of personal safety, assaulting their dignity and emotional tranquillity, and denying their equal status as human beings and members of the community. Second, although some forms of political speech should be protected despite their impact on other rights, this is not true of hate speech because it falls outside of a proper understanding of political debate.[67] For these reasons, public hate speech is not deserving of constitutional protection.

This conclusion is consistent with the view taken by the international community. For example, the International Covenant on Civil and Political Rights requires nations to prohibit "[a]ny advocacy of national, racial or religious hatred that constitutes incitement to discrimination, hostility or violence." Other international agreements take the same position. Many liberal democratic nations have enacted laws restricting certain forms of public hate speech, and they regard those laws as consonant with national and international guarantees of freedom of expression.[68]

My position on public hate speech is subject to four important qualifications. First, although I have argued that individuals have a right to recognition, that right can provide a justification for hate speech laws only if it is accepted by the political community. Thus, the controversy over hate speech cannot be resolved purely on the level of legal theory or doctrine but must also play out in the political arena. Those who support or oppose hate speech laws must persuade the community to adopt their views. The courts should allow this debate to proceed and not be too forward in imposing a solution. In particular, they should not reject hate speech laws out of hand on the ground that they are inconsistent with the American understanding of freedom of speech. As the ongoing debate over the issue makes clear, this understanding is not a monolithic one. Moreover, our conception of free speech and other rights evolves over time. If the community comes to believe that individuals have a fundamental right to respect as human beings and citizens, and if (as I have tried to show) this right is justified in principle, the courts should not simply hold that no such right exists. Instead, as in other cases, they should consider whether hate speech regulation is justified in view of the competing rights at stake.[69]

Second, in determining whether regulation is appropriate, courts and legislatures must take into account not only the substantive value of the rights, but also practical and institutional considerations. For example, hate speech laws are acceptable only if they can be drafted in a way that clearly distinguishes between lawful and unlawful conduct. Moreover, such laws should not be adopted if they are unnecessary or if they are likely to be counterproductive, for example, by provoking a backlash against minority groups.[70]

This discussion leads to a third qualification. On the view I have presented, the law is justified in regulating public hate speech when it causes concrete and serious injury to other rights that are recognized by the community and when such regulation makes sense from a practical standpoint. But whether this is true will vary from one situation to another. It follows that context is crucial in assessing the constitutionality and desirability of hate speech regulation.

This point becomes clear if we consider several variations on the problem of public hate speech. First, suppose that the Ku Klux Klan burns a cross in the yard of an African American family. Earlier, I discussed this case as an example of private hate speech that was intended to terrorize the family and force them to move.[71] Now imagine that the Klan's purpose was also to convey an ideological message to African Americans and to the public in general — say, a message that blacks are inferior and degraded beings who have no place in a white nation. In that case, the expression would also have a political dimension. It seems clear, however, that we would still have no difficulty in holding the expression unprotected by the First Amendment. As I have argued, the cross burning constitutes a serious invasion of the family members' rights to person and property as well as their rights to personality and equality. From a rights-based perspective, the fact that the conduct was also intended to send a political message does nothing to ameliorate the injuries they suffer. On the contrary, it aggravates those injuries, for in this case the speech also violates their rights of citizenship by attacking their status as members of the community.

Now suppose that, as in *Brandenburg v. Ohio* (1969), the Klan burns a cross at a small rally on a private farm that is not visible to others. Although this conduct may be intended to deny recognition to African Americans, it does so in a way that has far less impact on their rights. At the same time, the cross burning has some value as a means of self-expression and affirmation of group identity. Although those values are not strong enough to justify First Amendment protection for cross burning in front of a family's house, they are sufficient to justify protection in the context of a rally of this sort.

The case I have been focusing on — a march by Nazis or Klansmen through a Jewish or African American neighborhood — falls between these two extremes. How this issue should be resolved depends on one's assessment of the value of the speech and its impact on other rights. As I have indicated, my own judgment is that this speech causes profound injury to its targets and that it fails to meet the minimum standards of respect that citizens are entitled to demand of one another in public discourse. For these reasons I would hold the speech unprotected by the First Amendment. This conclusion is far from inevitable, however. One could accept the rights-based approach and nevertheless reach the opposite result if one thought that the injuries inflicted by the speech were not concrete and serious enough to justify depriving it of constitutional protection. Ultimately, the issue will turn on whether one believes that allowing the speech or restricting it will best promote the values of human freedom and dignity. As I have acknowledged, questions of this sort are deeply controversial. The goal of the liberal humanist approach is not to impose a particular answer to such questions, but to provide a framework within which we can reasonably debate them. In this way, it seeks to focus our attention on the substantive values at stake in First Amendment cases.

In sum, controversial issues like hate speech need not be resolved in an all-or-nothing fashion. We can allow regulation of public hate speech in situations where we believe it causes the most serious injury to other rights, while protecting it in other situations. I believe that a view like this, which is sensitive to context, is preferable to one that holds that speech may never (or hardly ever) be regulated on the basis of its content or communicative impact.

Fourth, while people have a right to be free from hate speech, they have no right to be free from expression that challenges their ideas or beliefs. This distinction goes to the heart of the recent controversy over Danish newspaper cartoons that depicted the Prophet Muhammad in ways that many Muslims found blasphemous and disrespectful and that sparked protests and rioting in countries around the world.[72] Although some of the cartoons' critics described them as hate speech against Muslims, this charge was unfounded. Many of the drawings were innocuous and were regarded as offensive only because they violated a belief held by some Islamic sects that forbids any representation of the prophet. In a liberal democratic society, however, public discourse may not be restricted merely because it fails to conform to the religious principles of some members of the society.[73] Several of the other cartoons — such as a drawing of the prophet wearing a turban shaped like a bomb, and another showing him holding a dagger while standing in front of two women clad in burkas — were more provocative. Nevertheless, these drawings did not attack the humanity of Muslims or call for any form of violence or discrimination against them. Instead, the drawings were intended to criticize those aspects of Islamic culture or belief that the artists viewed as promoting terrorism or the subordination of women. This does not constitute hate speech. It is true that religious beliefs are central to many people's identity and that an attack on those beliefs may therefore be experienced as an attack on their personality. But insofar as one's identity is based on beliefs of this sort, it must be open to revision and transformation in light of criticism. For the liberal tradition, this is an essential part of what it means to be rational and autonomous. The right to criticize one's own tradition as well as the views of others is fundamental to the liberal conception of free speech.[74] It follows that such speech falls within the principle of free expression.[75]

In short, individuals must enjoy absolute freedom to advocate and debate ideas, so long as they refrain from attacking the rights of others or their status as human beings and members of the community. To use Habermas's language, speech may never be restricted merely because of its cognitive content, but only when it is directed in a practical way toward violating the rights of others.[76]

This distinction also provides the key to a proper approach to the ongoing controversy over campus speech codes. As academic institutions, colleges and universities should promote the broadest freedom of intellectual inquiry. At the same time, they are communities whose members owe one another a minimum degree of respect. This point is by no means limited to hate speech, but extends to all forms of speech and conduct that wrongfully abuse or harass others. As we have seen, however, it is reasonable to believe that hate speech causes greater injury than many other forms of disrespectful speech and conduct.[77] Thus, it is appropriate for academic institutions to adopt policies that treat hate speech as an especially serious breach of the community's standards of conduct. At the same time, such policies must be carefully drawn to avoid interfering with the legitimate expression of ideas. Once more, context is important: as Post has suggested, it may be reasonable to apply different rules to the dormitories, classrooms, and open spaces of universities.[78]

Conclusion

In this chapter, I have argued that hate speech should often be held outside the protection of the First Amendment. Private hate speech may be restricted when it invades its targets' rights of personal security, personality, or equality by violating laws against assaults, threats, fighting words, incitement, intentional infliction of emotional distress, invasion of privacy, or discrimination. Moreover, because hate speech inflicts deeper injuries than other forms of wrongful speech, it is reasonable to subject it to greater regulation. At first glance, public hate speech, such as the Nazi march in Skokie, should receive protection as a form of political discourse. However, by refusing to treat its targets as members of the community, public hate speech violates their rights of citizenship as well as the basic principles that should govern democratic debate, which depends on mutual respect among free and equal citizens. In these ways, both private and public hate speech violate the most basic right of all, the right to recognition as a human being.

I I

Pornography

How should the First Amendment apply to sexually explicit material in magazines, books, films, and electronic media such as the Internet? Conservatives and liberals have long been divided over this question. The conservative position prevailed in *Miller v. California* (1973) and *Paris Adult Theatre I v. Slaton* (1973), which reaffirmed the power of the states to regulate obscene material "to protect *the social interest in order and morality.*" In an opinion by Chief Justice Burger, the Supreme Court declared that state legislatures reasonably could conclude that the distribution of such material had a corrupting and debasing effect on individual character, as well as "a tendency to injure the community as a whole" by endangering public safety and by undermining the right of the states "to maintain a decent society."[1]

By contrast, liberals contend that individuals should be free to decide for themselves what they want to read or view.[2] To be sure, many liberals would allow the state to regulate the display and distribution of sexually explicit material to protect children and unwilling viewers.[3] From a liberal perspective, however, any broader effort to suppress such material violates constitutional guarantees of freedom of expression and constitutes an illegitimate attempt to impose the majority's moral beliefs on other people.

In recent decades, this traditional debate between liberals and conservatives has been transformed by the rise of a new perspective that asserts that pornography is harmful because it subordinates and degrades women.[4] This position is best represented by the model ordinance drafted by Catharine A. MacKinnon and Andrea Dworkin, which declares pornography to be a violation of women's civil rights.[5] At times, antipornography feminists have joined with moral conservatives to support the regulation of sexual material.[6] Some other feminists oppose such regulation, either out of a commitment to free speech or on the ground that such material tends to promote sexual liberation and gender equality by undermining traditional moral views that have been harmful to women.[7] On the other hand, regulation finds some support among communitarians who are concerned with the impact pornography may have on our common life, as well as among neorepublicans whose conception of free speech focuses on its importance for democratic deliberation.[8]

In short, the contemporary debate over pornography appears to involve a conflict between sharply divergent and even irreconcilable perspectives. In this chapter, I want to see whether it is possible to bring these disparate views together within the framework of a rights-based theory of the First Amendment. In accord with the liberal position, I argue in the first section that the fundamental right to free expression includes the liberty to make and view sexually oriented materials. It follows that this liberty may be restricted only to protect the rights of others. The second section contends that, while sexual depictions should generally be protected, material that glorifies violence against women should be regarded as an invasion of their rights to dignity, equality, and personal security as well as the fundamental right to recognition. As the final section demonstrates, violent pornography also infringes the rights of the community as a whole. In addition, the community should be allowed to ban the display of pornography in public places as well as to shield children from pornography. In this way, I hope to develop a view that incorporates what is most persuasive in each of the leading positions: the liberal focus on autonomy, the feminist demand for equality, and the conservative concern for community.

Pornography and Freedom of Expression

In this chapter, I shall use the term *pornography* in a broad sense to refer to all sexually explicit material whose predominant purpose is to stimulate or satisfy the sexual desires of its audience. The threshold question is whether material of this sort falls within the fundamental freedoms of speech and press protected by the First Amendment.

In its first major obscenity decision, *Roth v. United States* (1957), the Supreme Court declared that obscene materials — which it defined as those that appealed to a prurient interest in sex — "were utterly without redeeming social importance" because they did nothing to advance the purpose of the First Amendment: "to assure unfettered interchange of ideas for the bringing about of political and social changes desired by the people." Balancing the social interests at stake, the Court concluded that obscene materials were entitled to no constitutional protection, for they were " 'of such slight social value as a step to truth that any benefit that may be derived from them is clearly outweighed by the social interest in order and morality.' "[9]

In contrast to *Roth,* I have argued that expression has intrinsic as well as instrumental value: free speech is not merely a means to promote social welfare, but also an inherent right. As the Court has come to recognize, the First Amendment protects the individual's "autonomy to choose the content of [his] own speech" as well as "the right to read or observe what he pleases." And freedom of expression serves not only "[t]o permit the continued building of our politics and culture," but also "to assure self-fulfillment for each individual."[10]

If these are the values that underlie the First Amendment, it is difficult to see how pornography can be excluded from its scope. The choice to make or view sexual material falls within the notion of individual autonomy, or the right to determine the content of one's own expression. Many people derive self-fulfillment from sexual material.[11] In addition, while the acts of making and viewing pornography may contribute little to democratic debate, they do influence the society and its culture, whether for good (as some liberals and anticensorship feminists believe) or for ill (as conservatives and antipornography feminists claim). Thus, these acts may be regarded as a form of participation in and shaping of the social and cultural life of the community.[12] Finally, as we saw in chapter 4, the search for truth takes place on an individual as well as on a social level. It has been persuasively argued that for some people, especially sexual minorities, pornography can play an important role in promoting self-knowledge with regard to sexuality.[13]

Pornography and the Rights of Women

For these reasons, I believe that the fundamental right to free expression extends to pornography. Under the liberal humanist approach, the next question is whether this form of expression violates the rights of others.

DOES PORNOGRAPHY INFRINGE THE RIGHTS OF WOMEN?

The right to recognition. As we saw in chapter 10, human beings have a basic right to recognition.[14] The radical feminist critique of pornography can be understood in these terms. According to MacKinnon and Dworkin, pornography is a form of sex discrimination which subordinates women and denies them equality. This denial of equality is not simply a matter of treating women less favorably than men, or even of according women inferior status and power in society. Instead, at the most fundamental level, the claim is that pornography denies recognition to women by treating them as mere objects for sexual gratification.[15]

In my view, this is not true of all forms of pornography. To represent a woman as a sex object is not necessarily to portray her as a *mere* sex object rather than a person. In this way the radical feminist claim seems too broad. And the same is true of any definition of pornography that would embrace all material that portrays women as sex objects.[16]

Nevertheless, I believe that the radical feminist position contains an essential core of truth. Some pornography does represent women as mere sex objects and not as persons. In particular, this is true of violent pornography — pornography that shows women being battered, raped, tortured, or killed, in a way that is intended to be sexually appealing to the viewer.[17] Representing women in this way violates their right to recognition by portraying them as mere objects which can be used or destroyed for the pleasure of others.

This is clearly true in the case of pornography that depicts a specific woman in this way. For example, in one notorious case, a student at the University of Michigan wrote, and posted to the Internet, a pornographic story that described in horrific detail how he desired to sexually torture, rape, and murder one of his classmates — a woman he identified by name.[18] Surely, this act of speech violated the woman's rights by representing her in a way wholly inconsistent with her dignity as a human being.

The Michigan case is highly unusual. Most works of violent pornography portray the infliction of harm on fictional characters rather than on real individuals. Such works may employ women as actresses, however. According to MacKinnon, women are frequently coerced into performing in pornographic films, and the violence done to them is often real rather than simulated.[19] Of course, to the extent this is true, pornography presents an easy case: no one would deny that to coerce an individual in this way or to inflict actual violence on her against her will is wrongful, nor would anyone claim that the First Amendment's protections extend to such conduct. The difficult problem arises only when a work of violent pornography is fictional and is made without coercion or violence against real people. In that case, the work does not seem to deny recognition to the individual women involved in its production.

I believe, however, that a strong argument can be made that violent pornography is wrongful in that it denies recognition to women in general. This argument rests on the following propositions. First, what is represented in pornography is not merely the image of *this* woman (the individual who performs in a film), but also the image of women in general. The viewer's deepest and most powerful desire is to see women's bodies or women engaged in sexual activity, rather than to see any particular woman. At its core, then, what pornography portrays is generic female sexuality. Second, the image of women in general is something that is shared by all women. Thus, the representations contained in pornography implicitly refer not only to the particular woman who is portrayed, but also to women in general and to all members of the group. Third, as I argued above, violent pornography infringes the rights of those it portrays to recognition as human beings. From these premises, it follows that violent pornography infringes women's right to recognition.[20]

Clearly, the notion of groups plays an essential role in this argument. But it is important to consider exactly how it does so. The argument does not rest on an assertion that women as a group have some special rights that others do not have. Instead, it is predicated on the fundamental right of all human beings to dignity and recognition. The thrust of the argument is that, in the case of violent pornography, this right is being denied to all of the members of a particular group. To put it another way, what is at issue here is not so much a *group right* as a *group-based wrong*. We may describe this either as a wrong to women as a class, or as a wrong to all of the individuals who belong to the class. In either case, the basic point is that an injury is being done to a number of people on the basis of group membership. When the argument is put in these terms, I believe it is consistent with liberal political and constitutional theory. Whether or not group status can provide the basis for positive entitlements (an issue that has generated intense debate in areas such as affirmative action), it is widely accepted that people have a negative right to be free from injury based on group status — a principle that lies at the heart of the Equal Protection Clause of the Fourteenth Amendment as well as other provisions that forbid discrimination against individuals or groups on the basis of race, religion, gender, or other grounds.[21]

Rights of personality. Violent pornography also infringes personality rights, especially the right to one's image. As I argued in chapter 4, people relate to one another only through the images they have of each other. Thus a person's image may be said to constitute her social personality or her personality in relation to others. The right to one's image embraces several specific rights under the common law: the right to reputation, the right not to be placed in a false light before the public, and the right to control the use of one's name and likeness.[22] More generally, the right to one's image should be understood to include all legitimate claims that individuals have with respect to the way they are portrayed by others.

To see how violent pornography can invade this right, we need to explore the nature of personality in more depth.[23] On one level, every person is unique. Yet every individual also shares some characteristics with others, including race, nationality, religion, gender, and so on.[24] Insofar as an individual accepts and affirms these characteristics, they become part of her personal identity. Similarly, insofar as other people attribute these characteristics to an individual, they become part of her social identity or image.

It follows that a person's image includes not only what is unique to her, but also the view that is commonly held of the characteristics she shares with others, such as her gender. As we have seen, however, what is represented in pornography includes the image of women in general, and violent pornography portrays this image in a way that is inconsistent with human dignity. It follows that violent pornography infringes the rights of women in general to their image.[25] Material of this sort may also inflict psychological and dignitary injury on individuals who are exposed to it without their consent.[26]

The right to personal security. Thus far, I have been focusing on the dignitary injuries that result from pornography. But radical feminists also argue that pornography harms women by promoting sexual assault and other forms of abuse.[27] In the language I am using, the claim is that pornography undermines the fundamental right to personal security or immunity from violence.

In assessing this claim, we must again distinguish between different kinds of pornography. The claim that pornography in general promotes violence against women may be too broad.[28] As applied to violent pornography, on the other hand, it may well have force. As I have said, violent pornography portrays women not as human beings with rights, but as mere objects that can be violated, abused, or killed, and it represents this violence in an erotically powerful way. It is reasonable to suppose that material of this kind tends to promote acts of violence against women by stimulating or reinforcing viewers' desires to commit such acts, while weakening their moral and psychological inhibitions against doing so. This view finds some support in social science research that suggests that "exposure to violent pornography [tends to] increase aggression against women."[29] This evidence is far from conclusive, however.[30] Thus, the question whether violent pornography leads to increased violence against women remains a deeply controversial one.

That is not the only important question, however. As we have seen, personal security includes not only the right to be safe from violence, but also the right to feel safe. For example, the law protects individuals against assaults and threats even when they do not lead to actual violence.[31]

Whether or not it can be convincingly shown that violent pornography causes violence against women, one can reasonably argue that it impinges on their right to feel secure against violence.[32] Of course, to enjoy this security, one must believe one is safe from harm. But the sense of security runs much deeper than that. It consists in a sense of trust in others, rooted in a belief that they recognize one as a person and a member of the community. But violent pornography denies recognition to women and portrays violence against them as legitimate and desirable. To the extent that men who consume such pornography accept the view it presents, they do not recognize women as persons with a right to be free from violence. It is entirely reasonable for women not to trust such men to respect their safety. Thus, by violating the right to recognition, violent pornography also tends to undermine the right to personal security. This effect does not seem powerful enough, standing alone, to make violent pornography wrongful. But it does reinforce the other reasons for reaching this conclusion.

The right to equality. Finally, rights theory lends support to the radical feminist claim that violent pornography subordinates women and denies them equality. As we have seen, the natural rights tradition holds that human beings are obligated to recognize and treat one another as equals.[33] According to Locke, this principle of equality is violated by any effort to impose domination or *"Subordination"* on others, by dealing with them as though they were "inferior" beings who were "made for [our own] uses" rather than "equal and independent" persons. By portraying women as mere sexual objects who can be used or even "destroy[ed]" at the "[p]leasure" of others, violent pornography denies them recognition as human beings.[34] In this way, it violates their right to equality. This right is also denied to the extent that violent pornography infringes women's substantive rights on the basis of gender.

ARE THESE INJURIES TO WOMEN OUTWEIGHED BY
THE VALUE OF THE SPEECH?

Violent pornography in general. In the preceding section, I argued that violent pornography infringes women's rights in several ways: by denying them recognition, inflicting injury to personality, threatening personal security, and undermining equality. Under the liberal humanist approach, the next question is whether this form of expression is nevertheless entitled to protection under the First Amendment. To answer this question, one must assess the rights involved on both sides.

One of the strongest arguments for protecting pornography is that it promotes individual self-fulfillment.[35] Thus, opponents of regulation might say that even if violent pornography does infringe women's rights, this injury is outweighed by the contribution it makes to the fulfillment of those who produce and consume it.

This argument is unconvincing for several reasons. First, as we saw in chapter 5, the balancing of rights is subject to an important constraint: a putative right can derive no value from its negation of another right.[36] Although some consumers of pornography derive satisfaction from depictions of violence against women, that cannot count as a reason to protect it, for that is precisely what makes the material wrongful in the first place. Some analogies should make this point crystal clear. No one would contend that an individual's right to be free from rape should be balanced against the pleasure a rapist might derive from it. If there is a right to be free from coerced sex, then the desire to force sex on another is wrongful in itself and cannot count as a reason to protect this conduct. This point is not limited to physical wrongs but extends to dignitary ones as well. Thus, no one would claim that an individual's right to privacy should be balanced against the pleasure a voyeur might take in invading it. The same is true of violent pornography: if it infringes women's rights, then the fact that some people derive pleasure from that violation cannot count as a reason to protect it.

On one level, this discussion merely highlights the point that individuals have no right to pursue their own self-realization in a way that interferes with the rightful self-realization of others. But one may also question the value of the fulfillment that can be derived from violent pornography. As I have suggested, the self is a unity of the general and the particular: it consists not only of what makes one unique, but also of the general qualities one shares with others.[37] The most basic of these is humanity. To fully realize this quality, one must recognize one's kinship with other people. But violent pornography disrespects the humanity of others and is therefore at odds with one's own humanity. Although viewing violent pornography may satisfy one's particular desires, it does so only at the expense of another, deeper aspect of self-fulfillment, the realization of one's nature as a human being.

To put this point a different way, the self has a social as well as an individual side. As Mill observes, rules that require individuals to respect the rights of others tend to develop "the social part of [one's] nature" by cultivating "the feelings and capacities which have the good of others for their object." At the same time, such rules are necessary to protect the ability of others to engage in self-realization. It follows that rules of this sort do not undermine human development but rather promote it.[38]

The self-fulfillment argument is also unpersuasive for another reason—one that has to do with the nature of sexual desire. In contrast to hunger and thirst, sexual desire is (at least characteristically) not a desire for a nonhuman object but a desire for another human being. In other words, sexual desire is inherently relational. Similarly, the right to fulfill one's desires through relations with another person is what I have called a relational right—a right to interact with others in a certain way or to participate in a common activity or good. As a relational right, it must be exercised in a way that is consistent with the rights of the other participants.[39] It follows that sexual freedom does not include the ability to satisfy one's desires in a way that infringes the rights of other persons who are the objects of those desires. Once again, this is clear in the case of rape and invasion of privacy. It is also true of violent pornography, which portrays women collectively in a way that is inconsistent with their fundamental rights.[40] For all of these reasons, a ban on violent pornography would not interfere with the right to pursue self-fulfillment.

At the same time, such a ban would undeniably impose some limits on individual autonomy, that is, on the freedom to determine one's own expression, whatever its content. But while autonomy is an important value, it has considerably less weight when divorced from the value of self-fulfillment. In this situation, the autonomy value does not seem substantial enough to outweigh the serious impact that violent pornography has on women's rights. As a general rule, then, violent pornography is not entitled to protection under the First Amendment.

Material that has serious value. What of sexual material that portrays violence against women but that nevertheless has serious literary or artistic value? Should this material receive protection under a liberal humanist approach to the First Amendment? In many cases, works with serious value do not violate the rights of women at all. Consider a film that graphically portrays rape for the purpose of showing how brutal and degrading it is. Although this work depicts violence against women, it does not do so in a way that is intended to represent such violence as legitimate or desirable.[41] For this reason, the work does not violate the right to recognition or the other rights I have discussed.

The same is true of many other works with serious value. For the most part, such works portray people not as generic types, but as individual characters with distinctive traits and personalities. Because as readers or viewers we tend to care about such characters, such works generally do not portray violence against them as legitimate or desirable (except in cases where violence is legally or morally justified).[42] Moreover, even in cases where violence is portrayed as legitimate or desirable, if the violence is directed against individualized characters, the work is best understood as a story about *those particular characters,* rather than about *women in general.* Because the work does not explicitly or implicitly refer to women in general, it does not violate their rights.

In cases like this, the work does not injure others at all, and so there is no need to reach the question of whether the injury is outweighed by the value of the speech. Suppose, however, that there are works that do portray women in a generic way and that represent violence against them as legitimate and desirable, but that nevertheless have serious literary or artistic value. Should works of this sort (say, those of the Marquis de Sade) be protected by the First Amendment? On one side, it might be argued that, because the right to recognition is the foundation of all other rights, it should prevail whenever it conflicts with other rights, including the freedom of speech. To put the point a different way, all of the rights an individual has ultimately depend on his right to recognition. But this right carries with it a duty to recognize others as persons. Individuals can have no rights that conflict with this fundamental obligation. It follows that the freedom of speech does not extend to speech that denies recognition to others.[43]

Although these arguments have great force as applied to violent pornography in general, I believe that the opposite view is more persuasive as applied to works that have serious literary or artistic value, in the sense that they seek to affect our basic understanding of human life and the world. Works of this sort make some contribution to the intellectual realm, while their impact on the rights of others is limited. Under these circumstances, it is reasonable to afford them constitutional protection.

I should make clear that, in saying this, I do not mean to imply that such works should be protected because they may turn out to be true. Recognition is not only the most fundamental right: it is also a basic condition for the pursuit of truth.[44] The search for truth requires a willingness to move beyond the bounds of one's subjective standpoint and to engage in dialogue with others in order to develop a deeper understanding of oneself and the world. To do so, one must recognize others as human beings who are capable of taking part in such a dialogue. Indeed, mutual recognition is not merely an essential condition for the search for truth; it will also be an integral part of any truth that is arrived at through this process.

Thus, there are strong reasons to conclude that recognition-denying speech is contrary to the fundamental truth about human beings. Nevertheless, as Mill argues, even false speech can add to the discussion, if only by leading to a clearer perception of the truth and by giving us greater assurance that all viewpoints have been considered.[45] Moreover, serious works of art or literature generally express some truths, even if they also deny recognition to other people. In this way, they contribute to a more comprehensive understanding. Critical engagement with such works also promotes the development of our intellectual and moral faculties. Finally, in addressing the reader or viewer as an intelligent person, a serious work of art or literature may be said to recognize her humanity in a practical way — even when she turns out to be one of the very people whose humanity the work means to deny. In this deeply ironic sense, serious works of art and literature are compelled to recognize the humanity of others, even when they are intended to do the opposite.

In short, while the law should generally be allowed to restrict violent pornography, works that have serious value should be protected under the First Amendment, either on the ground that they do not injure the rights of others or on the ground that the injury they cause is outweighed by their value. Of course, this does not imply that feminists are not justified in criticizing such works and combating their influence. Indeed, the Millian arguments for freedom of speech and thought depend on the notion that false beliefs will be subjected to vigorous criticism. Although serious works have a right to constitutional protection, those works that deny recognition to others are properly regarded as immoral and injurious to the social and cultural life of the community. These effects should be combated through means other than legal regulation. To put it another way, the struggle for recognition is one that takes place on many levels — legal, political, moral, social, and cultural. Law plays an essential part in this effort, but other forms of action are no less important.[46]

JUDICIAL DECISIONS

Now let us see how feminist concerns about pornography have fared in the courts. In *Butler v. Regina* (1992), the Supreme Court of Canada adopted a position much like the one I have argued for in this section. *Butler* was a challenge to the validity of a federal law banning various forms of obscene material. Although the statute was originally based on the traditional view that such materials undermine public morality, the court held that this rationale was no longer sufficient to justify the law after the adoption of the Canadian Charter of Rights and Freedoms in 1982. Because the statute restricted communication on the basis of content, the court found that it infringed the right to freedom of expression secured by section 2(b) of the Charter. The dispositive question then became whether this restriction was permissible under section 1, which provides that all Charter rights are subject to "such reasonable limits prescribed by law as can be demonstrably justified in a free and democratic society." On this point, the court ruled that although a general ban on pornography could not be justified, the legislature could properly ban violent and degrading material. On one hand, such material generally had little value. On the other hand, the legislature could reasonably believe that the material caused substantial harm to women by undermining their rights to dignity, equality, and freedom from violence — values that were "of fundamental importance in a free and democratic society." In these ways, violent and degrading pornography also contravened the fundamental norms of the community. The court concluded that such pornography fell outside the Charter's protection. At the same time, the court recognized an exception for works of serious value.[47]

In the United States, the courts have taken a very different approach to pornography. In *Miller* and *Paris,* the Supreme Court upheld the traditional morality-based view.[48] At least thus far, however, the courts have rejected an approach based on feminist concerns. The leading case is *American Booksellers Association v. Hudnut* (1985), in which Judge Easterbrook, writing for a panel of the U.S. Court of Appeals for the Seventh Circuit, ruled that an Indianapolis ordinance based on the MacKinnon–Dworkin model violated the First Amendment. Remarkably, Easterbrook did not deny that pornography causes serious harm to women. On the contrary, he wrote, "[W]e accept the premises of this legislation. Depictions of subordination tend to perpetuate subordination. The subordinate status of women in turn leads to affront and lower pay at work, insult and injury at home, battery and rape on the streets. In the language of the legislature, 'pornography is central in creating and maintaining sex as a basis of discrimination. Pornography is a systematic practice of exploitation and subordination based on sex which differentially harms women. The bigotry and contempt it produces, with the acts of aggression it fosters, harm women's opportunities for equality and rights [of all kinds].' "[49]

Yet all of this, Easterbrook continued, "simply demonstrates the power of pornography as speech." Under the First Amendment, that is a matter for the people to determine: "[A]n idea is as powerful as the audience allows it to be." Easterbrook acknowledged that ideas could be "pernicious": "The beliefs of the Nazis led to the death of millions, those of the Klan to the repression of millions." But he argued that the First Amendment does not permit speech to be restricted on this ground. Any other approach would "leave[] the government in control of all the institutions of culture, the great censor and director of which thoughts are good for us."[50]

In general terms, then, Easterbrook's objection to the Indianapolis ordinance was that it restricted speech because of the ideas it contained, or because of the danger that those ideas would lead to "unhappy consequences" such as violence and discrimination. But Easterbrook's objection also took a more specific form. By defining pornography in terms of the subordination of women, the ordinance had "establishe[d] an 'approved' view of women, of how they may react to sexual encounters, of how the sexes may relate to each other. Those who espouse the approved view may use sexual images; those who do not, may not." In this way, the ordinance favored one perspective over another in violation of the fundamental First Amendment rule against view-point discrimination.[51]

The rights-based theory provides a response to both objections. It is certainly true, as Easterbrook argues, that under the First Amendment government may not restrict speech merely because it disapproves of the ideas expressed or because it fears that the speech may be effective. But the First Amendment should not be interpreted to protect speech that invades the rights of others. The central question in a case like *Hudnut* should be whether particular forms of pornography infringe those rights without adequate justification. If so, then the speech may be regulated without violating either the general principles of the First Amendment or the rule against viewpoint discrimination in particular.[52]

RESTRICTIONS ON VIOLENT PORNOGRAPHY AND THE *MILLER* DOCTRINE

If my argument is correct, then as a matter of principle violent pornography should be regarded as outside the protection of the First Amendment. As we have seen, however, even when a regulation is justifiable on substantive grounds, it may be improper for other reasons. In particular, a regulation must be carefully reviewed for vagueness and overbreadth to ensure that it draws the line between lawful and unlawful speech in a reasonably clear way and that it sweeps no more broadly than necessary to protect the rights of others.[53] In my view, the Indianapolis ordinance was objectionable on these grounds.[54] Would the same be true of laws that were limited to violent pornography? Like so many aspects of the pornography debate, this question is certain to be controversial.[55] One point seems clear, however: the approach I am advocating is less problematic in this regard than the Supreme Court's current doctrine. Under the test formulated in *Miller v. California,* a work may be banned as obscene if "(a) . . . the average person, applying contemporary community standards would find that the work, taken as a whole, appeals to the prurient interest, (b) . . . the work depicts or describes, in a patently offensive way, sexual conduct specifically defined by the applicable state law; and (c) . . . the work, taken as a whole, lacks serious literary, artistic, political, or scientific value."[56]

The restrictions I have defended would regulate only material that falls within this definition, and would further be limited to material that portrays sexual violence against a group of people. A law of this sort not only would be consistent with the *Miller* standard, it would be *narrower* than the obscenity laws that are permitted by that standard.[57] Thus, even from a civil libertarian perspective, this approach would seem to represent an advance over current law.

As this discussion shows, antipornography laws that focus on harm to women need not conflict with the traditional doctrine set forth in *Miller*. To put it another way, the approach I am advocating seeks to develop some common ground between the traditional and feminist positions, by contending that the portrayals that are most contrary to contemporary community standards are those that glorify sexual violence. Among other advantages, an approach of this sort is likely to be far more effective in moving the law in a feminist direction than a position that emphasizes the differences between the feminist view and traditional law.[58]

Pornography and the Rights of the Community

I now want to turn to conservative concerns about obscenity and pornography. Traditionally, obscenity was banned on the ground that it tended "to deprave and corrupt those whose minds are open to such immoral influences."[59] Insofar as the conservative position is based on this view, it is at odds with the theory I have developed in this book. That theory does not allow expression to be restricted merely because the community regards it as improper or wants to protect individuals who choose to view it from moral harm.

To what extent can the conservative position be accommodated within a rights-based framework? When recast in these terms, the conservative view focuses on the rights of communities. It asserts that the society should have some power to regulate pornography to protect the quality of our common life. Although this position is primarily identified with moral conservatives, it may also be regarded as a communitarian view.[60]

In this section, I argue that the notion of community rights justifies the regulation of pornography in three ways. First, *violent pornography* constitutes a wrong not only to women, but also to the community as a whole. Such material may be banned without violating the First Amendment. Second, the law may restrict the display of sexual material in order to protect the public environment as well as the rights of unwilling viewers. Finally, the community should have the power to shield children from exposure to pornography. In these ways, I believe that a liberal humanist approach can meet some of the conservative and communitarian concerns about pornography while at the same time protecting a broad right to free expression.

VIOLENT PORNOGRAPHY

The previous section argued that, by portraying women as mere objects that can be used or destroyed at will, violent pornography denies them recognition as human beings. As I explained in chapter 10, however, recognition is not only an individual right but also the bond that holds the community together. In Lockean terms, speech that denies recognition to others "undermines the Foundations of Society."[61] For this reason, it constitutes a wrong to the community as well as to the particular people who are affected.

Violent pornography also infringes women's rights in several other ways. But wrongs to individuals often constitute wrongs to the community as well. From a rights-based perspective, the deepest explanation for this is that fundamental rights belong to all persons or members of society. Thus, an act that violates such a right injures all who share that right — the entire community — and not merely the victim himself. It is for this reason that many violations of individual rights are regarded not only as torts but also as crimes.[62]

As I argued above, violent pornography diminishes women's personal security, invades their dignity, and undermines their right to equality. In these ways it infringes rights that belong not merely to women but to all members of society. For this reason as well, violent pornography may be regarded as a wrong against the community as a whole.

PUBLIC PLACES

Another concern shared by conservatives and communitarians relates to the impact of pornography on the public environment. I believe this concern too can be met, at least in part, under a rights-based approach. In particular, communities should have the right to outlaw pornographic displays in public places.

This argument draws on the account of First Amendment activity I presented in chapter 6. In addition to inward thought and feeling, the First Amendment protects outward expression and communication. The function of communication is not merely to convey ideas from one person to another, but also to develop a shared understanding, by transforming a matter of individual awareness and concern into a matter of common awareness and concern. At the same time, communication establishes, or takes place within, a relationship between the participants. In these ways, communication has a social as well as an individual dimension.[63]

On this view, communication can be a matter of common concern to smaller or larger groups of people — from two or more individuals to social groups or organizations to all citizens or human beings in general. Thus, whether speech is "public" or "private" is a matter of degree. In rough terms, however, one can distinguish between expression that is private, in the sense that it is of concern to an individual or a small circle of people, and expression that is public, in the sense that it is of common concern to a substantial portion of the community.[64]

In general, pornography should be regarded as falling on the private side of the spectrum. Because the predominant goal of pornography is to stimulate or satisfy the sexual desires of individuals, it relates to a matter that is intensely personal. Pornographic material may have value for those who choose to view it, but it is not a matter of public interest in the way that political, literary, artistic, scientific, and other forms of discourse are. Likewise, the activity of viewing pornography is a private form of activity which is directed toward individual self-fulfillment.

Several important conclusions follow. First, as the Supreme Court held in *Stanley v. Georgia* (1969), the state may not ban the mere private possession of pornography. The First Amendment and the right to privacy protect the individual's liberty "to read or observe what he pleases" as well as "the right to satisfy his intellectual and emotional needs in the privacy of his own home."[65]

Second, just as individuals should be free to view pornography, they also should be free *not* to. It follows that one has no right to expose other people to such material without their consent. Precisely because such material is so deeply personal, individuals should be allowed to decide for themselves whether or not to watch it. To put the point another way, the activity of viewing pornography may be regarded not only as a kind of expression, but also as a kind of sexual experience. But no one has a right to force a sexual experience on another against her will. To expose an unwilling viewer to pornography is an invasion of privacy, or the right to be free from highly offensive intrusions into one's personal life. Such conduct may also violate the right to be free from unjustified infliction of emotional distress.[66] In a workplace setting, this conduct may constitute a form of sexual harassment.[67] Finally, far from deserving constitutional protection, this conduct runs counter to the basic principle of *Stanley* — that individuals should have the autonomy to decide for themselves what to read or view. In this situation, then, the law is clearly justified in protecting what the Court has called "[t]he unwilling listener's interest in avoiding unwanted communication."[68]

Third, and somewhat more controversially, the right of individuals to be free from unwanted exposure to pornography should apply in the public as well as in the private sphere. It is true, as Justice Harlan remarked in *Cohen v. California* (1971), "that we are often 'captives' outside the sanctuary of the home and subject to objectionable speech."[69] But this observation was made in the context of expression that was public in character, namely, a protest against the Vietnam War. Speech that is intended as a contribution to public debate and that does not violate the rights of others may not be restricted merely to protect individual sensibilities. But the act of exposing unwilling viewers to pornographic material does violate their rights.[70] And because such material is private in nature, it is not entitled to the same immunity as public speech in public places.

Up to this point, my argument has focused on the private rights of individuals. It is on this ground that many liberals would support a ban on public display.[71] At the same time, I believe that such a ban can also be justified by reference to the rights of the community and its members, as conservatives and communitarians would urge. This argument can be made in two ways. The first is based on the right to control the public environment. That environment is a matter of common awareness and therefore a matter of concern to the entire community. For this reason, the community should generally be allowed to regulate activities that affect the public environment — for example, by adopting various forms of aesthetic regulation.[72] Under the First Amendment, this power does not extend to content-based regulation of speech on matters of common concern.[73] As I have argued, however, pornography is not a public but a private form of expression. For these reasons, the community should have the right to regulate the public display of pornography.

A second argument is more substantive in nature. Just as private places such as the home allow individuals to develop their inner lives, public spaces enable us to develop a shared life as a community. For this reason, speech or conduct that relates to matters of common concern has a strong claim to protection in public places. Conversely, speech or conduct that is intensely personal is inappropriate in the public sphere.[74] For example, individuals have no right to engage in sex acts in public places. As Mill observes, while such acts may be perfectly appropriate in themselves, when they are performed in public they violate accepted standards of decency and propriety. In this way they constitute an offense against other persons who are exposed to them without their consent.[75] Moreover, because indecent acts have an adverse impact on the public environment, they constitute an offense against the community as well.

Similar considerations support a ban on the public display of pornographic material. Because such material is highly personal, it is out of place in the public realm. In addition, because pornography represents some people primarily as sexual objects, the display of this material is inconsistent with the respect citizens ought to show one another in the public sphere. It follows that the community should have the power to ban such displays in the interest of the public environment as well as to safeguard the rights of unwilling viewers.[76]

Conservatives go further and contend that the government should be allowed to outlaw obscenity in order to protect the ethos of the community, that is, its moral standards and way of life.[77] As Chief Justice Burger expressed it in *Paris,* the claim is that the nation and the states have "a right . . . to maintain a decent society."[78] But it is one thing to restrict pornography because of its direct impact on the public environment, and quite another thing to restrict it because of the indirect effects that may flow from private choices to make or view this material. If, as I have argued, those choices fall within the fundamental freedoms protected by the First Amendment, then to restrict them on this ground would violate the autonomy of individuals to determine the content of their own expression and to control their own inner lives. Although the state can promote cultural values in a positive way by means of education and public support for the arts, it should not be permitted to shape the culture in a coercive manner by interfering with private decisions of this sort, so long as they do not violate the concrete rights of others.

SHIELDING CHILDREN FROM PORNOGRAPHY

Finally, the community should have the authority to protect children from exposure to pornography. Although individuals should generally have the right to read or view whatever they please, this right does not apply with the same force to children. In the liberal tradition, rights are grounded in the capacity for rational self-direction. Because children do not fully possess this capacity, their autonomy is limited. Instead, others must care for them, not only to safeguard their physical well-being, but also to promote their intellectual, emotional, and moral development and to enable them to develop into autonomous individuals.[79] In a liberal society, this responsibility primarily belongs to parents, who have a right "to direct the upbringing and education of [their] children."[80] It follows that parents should have some authority to decide what forms of expression their children are exposed to and to shield them from material the parents reasonably believe to be harmful, such as material that contains graphic sex or violence.[81]

It may seem that this responsibility should rest solely with parents, and that the state should have no role. But the widespread availability of such material in the larger society makes it virtually impossible for parents to act effectively on their own. Instead, if parents are to have meaningful rights in this area, the community must have the power to regulate the manner in which such material is distributed.[82] Moreover, the society and its culture inevitably have a pervasive influence on the character of its members. Although liberalism presumes that adults are sufficiently autonomous to resist harmful social and cultural influences, this assumption cannot be made with regard to children. The society should therefore have a duty to restrain itself and its members (including those who make and sell pornography) from exposing minors to material the community reasonably believes to be harmful.

In short, the community's authority in this area rests on two related justifications: (1) it is legitimate for the state to assist parents in the exercise of their own authority to protect against material they reasonably consider to be harmful; and (2) the society has an independent duty to restrain itself and its members from exposing children to material it reasonably believes to be harmful. In both cases, the community must make a judgment about what material is harmful to children. At the same time, the community must determine how much value a particular form of material has, for regulation is justified only when it is reasonable to believe that the harm that flows from the material outweighs its value. Restrictions that cannot be justified in this way are not only improper, but may also violate the First Amendment rights of older minors to decide for themselves what forms of expression to see or hear.[83] Although children are not fully autonomous, their capacity for self-determination grows over time. As they approach adulthood, they develop an increasing capacity to exercise rights to express themselves and to receive information and ideas. While parents and the state retain the authority to impose appropriate restrictions, regulations that are unreasonable may violate the First Amendment.

Of course, the question of what material is harmful to children is a controversial one. This is especially true in the area of sexuality. Some people doubt that minors are harmed by exposure to pornographic material or that such material can reasonably be distinguished from other forms of expression (such as information regarding contraception, reproductive health services, and sexually transmitted diseases) that minors should have access to.[84] It is fair to say, however, that most people in American society believe that children should not be exposed to pornography. To be sure, they would give different explanations for this position. Conservatives hold that pornography conflicts with appropriate moral attitudes toward sexuality, while many feminists believe the material is degrading to women. Finally, while liberals are less inclined to regard pornography as harmful in general, many would regard it as inappropriate for children — for example, on the ground that it portrays sexuality in a depersonalized way that undermines the connection between sex and love. Although these views differ in rationale, they agree in the ultimate position they take. This strengthens the case for regulation, by showing that multiple perspectives lead to the same result.[85] Moreover, these views are not mutually exclusive: many people believe that pornography is harmful to children for several or even all of these reasons. Although this position is controversial, it is far from unreasonable. Thus, laws that shield children from pornography should be regarded as falling within the community's authority to make reasonable judgments about what material is harmful to them, so long as such laws do not unduly infringe other interests of minors or adults.

The view I have outlined is broadly consistent with the Supreme Court's decisions in this area. In a leading case, *Ginsberg v. New York* (1968), Justice Brennan declared that a state legislature "could properly conclude that parents and others . . . who have . . . primary responsibility for children's well-being are entitled to the support of laws designed to aid discharge of that responsibility." Moreover, "[t]he State . . . has an independent interest in the well-being of its youth." Deferring to the legislature's determination that exposure to pornography tends to "impair[] the ethical and moral development" of young people, Brennan sustained the constitutionality of a New York law that barred the sale to persons under the age of seventeen of material that met the prevailing test for obscenity, as adapted to apply to minors.[86] In subsequent cases, the Court has repeatedly recognized that the state has "a compelling interest in protecting the physical and psychological well-being of minors," and that "[t]his interest extends to shielding [them] from the influence of [material] that is not obscene by adult standards." At the same time, the Court has made clear that this "interest does not justify an unnecessarily broad suppression of speech addressed to adults."[87]

How should the First Amendment apply to cases where the interests of both adults and children are involved? In some situations this problem poses little difficulty. For example, it is possible to require identification for entry to adult bookstores and establishments and in this way to effectively exclude most minors. However, in some other contexts, such as the Internet, it is not yet technologically feasible to shield children from exposure to sexual material without imposing some burdens on adult access.[88] In several recent cases, the Court has shown a strong tendency to protect the interests of adults in this situation.[89] Treating laws designed to protect children as content-based restrictions on the First Amendment rights of adults, the Court has subjected those laws to "the most stringent review" and has struck them down if they are unable to meet the demanding requirements of strict scrutiny.[90] In my view, however, a more nuanced approach is called for. From a liberal humanist perspective, the problem is one of reconciling competing claims: the rights of adults to view pornography, on one hand, and the rights of parents and the community to shield children from such material, on the other. Resolving this problem calls for a careful consideration of the nature and value of the rights on both sides, as well as of the alternative ways in which each interest can be satisfied.[91]

On this view, the Court in *Reno v. ACLU* (1997) was clearly justified in striking down Congress's first effort to regulate Internet pornography, the Communications Decency Act of 1996 (CDA), for that statute was far broader than necessary to shield children from harmful material.[92] In response to that decision, Congress passed the Child Online Protection Act of 1998 (COPA). In contrast to the CDA, COPA was drafted in a careful and narrow manner. The Act imposed criminal penalties for posting on the World Wide Web material that was "harmful to minors," a term that was defined to incorporate the obscenity standard of *Miller v. California,* as adapted to children under the age of seventeen. The statute applied only to material that was posted for commercial purposes and it exempted material that had serious value for minors. At the same time, in order to protect free speech interests, COPA allowed material that was harmful to minors to be posted on the Web so long as it was placed behind "identification screens" designed to limit access to adults (for example, by requiring the use of a credit card or an adult personal identification number). After COPA was enacted, the ACLU and others filed a federal lawsuit challenging the statute under the First Amendment. Ruling that the plaintiffs were likely to succeed on their claim, the lower courts barred enforcement of the law pending trial, and the government appealed to the Supreme Court.[93]

Writing for a five to four majority in *Ashcroft v. ACLU* (2004), Justice Kennedy held that COPA was unlikely to satisfy the demands of strict scrutiny because the government had failed to prove that a criminal statute was the least restrictive way to protect minors from harmful material. In particular, he asserted that the use of filtering software by parents might well prove more effective, without imposing any restriction on the First Amendment freedoms of adults. For these reasons, he concluded that the statute was probably unconstitutional and upheld the injunction.[94]

This analysis was misguided. As Justice Breyer pointed out in dissent, "the presence of filtering software is not an *alternative* legislative approach to the problem," but "is part of the status quo, *i.e.,* the backdrop against which Congress enacted the present statute." In other words, filtering software is already available. The question is whether it provides an adequate solution to the problem, and if not, whether COPA would afford further protection without imposing an unwarranted burden on the First Amendment rights of adults. As Breyer explained, at least in its current form, filtering software is inadequate in several respects: it imposes a significant monetary cost on families; it depends on the ability and willingness of parents to monitor their children's Internet use; and it lacks precision, blocking much valuable material while failing to block some pornography. Under these circumstances, it is reasonable to believe that COPA would provide significant additional protection. Moreover, while COPA would impose some burden on adults who wish to view pornography, that burden is a relatively modest one.[95]

For these reasons, the Court should have upheld COPA as a reasonable effort to reconcile the competing values at stake. The majority's position seems to reflect the view that protecting children in this area is a task for parents and not for the government. As I have suggested, however, this view is unrealistic. However diligent parents may be, they lack the ability to effectively shield their children from harmful influences in the broader culture. Thus, society as a whole cannot escape its own responsibility in this area.[96]

Conclusion

In recent years, the debate over pornography has been dominated by three perspectives: conservative, liberal, and radical feminist. Although each position has considerable force, none fully captures our intuitions on the subject. Instead, we should seek to reconcile these conflicting perspectives within a more complex view. In this chapter, I have argued that the rights-based theory is capable of performing this task. Under this approach, individuals should enjoy broad freedom to make and view sexually oriented materials. But this protection should not extend to material that invades the rights of others. By denying recognition to women, violent pornography infringes their rights as well as those of the community as a whole. The community should also have the authority to exclude pornography from the public sphere and to shield children from such material. Contrary to the Court's traditional doctrine, however, the state should have no general authority to ban material it considers obscene, for that would violate the autonomy of individuals to determine the content of their own thought and expression. In this way, we can ensure broad protection for free speech without unduly sacrificing the values of equality and community that lie at the core of the feminist and conservative positions.

Conclusion

Law is not merely an instrument of social control but an embodiment of our fundamental values and aspirations. The law reflects our image of ourselves as individuals and as a community. At the same time, by shaping our lives in particular ways, the law seeks to realize that image in the social world.

As Americans, we conceive of ourselves as being free. Although the American idea of freedom is sometimes equated with negative liberty or the absence of governmental oppression, it is actually much broader than that.[1] Our conception of liberty includes the ability to direct our own lives, to pursue self-fulfillment, to participate in the social and political life of the community, and to search for meaning in the world. At the deepest level, our conception of liberty is bound up with our sense of self-worth, that is, with the belief that we count for something, that we are persons who are entitled to dignity and respect. This rich and complex understanding of freedom lies at the core of the modern liberal defense of free speech. On this view, speech should be protected not only as a form of external liberty, but also because it is essential for individual self-realization, democratic self-government, and the pursuit of truth.

As many critics have argued, however, free speech also has a dark side. Although expression can be used to promote the development of individual personality and democratic community, it can also be used to undermine those values. That is the case when speech is used to threaten or incite violence against others, to obstruct their self-realization, or to deny their equal status as human beings and citizens. To combat these evils, the critics contend that the law should restrict these forms of "assaultive speech."[2] Yet they have been unable to fully explain how such restrictions can be reconciled with our constitutional commitment to freedom of expression. In this way, we seem to be faced with an inescapable conflict between free speech and human dignity — a conflict that goes to the heart of our conception of ourselves and our constitutional order.

In this book, I have developed a liberal humanist theory of the First Amendment. According to this view, liberty and dignity are not opposing values but integral elements of a unified conception of the person as a free being of intrinsic worth — a conception that forms the basis of a liberal democratic society. It follows that there is no inherent conflict between free speech and human dignity. Instead, expressive liberty should be understood within a broader framework of rights, ranging from personal security and personality to citizenship and equality. Speech that criticizes the government or the existing political order should receive the strongest possible protection. At the same time, the law should be allowed to restrict speech that invades the rights of other people. Restrictions of this sort do not detract from the freedom of speech but rather enhance it, by requiring individuals to use their rights in ways that are consistent with the principles of dignity and autonomy on which they are based. It is in this way that we can best achieve the goals of First Amendment jurisprudence: to promote "the continued building of our politics and culture, and to assure self-fulfillment for each individual."[3]

Appendix

Overview of Free Speech and Other Rights*

Category of Rights	Rationale for Freedom of Speech	Other Individual Rights
Rights of Recognition	Demand for recognition (172)	Right to recognition (170–72)
External Rights of Life, Liberty, and Property	External freedom (48)	Personal security (48–50)
Rights of Personality	Individual self-realization (52–54)	Emotional tranquillity (54–55) Privacy (55–57, 149–63) Personal dignity (144–46) Reputation (57–59, 73–77)
Rights of Community	Political freedom (62–64)	Rights of citizenship (61–64, 170–72)
Rights of Intellectual and Spiritual Freedom	Search for truth (64–68)	Search for truth (64–68)
Rights of Equality	Content neutrality (86–87)	Equality (68)

* References in parentheses are to pages.

Other Community Rights	Infringements of Other Rights
Mutual recognition as bond of community (170–72)	Hate speech (170–72) Violent pornography (186–88, 197–98)
The public peace (50–51)	Assaults (49–51) Threats (49–51, 131–36) Fighting words (142–44) Incitement (127–30)
	Intentional infliction (54–55) Invasion of privacy (55–57, 149–63) Insulting words (144–46) Defamation (57–59, 73–77)
Bonds of community (170–72) Democratic self-government (41, 114–15)	Hate speech (170–72) Incitement to imminent overthrow of government (114–15)
Search for truth (64–68)	Hate speech (67–68, 279 n.67)
	Hate speech (166, 172) Violent pornography (190)

Notes

Introduction

1. W. Va. State Bd. of Educ. v. Barnette, 319 U.S. 624, 642 (1943).

2. Police Dep't v. Mosley, 408 U.S. 92, 95–96 (1972).

3. Mari J. Matsuda et al., Words That Wound: Critical Race Theory, Assaultive Speech, and the First Amendment (1993).

Chapter 1. Free Speech and the Natural Rights Tradition

1. For some leading works, see Michael Kent Curtis, Free Speech, "The People's Darling Privilege" (2000) [hereinafter Curtis, Free Speech]; Mark A. Graber, Transforming Free Speech (1991); Harry Kalven, Jr., A Worthy Tradition (Jamie Kalven ed., 1988); Leonard W. Levy, Emergence of a Free Press (1985); David M. Rabban, Free Speech in its Forgotten Years (1997); Geoffrey R. Stone, Perilous Times (2004). For a superb collection of materials that explores many of the authors and ideas discussed in this book, see Vincent Blasi, Ideas of the First Amendment (2006).

2. I should emphasize that this history is merely a starting point: I do not subscribe to the originalist view that the Constitution must be interpreted in accord with the intentions or the understanding of those who adopted it. For a discussion of the role that history should play in constitutional interpretation, see p. 223 n.54.

3. John Locke, Two Treatises of Government bk. II, §§ 4, 6, 123–31 (Peter Laslett ed., Cambridge Univ. Press 1988) (1690) [hereinafter Locke, Government].

4. See, e.g., John Locke, A Letter Concerning Toleration 47 (James Tully ed., Hackett 1983) (William Popple trans., 1689).

5. As Locke explains, "[T]hough Men uniting into politick societies, have resigned up to the publick the disposing of all their Force . . . : yet they retain still the power of Thinking" as they like. John Locke, An Essay Concerning Human Understanding bk. II, ch. XXVIII, at 353 (Peter H. Nidditch ed., Clarendon 1975) (1700). To establish peace and order in civil society, individuals must give up the unrestricted freedom to act and to use force as they see fit. But it is neither necessary nor possible for them to give up the power to think for themselves.

6. *Id.* bk. II, ch. XXI; *id.* bk. IV, ch. XX, at 708; Locke, Government, *supra* note 3, bk. II, § 63; John Locke, Of the Conduct of the Understanding § 6 (1706), *in* Some Thoughts Concerning Understanding and Of the Conduct of the Understanding 178 (Ruth W. Grant & Nathan Tarcov eds., Hackett 1996).

7. *See* Locke, Government, *supra* note 3, bk. II, §§ 87–88, 91, 127–31, 149, 240.

8. John Trenchard & Thomas Gordon, Cato's Letters (Ronald Hamowy ed., Liberty Fund 1995) (1755) [hereinafter Cato's Letters]. On *Cato's Letters* and their influence on the eighteenth-century American understanding of freedom of speech, see David S. Bogen, Bulwark of Liberty 16–21 (1984); Levy, *supra* note 1, at 109–14 (observing that "[i]n the history of political liberty as well as of freedom of speech and press, no eighteenth century work exerted more influence than *Cato's Letters*").

9. *See* Michael P. Zuckert, Natural Rights and the New Republicanism 289–319 (1994).

10. 1 Cato's Letters, *supra* note 8, No. 15, at 111, 114.

11. *Id.* at 113; No. 32, at 228, 231; No. 62, at 428; 2 *id.*, No. 100, at 713–17. The radical Whig ideology of natural rights and resistance to tyranny was also central to the most influential defense of free expression written in colonial America. See James Alexander, A Brief Narrative of the Case and Trial of John Peter Zenger (Stanley Nider Katz ed., Harvard Univ. Press, 2d ed. 1972) (1736).

12. 4 William Blackstone, Commentaries on the Laws of England *151–53 (St. George Tucker ed., Philadelphia, Young & Small 1803).

13. 1 *id.* at *124, *129–40, *145.

14. *Id.* at *41–42, *125; 4 *id.* at *152. Accordingly, Blackstone defined civil liberty as "natural liberty so far restrained by human laws (and no farther) as is necessary and expedient for the general advantage of the public." 1 *id.* at *125.

15. *Id.* at *48, *50–51, *190.

16. *Id.* at *38, *157–58, *271.

17. *Id.* at *127–28, *141, *161–62, *211–15.

18. *Id.* at *241; 4 *id.* at *150–53. Blackstone did acknowledge that human laws could not properly regulate some aspects of natural liberty, including freedom of conscience and thought, so long as they remained strictly private. *See, e.g.,* 4 *id.* at *45, *49, *51–52, *152. More generally, he asserted that civil government had no business interfering with purely private conduct that did not affect other individuals or the society itself. *See* 1 *id.* at *123–24; 4 *id.* at *41–42. Yet his political theory precluded him from treating even these narrowly defined rights as legal limits on government power. According to Blackstone, in all governments there must be some body that possesses sovereign authority. Under the English constitution, this "absolute despotic power" was vested in Parliament, whose authority extended even to altering the constitution itself. 1 *id.* at *48–49, *160–61. For

this reason, if Parliament were to pass a law contrary to reason or justice, the judiciary would not be free to reject it, "for that were to set the judicial power above that of the legislature, which would be subversive of all government." *Id.* at *91.

19. *See* Bernard Bailyn, The Ideological Origins of the American Revolution (enlarged ed., 1992); Gordon S. Wood, The Creation of the American Republic, 1776–1787 (1969). For an account of the influence of radical Whig thought on the early American conception of free speech, see David M. Rabban, *The Ahistorical Historian: Leonard Levy on Freedom of Expression in Early American History,* 37 Stan. L. Rev. 795, 821–36 (1985) (book review). For a valuable discussion of free speech and natural rights in eighteenth-century America, see Philip A. Hamburger, *Natural Rights, Natural Law, and American Constitutions,* 102 Yale L.J. 907 (1993).

20. Pa. Declaration of Rights of 1776, arts. I, IV, XII. Article XIV of the Vermont Declaration of 1777 contained virtually identical language on speech and press. The state declarations may be found in 1 Bernard Schwartz, The Bill of Rights: A Documentary History (1971).

21. Va. Declaration of Rights of 1776, art. 12; Mass. Const. of 1780, pt. 1, arts. X, XI, XVI (emphasis added). On the centrality of reputation and honor in late eighteenth-century American political culture, see Joanne B. Freeman, Affairs of Honor (2001).

22. *See, e.g.,* Petition to Va. House of Delegates (Aug. 1797) (asserting that the people have a "natural right of communicating their sentiments to one another by speaking and writing"), *in* Freedom of the Press from Zenger to Jefferson 349 (Leonard W. Levy ed., 1966) [hereinafter From Zenger to Jefferson]; Letter from Thomas Jefferson to Noah Webster (Dec. 4, 1790) (characterizing freedom of the press as among the "fences which experience has proved peculiarly efficacious against wrong"), *in id.* at 342.

23. *See, e.g.,* Draft Const. for Va. art. IV (June 1776) ("Printing presses shall be free, except so far as by commission of private injury cause may be given for private action."), *in* Thomas Jefferson, Writings 344 (Merrill D. Peterson ed., Library of Am. 1984); Letter from Thomas Jefferson to Rabout de St. Etienne (June 3, 1789) (enclosing a draft charter of rights for France containing a similar provision), *in id.* at 956; Letter from Thomas Jefferson to James Madison (Aug. 28, 1789) (proposing that Madison's draft of the First Amendment be altered to read: "The people shall not be deprived or abridged of their right to speak to write or *otherwise* to publish any thing but false facts affecting injuriously the life, liberty, property, or reputation of others or affecting the peace of the confederacy with foreign nations"), *in* From Zenger to Jefferson, *supra* note 22, at 340. For a persuasive demonstration that eighteenth-century Americans regarded free speech as limited by the rights of others, see Hamburger, *supra* note 19, at 920 & n.41, 928, 936 & n.83, 948–53.

24. *See, e.g.,* Letters of Centinel No. 2, *in* 2 The Complete Anti-Federalist 143–44 (Herbert J. Storing ed., 1981); Letters from the Federal Farmer Nos. 2, 6, *in id.* at 231–32, 262; Speech of Patrick Henry in Va. Ratifying Convention, 3 The Debates in the Several State Conventions on the Adoption of the Federal Constitution 449 (Jonathan Elliot ed., 2d ed. 1836) [hereinafter Elliot's Debates].

25. James Wilson, Speech at a Public Meeting in Philadelphia (Oct. 6, 1787), *in* 1 The Debate on the Constitution 64 (Bernard Bailyn ed., Library of Am. 1993). Wilson added that it would have been not merely useless but dangerous to have included a declaration

on liberty of the press in the Constitution, because such a provision "might have been construed to imply that some degree of power was given, since we undertook to define its extent." *Id.* For similar arguments, see The Federalist No. 84 (Alexander Hamilton).

26. Va. Ratifying Convention, Proposed Bill of Rights, arts. 12th, 16th, *in* 3 Elliot's Debates, *supra* note 24, at 658–59; *see* Hamburger, *supra* note 19, at 950–51. North Carolina called for identical amendments before it would ratify the Constitution. *See* N.C. Ratifying Convention, Proposed Declaration of Rights, arts. 12th, 16th, in 4 Elliot's Debates, *supra* note 24, at 244. For other state proposals on speech and press, see The Complete Bill of Rights 92–93 (Neil H. Cogan ed., 1997).

27. James Madison, Speech to House of Representatives (June 8, 1789), *in* Creating the Bill of Rights: The Documentary Record from the First Federal Congress 77, 78, 80–81, 83 (Helen E. Veit et al. eds., 1991) [hereinafter Madison Speech].

28. Madison Resolution (June 8, 1789), *in* Creating the Bill of Rights, *supra* note 27, at 12; James Madison, Notes for Amendments Speech (1789), *in* 2 Schwartz, *supra* note 20, at 1042.

29. Roger Sherman's Proposed Committee Report (July 21–28, 1789), *in* Creating the Bill of Rights, *supra* note 27, at 266; *id.* at 159 (remarks of Rep. Sedgwick).

30. *See* Wood, *supra* note 19, at 393–518.

31. 2 Elliot's Debates, *supra* note 24, at 449 (remarks of James Wilson).

32. *See* Steven J. Heyman, *Ideological Conflict and the First Amendment,* 78 Chi.-Kent L. Rev. 531, 537–47 (2003).

33. Creating the Bill of Rights, *supra* note 27, at 167–68, 176 (remarks of Rep. Madison); *id.* at 172 (remarks of Rep. Sedgwick).

34. For a comprehensive account of the period, see Stanley Elkins & Eric McKitrick, The Age of Federalism (1993).

35. 1 Stat. 596, § 2 (1798). On the history of the Act, see Curtis, Free Speech, *supra* note 1, chs. 2–4; Elkins & McKitrick, *supra* note 34, ch. XV; Norman L. Rosenberg, Protecting the Best Men ch. 4 (1986); James Morton Smith, Freedom's Fetters (1956); Stone, *supra* note 1, ch. I. For an interesting discussion of its ideological background, see James P. Martin, *When Repression Is Democratic and Constitutional: The Federalist Theory of Representation and the Sedition Act of 1798,* 66 U. Chi. L. Rev. 117 (1999).

36. John Marshall, Report of the Minority on the Virginia Resolutions (Jan. 22, 1799), *in* 5 The Founders' Constitution 136, 138 (Philip B. Kurland & Ralph Lerner eds., 1987).

37. For Wilson's view, see pp. 14–15.

38. Marshall, *supra* note 36, at 137–38. Some other Federalists recast Blackstone in the same way. *See, e.g.,* H. Select Comm., Report on Petitions for Repeal of Alien and Sedition Laws, *in* 9 Annals of Cong. 2986, 2988 (1799) (asserting that liberty of the press consists in "a permission to publish, without previous restraint, whatever [one] may think proper, being answerable to the public and individuals, for any abuse of this permission to their prejudice"). Other Federalists endorsed the Blackstonian view in its pure form. *See, e.g.,* In re Fries, 9 F. Cas. 826, 839–40 (C.C.D. Pa. 1799) (No. 5,126) (charge of Iredell, J., to grand jury).

39. James Madison, Report on the Virginia Resolutions (Jan. 1800), *in* 5 The Founders' Constitution, *supra* note 36, at 141, 142 [hereinafter Madison Report].

40. *Id.* at 144–45.

41. *See, e.g., id.* at 143–44.

42. *See, e.g.,* Akhil Reed Amar, The Bill of Rights 36 & 326 n.78 (1998). That is not to say that the Republican position on this point was beyond dispute. After all, those who advocated a bill of rights during the ratification struggle did not take these Federalist assertions at face value or find them convincing. They feared that some provisions of the Constitution, such as the taxation and necessary-and-proper clauses of article I, section 8, might give Congress power to interfere with the press. In addition, the Republicans' position rested to a considerable extent on their strong commitment to state power and their strict-constructionist approach to constitutional interpretation, both of which were highly controversial. Finally, while it is clear that the Constitution granted no express power over the press, it does not follow that Congress's incidental powers could never extend to speech or press. An example may be found in the Sedition Act itself. Although the Republicans strenuously attacked section 2 of the Act, which punished seditious libels, they rarely objected to section 1, which among other things made it an offense to counsel riot or insurrection with the intent to oppose any law of the United States or to prevent any federal officer from performing his duty. 1 Stat. 596, § 1; *see* Martin, *supra* note 35, at 122 n.7. Of course, it would have been very difficult to argue that no provision of the Constitution, including the necessary-and-proper clause, gave Congress the power to punish expression of this sort (at least if it took the form of direct and immediate incitement), or that such expression was protected by the First Amendment.

43. *See* Madison Report, *supra* note 39, at 143.

44. *See* pp. 11–14; David A. Anderson, *The Origins of the Press Clause,* 30 UCLA L. Rev. 455, 508 (1983). In his 1800 Report, Madison emphasized that when the Virginia Convention ratified the Constitution, it declared "that, among other essential rights, the liberty of conscience and of the press cannot be cancelled, abridged, restrained, or modified, by any authority of the United States." Although this statement did indeed constitute a "positive denial" that Congress had any power over the press, Virginia's proposal for a constitutional amendment did not take this form, but instead followed the language of the state declarations of rights. *See* p. 13; Anderson, *supra,* at 502.

45. Madison Resolution, *supra* note 28, at 13; Madison Speech, *supra* note 27, at 80–83, 85. Madison added that, while some states already protected those rights in their own constitutions, others did not, and that no harm would be done by providing "a double security on those points." *Id.* at 85.

46. *See* Creating the Bill of Rights, *supra* note 27, at 38, 41.

47. *See* The Complete Bill of Rights, *supra* note 26, at 86–87.

48. For modern defenses of the federalism reading, see Amar, *supra* note 42, at 36–41; Levy, *supra* note 1, at 269–71; William T. Mayton, *Seditious Libel and the Lost Guarantee of a Freedom of Expression,* 84 Colum. L. Rev. 91 (1984). For an effective critique of this view, see Anderson, *supra* note 44, at 500–09.

49. *Compare* Letter from Thomas Jefferson to Abigail Adams (Sept. 11, 1804) (reaffirming the states' power to restrain "the overwhelming torrent of slander, which is confounding all vice and virtue, all truth & falsehood, in the U.S."), *in* From Zenger to Jefferson, *supra* note 22, at 367, *with* Minority Report on Repeal of Sedition Act, 9 Annals of Cong. 3003–14 (1799) (arguing that the doctrine of seditious libel is "obsolete" and "inconsistent with the nature of our Government"), *reprinted in id.* at 176–86.

50. St. George Tucker, *Of the Right of Conscience; and of the Freedom of Speech and of the Press, in* 1 Blackstone, *supra* note 12, app., note G, at 11 (emphasis added); *see also id.* at 28–30. Similarly, George Hay, a Republican lawyer and member of the Virginia House of Delegates, contended that liberty of the press consisted in the "absolute freedom" to publish whatever one pleases, *"provided he does no injury to any other individual"* through "slander and defamation." Hortensius [George Hay], An Essay on the Liberty of the Press 23 (2d printing 1803), *reprinted in* George Hay, Two Essays on the Liberty of the Press (Da Capo 1970). Thus, almost all Republicans believed that free speech could be restricted to protect the right to reputation. *See* Rosenberg, *supra* note 35, at 93–94. *But see id.* at 97–98 (discussing the views of the radical democrat John Thomson, who argued that the government should never restrict free expression even in the case of defamation).

51. Madison Report, *supra* note 39, at 144; *see also* 9 Annals of Cong. 3014 (1799) (remarks of Rep. Nicholas). Federalists and other defenders of the Sedition Act also held that free speech was limited by the rights of others. *See, e.g.,* 8 Annals of Cong. 2112 (1798) (remarks of Rep. Dana); *id.* at 2151 (remarks of Rep. Otis); *id.* at 2167 (remarks of Rep. Harper); Liberty of Speech and of the Press, 1 Add. 270 (Pa. 1798) (charge of McKean, C.J., to grand jury); Curtis, Free Speech, *supra* note 1, at 65–66, 78–79.

52. *See, e.g.,* In re Fries, 9 F. Cas. 826, 839–40 (C.C.D. Pa. 1799) (No. 5,126) (charge of Iredell, J., to grand jury); Elkins & McKitrick, *supra* note 34, ch. XV; Smith, *supra* note 35, at 268.

53. 4 Annals of Cong. 934 (1794) (remarks of Rep. Madison).

54. *See* Levy, *supra* note 1; Rabban, *supra* note 1, ch. 3.

55. *See* pp. 105–08.

56. 376 U.S. 254, 276 (1964). The *New York Times* case is discussed in chapter 5 at pp. 73–75. As we shall see in chapter 7, in some respects the conflict between the libertarian-republican and conservative approaches to antigovernment speech continues to this day.

57. This belief was consistent not only with the conservative view, but also with the view of many libertarians, who agreed with *Cato's Letters* that speech was entitled to protection so long as it "injure[d] neither the society, nor any of its members." Cato's Letters, *supra* note 8, No. 62, at 428. By contrast, some libertarians asserted that freedom of expression was limited only by the rights of other individuals. *See, e.g.,* p. 19 (quoting St. George Tucker). However, those statements were generally directed against the law of seditious libel, and do not necessarily indicate that their authors believed that such freedom could never be restricted to protect public rights. For example, while Tucker condemned section 2 of the Sedition Act, which punished seditious libels, he did not take issue with section 1, which made it an offense, among other things, to counsel or advise insurrection against the United States. *See* 4 Blackstone, *supra* note 12, at *123 n.9 (Tucker's note). Similarly, Tucker accepted the common law rule that a challenge to fight amounted to a breach of the public peace (the source of the modern "fighting words" doctrine discussed in chapter 8). *See id.* at *150 n.17 (Tucker's note).

58. *Gitlow v. New York*, 268 U.S. 652 (1925), was the first case in which the Supreme Court recognized that "freedom of speech and of the press—which are protected by the First Amendment against abridgment by Congress—are among the fundamental per-

sonal rights and 'liberties' protected by the due process clause of the Fourteenth Amendment from impairment by the States." *Id.* at 666. Over time, the Court has held that most other protections of the Bill of Rights are also "incorporated" by the Fourteenth Amendment. *See* Erwin Chemerinsky, Constitutional Law: Principles and Policies § 6.3.3 (3d ed. 2006).

59. *See generally* Eric Foner, Free Soil, Free Labor, Free Men (1970); Jacobus tenBroek, Equal Under Law (rev. ed. 1965); William M. Wiecek, The Sources of Antislavery Constitutionalism in America, 1760–1848 (1977); Daniel A. Farber & John E. Muench, *The Ideological Origins of the Fourteenth Amendment,* 1 Const. Comm. 235 (1984).

60. *See, e.g.,* Curtis, Free Speech, *supra* note 1, at 185–86, 209, 239.

61. On Birney, see *id.* at 144–45.

62. *The Cincinnati Preamble and Resolutions, No. 2,* The Philanthropist, Feb. 26, 1836, at 2 [hereinafter Philanthropist]. I am grateful to Michael Kent Curtis for providing me with a copy of this article. For similar views of slavery opponents and their Northern supporters, see Curtis, Free Speech, *supra* note 1, at 190–91, 207–08, 226–27, 237, 239, 253, 255; Joseph C. Lovejoy & Owen Lovejoy, Memoir of the Rev. Elijah Lovejoy 279–80 (New York, J. S. Taylor 1838) (quoting speech of the abolitionist Elijah Lovejoy to the people of Alton, Illinois, demanding to be protected in his God-given and constitutional right to free expression, but acknowledging that this right was properly limited by laws protecting the reputation of others), *quoted in* tenBroek, *supra* note 59, at 38 n.6.

63. For example, in response to the assertion that abolitionist speech should be suppressed because it "injure[d] the acknowledged rights of others" to hold slaves, Philanthropist, *supra* note 62 (quoting a resolution adopted by a Cincinnati antiabolition meeting), Birney denied that slaveholding was a right—since it was contrary to "the truth . . . that all men are created equal"—or that efforts to persuade slaveholders of its wrongfulness injured any such right. *See id.*

64. This party was not descended from the Republican party of Jefferson and Madison, which by this time had become known as the Democratic party.

65. *See* Amar, *supra* note 42, at 163–214; Michael Kent Curtis, No State Shall Abridge: The Fourteenth Amendment and the Bill of Rights (1986) [hereinafter Curtis, Fourteenth Amendment].

66. *See, e.g.,* Curtis, Fourteenth Amendment, *supra* note 65, at 49–54.

67. *See, e.g.,* Cong. Globe, 36th Cong., 1st Sess. 64 (1859–60) (remarks of Sen. Wilson) (implying that incitement and threats are not protected by the principle of free speech); *id.* app. at 205 (remarks of Rep. Lovejoy) (suggesting that freedom of speech does not extend to threats or incitement and must be exercised in "peaceful," "orderly and legal way"); *id.* at 270–71 (remarks of Rep. Wade) (implying that incitement is not protected). The most careful student of the period, Professor Curtis, observes that "[a]dvocates of free speech often accepted the idea that rights were limited by other rights" and that categories of speech such as "treason, defamation of private character, and incitement to violate the law were not protected." Curtis, Free Speech, *supra* note 1, at 421–22. As Curtis emphasizes, however, these individuals believed that such exceptions "must be narrowly confined to protect the democratic and truth-declaring function of free speech." *Id.* at 421. *See also id.* at 368 (describing the views of slavery opponents in similar terms).

68. *See, e.g.,* Nathaniel Chipman, Principles of Government 103–06 (Burlington, Ed-

218 Notes to Pages 24–25

ward Smith 1833) (observing that the right of free speech is limited only by the condition that an individual "violate not the rights of others, or injure the community, of which he is a member"); Thomas M. Cooley, A Treatise on the Constitutional Limitations Which Rest Upon the Legislative Power of the States of the American Union 422 (Boston, Little, Brown 1868) (noting that "the constitutional liberty of speech and of press" does not protect false and malicious publications that "injuriously affect the private character of individuals"); William Rawle, A View of the Constitution of the United States of America 123–24 (2d ed., Philadelphia, Philip H. Nicklin 1829) (asserting that remedies for the abuse of liberty of speech and press "will always be found while the protection of individual rights and the reasonable safeguards of society itself form parts of the principles of our government"); 3 Joseph Story, Commentaries on the Constitution §§ 1874, 1882 (Boston, Hilliard, Gray & Co. 1833) (interpreting the First Amendment to mean "that every man shall have a right to speak, write, and print his opinions upon any subject whatsoever, without any prior restraint, so always, that he does not injure any other person in his rights, person, property, or reputation; and so always, that he does not thereby disturb the public peace, or attempt to subvert the government").

Chapter 2. The Transformation of Free Speech Jurisprudence

1. Morton J. Horwitz, The Transformation of American Law, 1870–1960, at 116 (1992) (quoting Saul Touster, In Search of Holmes from Within, 18 Vand. L. Rev. 437, 449 (1965)).

2. See, e.g., Oliver Wendell Holmes, The Common Law 37–38 (Mark deWolfe Howe ed., Harvard Univ. Press 1963) (1881); O. W. Holmes, Ideals and Doubts, 10 Ill. L. Rev. (now Nw. U.L. Rev.) 1 (1915); Letter from O. W. Holmes to John C. H. Wu (Aug. 26, 1926), in The Mind and Faith of Justice Holmes 431–32 (Max Lerner ed., Modern Library ed. 1954); David M. Rabban, Free Speech in Its Forgotten Years 287 (1997). By the same token, Holmes rejected efforts to ascertain the bounds of liberty by reference to the rights of others. See O. W. Holmes, The Path of the Law, 10 Harv. L. Rev. 457, 466 (1897).

3. Holmes, Path of the Law, supra note 2, at 457–61, 466–67, 469, 474.

4. Roscoe Pound, Interests of Personality (pts. 1 & 2), 28 Harv. L. Rev. 343, 445, at 346, 347, 355, 357 (1915). The internal quotation is from John Dewey & James H. Tufts, Ethics 482–83 (1908). On Pound, sociological jurisprudence, and freedom of speech, see Mark A. Graber, Transforming Free Speech 69–74 (1991); Rabban, supra note 2, at 184–89.

5. Pound, supra note 4, at 344, 354–55.

6. See Graber, supra note 4, at 65–74; Horwitz, supra note 1; Rabban, supra note 2, at 211–47. I do not mean to suggest that all progressives shared these views. As recent scholarship has shown, progressivism was a broad, diverse movement. Although some progressives were critical of rights discourse, others employed it to advance progressive ends. See, e.g., Linda Gordon, Pitied But Not Entitled: Single Mothers and the History of Welfare, 1890–1935, at 160–61 (1994) (describing how some early twentieth-century social reformers drew inspiration from the natural rights tradition and argued for a series of new rights, including health, education, housing, a living wage, and women's and children's rights). In the context of the constitutional and jurisprudential debates of the

Lochner era, however, progressives often criticized traditional notions of individual rights.

7. Lochner v. New York, 198 U.S. 45 (1905); Rabban, *supra* note 2, at 211–12.

8. *See, e.g.,* Pound, *supra* note 4, at 454–56.

9. 249 U.S. 47 (1919). On free speech jurisprudence prior to *Schenck,* see Rabban, *supra* note 2.

10. 249 U.S. at 52.

11. *See, e.g.,* Debs v. United States, 249 U.S. 211, 216 (1919) (upholding the conviction of a political speaker for attempting to obstruct military recruitment where "the words used had [this] as their natural tendency and reasonably probable effect"); Rabban, *supra* note 2, at 279–85. Holmes's opinion in *Schenck* was consistent with his long-standing view that individual interests must be sacrificed where necessary to promote the common good. *See* Holmes, Common Law, *supra* note 2, at 37, 40–41, 86–87; Horwitz, *supra* note 1, at 110–11; Rabban, *supra* note 2, at 285–93.

12. Traces of the older view may be found in the Supreme Court's jurisprudence as late as the 1930s. *See* Grosjean v. Amer. Press Co., 297 U.S. 233, 243 (1936) (asserting that unwarranted burdens on freedom of the press strike at "the heart of the natural right of the members of an organized society, united for their common good, to impart and acquire information about their common interests").

13. Zechariah Chafee, Jr., Freedom of Speech 34, 37 (1920) [hereinafter Chafee book]; Chafee, *Freedom of Speech in War Time,* 32 Harv. L. Rev. 932, 956, 959, 968–69 (1919) [hereinafter Chafee, *War Time*]. In emphasizing the importance of free discussion to the "social interest in the attainment of truth," Chafee book, *supra,* at 36, Chafee followed a course that had been marked out half a century earlier, in John Stuart Mill's comparable effort to defend freedom of speech and thought on grounds of utility rather than "abstract right." John Stuart Mill, On Liberty 12 (David Spitz ed., W. W. Norton 1975) (1859). For discussions of Chafee, see Graber, *supra* note 4, at 122–64; Rabban, *supra* note 2, at 316–35.

14. 250 U.S. 616, 630 (1919) (Holmes, J., joined by Brandeis, J., dissenting). For an insightful discussion of this opinion, see Rabban, *supra* note 2, at 346–55.

15. Chafee book, *supra* note 13, at 34, 36; Chafee, *War Time, supra* note 13, at 956, 958.

16. 274 U.S. 357, 373–79 (1927) (Brandeis, J., joined by Holmes, J., concurring); *Abrams,* 250 U.S. at 630–31 (Holmes, J., dissenting). For a fuller discussion of *Schenck, Abrams, Whitney,* and other decisions on subversive speech, see pp. 104–08.

17. *See* Graber, *supra* note 4, at 122–64; Rabban, *supra* note 2, at 211–47. In this respect, progressives rejected not only the classical libertarian rationale for free speech discussed in chapter 1, but also the views of late nineteenth- and early twentieth-century laissez-faire conservatives and libertarian radicals, who continued to defend free speech on individualist grounds, *see* Graber, *supra* note 4, at 17–49, 53–65; Rabban, *supra* note 2, at 23–76.

18. 304 U.S. 144, 152–53 n.4 (1938). For a contemporary version of this approach to the First Amendment, see John Hart Ely, Democracy and Distrust 93–94, 105–16 (1980).

19. Chafee book, *supra* note 13, at 36.

20. *Id.* at 37; *see also* Pound, *supra* note 4, at 454–56.

21. 274 U.S. 357, 373–75 (1927) (Brandeis, J., concurring); *see* Rabban, *supra* note 2, at 368–70; pp. 106–07 (discussing the *Whitney* opinion). Brandeis's belief in individual rights was expressed even more clearly the following year in *Olmstead v. United States,* 277 U.S. 438 (1928). In arguing for broad constitutional protection for personal privacy, Brandeis wrote, "The makers of our Constitution undertook to secure conditions favorable to the pursuit of happiness. They recognized the significance of man's spiritual nature, of his feelings and of his intellect. They knew that only a part of the pain, pleasure and satisfactions of life are to be found in material things. They sought to protect Americans in their beliefs, their thoughts, their emotions and their sensations. They conferred, as against the Government, the right to be let alone — the most comprehensive of rights and the right most valued by civilized men." *Id.* at 478 (Brandeis, J., dissenting).

22. 319 U.S. 624, 642 (1943).

23. For some leading statements of this view, see C. Edwin Baker, Human Liberty and Freedom of Speech (1989); Martin H. Redish, Freedom of Expression ch. 1 (1984); David A. J. Richards, Toleration and the Constitution 165–230 (1986); Thomas I. Emerson, *Toward a General Theory of the First Amendment,* 72 Yale L.J. 877, 879–81 (1963) [hereinafter Emerson, *General Theory*]; Thomas Scanlon, *A Theory of Free Expression,* 1 Phil. & Pub. Aff. 204 (1972).

24. As we have seen, the Blackstonian conservative tradition also played an important role during the founding period as well as in nineteenth-century American law. Nevertheless, the impetus and rationale for adopting the First Amendment came primarily from the libertarian tradition. Moreover, this is the body of thought I shall use as a starting point for developing a normative theory of freedom of expression. For these reasons, the present section focuses on the contrast between modern free speech jurisprudence and classical libertarianism rather than Blackstonian conservatism.

25. *See, e.g.,* Alexander Meiklejohn, Political Freedom 54–55 (1960) (rejecting Chafee's view that the First Amendment protects an individual as well as a social interest); Robert H. Bork, *Neutral Principles and Some First Amendment Problems,* 47 Ind. L. J. 1, 24–26 (1971) (contending that the First Amendment protects only explicitly political speech).

26. *See, e.g.,* Emerson, *General Theory, supra* note 23, at 878–86.

27. Abrams v. United States, 250 U.S. 616, 630 (1919) (Holmes, J., dissenting). Indeed, on this view our current acceptance of free speech does not even guarantee the continued existence of a constitutional form of government. *See* Gitlow v. New York, 268 U.S. 652, 673 (1925) (Holmes, J., dissenting).

28. *See* Chafee book, *supra* note 13, at 35 (equating interests with "desires and needs"); John Chipman Gray, The Nature and Sources of the Law 18 (Roland Gray ed., 2d ed. 1921) ("By the interests of a man is meant the things which he may desire."); Pound, *supra* note 4, at 343 (referring to individual interests as "the demands which individuals may make"); *id.* at 344 (defining an interest as "a claim which a human being or a group of human beings may make").

29. For a classic statement to this effect, see Holmes, *Path of the Law, supra* note 2, at 466 (observing that judicial decisions ultimately rest on policy considerations that are

"not capable of exact quantitative measurement" and that such decisions therefore "can do no more than embody the preference of a given body in a given time and place").

30. *See* Pound, *supra* note 4, at 345.

31. For a dramatic illustration, see pp. 156–58 (discussing *Florida Star v. B.J.F.*).

My discussion in this chapter has focused on the ways in which changes in political and legal theory contributed to the development of modern First Amendment jurisprudence. But other factors also played an important role, including the evolution of legal doctrine. As I have noted, the Blackstonian conservative view long retained a strong influence on American law. *See* p. 20. According to that view, the state could regulate speech not only to protect the rights of others, but also to promote the common good. *See* pp. 9–11. During the nineteenth century, this position was amalgamated with the emerging legal doctrine that individual liberty was subject to regulation under the police power of the state to promote public health, safety, welfare, and morals. *See* Rabban, *supra* note 2, at 132–34. In this way, American courts came to view many free speech issues in terms of an opposition between individual liberty and the state's power to promote the common good. The Supreme Court took a similar approach when it began to grapple with free speech issues. *See, e.g.*, Patterson v. Colorado, 205 U.S. 454, 462 (1907) (Holmes, J.) (stating that constitutional protections for speech and press do not prevent the state from punishing "such [publications] as may be deemed contrary to the public welfare"); *see also* p. 25 (discussing *Schenck*).

In this respect, there is an important continuity between the nineteenth-century legal tradition and the modern approach to the First Amendment. *See* Rabban, *supra* note 2, ch. 6. At the same time, however, there are significant divergences between them. First, to the extent that nineteenth-century courts accepted the jurisprudential underpinnings of Blackstone's view, or of the state or federal constitutional provisions at issue, they considered freedom of expression to be an inherent right — a position not necessarily taken by the modern approach. Second, although the nineteenth-century tradition held that freedom of speech could be regulated to promote the common good, it also accepted the principle that this freedom was limited by the rights of others. In this way, the tradition stands in sharp contrast to modern First Amendment jurisprudence, from which this principle for the most part has disappeared.

32. This was the effect of the clear-and-present-danger test in its original form. *See* p. 25. For a contemporary version of the statist view, as applied to all but explicitly political speech, see Bork, *supra* note 25, at 20–35. For a critique of Bork's position, see pp. 108–13.

33. For valuable histories of the modern civil libertarian movement, see Judy Kutulas, The American Civil Liberties Union and the Making of Modern Liberalism, 1930–1960 (2006); Rabban, *supra* note 2; Samuel Walker, In Defense of American Liberties: A History of the ACLU (2d. ed. 1999).

34. The leading proponent of this view was Justice Hugo L. Black. *See, e.g.*, Konigsberg v. State Bar of Cal., 366 U.S. 36, 60–62, 75 (1961) (Black, J., dissenting); Smith v. California, 361 U.S. 147, 157–58 (1959) (Black, J., concurring); Beauharnais v. Illinois, 343 U.S. 250, 274–75 (1952) (Black, J., dissenting). For similar reliance on the "absolute" language of the First Amendment, see Meiklejohn, Political Freedom, *supra* note 25, at 20–21.

35. In several opinions, Black relied on the Republican position during the Sedition Act controversy of 1798–1800 to show that the First Amendment was an absolute. He further contended that, under the Fourteenth Amendment, the same absolute prohibition applied to the states. *See, e.g.,* New York Times Co. v. Sullivan, 376 U.S. 254, 295–97 (1964) (Black, J., concurring); *Smith,* 361 U.S. at 157–58 (Black, J., concurring). This argument is unpersuasive for two reasons. First, as we have seen, at the time the First Amendment was adopted, there was no clear understanding that it was an absolute. *See* pp. 18–19. Second, even if one accepted the Jeffersonian Republican view of the original understanding, that would not support an originalist argument for holding that the First Amendment is equally absolute as applied to the states. The Republicans' absolutism was based on notions of federalism, rather than on a substantive conception of the liberties of speech and press. As a substantive matter, Republicans believed that those liberties were limited by the rights of others. They insisted, however, that the First Amendment was intended to deny the federal government all power over the press, while leaving any legitimate power to the states. *See id.* The framers of the Fourteenth Amendment appear to have shared this substantive view of the scope of free expression. *See* pp. 21–22. When the freedoms of speech and press are applied to the states through the Fourteenth Amendment, it is the substantive meaning of those freedoms that should govern, rather than any special federalism-based restrictions the First Amendment may have been intended to impose on the national government. *See* Akhil Reed Amar, The Bill of Rights 233–34 (1998).

36. Meiklejohn, Political Freedom, *supra* note 25, at 57; *see also* Emerson, *General Theory, supra* note 23, at 916. In *Konigsberg,* Black asserted that "the First Amendment's unequivocal command . . . shows that the men who drafted our Bill of Rights did all the 'balancing' that was to be done in this field." 366 U.S. at 61; *see also Beauharnais,* 343 U.S. at 275 (Black, J., dissenting). In this form, the argument simply projects modern interest analysis back onto the eighteenth century.

37. *See, e.g., Konigsberg,* 366 U.S. at 49–50 n.10 (Harlan, J.).

38. Meiklejohn, Political Freedom, *supra* note 25, at 18, 55, 60.

39. Emerson, *General Theory, supra* note 23, at 880; Thomas I. Emerson, The System of Freedom of Expression 17 (1970) [hereinafter Emerson, System].

40. In a later section of *General Theory,* Emerson recognizes this point, holding that individual interests should be treated differently from social goals in general and that some individual interests, such as reputation and privacy, may justify restrictions on speech. *See* Emerson, *General Theory, supra* note 23, at 920–28. Of course, this view stands in some tension with his more general claim that speech should enjoy full protection. It is therefore not surprising that, in his later work, Emerson sharply retreats from this view and adheres more closely to an absolutist position. *See* Emerson, System, *supra* note 39, at v, 517–62.

41. *See* Emerson, System, *supra* note 39, at 6–9.

42. This is how Emerson appears to present the argument in his later work. *See id.*

43. *See* pp. 71 & 243 n.5 (discussing John Rawls's conception of "the priority of liberty").

44. *See, e.g.,* Chafee book, *supra* note 13, at 34; Redish, *supra* note 23, at 52–55.

45. *See* p. 33.

46. Young v. Am. Mini Theatres, 427 U.S. 50, 88 (1976) (Stewart, J., joined by Brennan, Marshall & Blackmun, JJ., dissenting); *see also* Ronald Dworkin, Taking Rights Seriously 193 (paperback ed. 1978).

47. For example, the ACLU strongly defends the right to privacy against governmental actions disclosing private information about individuals. *See, e.g.*, E.B. v. Verniero, 119 F.3d 1077 (3d Cir. 1997) (litigation challenging New Jersey's Megan's Law). At the same time, the ACLU holds that publication of private facts by the media falls within the freedom of speech and press, and it therefore opposes laws allowing recovery for invasion of privacy in such cases. *See* American Civil Liberties Union, Policy Guide, policy # 6(d)(4) (2007).

48. Insofar as free speech is viewed as one social interest in competition with others, its supporters cannot be faulted for making the strongest possible claims in its favor, in the knowledge that other interests will also have strong advocates. In the case of free speech, however, those claims generally are — and must be — made in terms of *principle*. Excessive claims of this kind may be self-defeating, at least in the long run, because they tend to discredit the principle they contend for.

49. Chafee book, *supra* note 13, at 34–35. The leading contemporary exponent of this approach is Richard A. Posner. *See, e.g.*, Richard A. Posner, *The Speech Market and the Legacy of* Schenck, *in* Eternally Vigilant 121 (Lee C. Bollinger & Geoffrey R. Stone eds., 2002).

50. *See* p. 28; *see also* Posner, *supra* note 49, at 126–27 ("The problems of operationalizing the instrumental (or any) approach to free speech are formidable, because of the indeterminacies that pervade the field. We just don't know a great deal about the social consequences of various degrees of freedom of speech.").

51. *See* Dennis v. United States, 341 U.S. 494, 525 (1951) (Frankfurter, J., concurring in judgment).

52. *Id.* at 510. For a contemporary example, see Richard A. Posner, Not a Suicide Pact: The Constitution in a Time of National Emergency 120–25 (2006), which endorses the *Dennis* approach and argues in the context of the war on terror that the government has the constitutional power to ban "generalized advocacy of violence against the United States."

53. *See* pp. 30–32 (discussing Meiklejohn and Emerson). As we have seen, those arguments were often directed to showing that freedom of speech should receive absolute protection. Although they were unconvincing in this respect, they nevertheless succeeded in showing the ways in which free speech differs from other social interests.

54. Thus, the argument I am making is not an originalist one. I do not believe that, in interpreting the Constitution, we are bound by the intentions or the understanding of those who adopted it. Instead, constitutional meaning develops over time. One reason has to do with the nature of the language used in the document. As we saw in chapter 1, the First Amendment was meant to declare general principles, not to specify their meaning. As a result, the Amendment has always been subject to competing interpretations. The same is true of many other sections of the Constitution and the Bill of Rights. The meaning of such "open-textured" provisions was not definitively established at the time they were adopted but emerges through political and constitutional debate — a debate that began during the founding period and continues to the present day. *See* Steven J.

Heyman, *Ideological Conflict and the First Amendment*, 78 Chi.-Kent L. Rev. 531 (2003).

A similar conclusion follows if we consider the relationship between particular provisions and the broader constitutional order. Open-textured provisions like the First Amendment cannot properly be understood in isolation. *See* Ely, *supra* note 18, ch. 2 (criticizing this approach). Instead, they must be interpreted in the context of the Constitution as a whole. In turn, the Constitution is not merely a formal written document, but a framework for our national life. For this reason, the document must be construed in light of our understanding of the nation's character, its social and political order, and the values to which it is committed. (For a classic statement of this position, see Montesquieu, The Spirit of the Laws (Anne M. Cohler et al. trans. & eds., Cambridge Univ. Press 1989) (1748); for a contemporary statement, see Robert C. Post, Constitutional Domains 35– 50 (1995).) Because our understanding of the nation changes over time, the same is true of our conception of the Constitution as a whole as well as our interpretation of particular provisions.

Finally, as I argued in chapter 1, some constitutional provisions, such as the First and the Fourteenth Amendments, reflect a conception of the inherent rights that individuals enjoy as human beings and as citizens of a democratic society. As our understanding of those rights changes, so does our understanding of the provisions that secure them. For all of these reasons, contemporary constitutional interpretation should not be bound by the original understanding or intent. (For a variety of perspectives on originalism, see the essays in Interpreting the Constitution (Jack N. Rakove ed., 1990) and in Antonin Scalia, A Matter of Interpretation (Amy Gutmann ed., 1997).)

At the same time, however, I believe that history can play an important role in several ways. First, it can be used to dispel misconceptions that may lead originalists — and others who do not consider themselves to be originalists — to adopt inappropriate interpretations of the Constitution. For example, many people think that those who adopted the First Amendment held a very narrow view of freedom of expression. By contrast, the Amendment's broad language has led many others to believe that it was intended to provide virtually absolute protection for speech. As I argued in chapter 1, both views are mistaken. Although there were deep disagreements during the founding period over the scope of expressive freedom, even conservatives acknowledged that the liberties of speech and press were inherent rights of human nature and republican citizenship. On the other hand, there was also broad agreement that those liberties were not absolute but were limited by the rights of others.

In addition to this negative function of dispelling misconceptions, history can play a positive role in constitutional interpretation. First, although the meaning of a constitutional provision does not end with the original understanding, it does begin there: that understanding provides a starting point for the process of constitutional development that extends from the founding to the present. Thus, the way a provision was understood when it was adopted may shed important light on how it should be understood today. Second, tracing the historical development of a provision is essential to understanding our current situation and where we ought to go from here. For example, I have argued in this part of the book that the history of First Amendment jurisprudence helps to explain why our current discourse is so unsatisfactory and how we can escape from this difficulty.

Third, although we often do not realize it, our contemporary understandings of concepts like freedom of speech are often deeply influenced by the ways in which those concepts were understood in the past. Thus, an exploration of the history can serve the hermeneutical function of illuminating and enriching our current understanding. *See* Hans-Georg Gadamer, Truth and Method (Joel Weinsheimer & Donald G. Marshall trans., 2d rev. ed. 2004). Finally, by exploring the past, we can sometimes discover conceptions of rights that are normatively attractive today and that can be used to construct a theory of those rights for our own time.

Chapter 3. The Basic Approach

1. For some leading contemporary works on rights theory, see Ronald Dworkin, Taking Rights Seriously (paperback ed. 1978) [hereinafter Dworkin, Rights]; Alan Gewirth, Reason and Morality (1978); Jürgen Habermas, Between Facts and Norms: Contributions to a Discourse Theory of Law and Democracy (William Rehg trans., 1996); John Rawls, A Theory of Justice (rev. ed. 1999); John Rawls, Political Liberalism (1993); Joseph Raz, The Morality of Freedom (1986); Theories of Rights (Jeremy Waldron ed., 1984); Judith Jarvis Thomson, The Realm of Rights (1990).

2. For some other recent work that uses the natural rights tradition to illuminate contemporary legal problems, see Alan Brudner, Constitutional Goods (2004); Alan Brudner, The Unity of the Common Law (1995); Ernest J. Weinrib, The Idea of Private Law (1995).

3. Prominent examples of the former include *Griswold v. Connecticut*, 381 U.S. 479 (1965) (recognizing a constitutional right to privacy that includes the use of contraception); *Roe v. Wade*, 410 U.S. 113 (1973) (holding that the right to privacy extends to abortion); *Planned Parenthood of Southeastern Pennsylvania v. Casey*, 505 U.S. 833 (1992) (reaffirming the basic holding of *Roe*); and *Lawrence v. Texas*, 539 U.S. 558 (2003) (striking down antisodomy laws under the Fourteenth Amendment). The revival of contractarian political philosophy was sparked by Rawls, Theory of Justice, *supra* note 1 (1st ed. 1971), and Robert Nozick, Anarchy, State, and Utopia (1974).

4. This account of negative and positive liberty is implicit in the writings of Locke, *see* John Locke, An Essay Concerning Human Understanding bk. II, ch. XXI (Peter H. Nidditch ed., Clarendon 1975) (1700) [hereinafter Locke, Human Understanding], and is more fully developed in the works of Kant and G. W. F. Hegel, *see* Immanuel Kant, Foundations of the Metaphysics of Morals *446–47 (Lewis W. Beck trans., 2d ed., Macmillan 1990) (1785) [hereinafter Kant, Foundations]; Immanuel Kant, The Metaphysics of Morals *213–14 (Mary Gregor trans., Cambridge Univ. Press 1991) (1797); G. W. F. Hegel, Elements of the Philosophy of Right §§ 5–7 (Allen W. Wood ed., H. B. Nisbet trans., Cambridge Univ. Press 1991) (1820) [hereinafter Hegel, Philosophy of Right]. *See also* Steven J. Heyman, *Positive and Negative Liberty,* 68 Chi.-Kent L. Rev. 81 (1992) (exploring these two aspects of liberty in classical liberal political thought).

5. *See, e.g.,* John Locke, Two Treatises of Government bk. II, §§ 4, 6, 57, 63 (Peter Laslett ed., Cambridge Univ. Press 1988) (1690) [hereinafter Locke, Government]. For a contemporary statement of this position, see Gewirth, Reason and Morality, *supra* note 1.

6. *See* Locke, Government, *supra* note 5, § 57; 1 William Blackstone, Commentaries

on the Laws of England *125; Kant, Metaphysics of Morals, *supra* note 4, at *230–33; Alan Gewirth, The Community of Rights 174–75, 317 (1996).

7. *See* Kant, Metaphysics of Morals, *supra* note 4, at *230; *see also* Habermas, *supra* note 1, at 82–83. Compare Rawls's first principle of justice: "Each person has an equal right to a fully adequate scheme of equal basic liberties which is compatible with a similar scheme of liberties for all." Rawls, Political Liberalism, *supra* note 1, at 291.

8. *See, e.g.,* 1 Blackstone, *supra* note 6, at *125, *129.

9. *See, e.g.,* International Covenant on Civil and Political Rights preamble [hereinafter ICCPR] (declaring that all human beings have "equal and inalienable rights" that "derive from the inherent dignity of the human person").

10. Kant, Metaphysics of Morals, *supra* note 4, at *434–35; *see also* Kant, Foundations, *supra* note 4, at *428–29.

11. *See* Hegel, Philosophy of Right, *supra* note 4, §§ 36, 95 (arguing that an intentional wrong constitutes not merely an infringement of a particular right but also a denial of the victim's *"capacity for rights,"* contrary to "[t]he commandment of right" to *"respect others as persons"*).

12. John Milton, Areopagitica, *in* Areopagitica and Of Education 29–30 (George H. Sabine ed., Harlan Davidson 1951) (1644).

13. In the natural rights tradition, the concept of human dignity rests on a fundamental distinction between persons and things. *See, e.g.,* Locke, Government, *supra* note 5, bk. II, §§ 6, 163; Kant, Foundations, *supra* note 4, at *428–29; Kant, Metaphysics of Morals, *supra* note 4, at *223, *331, *462; Hegel, Philosophy of Right, *supra* note 4, §§ 41–42.

14. Restatement (Second) of Torts § 19 (1965).

15. *See, e.g.,* pp. 55–59, 144–46 (discussing rights to privacy, reputation and image, and personal dignity). I should emphasize that this distinction between the substantive and the formal dimensions of a right is not meant to imply that the latter is "merely formal" and thus less essential or deserving of protection than the former. Indeed, there is a sense in which the opposite is true: the formal element of a right may be regarded as paramount because it is rooted most directly in the principle of respect for the freedom and dignity of others. In the case of bodily security, for example, this principle gives rise first and foremost to a duty to refrain from actions that invade another person's bodily integrity. Infringements of this sort are wrongful even if they do not cause any substantive harm to the body, such as physical damage or pain. Similarly, harmful battery is wrongful not merely because of the substantive harm that it causes, but above all because of its disrespect for the victim's bodily integrity. *See* Axel Honneth, Disrespect 133–34 (2007). Thus, the right to formal inviolability should not be regarded as less fundamental than the right to be free from substantive harm. Instead, as we shall see in later chapters, both the substantive and the formal aspects should be seen as integral elements of a comprehensive theory of rights.

16. For valuable comparative law studies of the United States and other liberal democratic societies, see Edward J. Eberle, Dignity and Liberty: Constitutional Visions in Germany and the United States (2002); Ronald J. Krotoszynski, Jr., The First Amendment in Cross-Cultural Perspective (2006); James Q. Whitman, *Enforcing Civility and Respect: Three Societies,* 109 Yale L.J. 1279 (2000); James Q. Whitman, *The Two Western Cultures of Privacy: Dignity Versus Liberty,* 113 Yale L.J. 1151 (2004).

17. Universal Declaration of Human Rights preamble (1948); *see also id.* § 1 ("All human beings are born free and equal in dignity and rights.").

18. For some constitutional provisions affirming the value of human dignity, see Const. of Italy § 3 ("All citizens have equal social dignity and are equal before the law . . . ."); Basic Law of the Federal Republic of Germany, art. 1(1) (1949) [hereinafter German Basic Law] ("Human dignity shall be inviolable. To respect and protect it shall be the duty of all state authority."); Basic Law of Israel: Human Dignity and Liberty, §§ 2, 4 ("All persons are entitled to protection of their life, body and dignity."); S. Afr. Const. 1996, § 10 ("Everyone has inherent dignity and the right to have their dignity respected and protected.").

19. *See* sources cited in note 16 above.

20. *See, e.g.,* The Constitution of Rights: Human Dignity and American Values (Michael J. Meyer & William A. Parent eds., 1992); Maxine D. Goodman, *Human Dignity in Supreme Court Constitutional Jurisprudence,* 84 Neb. L. Rev. 740 (2006). This value played an especially prominent role in the jurisprudence of Justice William J. Brennan, Jr., one of the leading liberal members of the Court during the second half of the twentieth century. *See, e.g.,* William J. Brennan, Jr., *The Constitution of the United States: Contemporary Ratification, in* Interpreting the Constitution (Jack N. Rakove ed., 1990); Stephen J. Wermiel, *Law and Human Dignity: The Judicial Soul of Justice Brennan,* 7 Wm. & Mary Bill Rts. J. 223 (1998).

21. 403 U.S. 15, 24 (1971) (citing Whitney v. California, 274 U.S. 357, 375–77 (1927) (Brandeis, J., concurring)); *see also* Procunier v. Martinez, 416 U.S. 396, 427–28 (1974) (Marshall, J., concurring) ("To suppress expression is to reject the basic human desire for recognition and affront the individual's worth and dignity.") (citing Thomas I. Emerson, *Toward a General Theory of the First Amendment,* 72 Yale L.J. 877, 879–80 (1963)); Dun & Bradstreet, Inc. v. Greenmoss Builders, Inc., 472 U.S. 749, 787 (1985) (Brennan, J., dissenting) ("[F]reedom of expression is not only essential to check tyranny and foster self-government but also intrinsic to individual liberty and dignity and instrumental in society's search for truth.").

22. *See, e.g.,* Winston v. Lee, 470 U.S. 753, 760 (1985) (declaring that "[the] overriding function of the Fourth Amendment is to protect personal privacy and dignity against unwarranted intrusion by the State") (internal quotation marks and citation omitted).

23. *See, e.g.,* Miranda v. Arizona, 384 U.S. 436, 460 (1966) (asserting that "the constitutional foundation underlying the privilege is the respect a government — state or federal — must accord to the dignity and integrity of its citizens" as well as "the inviolability of the human personality").

24. *See, e.g.,* Atkins v. Virginia, 536 U.S. 304, 311–12 (2002) (" 'The basic concept underlying the Eighth Amendment is nothing less than the dignity of man. . . . The Amendment must draw its meaning from the evolving standards of decency that mark the progress of a maturing society.' ") (quoting Trop v. Dulles, 356 U.S. 86, 100–01 (1958) (plurality opinion)).

25. *See, e.g.,* Roberts v. U.S. Jaycees, 468 U.S. 609, 625 (1984) (observing that sex discrimination "both deprives persons of their individual dignity and denies society the benefits of wide participation in political, economic, and cultural life"). In recent years, a narrow majority of the Court has struck down many affirmative action programs and other race-conscious measures on the ground that "it demeans the dignity and worth of a

person to be judged by ancestry instead of by his or her own merit and essential qualities." Parents Involved in Cmty. Sch. v. Seattle Sch. Dist. No. 1, 127 S. Ct. 2738, 2767 (2007) (plurality opinion) (internal quotation marks and citation omitted). Of course, the majority is right that the Fourteenth Amendment and other civil rights guarantees are centrally concerned with the protection of human dignity. For example, the Court's condemnation of school segregation in *Brown v. Board of Education,* 347 U.S. 483, 494 (1954), was based on the dignitary and psychological harm it inflicted on African American school children. *See also* Martin Luther King, Jr., *The Rising Tide of Racial Consciousness* (1960), *in* A Testament of Hope 145, 145–46 (James Melvin Washington ed., 1986) (observing that *Brown* contributed to "new sense of dignity and self-respect" on the part of African Americans); Heart of Atlanta Motel v. United States, 379 U.S. 241, 291–92 (1964) (Goldberg, J., concurring) ("The primary purpose of the Civil Rights Act of 1964 . . . is the vindication of human dignity and not mere economics.") (citing Senate committee report on the Act). The problem with the Court's current position on affirmative action is that it fails to recognize that, far from denying human dignity, race-conscious measures may be essential to promote the dignity and equality of historically disadvantaged groups.

26. *See, e.g.,* Lawrence v. Texas, 539 U.S. 558, 567 (2003) (holding that "adults may choose to enter upon [intimate sexual] relationship[s] in the confines of their homes and their own private lives and still retain their dignity as free persons"); Planned Parenthood of Se. Pa. v. Casey, 505 U.S. 833, 851 (1992) (explaining that the Court has accorded protection to rights related to "marriage, procreation, contraception, family relationships, child rearing, . . . education," and abortion because these matters involve "the most intimate and personal choices a person may make in a lifetime, choices central to personal dignity and autonomy").

27. Locke, Government, *supra* note 5, bk. II, § 95; Locke, Human Understanding, *supra* note 4, bk. III, ch. I, at 402. Locke writes: "God having designed Man for a sociable Creature, made him not only with an inclination, and under a necessity to have fellowship with those of his own kind; but furnished him also with Language, which was to be the great Instrument, and common Tye of Society." *Id.; see also* Locke, Government, *supra* note 5, bk. II, § 77. This account of language suggests that, rather than understanding speech in strictly individualist terms, Locke believed that speech was essential to human community — a view that traces back to Aristotle's *Politics.* According to Aristotle, "man is by nature a political animal" because man "has speech." Speech "serves to reveal . . . [what is] good and bad and just and unjust . . . and partnership in these things is what makes a household and a city [*polis*]." Aristotle, Politics bk. 1, ch. 2, 1253a1–18 (Carnes Lord trans., Univ. of Chicago Press 1984).

28. Locke, Government, *supra* note 5, bk. II, § 128; *see also id.* §§ 6, 172.

29. *See id.* §§ 87, 123–31, 135; *see also* Gordon S. Wood, The Creation of the American Republic, 1776–1787, at 24 (1969) (observing that in eighteenth-century Whig political theory "[p]ublic liberty was . . . the combining of each man's individual liberty into a collective governmental authority, the institutionalization of the people's personal liberty, making public or political liberty equivalent to democracy or government by the people themselves").

30. Locke, Government, *supra* note 5, bk. II, § 96. This point was widely accepted in eighteenth-century America. As Jack N. Rakove has explained, "Rights did not pertain to

individuals alone . . . . The people as a whole had a right [to govern themselves and] to be ruled by law. Communities, corporate bodies, and governing institutions all had rights, which they exercised on behalf both of the collective groups so constituted and their individual members." Jack N. Rakove, Original Meanings 291, 307 (1996).

Further insight into the eighteenth-century view may be derived from the Massachusetts Declaration of Rights of 1780, which draws a consistent distinction between the rights of individuals and the collective rights of the people. *See* Mass. Const. of 1780, pt. I. Among other collective rights, the people are said to have "the sole and exclusive right of governing themselves as a free, sovereign, and independent State," *id.* art. IV; the inalienable right to institute and reform the government, *id.* art. VIII; the right to freely elect public officers, *id.* arts. VIII–IX; the right to be subject only to those laws and taxes made with "the consent of the people, or their representatives in the legislature," *id.* arts. X, XXIII; and the "right, in an orderly and peaceable manner, to assemble to consult upon the common good" and to petition the legislature for redress, *id.* art. XIX. For further discussion of this document, see Steven J. Heyman, *Natural Rights and the Second Amendment,* 76 Chi.-Kent L. Rev. 237, 260–63, 284–90 (2000).

31. ICCPR, *supra* note 9, art. 1. For endorsements of this right, see John Rawls, The Law of Peoples 38, 61–62, 111–12 (1999); Raz, *supra* note 1, at 207–09.

32. *See, e.g.,* Gewirth, The Community of Rights, *supra* note 6, at 317 (contending that "the right to political democracy is a collective right" because "it is a political expression of the right to freedom for all persons"); Rawls, Political Liberalism, *supra* note 1, at 136 (stating that "[i]n a constitutional regime . . . political power is ultimately the power of the public, that is, the power of free and equal citizens as a collective body").

33. For further discussion, see pp. 62–64, 174–79.

34. This distinction was central to the organization of Blackstone's *Commentaries,* the most influential legal text in eighteenth- and nineteenth-century America. Volume III was concerned with "*private wrongs,*" or "infringement[s] . . . of the private or civil rights belonging to individuals," while volume IV dealt with "*crimes* and *misdemesnors,*" or "violation[s] of public rights and duties, which affect the whole community." 3 Blackstone, *supra* note 6, at *2.

35. *See* pp. 50–51.

36. For further discussion, see pp. 62–64, 65–66, 86, 174–79.

37. *See pp.* 50–51 (assaults and threats); pp. 114–15 (incitement to imminent revolution or unlawful action); chapter 8 (incitement, threats, murder manuals, and fighting words).

38. *See* pp. 29–34.

39. *See* pp. 108–16.

40. *See* Locke, Government, *supra* note 5, bk. II, §§ 123–31; Kant, Metaphysics of Morals, *supra* note 4, at *305–13; Hegel, Philosophy of Right, *supra* note 4, §§ 3, 211–12.

41. *See, e.g.,* Kant, Metaphysics of Morals, *supra* note 4, at *230 (noting that the positive laws of a society "can serve as excellent guides" to determining what is right in itself); John Rawls, Justice as Fairness 5 (Erin Kelly ed., 2001) (observing that "we look to the public political culture of a democratic society, and to the traditions of interpretation of its constitution and basic laws, for certain familiar ideas that can be worked up into a conception of political justice").

42. Lochner v. New York, 198 U.S. 45 (1905) (striking down a maximum-hours law for bakery workers as a violation of liberty of contract); Planned Parenthood of Se. Pa. v. Casey, 505 U.S. 833 (1992) (protecting reproductive freedom); Lawrence v. Texas, 539 U.S. 558 (2003) (holding antisodomy laws unconstitutional).

43. *See, e.g.,* Roper v. Simmons, 543 U.S. 551, 575–78 (2005) (acknowledging "the overwhelming weight of international opinion against the juvenile death penalty"); *Lawrence,* 539 U.S. at 573 (citing an opinion of the European Court of Human Rights as support for a decision striking down ban on consensual sodomy).

44. Federal News Service, Morning Session of a Hearing of the Senate Judiciary Committee [on the] Nomination of Samuel A. Alito Jr., Jan. 11, 2006, LEXIS, News, All.

45. *See Roper,* 543 U.S. at 624–28 (Scalia, J., dissenting).

46. Creating the Bill of Rights: The Documentary Record from the First Federal Congress 78, 81 (Helen E. Veit et al. eds., 1991) (remarks of Rep. Madison in House speech of June 8, 1789).

47. *Cf.* Letter of Thomas Jefferson to James Madison (Dec. 20, 1787), *in* Thomas Jefferson, Writings 916 (Merrill D. Peterson ed., Library of Am. 1984) (asserting that "a bill of rights is what the people are entitled to against every government on earth, . . . & what no just government should refuse, or rest on inferences").

48. For a similar argument, see Daniel A. Farber, Retained by the People ch. 19 (2007). Of course, to say that one should consider the views of other nations does not mean that one should always follow those views. Although I believe that American law can learn much from other legal systems on some points — including the principle that free speech is limited by the rights of others, *see* p. 45 — American law also has some unique virtues — such as the strong protection that it affords to political dissent, *see* pp. 73–75 & chapter 7.

49. *See, e.g.,* Ronald Dworkin, Law's Empire (1986).

50. For a fuller discussion of this approach to constitutional interpretation, see Steven J. Heyman, *Ideological Conflict and the First Amendment,* 78 Chi.-Kent L. Rev. 531, 535–64 (2003).

51. As we saw in chapter 1, Americans inherited two versions of natural rights theory from England. The libertarian-republican view held that the freedoms of speech and press were inalienable rights which were limited only by the rights of other individuals and of the community itself. By contrast, the Blackstonian conservative view treated speech and press as alienable forms of liberty which could be regulated not only to protect other rights, but also to promote the common good. *See* pp. 7–11.

For several reasons, my theory draws its inspiration from the libertarian rather than the conservative view. First, the basic impulse or motivation for protecting freedom of expression was — and continues to be — a libertarian one. It was writers like Locke and Cato who first advocated strong protection for that right. Blackstone's view was essentially a reaction against this position and an effort to confine freedom of expression within narrower bounds. *See* pp. 9–11. Similarly, although the movement to adopt the Federal Constitution drew strong support from conservatives who were concerned about an excess of popular liberty, the demand for a bill of rights represented a reassertion of the radical Whig ideology that animated the American Revolution. *See* pp. 12–14; Bernard Bailyn, *Fulfillment: A Commentary on the Constitution, in* The Ideological Origins of the

American Revolution 321, 331–51 (enlarged ed., 1992). Of course, libertarian ideology also provided the rationale for the Fourteenth Amendment, which protected fundamental rights against the states. *See* pp. 20–22.

A second reason for following the libertarian tradition has to do with the nature and purpose of the Bill of Rights. As Madison explained, that document was meant to protect inalienable rights such as speech by placing them beyond the government's power to abridge. *See* p. 13. In this way, the Bill of Rights follows the logic of the libertarian rather than the Blackstonian view. Third, the libertarian approach is better suited to modern America, which is far more liberal and democratic than the society for which Blackstone wrote. Finally, modern First Amendment jurisprudence is much closer to the libertarian-republican than to the Blackstonian conservative view. *See* pp. 73–77 (discussing the constitutional revolution in defamation law that began with *New York Times Co. v. Sullivan*); chapter 6 (discussing current First Amendment doctrine in general).

Although my theory is rooted in the libertarian-republican position, it seeks to accommodate the conservative view in two ways. First, because the theory recognizes some rights on the part of the community, one can argue that a particular form of speech should be regulated to protect those rights. *See, e.g.,* pp. 198–200 (contending that the state may restrict public display of pornography to protect the community's right to the public environment as well as the rights of unwilling viewers). Second, although freedom of speech generally should be regarded as a fundamental or inalienable right, in some cases it should be treated as a nonfundamental right which is subject to legislative regulation for the common good. *See* p. 46 (discussing commercial advertising).

52. Abrams v. United States, 250 U.S. 616, 628, 630–31 (1919) (Holmes, J., dissenting) ("It is only the present danger of immediate evil or an intent to bring it about that warrants Congress in setting a limit to the expression of opinion *where private rights are not concerned.*") (emphasis added); W. Va. State Bd. of Educ. v. Barnette, 319 U.S. 624, 630 (1943). Likewise, in *Tinker v. Des Moines Independent Community School District,* 393 U.S. 503 (1969), the Court held that the First Amendment allows public school students to express their views on controversial subjects so long as they do so "without materially and substantially interfer[ing] with the requirements of appropriate discipline in the operation of the school and *without colliding with the rights of others.*" *Id.* at 513 (emphasis added, internal quotation marks and citation omitted).

53. *See, e.g.,* Hill v. Colorado, 530 U.S. 703 (2000) (privacy); Time, Inc. v. Hill, 385 U.S. 374, 411–16, 420 (1967) (Fortas, J., dissenting) (privacy and reputation); Nebraska Press Ass'n v. Stuart, 427 U.S. 539 (1976) (fair trial).

54. In several recent opinions, Justice Stephen G. Breyer has argued that First Amendment interests are present on both sides of the case. *See, e.g.,* Bartnicki v. Vopper, 532 U.S. 514, 535 (2001) (Breyer, J., concurring); Nixon v. Shrink Mo. Gov't PAC, 528 U.S. 377, 399 (2000) (Breyer, J., concurring); Turner Broad. Sys. v. FCC, 520 U.S. 180, 226–27 (1997) (Breyer, J., concurring in part). For other opinions that take this view, see *Bartnicki,* 532 U.S. at 518 (majority opinion); *id.* at 553–54 (Rehnquist, C.J., dissenting); Harper & Row, Publ'rs v. Nation Enters., 471 U.S. 539, 559–60 (1985); First Nat'l Bank v. Bellotti, 435 U.S. 765, 802–22 (1978) (White, J., dissenting); CBS v. Dem. Nat'l Comm., 412 U.S. 94, 170–204 (1973) (Brennan, J., dissenting); Red Lion Broad. Co. v. FCC, 395 U.S. 367, 389–90 (1969).

55. *See, e.g.,* Gertz v. Robert Welch, Inc., 418 U.S. 323 (1974) (balancing the interest in free speech against the state interest in protecting individual reputation).

56. A classic statement of the principle may be found in the Declaration of the Rights of Man and the Citizen adopted by the French National Assembly at the outset of the Revolution of 1789. Article 4 asserts that "[l]iberty consists in the freedom to do everything which injures no one else; hence the exercise of the natural rights of each man has no limits except those which assure to the other members of the society the enjoyment of the same rights. These limits can only be determined by law." Article 11 applies this principle to "[t]he free communication of ideas and opinions," which it describes as "one of the most precious of the rights of man." The declaration is reaffirmed in the preamble to the present French constitution. For a valuable account of the human rights tradition, see Lynn Hunt, Inventing Human Rights (2007).

57. *See* ICCPR, *supra* note 9, art. 19(3); European Convention on Human Rights art. 10(2); *see also* German Basic Law, *supra* note 18 (providing that rights of expression "are limited by the provisions of the general laws, the provisions of law for the protection of youth and by the right to inviolability of personal honor"). For an overview of free speech jurisprudence under the European Convention, see Clare Ovey & Robin C.A. White, Jacobs and White, The European Convention on Human Rights ch. 13 (4th ed. 2006).

The principle that free speech may be restricted to protect the rights of others, or to prevent harm to them, also finds support in the work of some contemporary philosophers and political theorists. *See, e.g.,* Brudner, Constitutional Goods, *supra* note 2, at 90 (developing a Hegelian view); Joel Feinberg, *Limits to the Free Expression of Opinion* (1975), *reprinted in* Freedom and Fulfillment 124 (1992) (presenting an account based on Mill's harm principle); D. F. B. Tucker, Law, Liberalism and Free Speech (1985) (formulating a Rawlsian deontological approach); *see also* pp. 71 & 243 n.5 (discussing Rawls's position). This principle has also been used in various ways in the work of some American constitutional scholars. *See* C. Edwin Baker, Human Liberty and Freedom of Speech 56–60, 73–74 (1989); Dworkin, Rights, *supra* note 1, at 193–94; David A. J. Richards, Toleration and the Constitution 195–203 (1986).

58. As we shall see, there are cases in which a speaker can properly be held responsible for the infringement of another right even though she did not cause it in a strict sense. In particular, under well-established principles of tort and criminal law, a speaker who provides another person with substantial assistance or encouragement in the commission of a wrongful act may be held responsible for that act, regardless of whether the speech caused the act in the sense that if the speech had not occurred, the act would not have occurred. I shall discuss this issue in chapter 8 in connection with the doctrines of incitement and complicity. *See* pp. 127–30.

59. Thus, modern First Amendment jurisprudence properly rejects the common law doctrine that speech is unlawful whenever it has a mere "tendency" to bring about illegal action or other social harms. For the traditional doctrine, see 4 Blackstone, *supra* note 6, at *152.

60. For instance, in view of the high value of political expression under the First Amendment, the Supreme Court has held that states may not proscribe the advocacy of law violation unless it is both intended and likely to produce "*imminent* lawless action." Brandenburg v. Ohio, 395 U.S. 444, 447 (1969) (per curiam) (emphasis added). Presumably, however, this strict standard would not apply to private criminal solicitation, since

such speech has far less value, while the threat it poses to other rights is likely to be greater. *See* p. 115.

61. This is especially true where criminal sanctions are at stake. *See, e.g.,* note 60 above (describing the *Brandenburg* standard for criminal incitement).

62. For example, under *New York Times Co. v. Sullivan,* 376 U.S. 254 (1964), liability for defamation of a public official may be based on reckless disregard for the truth, while under *Gertz v. Robert Welch, Inc.,* 418 U.S. 323 (1974), private figures may recover on a showing of negligence, that is, conduct that is unreasonable under the circumstances.

63. 376 U.S. 255 (1964).

64. *See* Hegel, Philosophy of Right, *supra* note 4, § 222; Kant, Metaphysics of Morals, *supra* note 4, at *296–305; Weinrib, *supra* note 2, at 106–07; *see also* Locke, Government, *supra* note 5, bk. II, § 205.

65. *Cf.* John Stuart Mill, On Liberty ch. 1, at 13 (David Spitz ed., W. W. Norton, 1975) (1859) (making this point in utilitarian terms).

66. Once more, *New York Times* is a good example. For some defenses of free speech that focus on the tendency of the government or society to improperly restrict expression, see Larry Alexander, Is There a Right to Freedom of Expression? 191–93 (2005); Frederick Schauer, Free Speech: A Philosophical Enquiry (1982); Vincent Blasi, *The Pathological Perspective and the First Amendment,* 85 Colum. L. Rev. 449 (1985); Thomas I. Emerson, *supra* note 21, at 889–95.

67. For some arguments to this effect, see Baker, *supra* note 57, at 194–224; John Rawls, Political Liberalism, *supra* note 1, at 363–68; Thomas H. Jackson & John Calvin Jeffries, Jr., *Commercial Speech: Economic Due Process and the First Amendment,* 65 Va. L. Rev. 1 (1979); see also Richard A. Posner, *The Speech Market and the Legacy of Schenck, in* Eternally Vigilant 121, 143 (Lee C. Bollinger & Geoffrey R. Stone eds., 2002) ("[B]ecause the commercial speaker normally expects to recoup the full economic value of his speech in the form of [profits,] . . . it is far from obvious that commercial speech should get any greater constitutional protection than commercial activity generally.").

68. On the distinction in First Amendment jurisprudence between content and non-content-based regulation, see chapter 6. For the standards that courts apply to the latter, see p. 247 n.9.

Chapter 4. Free Speech in a Framework of Rights

1. For an overview of this framework, see the appendix, pp. 208–09.

2. For a classic discussion of these rights, see 1 William Blackstone, Commentaries on the Laws of England *121–45 (St. George Tucker ed., Philadelphia, Young & Small 1803). For a modern affirmation, see Universal Declaration of Human Rights arts. 3, 17 (1948) [hereinafter UDHR]. Of course, in the American legal system, these rights are recognized (among other places) in the Due Process Clauses of the Fifth and Fourteenth Amendments as well as in corresponding state constitutional provisions.

3. *See, e.g.,* St. George Tucker, *Of the Right of Conscience; and of the Freedom of Speech and of the Press, in* 1 Blackstone, *supra* note 2, app., note G, at 3.

4. *See, e.g.,* John Trenchard & Thomas Gordon, Cato's Letters No. 62, at 429 (Ronald Hamowy ed., Liberty Fund 1995) (1755) (arguing that the magistrate has no legiti-

mate concern with "what gestures I use, or what words I pronounce, when they please me, and do him and my neighbour no hurt"); Roscoe Pound, *Interests of Personality* (pt. 2), 28 Harv. L. Rev. 445, 453 (1915) (describing liberty of belief and expression as "a sort of free mental motion and locomotion").

5. In shutting down the clinic, the protesters also interfere with the patients' right to reproductive freedom, which is a part of the personal security and liberty protected against state interference by the Fourteenth Amendment under the Supreme Court's decisions in *Roe v. Wade*, 410 U.S. 113 (1973), and *Planned Parenthood of Southeastern Pennsylvania v. Casey*, 505 U.S. 833 (1992).

6. On the distinction between communicative and noncommunicative impact, see chapter 6.

7. The analysis in the following two paragraphs is derived largely from G. W. F. Hegel, Elements of the Philosophy of Right §§ 47–48, 57 (Allen W. Wood ed., H. B. Nisbet trans., Cambridge Univ. Press 1991) (1820) [hereinafter Hegel, Philosophy of Right].

8. *Id.* § 48R.

9. Of course, this idea is central to the women's movement. *See, e.g.,* Linda Gordon, Woman's Body, Woman's Right (rev. & updated ed. 1990).

10. For discussion of the negative and positive aspects of freedom, see p. 38.

11. Restatement (Second) of Torts § 19 (1965).

12. Communicative impact can, however, bring about such injury indirectly — for example, by frightening a coronary patient so that he has a heart attack, *see* Wilkinson v. Downton, [1897] 2 Q.B. 57, 60–61, or by inciting a crowd to lynch a prisoner, *see* pp. 127–30. Communicative impact can also play an integral role in offensive battery. For example, in *Fisher v. Carrousel Motor Hotel*, 424 S.W.2d 627 (Tex. 1967), a NASA employee was standing in line at a luncheon buffet during a scientific conference when the restaurant's manager snatched a plate out of his hand and "shouted in a loud and offensive manner" that he could not be served there because he was black. *Id.* at 628–29. This conduct constituted an offensive battery because of the "humiliation and indignity" that it inflicted. *Id.* at 629.

13. This is the rule in tort law. *See* Restatement, *supra* note 11, § 31. Criminal law might reach the same result. *See* Wayne R. LaFave, Criminal Law 826 & n. 32 (4th ed. 2003).

Like battery, assault has a dignitary dimension. This is true in two respects. First, the concept of assault encompasses not only acts that threaten harmful battery, but also those that threaten offensive battery. Second, although the victim of an assault typically suffers fear, this is not necessary to constitute the wrong. Instead, it is enough that the defendant intentionally caused the victim to experience "apprehension," that is, to perceive an imminent danger to her personal security, even though she may be so brave or skilled in self-defense that she is not afraid. *See* Restatement, *supra* note 11, § 24, cmt. b. In this way, the law of assault protects the inviolability of consciousness, just as the law of battery protects bodily integrity.

14. *See* Virginia v. Black, 538 U.S. 343, 359 (2003).

15. *See* Hegel, Philosophy of Right, *supra* note 7, § 99A (describing a threat as "the representation of an evil").

16. *See, e.g., Black,* 538 U.S. at 359–60; NAACP v. Claiborne Hardware Co., 458 U.S. 886, 916 (1982). For further exploration of threats, see pp. 131–36.

17. *See* pp. 40–41; John Locke, Two Treatises of Government bk. II, §§ 7–8, 87–89, 95, 123–31 (Peter Laslett ed., Cambridge Univ. Press 1988) (1690) [hereinafter Locke, Government]. For other discussions of peace, see Thomas Hobbes, Leviathan ch. XIV, at 92 (Richard Tuck ed., Cambridge Univ. Press 1991) (1651) (asserting that the duty "*to seek Peace*" is "the first, and Fundamentall Law of Nature"); *id.* ch. XV, at 111 (describing the laws of nature as "the meanes of peaceable, sociable, and comfortable living"); Immanuel Kant, The Metaphysics of Morals *307–08, *312 (Mary Gregor trans., Cambridge Univ. Press 1991) (1797) (discussing the duty to reject violence and to enter into a rightful condition); Immanuel Kant, Perpetual Peace (1795), *in* Political Writings (Hans Reiss ed., H. B. Nisbet trans., 2d enlarged ed. 1991).

18. Locke, Government, *supra* note 17, bk. II, §§ 6, 19. These passages describe the condition of peace that ideally should obtain in a state of nature and that civil society is formed to secure.

19. *See* Hegel, Philosophy of Right, *supra* note 7, § 268A.

20. The idea of sympathy plays an important role in eighteenth-century moral thought. *See, e.g.,* David Hume, A Treatise of Human Nature (L. A. Selby-Bigge & P. H. Nidditch eds., Oxford Univ. Press, 2d ed. 1978) (1739–40); Adam Smith, The Theory of the Moral Sentiments (D. D. Raphael et al. eds., Oxford Univ. Press 1976) (1759). This idea is also central to Adam Smith's theory of criminal justice. *See id.* pt. II, § II; Adam Smith, Lectures on Jurisprudence 17, 104, 130, 294, 475 (R. L. Meek et al. eds., Oxford Univ. Press 1978). On the connection between sympathy and the rise of a modern social order based on equality and rights, see Lynn Hunt, Inventing Human Rights ch. 1 (2007).

21. *See* Hegel, Philosophy of Right, *supra* note 7, § 218R.

22. *See, e.g.,* Virginia v. Black, 538 U.S. 343, 360 (2003).

23. [1897] 2 Q.B.D. 57, 58; *see* Restatement, *supra* note 11, § 46(1) & cmt. k.

24. Samuel Warren & Louis D. Brandeis, *The Right to Privacy,* 4 Harv. L. Rev. 193, 195, 205 (1890). For an affirmation of this value, see UDHR, *supra* note 2, art. 22 (stating that every member of the community is "entitled to realization . . . of the economic, social and cultural rights indispensable for his dignity and the free development of his personality"). The right to personality also holds a central place in the German legal order. *See* Basic Law of the Federal Republic of Germany art. 2(1) [hereinafter German Basic Law] ("Everyone has the right to the free development of his personality insofar as he does not violate the rights of others or offend against the constitutional order or the moral code."); Edward J. Eberle, Dignity and Liberty: Constitutional Visions in Germany and the United States chs. 3–5 (2002) (discussing this right in German law).

25. *See* Georg Wilhelm Friedrich Hegel, Lectures on Natural Right and Political Science § 45, at 97 (J. Michael Stewart & Peter C. Hodgson trans., 1995) (discussing honor in these terms). Kant captures the twofold nature of reputation when he describes it as "an innate external belonging." Kant, Metaphysics of Morals, *supra* note 17, at *295.

26. *Cf.* James Wilson, Lectures on Law (1790–91), *in* 1 & 2 The Works of James Wilson 67, 593, 595–96 (Robert Green McCloskey ed., Harvard Univ. Press 1967) (1804) (comparing reputation with property).

27. For leading accounts of free speech as self-realization, see C. Edwin Baker, Human Liberty and Freedom of Speech (1989); Martin H. Redish, Freedom of Expression (1984); David A. J. Richards, Toleration and the Constitution 165–230 (1986).

28. This concept plays an important part in Mill's defense of liberty of expression, which he regards as essential to the mental development of mankind. *See* John Stuart Mill, On Liberty ch. 2, at 32–33 (David Spitz ed., W. W. Norton 1975) (1859).

29. *See* Thomas I. Emerson, *Toward a General Theory of the First Amendment,* 72 Yale L.J. 877, 879–81 (1963).

30. On free speech as a personality right, see United States v. Playboy Entm't Group, 529 U.S. 803, 817 (2000) ("It is through speech that our personalities are formed and expressed."); Doe v. Bolton, 410 U.S. 179, 211 (1973) (Douglas, J., concurring) (asserting that the First Amendment guarantees *"autonomous control over the development and expression of one's intellect, interests, tastes, and personality"*); Police Dep't v. Mosley, 408 U.S. 92, 95–96 (1972) (declaring that the First Amendment is intended "to assure self-fulfillment for each individual"). The German Constitutional Court has also emphasized the relationship between free speech and personality. *See, e.g.,* Lüth, 7 BverfGE 198 (F.R.G. 1958), *in* Donald P. Kommers, The Constitutional Jurisprudence of the Federal Republic of Germany 361, 364 (2d ed. 1997) ("The basic right to freedom of opinion is the most immediate expression of the human personality [living] in society and, as such, one of the noblest rights."); Eric Barendt, Freedom of Speech 61 (2d ed., paperback ed. 2007); Eberle, *supra* note 24, at 198–99, 212.

31. One way to square this position with the constitutional text is as follows. When one aspect of a right is more controversial than another, a statutory or constitutional provision that protects that right may be drafted in such a way as to expressly refer only to the former. In cases like this, one can reasonably conclude that if the provision was intended to protect the more controversial form of the right, it was also intended to protect the less controversial one.

We can understand the First Amendment's application to freedom of thought in these terms. In protecting freedom of speech and press, the First Amendment did not mean to leave one's inner thoughts unprotected. Instead, this right was hardly in dispute in the late eighteenth century—even those who accepted substantial limitations on speech recognized that liberty of thought and belief were inalienable rights. *See* p. 212 n.18 (discussing Blackstone's view). Thus, it is reasonable to hold that if the First Amendment protects freedom of speech, *a fortiori* it also protects freedom of thought. For an analogous argument, see Robert A. Gorman & Mathew W. Finkin, *The Individual and the Requirement of "Concert" Under the National Labor Relations Act,* 130 U. Pa. L. Rev. 286 (1981).

Of course, freedom of belief also derives some protection from the First Amendment's guarantee of the free exercise of religion. For other affirmations of freedom of thought, opinion, and belief, see UDHR, *supra* note 2, preamble; *id.* art. 19; International Covenant on Civil and Political Rights art. 19 [hereinafter ICCPR]; European Convention on Human Rights art. 10(1) [hereinafter ECHR]; Canadian Charter of Rights and Freedoms § 2(b).

32. *See, e.g.,* Texas v. Johnson, 491 U.S. 397, 404 (1989) (holding that conduct may constitute speech for First Amendment purposes if it is intended to convey a particular message and this message is likely to be understood by those who view it); John Hart Ely, *Flag Desecration: A Case Study in the Roles of Categorization and Balancing in First Amendment Analysis,* 88 Harv. L. Rev. 1482, 1497 (1975); Thomas Scanlon, *A Theory of Free Expression,* 1 Phil. & Pub. Aff. 204, 206 (1972).

33. *See* Baker, *supra* note 27, at 51–52.

34. *See, e.g.,* Wooley v. Maynard, 430 U.S. 705 (1977); W. Va. State Bd. of Educ. v. Barnette, 319 U.S. 624, 642 (1943). The same result follows when liberty is understood in external terms. As Locke explains, liberty should be understood as a power to act or not act, according to one's own choice. *See* John Locke, An Essay Concerning Human Understanding bk. II, ch. XXI, §§ 7–12 (Peter H. Nidditch ed., Clarendon 1975) (1700) [hereinafter Locke, Human Understanding]. For this reason, the right to personal liberty encompasses not only the right to speak, but also the right to remain silent.

35. This is one of the original meanings of "information," which referred to the formation of the mind through external means such as instruction. *See* Oxford English Dictionary (2d ed. 1989), s.v. inform, information. For an illustration, see Locke, Government, *supra* note 17, bk. II, § 58 (maintaining that parents have a duty to "inform the Mind, and govern the Actions" of their children until they reach the age of reason). For the Supreme Court's recognition of a First Amendment "right to receive information and ideas," see Board of Educ. v. Pico, 457 U.S. 853, 866–68 (1982) (plurality opinion), and cases cited. For other affirmations of this right, see UDHR, *supra* note 2, art. 19; ICCPR, *supra* note 31, art. 19; ECHR, *supra* note 31, art. 10(1); German Basic Law, *supra* note 24, art. 5(1)(b); S. Afr. Const. 1996, § 16(1)(b).

36. For further discussion of this point, see pp. 92–93, 149–55.

37. Moreover, as I suggested at the end of chapter 3, some speech, such as commercial advertising, should also be subject to broader regulation for the public good.

38. The argument of this paragraph is derived primarily from Hegel, Philosophy of Right, *supra* note 7, §§ 33A, 71, 73, 112.

39. *See* Immanuel Kant, Foundations of the Metaphysics of Morals *429 (Lewis W. Beck trans., 2d ed., Macmillan 1990) (1785) [hereinafter Kant, Foundations].

40. Restatement, *supra* note 11, § 46. A recent draft of the Third Restatement sets forth substantially the same doctrine, although the tort is relabeled as intentional infliction of emotional disturbance. *See* Restatement (Third) of Torts: Liability for Physical and Emotional Harm § 45 (Tentative Draft No. 5, 2007).

41. *See, e.g.,* Locke, Government, *supra* note 17, bk. II, § 63; Locke, Human Understanding, *supra* note 34, bk. II, ch. XXI; Kant, Foundations, *supra* note 39.

42. *See* Mill, *supra* note 28, ch. 2.

43. On *Wilkinson*, see p. 51. For another striking example of the infliction of emotional distress through speech, see pp. 143–45 (discussing *Gomez v. Hug*).

44. Similarly, Rawls observes that the category of basic liberties includes both the physical and the psychological "integrity . . . of the person." John Rawls, Justice as Fairness 113 (Erin Kelly ed., 2001). Somewhat surprisingly, however, he treats these rights merely as "supporting" liberties that are necessary if individuals are to develop and exercise what he regards as their two fundamental moral powers—implementing a sense of justice and forming and pursuing a conception of the good. *Id.* at 112–13. By contrast, this chapter argues that rights like personal security and psychological integrity should be protected for their own sake, and that this is an essential part of what it means to respect others as persons.

45. In chapter 8, I shall argue that profound insults also violate the dignity and integrity of personality. *See* pp. 144–46.

46. For an illuminating history of privacy and related issues in modern American life, see Rochelle Gurstein, The Repeal of Reticence (1996).

47. This account draws on the discussion of subjectivity in Hegel, Philosophy of Right, *supra* note 7, §§ 94A, 105–41. For a similar view of the internal sphere, see Eberle, *supra* note 24, at 61.

48. For recognitions of this right, see UDHR, *supra* note 2, art. 12; ICCPR, *supra* note 31, art. 17; ECHR, *supra* note 31, art. 8; Basic Law of Israel: Human Dignity and Liberty § 7; Netherlands Const. arts. 10, 12, 13; S. Afr. Const. 1996, § 14. The right to privacy is expressly protected in a number of American state constitutions. *See, e.g.,* Alaska Const. art. I, § 22; Cal. Const. art. I, § 1.

49. For an insightful discussion on which this paragraph draws, see Harry M. Clor, *Obscenity and Freedom of Expression, in* Censorship and Freedom of Expression 97, 102–04 (Harry M. Clor ed., 1971).

50. For explorations of the relationship between privacy and dignity, see Robert C. Post, Constitutional Domains ch. 2 (1995); Edward J. Bloustein, *Privacy as an Aspect of Human Dignity: An Answer to Dean Prosser,* 39 N.Y.U. L. Rev. 962 (1964).

51. Restatement, *supra* note 11, § 652B.

52. *Id.* § 652D.

53. These facts are taken from the opinion of the Texas Supreme Court, where the case was called *Boyles v. Kerr. See* 855 S.W.2d 593, 594 (Tex. 1993). On the bizarre sequel to the case, see David Margolick, *For Texas Firm, the Price of Circulating a Videotape Proves Quite Steep,* N.Y. Times, June 1, 1990, at B6. After a jury awarded Kerr one million dollars for invasion of privacy (an amount that "could have been much higher"), employees of the defendants' law firm decided to celebrate by watching the videotape for their own entertainment. *Id.* When the plaintiff's attorneys learned of their conduct, the defendant's firm was compelled to pay Kerr an additional six hundred thousand dollars for violating her privacy anew. *Id.*

54. *See* Baker, *supra* note 27, at 54.

55. For an exploration of conflicts between privacy and freedom of expression, see chapter 9.

56. In this respect, they followed earlier writers. *See, e.g.,* Samuel Pufendorf, Elementa Jurisprudentiae Universalis bk. II, obs. iv., § 26 (William Abbot Oldfather trans., Oceana 1964) (1672); John Locke, Questions Concerning the Law of Nature qu. X, at 223 (Robert Horwitz et al. ed. & trans., Cornell Univ. Press 1990) (asserting that "the law of nature . . . command[s] . . . that what [one] says should not injure the good name or repute of another").

57. 1 Blackstone, *supra* note 2, at *129, *134; 3 *id.* at *123; 2 James Kent, Commentaries on American Law *16.

58. *See* 1 Blackstone, *supra* note 2, at *123; Kent, *supra* note 57, at *1.

59. Tucker, *supra* note 3, at 28.

60. *See* Joanne B. Freeman, Affairs of Honor: National Politics in the New Republic (2001); Robert C. Post, *The Social Foundations of Defamation Law: Reputation and the Constitution,* 74 Cal. L. Rev. 691, 699–707 (1986).

61. *See* Locke, Human Understanding, *supra* note 34, bk. II (making this point about our knowledge of the world in general).

62. *Cf.* 2 Wilson, *supra* note 26, at 593 (defining an individual's character as "the just result of those opinions, which ought to be formed concerning his talents, his sentiments, and his conduct").

63. *See* Oxford English Dictionary, *supra* note 35, s.v. person, persona.

64. On the right to reputation or honor, see UDHR, *supra* note 2, art. 12; ICCPR, *supra* note 31, art. 17; German Basic Law, *supra* note 24, art. 5(2). Many state constitutions also protect this right. *See, e.g.,* Ill. Const. art. I, § 12 ("Every person shall find a certain remedy in the laws for all injuries and wrongs which he receives to his person, privacy, property or reputation.").

65. Kant characterizes this as the right to be held "*beyond reproach* (*iusti*), since before [a person] performs any act affecting rights he has done no wrong to anyone." Kant, Metaphysics of Morals, *supra* note 17, at *238. According to Kant, this right is an aspect of the innate right to freedom. *Id.* at *237–38.

66. *See* 2 Wilson, *supra* note 26, at 594, 596.

67. *See id.*; 3 Blackstone, *supra* note 2, at *125.

68. *See* Laurence H. Tribe, American Constitutional Law 1389–90 (2d ed. 1988).

69. For a discussion of the First Amendment standards that should apply in the area of defamation, see pp. 73–77.

In exploring other rights, we saw that they could be violated not only in a substantive but also in a formal way. The same is true here. Falsely representing a person's character or conduct may not cause substantive harm to reputation in a particular case, but may nevertheless infringe her dignity. This is the subject of the tort known as "false light," which consists of misrepresenting an individual before the public in a way highly offensive to a reasonable person. *See* Restatement, *supra* note 11, § 652E. Although "false light" is often classified as a form of invasion of privacy, it is better understood as protecting the dignitary dimension of reputation.

The right to one's image may also be violated when one's name or likeness is appropriated by others without one's consent. This conduct may also violate the right to privacy, by involuntarily exposing the self to the world. *See id.* § 652C. For a classic case, see Roberson v. Rochester Folding Box Co., 64 N.E. 442 (N.Y. 1902).

70. The fullest statement of this view may be found in Vincent Blasi, *Free Speech and Good Character: From Milton to Brandeis to the Present, in* Eternally Vigilant 61 (Lee C. Bollinger & Geoffrey R. Stone eds., 2002) [hereinafter Blasi, *Character*]. This essay is reprinted in Blasi's casebook, Ideas of the First Amendment 929 (2006). *See also* Vincent Blasi, *Holmes and the Marketplace of Ideas,* 2004 Sup. Ct. Rev. 1 (arguing that a concern for character is present in Holmes's metaphor of the marketplace of ideas).

71. Blasi, *Character, supra* note 70, at 62.

72. *See* Kant, Metaphysics of Morals, *supra* note 17, at *387–88, *391–93, *444–47.

73. *See id.* at *383 ("To every duty there corresponds a right in the sense of an *authorization* to do something . . . .")

74. Blasi, *Character, supra* note 70, at 84.

75. On self-respect, respect for others, and the relationship between them, see Kant, Metaphysics of Morals, *supra* note 17, at *434–37, *462–68, as well as the essays in Dignity, Character, and Self-Respect (Robin S. Dillon ed., 1995).

76. *See* Kant, Metaphysics of Morals, *supra* note 17, at *231–32, *239, *466.

77. Blasi, *Character, supra* note 70, at 93–94.

78. *Id.*

79. *See* p. 46.

80. *See, e.g.,* Locke, Government, *supra* note 17, bk. II, § 95; Jean-Jacques Rousseau, The Social Contract bk. I, ch. VIII (Susan Dunn et al. trans.) (1762), *in* The Social Contract and The First and Second Discourses (Susan Dunn ed., Yale Univ. Press, 2002); Kant, Metaphysics of Morals, *supra* note 17, at *313–14; Jürgen Habermas, Between Facts and Norms: Contributions to a Discourse Theory of Law and Democracy 126, 449 (William Rehg trans., 1996).

81. On law and society as expanding freedom, see, for example, Locke, Government, *supra* note 17, bk. II, § 57; 1 Blackstone, *supra* note 2, at *125–26; [Thomas Tudor Tucker,] *Oration in Commemoration of American Independence* (1795), *quoted in id.* (ed. note).

82. Kant, Metaphysics of Morals, *supra* note 17, at *329–30.

83. *See, e.g.,* 1 Blackstone, *supra* note 2, at *125.

84. *See, e.g.,* ICCPR, *supra* note 31, art. 25; Habermas, *supra* note 80, at 123, 126–27; John Rawls, A Theory of Justice § 36 (rev. ed. 1999).

85. *See, e.g.,* International Covenant on Economic, Social and Cultural Rights [hereinafter ICESCR].

86. As I have argued elsewhere, these rights of citizenship are not limited to negative liberties, but should also be understood to embrace some positive rights, including protection against private violence and minimum guarantees of welfare. *See* Steven J. Heyman, *The First Duty of Government: Protection, Liberty and the Fourteenth Amendment,* 41 Duke L.J. 507 (1991); Steven J. Heyman, *Foundations of the Duty to Rescue,* 47 Vand. L. Rev. 673, 703–06 (1994). For recognition of these rights in international human rights law, see UDHR, *supra* note 2, arts. 8, 22, 25–26; ICESCR, *supra* note 85.

87. *See* Steven H. Shiffrin, Dissent, Injustice, and the Meanings of America (1999); Vincent Blasi, *The Checking Value in First Amendment Theory,* 1977 Am. B. Found. Res. J. 521.

88. 274 U.S. 357, 375–77 (1927) (Brandeis, J., concurring). Brandeis's view is set forth at greater length at pp. 106–07.

89. Alexander Meiklejohn, Political Freedom (1960) (originally published in 1948 as Free Speech and its Relation to Self-Government). For some other works that focus on the relationship between free speech and democracy, see George Anastaplo, The Constitutionalist (2004 ed.); John Hart Ely, Democracy and Distrust 105–16 (1980); Owen M. Fiss, The Irony of Free Speech (1996); Robert C. Post, Constitutional Domains, *supra* note 50; Cass R. Sunstein, Democracy and the Problem of Free Speech (1993); Robert H. Bork, *Neutral Principles and Some First Amendment Problems,* 47 Ind. L.J. 1, 20–35 (1971).

90. Meiklejohn, Political Freedom, *supra* note 89, at 14–19, 24–28, 88.

91. *Id.* at 13, 16, 75–76; Alexander Meiklejohn, *The First Amendment Is an Absolute,* 1961 Sup. Ct. Rev. 245, 255–57 [hereinafter Meiklejohn, *Absolute*]. Kant maintains that citizens possess dignity as "colegislating members of a state" who give laws to themselves. Kant, Metaphysics of Morals, *supra* note 17, at *313–16, *329–30, *345–46. This aspect of his political philosophy is rooted in his deeper moral conception of the autonomy of the will, which holds that individuals must view themselves as sovereign legisla-

tors in a "realm of ends" who impose moral laws on themselves. This is the foundation of "the Idea of the dignity of a rational being who obeys no law except one which he himself also gives." Kant, Foundations, *supra* note 39, at *433–35.

92. Meiklejohn, Political Freedom, *supra* note 89, at 24–25; Meiklejohn, *Absolute, supra* note 91, at 260; *see also* John Rawls, Political Liberalism 296 (1993) (endorsing Meiklejohn's view on the importance of "rules of order").

93. The distinction between these two kinds of rights is a traditional one. For example, Blackstone and Kent distinguish between "absolute" rights, which are inherent in individuals and would exist even in a state of nature, and "relative" rights, which belong to individuals "as members of society, and standing in various relations to each other." 1 Blackstone, *supra* note 2, at *123; 2 Kent, *supra* note 57, at *1. In these terms, personal liberty is an absolute right, while family and political relationships involve relative rights. To avoid misunderstanding, I should note that, in this traditional usage, "absolute" and "relative" refer to the *nature* rather than the *strength* of a right: although absolute rights were inherent in individuals, they were limited by the rights of others, and (except to the extent that the right was an inalienable one) were subject to regulation for the common good. *See* Heyman, *First Duty of Government, supra* note 86, at 532–33.

94. Meiklejohn, Political Freedom, *supra* note 89, at 25.

95. *See* pp. 8–9 (discussing Locke and Cato); Meiklejohn, Political Freedom, *supra* note 89, at 24–28; Meiklejohn, *Absolute, supra* note 91, at 255.

96. *See, e.g.,* Police Dep't v. Mosley, 408 U.S. 92, 95–96 (1972); Emerson, *supra* note 29, at 883; UDHR, *supra* note 2, art. 27(1) ("Everyone has the right freely to participate in the cultural life of the community, to enjoy the arts and to share in scientific advancement and its benefits."); ICESCR, *supra* note 85, art. 15(1) (similar provision).

97. Although this section has focused on the meaning of liberty within society as a whole, one should note that rights of community also apply within other groups, such as families, neighborhoods, workplaces, schools, and religious bodies. All of these communities involve interaction with others and require respect for their rights. In some cases, those rights are protected by public or private law, while in others they are governed by the internal rules or understandings of the group itself.

98. For a valuable exploration of the relationship between free speech and the search for truth, see Susan H. Williams, Truth, Autonomy, and Speech (2004).

99. *See, e.g.,* John Milton, Areopagitica, *in* Areopagitica and Of Education 29–30, 37 (George H. Sabine ed., Harlan Davidson 1951) (1644); John Locke, Of the Conduct of the Understanding § 6 (1706), *in* Some Thoughts Concerning Understanding and Of the Conduct of the Understanding 178 (Ruth W. Grant & Nathan Tarcov eds., Hackett 1996); Mill, *supra* note 28, at 11–12, 33–35, 55–56.

100. W. Va. State Bd. of Educ. v. Barnette, 319 U.S. 624, 642 (1943).

101. *See* p. 58.

102. The attainment of self-knowledge in these and other ways is a central theme in the novels of Jane Austen. *See, e.g.,* Jane Austen, Emma bk. III, ch. XI (R. W. Chapman ed., Oxford Univ. Press, 3d ed. 1969) (1816); Jane Austen, Pride and Prejudice bk. II, ch. XIII (R. W. Chapman ed., Oxford Univ. Press, 3d ed. 1969) (1813); *id.* bk. III, chs. VI, XVI.

103. *See, e.g.,* Michael J. Sandel, Liberalism and the Limits of Justice (1982); Charles Taylor, Sources of the Self (1989).

104. On moral knowledge of one's own humanity, see Kant, Foundations, *supra* note 39, at *450–53; Kant, Metaphysics of Morals, *supra* note 17, at *441–42, *483.

105. 250 U.S. 616, 630–31 (1919) (Holmes, J., dissenting). For a contemporary defense of this view, see Richard A. Posner, *The Speech Market and the Legacy of* Schenck, *in* Eternally Vigilant, *supra* note 70, at 121.

106. For other critiques of the marketplace theory, see Baker, *supra* note 27, ch. 1; Frederick Schauer, Free Speech: A Philosophical Enquiry ch. 2 (1982); James Boyd White, Living Speech 29–38 (2006); Steven H. Shiffrin, *The First Amendment and Economic Regulation: Away from a General Theory of the First Amendment*, 78 Nw. U.L. Rev. 1212, 1281 (1983).

107. *See* pp. 62–64.

108. *See* Meiklejohn, Political Freedom, *supra* note 89, at 27–28.

109. *Id.* at 79–81.

110. *See* Milton, *supra* note 99, at 17–19, 29–30, 37, 41–46; Locke, Human Understanding, *supra* note 34, bk. IV, ch. XVI, at 659–61; John Locke, A Letter Concerning Toleration 26–28, 38 (James Tully ed., Hackett 1983) (William Popple trans., 1689) [hereinafter Locke, Toleration]; Mill, *supra* note 28, at 33–35, 38–42, 44–50. For an illuminating account of the relationship between speech, dignity, and the pursuit of meaning in human life, see White, *supra* note 106.

111. *See, e.g.,* Mill, *supra* note 28, at 34–44 (arguing that even false beliefs have value in promoting a clearer perception of truth).

112. As Robert C. Post explains, the search for truth "requires an important set of shared social practices: the capacity to listen and to engage in self-evaluation, as well as a commitment to the conventions of reason, which in turn entail aspirations toward objectivity, disinterest, civility, and mutual respect." Robert C. Post, *Reconciling Theory and Doctrine in First Amendment Jurisprudence*, 88 Cal. L. Rev. 2353, 2365 (2000).

113. On the idea of relational rights, see p. 63.

114. *See, e.g.,* Locke, Toleration, *supra* note 110, at 46 ("[T]he business of Laws is not to provide for the Truth of Opinions, but for the Safety and Security of the Commonwealth, and of every particular mans Goods and Person."); Mill, *supra* note 28, ch. 2; *see also* 4 Annals of Cong. 934 (1794) (remarks of Rep. Madison) ("Opinions are not the objects of legislation.").

115. *See, e.g.* p. 279 n.67 (discussing this point in the context of hate speech).

116. *See, e.g.,* Locke, Government, *supra* note 17, bk. II, § 4 (discussing natural freedom and equality); Kant, Metaphysics of Morals, *supra* note 17, at *237 (explaining that the innate right to freedom contains within it an innate right to equality).

117. *See* Locke, Government, *supra* note 17, bk. II, §§ 4, 54.

118. *See id.* §§ 22, 59, 142. For a discussion of the roots of equal protection in the natural rights tradition, see Heyman, *First Duty of Government*, *supra* note 86, at 563–66.

119. *See, e.g.,* UDHR, *supra* note 2, art. 1 ("All human beings are born free and equal in dignity and rights.").

120. *See, e.g.,* N.Y. Const., art. I, § 11; Civil Rights Act of 1964, Pub. L. No. 88–352, 78 Stat. 241 (1964); Canadian Charter of Rights and Freedoms § 15; UDHR, *supra* note 2, art. 7; ICCPR, *supra* note 31, arts. 2(1), 3, 26.

Chapter 5. Conflicts of Rights

1. *See* Jeremy Waldron, *Rights in Conflict, in* Liberal Rights 203, 224 (1993).

2. The way the problem is conceived is also partly a function of the source of the rights and the jurisdiction of the court. When both rights derive from the same source (such as state law), the issue can often be viewed as one of adjusting competing rights. Many constitutional cases, on the other hand, involve conflicts between state law rights (such as privacy and reputation) and the First Amendment. In this situation, federal courts lack power to redraw the boundaries of rights that have been authoritatively defined by state law, and the courts can rule in favor of free speech only by finding a constitutional privilege to override other rights.

3. This sort of balancing is characteristic of many legal systems, especially those in Canada and Europe. *See, e.g.,* Eric Barendt, Freedom of Speech 39–73, 205–26 (2d ed., paperback ed. 2007); Ronald J. Krotoszynski, Jr., The First Amendment in Cross-Cultural Perspective (2006).

4. However, some forms of speech, such as commercial advertising, should be considered nonfundamental rights which are subject to regulation not only to protect the rights of others but also to promote the common good. *See* p. 46.

5. On the "priority of liberty," see John Rawls, A Theory of Justice § 39 (rev. ed. 1999); John Rawls, Political Liberalism lect. VIII (1993). This doctrine holds that basic liberties may never be traded off against social welfare. At the same time, Rawls explains that "the basic liberties are to be assessed as a whole, as one system." "Since the various basic liberties are bound to conflict with one another, . . . none of [them] is absolute." Instead, it is necessary "to balance one basic liberty against another" in order to formulate "the best total system of liberty." Rawls, Theory of Justice, *supra,* § 32, at 178; Rawls, Political Liberalism, *supra,* at 295. For a thoughtful application of this perspective to First Amendment issues, see James E. Fleming, Securing Constitutional Democracy ch. 8 (2006).

6. As applied to *New York Times Co. v. Sullivan,* 376 U.S. 254 (1964), for example, this approach would characterize the rights neither as "free speech" and "reputation," on one hand, nor as the right to publish this specific advertisement or to be free from these particular accusations, on the other hand. Instead, one should characterize the competing rights, as the Court did, at an intermediate level — as the right to criticize the conduct of public officials and the right to be free from false and defamatory statements about such conduct.

7. Melville Nimmer, *The Right to Speak from Times to* Time, 56 Cal. L. Rev. 935, 942 (1968). *But see* Steven H. Shiffrin, The First Amendment, Democracy, and Romance 13–17 (1990) (arguing that ad hoc decision making is necessary and desirable in some situations).

8. On this approach, see Waldron, *supra* note 1, at 220–24.

9. *See* p. 58.

10. *See* pp. 31–32.

11. *See* Palko v. Connecticut, 302 U.S. 319, 326–27 (1937) (observing that "freedom of thought, and speech . . . is the matrix, the indispensable condition, of nearly every other form of freedom").

12. *See, e.g.,* Texas v. Johnson, 491 U.S. 397, 409 (1989); Tinker v. Des Moines Indep. Cmty. Sch. Dist., 393 U.S. 503, 508–09 (1969).

13. 376 U.S. 254, 256–59, 279–80 (1964). On the common law, see Prosser and Keeton on the Law of Torts 804 (W. Page Keeton et al. eds., 5th ed. 1984).

14. Garrison v. Louisiana, 379 U.S. 64, 74–75 (1964); *New York Times,* 376 U.S. at 279; Gertz v. Robert Welch, Inc., 418 U.S. 323, 344 (1974).

15. *See* pp. 58–59 (discussing the right to reputation); p. 63 (defining relational rights).

16. For the historical basis of this view, see chapter 1.

17. In a concurring opinion, Justice Arthur J. Goldberg contended that, instead of adopting an "actual malice" standard, the Court should have recognized "an absolute, unconditional privilege to criticize official conduct despite the harm which may flow from excesses and abuses." 376 U.S. at 296 (Goldberg, J., joined by Douglas, J., concurring in result). Justice Black took a similar position. *See id.* at 297 (Black, J., joined by Douglas, J., concurring) ("An unconditional right to say what one wants about public affairs is what I consider to be the minimum guarantee of the First Amendment."). From the standpoint of substantive right, this position is unconvincing. As Brennan argued in *Garrison,* while good-faith criticism of government officials must be protected by the First Amendment, "calculated falsehood" undermines rather than promotes the community's ability to make informed judgments. 379 U.S. at 73–75. It follows that a rule of absolute protection would sacrifice legitimate claims to reputation without advancing the paramount rights of the public.

As we saw in chapter 3, however, the law must take account of institutional as well as substantive considerations. *See* pp. 45–46. The concurring Justices emphasized the difficulty of determining a speaker's state of mind as well as the danger that juries would use libel law to suppress unpopular views. *See* 376 U.S. at 293–95 (Black, J., concurring); *id.* at 300 (Goldberg, J., concurring in result). These concerns clearly justify the Court's adoption of a demanding "actual malice" standard of liability and a requirement of clear and convincing evidence as well as independent judicial review of libel awards. The question is whether these measures are sufficient or whether an absolute First Amendment privilege is necessary to ensure that citizens are not deterred from engaging in legitimate criticism of government officials.

Issues of this sort cannot be resolved on a theoretical level, but only through the exercise of informed practical judgment. In making such a judgment, it is important to remember that free speech and other rights are not sharply antithetical to one another but are integral elements of a broader system of constitutional liberty. The aim of constitutional adjudication should be to reconcile such rights as far as possible. Thus, a right that is justified in principle should be limited for institutional reasons only to the extent necessary to promote right as a whole. In the present context, my own view is that a rule of absolute protection would tend to diminish rather than to promote the quality of public discourse, by relieving speakers of even the possibility of liability for making knowingly or recklessly false accusations against public officials or candidates for office. For this reason, I believe that the majority in *New York Times* was correct to reject such a rule.

18. *See* Curtis Publ'g Co. v. Butts, 388 U.S. 130 (1967). In *Hustler Magazine v. Falwell,*

485 U.S. 46 (1988), the Court held that the same rule should apply when public officials or public figures sue for intentional infliction of emotional distress caused by publications that subject them to ridicule.

19. Rosenbloom v. Metromedia, Inc., 403 U.S. 29 (1971) (plurality opinion); *Gertz*, 418 U.S. 323.

20. *See Gertz*, 418 U.S. at 344–45.

21. *See* 403 U.S. at 43–44 (plurality opinion).

22. *See* Aristotle, Politics bk. II, ch. 3, at 1261b20–32 (Carnes Lord trans., Univ. of Chicago Press 1984).

23. *New York Times*, 376 U.S. at 274–75 (quoting Virginia Resolutions of 1798); Rosenblatt v. Baer, 383 U.S. 75, 92 (1966) (Stewart, J., concurring).

24. *See Gertz*, 418 U.S. at 347. In recent years, many nations have expanded the protection they afford to defamatory speech on public matters, although few go as far as the United States. *See* Eric Barendt, Freedom of Speech vii, 205–26 (2d ed., paperback ed. 2007).

25. For discussion of the standard of review that should apply in such cases, see pp. 95–97.

26. *See* p. 24.

27. Indeed, it can be argued that the Constitution not only authorizes but requires the government to protect fundamental rights. According to the natural rights tradition, government is obligated to protect its citizens against the invasion of their rights by others. This notion was a central feature of American constitutional thought between the Revolution and the Civil War. A strong case can be made that congressional Republicans, concerned about the denial of protection to Southern blacks and Unionists following the Civil War, intended to incorporate a right to protection into the first section of the Fourteenth Amendment. *See* Steven J. Heyman, *The First Duty of Government: Protection, Liberty and the Fourteenth Amendment,* 41 Duke L.J. 507 (1991). If the Amendment were interpreted in this way — contrary to the Supreme Court's position in *DeShaney v. Winnebago County Department of Social Services,* 489 U.S. 189 (1989) — then one could argue that the government has a constitutional duty to protect fundamental rights against violation by others, whether that violation takes the form of speech or conduct. One need not go that far for present purposes, however, for even if the Constitution does not *require* the government to regulate speech where necessary to protect the fundamental rights of others, it should be interpreted to *permit* the government to do so.

28. An exception is the Thirteenth Amendment, which outlaws slavery whether or not supported by state action.

29. On privacy and the Fourth Amendment, see Katz v. United States, 389 U.S. 347 (1967); Olmstead v. United States, 277 U.S. 438, 471 (1928) (Brandeis, J., dissenting). On rights of privacy under the Fifth and Fourteenth Amendments, see, for example, Whalen v. Roe, 429 U.S. 589, 599–600 (1977) (observing that the Court's decisions have recognized two distinct interests in privacy, "the individual interest in avoiding disclosure of personal matters" and "the interest in independence in making certain kinds of important decisions"); Roe v. Wade, 410 U.S. 113, 153 (1973) (holding that "the Fourteenth Amendment's concept of personal liberty" includes a "right of privacy" that "is broad enough to encompass a woman's decision whether or not to terminate her pregnancy").

30. *See, e.g.,* Planned Parenthood of Se. Pa. v. Casey, 505 U.S. 833, 851 (1992).

31. For an overview of the Supreme Court's decisions on the right to political participation, see Erwin Chemerinsky, Constitutional Law: Principles and Policies § 10.8 (3d ed. 2006).

32. On the Ninth Amendment, see Daniel A. Farber, Retained by the People (2007); 1 & 2 The Rights Retained by the People (Randy E. Barnett ed., 1989 & 1993).

33. 383 U.S. 75, 92 (1966) (Stewart, J., concurring).

34. *See, e.g.,* Abrams v. United States, 250 U.S. 616, 630 (1919) (Holmes, J., dissenting) (arguing that "the ultimate good desired" by members of society can best be achieved through freedom of speech).

Chapter 6. Content Neutrality and the First Amendment

1. 408 U.S. 92, 93, 99–102 (1972).

2. *Id.* at 95–96 (quoting New York Times Co. v. Sullivan, 376 U.S. 254, 270 (1964)) (additional citations omitted).

3. *See* Kenneth L. Karst, *Equality as a Central Principle in the First Amendment,* 43 U. Chi. L. Rev. 20, 28 & n.43 (1975); Erwin Chemerinsky, *Content Neutrality as a Central Problem of Freedom of Speech: Problems in the Supreme Court's Application,* 74 S. Cal. L. Rev. 49, 50 (2000).

4. Davenport v. Wash. Educ. Ass'n, 127 S. Ct. 2372, 2381 (2007); United States v. Playboy Entm't Group, 529 U.S. 803, 813 (2000); Hustler Mag. v. Falwell, 485 U.S. 46, 55–56 (1988).

5. Am. Booksellers Ass'n v. Hudnut, 771 F.2d 323 (7th Cir. 1985), *aff'd mem.,* 475 U.S. 1001 (1986), *discussed at* pp. 195–96; Simon & Schuster, Inc. v. Members of N.Y. State Crime Victims Bd., 502 U.S. 105 (1991), *discussed at* p. 249 n.40; Texas v. Johnson, 491 U.S. 397 (1989), and United States v. Eichman, 496 U.S. 310 (1990), *discussed at* pp. 122–26; Collin v. Smith, 578 F.2d 1197 (7th Cir.), *cert. denied,* 439 U.S. 916 (1978), and R.A.V. v. City of St. Paul, 505 U.S. 377 (1992), *discussed in* chapter 10.

6. For commentary that generally supports the doctrine, see Rodney A. Smolla, Free Speech in an Open Society 45–54 (1992); Laurence H. Tribe, American Constitutional Law ch. 12 (2d ed. 1988); Chemerinsky, *supra* note 3; Karst, *supra* note 3; Geoffrey R. Stone, *Content Regulation and the First Amendment,* 25 Wm. & Mary L. Rev. 189 (1983); Susan H. Williams, *Content Discrimination and the First Amendment,* 139 U. Pa. L. Rev. 615 (1991); *see also* John Rawls, Political Liberalism 295–96 (1993). The doctrine's strongest judicial critic is Justice John Paul Stevens. *See, e.g., R.A.V.,* 505 U.S. at 420–22 (Stevens, J., concurring in judgment); FCC v. Pacifica Found., 438 U.S. 726, 744–47 (1978) (plurality opinion); Young v. Am. Mini Theatres, Inc., 427 U.S. 50, 63–71 (1976) (plurality opinion). For other critiques of content neutrality, see Larry Alexander, Is There a Right to Freedom of Expression? ch. 4 (2005); Martin H. Redish, Freedom of Expression ch. II (1984); Steven H. Shiffrin, The First Amendment, Democracy, and Romance ch. 1 (1990); Daniel A. Farber, *Content Regulation and the First Amendment: A Revisionist View,* 68 Geo. L.J. 727 (1980); T. M. Scanlon, Jr., *Content Regulation Reconsidered, in* Democracy and the Mass Media 331 (Judith Lichtenberg ed., 1990);

Paul B. Stephan III, *The First Amendment and Content Discrimination,* 68 Va. L. Rev. 203 (1982).

7. 408 U.S. at 96, 99.

8. For the traditional view, see Chaplinsky v. New Hampshire, 315 U.S. 568, 572 (1942), *discussed at* p. 90. As the Court has observed, in recent decades the scope of these traditional categories has narrowed, but "a limited categorical approach has remained an important part of our First Amendment jurisprudence." *R.A.V.,* 505 U.S. at 383. Since the 1970s, the Court has also recognized some intermediate categories, such as commercial advertising and "adult" expression, which receive some constitutional protection but less than that accorded to fully protected speech. *See* p. 96.

9. *See, e.g., Simon & Schuster,* 502 U.S. at 118. For a rare Supreme Court decision sustaining a content-based regulation under this standard, see Burson v. Freeman, 504 U.S. 191 (1992) (plurality opinion) (holding that a ban on electioneering within one hundred feet of a polling place was necessary to advance compelling state interests in preventing voter intimidation and election fraud). For a valuable history of the strict scrutiny doctrine, see Stephen A. Siegel, *The Origin of the Compelling State Interest Test and Strict Scrutiny,* 48 Am. J. Legal Hist. (forthcoming).

By contrast, content-neutral regulations are reviewed under a less stringent standard. The Court has held that the government "may impose reasonable restrictions on the time, place, or manner of protected speech, provided that the restrictions are justified without reference to the content of the regulated speech, that they are narrowly tailored to serve a significant governmental interest, and that they leave open ample alternative channels for communication of the information." Ward v. Rock Against Racism, 491 U.S. 781, 791 (1989) (internal quotation marks and citations omitted). Similarly, under *United States v. O'Brien,* 391 U.S. 367 (1968), the government may regulate symbolic conduct (such as draft card burning) if the regulation "is within the constitutional power of the Government; if it furthers an important or substantial governmental interest; if the government interest is unrelated to the suppression of free expression; and if the incidental restriction on alleged First Amendment freedoms is no greater than is essential to the furtherance of that interest." *Id.* at 377. The Court has indicated that these two tests for content-neutral regulations are substantially similar, *see* Clark v. Community for Creative Non-Violence, 468 U.S. 288, 298 (1984), and that they amount to an intermediate standard of review (by contrast with strict scrutiny on one hand and the lenient rational-basis test on the other), *see* Turner Broad. Sys. v. FCC, 520 U.S. 180, 189 (1997).

10. For example, in her opinion for the Court in *Simon & Schuster,* Justice Sandra Day O'Connor declares in no uncertain terms that "[r]egulations which permit the Government to discriminate on the basis of the content of the message cannot be tolerated under the First Amendment," 502 U.S. at 116 (internal quotation marks and citation omitted), only to state two pages later that such regulations will be upheld if they are able to survive strict scrutiny, *id.* at 118. In a separate opinion, Justice Anthony Kennedy rejects the strict scrutiny exception and insists that "the sole question is, or ought to be, whether the restriction is in fact content based." *Id.* at 125 (Kennedy, J., concurring in judgment). Restrictions of this sort, he asserts, "amount[] to raw censorship . . . forbidden by the text of the First Amendment and well-settled principles protecting speech and press." *Id.* at 128. At the same time, however, he concedes that there are certain "historic and tradi-

tional categories," such as obscenity, defamation, and incitement, in which content-based regulation is permissible. *Id.* at 127.

11. Hill v. Colorado, 530 U.S. 703, 789 (2000) (Kennedy, J., dissenting) (accusing the majority of disregarding "the neutrality that must be the first principle of the First Amendment").

12. *See, e.g.*, Police Dep't v. Mosley, 408 U.S. 92, 96 (1972) (stating that the First Amendment precludes the government from discriminating among speakers "on the basis of what they intend to say").

13. This tripartite view of communication may be traced to Aristotle. *See* Aristotle, On Rhetoric (George A. Kennedy trans., Oxford Univ. Press 1991). Aristotle identifies three means of persuasion through speech, which he calls *ethos, logos,* and *pathos. Id.* bk. I, ch. II, §§ 3–6, 1365a, at 37–39. First, speech can seek to persuade through "the character [*ethos*] of the speaker," which occurs "whenever the speech is spoken in such a way as to make the speaker worthy of credence." *Id.* § 4, at 38. Second, speech can persuade through "the argument [*logos*] itself," "when we show the truth or the apparent truth from whatever is persuasive in each case." *Id.* § 6, at 39. Finally, speech can persuade through "disposing the listener in some way," which occurs when "the hearers . . . are led to feel emotion [*pathos*] by the speech." *Id.* § 5, at 38.

14. *See, e.g.*, Thomas I. Emerson, The System of Freedom of Expression 21–22 (1970). For the historical basis of this view, see pp. 8–9.

15. 394 U.S. 557, 565–66 (1969). In *Stanley,* the Court invoked this principle to strike down a Georgia law that criminalized the possession of obscene material even in a person's home.

16. *See* John Locke, A Letter Concerning Toleration 26–27 (James Tully ed., Hackett 1983) (William Popple trans., 1689); Immanuel Kant, The Metaphysics of Morals *214, *219, *230 (Mary Gregor trans., Cambridge Univ. Press 1991) (1797); John Stuart Mill, On Liberty 10–14 (David Spitz ed., W. W. Norton 1975) (1859).

17. W. Va. State Bd. of Educ. v. Barnette, 319 U.S. 624, 642 (1943). For an account of First Amendment freedoms that focuses on the inviolability of individual thought and belief, see David A. J. Richards, Toleration and the Constitution chs. 6–7 (1986).

18. Police Dep't v. Mosley, 408 U.S. 92, 96 (1972); Cohen v. California, 403 U.S. 15, 24 (1971); Hurley v. Irish-Am. Gay, Lesbian & Bisexual Group of Boston, 515 U.S. 557, 573 (1995). For Emerson's view, see Emerson, *supra* note 14, at 6.

19. *See* pp. 122–26.

20. *See* pp. 64–68.

21. *See* p. 53. For First Amendment theories that focus on listeners' autonomy, see Thomas Scanlon, *A Theory of Freedom of Expression,* 1 Phil. & Pub. Aff. 204 (1972) [hereinafter Scanlon, *Theory*]; David A. Strauss, *Persuasion, Autonomy, and Freedom of Expression,* 91 Colum. L. Rev. 334 (1991).

22. For a First Amendment theory that emphasizes this idea, see Redish, *supra* note 6, ch. 1.

23. 394 U.S. 557, 564 (1969).

24. *See* p. 197.

25. Charles Taylor, *Theories of Meaning, in* 1 Philosophical Papers 259–60, 263–66 (1985) (emphasis added); Charles Taylor, *Irreducibly Social Goods, in* Philosophical

Arguments 138–39 (1995); Charles Taylor, *Cross-Purposes: The Liberal-Communitarian Debate, in id.* 189–90. On the social and relational nature of communication, see Robin West, *Toward a First Amendment Jurisprudence of Respect: A Comment on George Fletcher's* Constitutional Identity, 14 Cardozo L. Rev. 759, 761 (1993).

26. For a discussion of the ways in which public discourse can function "to reconcile individual with collective autonomy" within a self-governing community, see Robert C. Post, Constitutional Domains 268, 280 (1995).

27. Alexander Meiklejohn, Political Freedom 26–27 (1960); Police Dep't v. Mosley, 408 U.S. 92, 96 (1972).

28. *See* Karst, *supra* note 3, at 23–26. For some defenses of content neutrality that focus on equality, see Ronald Dworkin, Sovereign Virtue 365–66 (2000); Karst, *supra* note 3; Williams, *supra* note 6, at 666–76.

29. Police Dep't v. Mosley, 408 U.S. 92, 99–102 (1972).

30. *See, e.g.,* Chemerinsky, *supra* note 3, at 51.

31. *See, e.g.,* Ward v. Rock Against Racism, 491 U.S. 781, 791 (1989); Young v. Am. Mini Theatres, Inc., 427 U.S. 50, 67 (1976) (plurality opinion). For the view that the *Mosley* doctrine should be limited to viewpoint discrimination, see Stephan, *supra* note 6; see also Marjorie Heins, *Viewpoint Discrimination,* 24 Hastings Const. L.Q. 99, 115 (1996).

32. *See, e.g.,* Hill, 530 U.S. at 723; *id.* at 770 (Kennedy, J., dissenting); R.A.V. v. City of St. Paul, 505 U.S. 377, 381 (1992); *Mosley,* 408 U.S. at 95, 97.

33. 391 U.S. 367, 369–70, 376, 382 (1968). For the standard adopted in *O'Brien,* see *supra* note 9.

34. John Hart Ely, *Flag Desecration: A Case Study in the Roles of Categorization and Balancing in First Amendment Analysis,* 88 Harv. L. Rev. 1482, 1496–1502 (1975) [hereinafter Ely, *Flag Desecration*].

35. For a discussion of these two approaches, see pp. 30–33.

36. Ely, *Flag Desecration, supra* note 34, at 1486–87, 1493 n.44, 1500–02.

37. John Hart Ely, Democracy and Distrust 109–110 (1980) [hereinafter Ely, Democracy].

38. Tribe, *supra* note 6, § 12–2, at 580–83 (1st ed. 1978). Tribe's analysis also drew on work by Thomas Scanlon and Melville Nimmer, who had previously developed versions of the distinction between communicative and noncommunicative impact. *Id.* § 12–2, at 580 n.9, 581 n.15 (citing Scanlon, *Theory, supra* note 21; Melville B. Nimmer, *The Meaning of Symbolic Speech Under the First Amendment,* 21 UCLA L. Rev. 29 (1973)).

39. Texas v. Johnson, 491 U.S. 397, 411–12 (1989); United States v. Eichman, 496 U.S. 310, 315–19 (1990).

40. Hustler Mag. v. Falwell, 485 U.S. 46, 55 (1988). For other expressions of this theme, see R.A.V. v. City of St. Paul, 505 U.S. 377, 394 (1992); *Johnson,* 491 U.S. at 411–12; Boos v. Barry, 485 U.S. 312, 321–22 (1988); NAACP v. Claiborne Hardware Co., 458 U.S. 886, 909–11 (1982); Collin v. Smith, 578 F.2d 1197, 1206 (7th Cir.), *cert. denied,* 439 U.S. 916 (1978).

This doctrine has sometimes been taken to remarkable lengths. For example, in *Simon & Schuster, Inc. v. Members of New York State Crime Victims Board,* 502 U.S. 105 (1991), the Court reviewed the New York Son-of-Sam law, which sought to prevent individuals from profiting from their crimes by selling their stories for publication. In an opinion holding the statute unconstitutional under the content neutrality doctrine, Justice O'Connor summarily rejected any justification for the law based on an "interest in limiting whatever anguish [a criminal's] victims may suffer from reliving their victimization." *Id.* at 118. To rely on such an interest, she said, would violate the "bedrock [First Amendment] principle . . . that the Government may not prohibit the expression of an idea simply because society finds the idea itself offensive or disagreeable." *Id.* (quoting *Eichman,* 496 U.S. at 319; *Johnson,* 491 U.S. at 414) (internal quotation marks and citations omitted).

Another striking example is provided by *Florida Bar v. Went for It, Inc.,* 515 U.S. 618 (1995), which involved a state bar association rule that prohibited targeted direct-mail solicitation of accident victims and their relatives for a thirty-day period. Although the Court upheld the rule under the First Amendment, four Justices dissented. Rejecting the notion that the regulation could be justified on the basis of a concern "that victims or their families will be offended by receiving a solicitation during their grief and trauma," the dissenters wrote that the Court's decisions "do not allow restrictions on speech to be justified on the ground that the expression might offend the listener. On the contrary, we have said that these are classically not justifications validating the suppression of expression protected by the First Amendment." *Id.* at 638 (Kennedy, J., dissenting) (internal quotation marks and citation omitted). For further criticism of this trend in First Amendment doctrine, see Catharine A. MacKinnon, Only Words 105 & 145 n.63 (1993).

41. *R.A.V.,* 505 U.S. at 382–83.

42. *See, e.g., id.* at 383 (characterizing exceptions as "traditional limitations" on First Amendment freedoms); *Simon & Schuster,* 502 U.S. at 127 (Kennedy, J., concurring in judgment) (describing exceptions as "historic and traditional categories long familiar to the bar").

43. 315 U.S. 568, 571–72 (1942). For some contemporary opinions that invoke *Chaplinsky*'s approach, see *R.A.V.,* 505 U.S. at 382–83; New York v. Ferber, 458 U.S. 747, 776 (1982) (Brennan, J., concurring in judgment).

44. As the *Chaplinsky* Court indicated, 315 U.S. at 572 nn.4 & 5, its dictum was drawn from Zechariah Chafee, Jr., Free Speech in the United States 149–50 (1941). In Chafee's work the balancing methodology is clear. *See id.* at 149 (explaining that the "social interest" injured by speech "must be weighed in the balance" against the "countervailing social interest in the attainment and dissemination of truth"). On Chafee and balancing in post–World War I progressive free speech jurisprudence, see chapter 2.

45. 458 U.S. 747, 763–64 (1982); *see also* Davenport v. Wash. Educ. Ass'n, 127 S. Ct. 2372, 2381 (2007) (asserting that "speech that is obscene or defamatory can be constitutionally proscribed because the social interest in order and morality outweighs the negligible contribution of those categories of speech to the marketplace of ideas").

46. Melville Nimmer, Nimmer on Freedom of Speech (1984); Nimmer, *Symbolic Speech, supra* note 38; Tribe, *supra* note 6, § 12–2, at 792–93 (2d ed. 1988). As Tribe expresses the point, "Any exclusion of a class of activities from first amendment safeguards represents an implicit conclusion that the governmental interests in regulating those activities are such as to justify whatever limitation is thereby placed on the free expression of ideas. Thus, [such] determinations . . . presuppose some form of 'balancing' whether or not they appear to do so." *Id.*

47. On Black and Douglas, see pp. 89, 221–22 nn.34–36; on Emerson and Meikle-john, see pp. 30–32, 85–86.

48. *See* p. 31.

49. *See* Ely, Democracy, *supra* note 37, at 109–16; Ely, *Flag Desecration, supra* note 34, at 1500–01; Simon & Schuster, Inc. v. Members of N.Y. State Crime Victims Bd., 502 U.S. 105, 118 (1991); *id.* at 124 (Kennedy, J., concurring in judgment).

50. Ely, *Flag Desecration, supra* note 34, at 1497.

51. *See* p. 64.

52. 403 U.S. 15, 21 (1971).

53. *See* p. 86.

54. Hill v. Colorado, 530 U.S. 703, 716–17 (2000) (quoting Olmstead v. United States, 277 U.S. 438, 478 (1928) (Brandeis, J., dissenting)). For an interesting discussion of the right to be free from unwanted speech, see Patrick M. Garry, Rediscovering a Lost Freedom (2006).

55. For further discussion of free speech and freedom from intrusion, see pp. 149–55.

56. *See* pp. 49–50, 51.

57. Ely, *Flag Desecration, supra* note 34, at 1497.

58. C. Edwin Baker, *Harm, Liberty, and Free Speech,* 70 S. Cal. L. Rev. 979, 989–92 (1997); Am. Booksellers Ass'n v. Hudnut, 771 F.2d 323, 327–29 (7th Cir. 1985), *aff'd mem.,* 475 U.S. 1001 (1986). For a philosophical defense of the position that individuals have no right to be free from injuries of this sort, see Judith Jarvis Thomson, The Realm of Rights chs. 10–11 (1990).

59. For example, under *Brandenburg v. Ohio,* 395 U.S. 444 (1969) (per curiam), speech that advocates law violation may be restricted only where it is "directed to inciting or producing imminent lawless action and is likely to incite or produce such action." *Id.* at 447.

60. *See* Restatement (Second) of Torts § 24, cmt. b (1965) (holding that this constitutes an assault).

61. Although listeners generally should not be allowed to recover for unreasonable reactions, the law arguably should recognize an exception in cases where the speaker deliberately exploits the listener's known peculiarity for the purpose of causing him injury. *See id.* § 46, cmt. f (adopting this position in cases of intentional infliction of emotional distress).

62. *See* J. L. Austin, How to Do Things with Words 101 (2d ed. 1975).

63. Baker rejects this view on the ground that the listener is capable of avoiding the harm by choosing how to respond to the speech. For example, a person who is subjected to racist speech can choose to regard it as reflecting badly on the speaker rather than on himself. Baker, *supra* note 58, at 992. This argument is unconvincing for two reasons. First, as Baker acknowledges, speech can "impose brutal injuries" on others and can cause them to be "distressed" and "humiliated" in "devastating" ways. *Id.* at 987, 989, 992. It is very difficult for an ordinary or reasonable person to shield himself from such injuries. Second, in many situations, the target suffers serious harm from the initial impact of the speech. Even if he is able to overcome this harm by reaffirming his sense of self-worth, that does not mean that no harm has occurred, any more than the healing of a physical wound means that no injury was suffered in the first place. Thus, the fact that

people are sometimes capable of overcoming the harms caused by abusive expression should not relieve speakers of responsibility for wrongfully causing them.

64. *See* pp. 49–51.

65. *See* Oxford English Dictionary (2d ed. 1989), s.v. injury.

66. Am. Booksellers Ass'n v. Hudnut, 771 F.2d 323, 329 (7th Cir. 1985), *aff'd mem.,* 475 U.S. 1001 (1986).

67. *See* pp. 127–30.

68. For a discussion of when regulations should be regarded as content-based, see Steven J. Heyman, *Spheres of Autonomy: Reforming the Content Neutrality Doctrine in First Amendment Jurisprudence,* 10 Wm. & Mary Bill of Rights J. 647, 706–07 (2002).

69. Police Dep't v. Mosley, 408 U.S. 92, 99 (1972); pp. 90–91.

70. 458 U.S. 747 (1982).

71. *See, e.g.,* Cent. Hudson Gas & Elec. Corp. v. Pub. Serv. Comm'n, 447 U.S. 557 (1980) (commercial advertising); City of Renton v. Playtime Theatres, Inc., 475 U.S. 41 (1986) (adult expression); Young v. Am. Mini Theatres, Inc., 427 U.S. 50 (1976) (plurality opinion) (same).

72. In *Chaplinsky v. New Hampshire,* 315 U.S. 568, 572 (1942), for example, the Court mentioned "the lewd and obscene, the profane, the libelous, and the insulting or 'fighting' words" as categories of unprotected speech, yet failed to include such obvious categories as threats and incitement.

73. Although I argue in chapter 7 that the rights-based theory offers the best way to ensure strong protection for antigovernment speech, in this area the theory would reach much the same results as the strict scrutiny doctrine. Thus, a second-best position would hold that strict scrutiny should apply to restrictions on antigovernment speech, while the rights-based theory should be used to evaluate limitations on speech that causes injury to individuals or groups.

74. In *Bartnicki v. Vopper,* 532 U.S. 514 (2001), Justice Breyer expresses a similar view: "What this Court has called 'strict scrutiny'—with its strong presumption against constitutionality—is normally out of place where . . . important competing constitutional interests are implicated." *Id.* at 537 (Breyer, J., concurring); *see also* United States v. Am. Library Ass'n, 539 U.S. 194, 217–18 (2003) (Breyer, J., concurring in judgment) (elaborating this view). In *Bartnicki,* the "constitutional interests" Breyer has in mind include the interests in privacy and in private speech. 532 U.S. at 537. Strictly speaking, however, the Constitution protects those interests only against the government, not against private parties. In this passage, therefore, Breyer appears to use "constitutional interests" in a broad sense, to refer to fundamental rights of the sort that are protected against governmental interference by the Constitution and against private interference by state and federal law. For a defense of the view that free speech may be regulated to protect other fundamental rights, whether those rights are protected by the Constitution or by other sources of law, see pp. 78–80. For further discussion of *Bartnicki,* see pp. 158–61.

75. In *R.A.V. v. City of St. Paul,* 505 U.S. 377 (1992), the Court dramatically expanded the content discrimination doctrine by holding that it applies not only to laws that restrict constitutionally protected speech, but also to laws that draw distinctions within an unprotected category of speech such as fighting words. For a critique of this holding, see p. 273 n.26.

76. *See, e.g.,* Rosenberger v. Rector of Univ. of Va., 515 U.S. 819, 833–34 (1995).

77. *See, e.g., id.* The most forceful statements of this position may be found in *National Endowment for the Arts v. Finley,* 524 U.S. 569, 600 (1998) (Souter, J., dissenting), and *Rust v. Sullivan,* 500 U.S. 173, 203 (1991) (Blackmun, J., dissenting).

78. *See, e.g., Rust,* 500 U.S. 173; Regan v. Taxation With Representation, 461 U.S. 540 (1983). The most uncompromising statement of this view appears in *Finley,* 524 U.S. at 590 (Scalia, J., concurring in judgment).

79. "The doctrine of unconstitutional conditions holds that government may not grant a benefit on the condition that the beneficiary surrender a constitutional right, even if the government may withhold that benefit altogether." Kathleen M. Sullivan, *Unconstitutional Conditions,* 102 Harv. L. Rev. 1413, 1419 (1989).

80. *See Rust,* 500 U.S. at 197.

81. For a fuller exploration of the issue, see Steven J. Heyman, *State-Supported Speech,* 1999 Wis. L. Rev. 1119.

Chapter 7. Subversive Speech

1. For in-depth treatments of the history recounted in this section, see Harry Kalven, Jr., A Worthy Tradition 119–236 (Jamie Kalven ed., 1988); Geoffrey R. Stone, Perilous Times chs. III–VI (2004).

2. 249 U.S. 47, 48–51 (1919); Kalven, *supra* note 1, at 131. The quoted language is taken from the Court's summary of the leaflets.

3. 249 U.S. at 48, 51–52.

4. *Id.* at 51–52; Frohwerk v. United States, 249 U.S. 204, 206–08 (1919); Debs v. United States, 249 U.S. 211, 212–14, 216 (1919).

5. 250 U.S. 616, 617–24 (1919).

6. *Id.* at 626–31 (Holmes, J., dissenting).

7. Gitlow v. New York, 268 U.S. 652, 656 & n.2, 667–71 (1925); Whitney v. California, 274 U.S. 357, 359–60, 363–66 (1927).

8. 274 U.S. at 375–77 (Brandeis, J., concurring) (footnote omitted). For an insightful reading of this opinion, see Vincent Blasi, *The First Amendment and the Ideal of Civic Courage: The Brandeis Opinion in* Whitney v. California, 29 Wm. & Mary L. Rev. 653 (1988).

9. 341 U.S. 494, 497, 510–11 (1951); *id.* at 579–81 (Black, J., dissenting); *id.* at 581–91 (Douglas, J., dissenting).

10. 395 U.S. 444, 444–49 (1969) (per curiam).

11. *See* pp. 127–30.

12. Bork's critique of *Brandenburg* appears in a 1971 lecture, *Neutral Principles and Some First Amendment Problems,* 47 Ind. L.J. 1, 20–35 (1971) [hereinafter Bork, *Neutral Principles*], and is reaffirmed in his book The Tempting of America 333–36 (1990).

13. Bork, *Neutral Principles, supra* note 12, at 2–3, 5–6, 8, 10–11, 14, 17, 23. On this ground, Bork sharply criticizes *Griswold v. Connecticut,* 381 U.S. 479 (1965), in which the Court held that a ban on the use of contraceptives by married couples violated their fundamental right to privacy—a right that is not expressly stated in the Constitution. According to Bork, such a law should receive no greater judicial scrutiny than one that

restricts economic activity, such as an environmental regulation that decreases the profits of an electric utility company. In each case, he argues, those challenging the law are merely asserting a right to pursue their own "pleasure" or "gratification," and "[t]here is no principled way to decide that one man's gratifications are more deserving of respect than another's." Bork, *Neutral Principles, supra* note 12, at 7–11. Together with his narrow view of free speech, Bork's attack on the right to privacy was a major reason the Senate rejected his nomination to the Supreme Court.

14. Bork, *Neutral Principles, supra* note 12, at 17, 25–26.

15. *Id.* at 26 (quoting Whitney v. California, 274 U.S. 357, 375 (1927) (Brandeis, J., concurring)).

16. *Id.* at 30–31.

17. *Id.* at 20, 26–28. In later writings, Bork abandons the view that the First Amendment protects only political speech, concluding that, while this view is correct in principle, it is "unworkable" in practice. Bork, The Tempting of America, *supra* note 12, at 333.

18. Bork, *Neutral Principles, supra* note 12, at 20, 29–35.

19. *Id.* at 31–33.

20. *See* chapter 1.

21. *See* John Locke, A Letter Concerning Toleration 55 (James Tully ed., Hackett 1983) (William Popple trans., 1689); John Locke, Two Treatises of Government bk. II, §§ 168, 208 (Peter Laslett ed., Cambridge Univ. Press 1988) (1690) [hereinafter Locke, Government].

22. *See, e.g.,* The Press and the American Revolution (Bernard Bailyn & John B. Hench eds., 1980); Bernard Bailyn, Pamphlets of the American Revolution, 1750–1776 (1965); Political Sermons of the American Founding Era, 1730–1805, at 369–681 (Ellis Sandoz ed., 1990); Pauline Maier, From Resistance to Revolution 224 (1972).

23. James Madison, *Report on the Virginia Resolutions* (Jan. 1800), *in* 5 The Founders' Constitution 141, 143 (Philip B. Kurland & Ralph Lerner eds., 1987); Va. Declaration of Rights of 1776, art. XII; N.C. Declaration of Rights of 1776, § XV. On the Antifederalists, see Herbert J. Storing, What the Antifederalists Were *For* 64–65 (1981). Proposals from the state ratifying conventions are collected in The Complete Bill of Rights 92–93 (Neil H. Cogan ed., 1997).

24. Dennis v. United States, 341 U.S. 494, 501 (1951) (plurality opinion).

25. *See, e.g.,* Sanford Levinson, Our Undemocratic Constitution (2006).

26. *See, e.g.,* Declaration of Independence para. 2; Va. Declaration of Rights of 1776, art. 3; Gordon S. Wood, The Creation of the American Republic, 1776–1787, at 532–36 (1969).

27. *See* pp. 8–9; Whitney v. California, 274 U.S. 357, 375 (1927) (Brandeis, J., concurring).

28. *See, e.g.,* Alexander M. Bickel, The Least Dangerous Branch (1962); Larry D. Kramer, The People Themselves (2004); Robert Post & Reva Siegel, *Roe Rage: Democratic Constitutionalism and Backlash*, 42 Harv. C.R.-C.L. L. Rev. (forthcoming).

29. *See, e.g.,* John Rawls, Political Liberalism 346 (1993).

30. *See* Gitlow v. New York, 268 U.S. 652, 673 (1925) (Holmes, J., dissenting).

31. *See, e.g.,* Lawrence Byard Solum, *Freedom of Communicative Action: A Theory of the First Amendment Freedom of Speech*, 83 Nw. U.L. Rev. 54, 121–22 (1989).

32. *See* Rawls, Political Liberalism, *supra* note 29, at 345–48.

33. *See, e.g.,* Roper v. Simmons, 543 U.S. 551, 575–78 (2005) (recognizing overwhelming international consensus against the juvenile death penalty); Mary Dudziak, *Desegregation as a Cold War Imperative,* 41 Stan. L. Rev. 61 (1988) (discussing the importance of *Brown v. Board of Education* for America's image in world).

34. Indeed, Bork's view suffers from an even more serious flaw, for it implies that the First Amendment's protections do not extend to general works of political philosophy. Although such works do not necessarily violate democratic principles in the way that Bork claims revolutionary speech does, they do not fall within the category of "explicitly political speech" as he defines it: "criticisms of public officials and policies, proposals for the adoption or repeal of legislation or constitutional provisions and speech addressed to the conduct of any governmental unit in the country." Bork, *Neutral Principles, supra* note 12, at 29. General works of political philosophy, whether classical or contemporary, frequently are not directed to "political truth" in Bork's sense, for they do not address the meaning of the American Constitution or seek to influence the ordinary political process. Instead, they are concerned with broader principles "that exist independently of Constitution or statute." *Id.* at 30–31. It appears, then, that Bork's view would deny First Amendment protection to works of this kind in the same way that it does to art, literature, and science. Clearly, however, any governmental effort to ban such texts would strike a crippling blow to our ability to discuss even the political and constitutional issues Bork regards as appropriate for public debate.

35. *See, e.g.,* John Rawls, A Theory of Justice § 57 (rev. ed. 1999).

36. *See, e.g.,* Martin Luther King, Jr., *Letter from Birmingham City Jail* (1963), *in* A Testament of Hope 289 (James Melvin Washington ed., 1986).

37. 539 U.S. 558, 574–75, 578 (2003).

38. Of course, this assumes that a speaker properly can be held responsible when she urges others to commit a wrongful act and when a sufficiently close connection exists between the speech and the act. For a defense of this view, see pp. 127–30.

39. *Whitney,* 274 U.S. at 373 (Brandeis, J., concurring).

40. For instance, as Justice Douglas suggested in *Dennis,* if individuals conspire against the government, they may be convicted of the crime of seditious conspiracy. Dennis v. United States, 341 U.S. 494, 581–82 (1951) (Douglas, J., dissenting). For a recent example, see United States v. Rahman, 189 F.3d 88 (2d Cir. 1999) (upholding the convictions of ten defendants for a 1993 conspiracy to bomb the World Trade Center and to levy war against the United States as an enemy of Islam), *cert. denied,* 528 U.S. 1094 (2000).

41. Brandenburg v. Ohio, 395 U.S. 444, 447 (1969) (per curiam). Other nations may reasonably draw the line between the two sets of rights in a somewhat different place. For example, after the atrocities of the Nazi era, it was reasonable for the new Federal Republic of Germany to impose a ban on political parties "which, by reason of their aims or the behavior of their adherents, seek to impair or destroy the free democratic basic order or to endanger the existence of the . . . Republic." Basic Law of the Federal Republic of Germany art. 21(2). Likewise, the European Court of Human Rights recently allowed Turkey to ban a political party that was dedicated to the establishment of Islamic supremacy, finding that the party posed a sufficiently imminent threat to democracy and to the rights and freedoms of others. *See* Refah Partisi (Welfare Party) v. Turkey, Eur. Ct. H.R. App. No. 41340/98, 37 Eur. H.R. Rep. 1 (2003). Restrictions like this would be out

of place in the United States, a long-established and stable democracy which is not seriously threatened by radical movements of this sort. For a thoughtful discussion of the problem of speech directed against the democratic order, together with a review of the European and American law on this subject, see Eric Barendt, Freedom of Speech 162–70 (2d ed., paperback ed. 2007).

42. For other arguments to this effect, see Kent Greenawalt, Speech, Crime, and the Uses of Language 116–17, 266–69 (1989); Rodney A. Smolla, Free Speech in an Open Society 112–16 (1992).

43. *See* Greenawalt, *supra* note 42, at 267; Martin H. Redish, Freedom of Expression 190–91 (1984); Smolla, *supra* note 42, at 114.

44. Greenawalt, *supra* note 42, at 116–17, 260–69.

45. *Id.* at 117, 269–70.

46. *See* p. 135.

47. In one controversial case, a Muslim cleric, Dr. Ali al-Timimi, was convicted of inciting several young followers to commit treason by telling them "that it was their Muslim duty to fight for Islam overseas and to defend the Taliban in Afghanistan against American forces." Eric Lichtblau, *Scholar Is Given Life Sentence in "Virginia Jihad" Case,* N.Y. Times, July 14, 2005, at A21. The U.S. Court of Appeals for the Fourth Circuit later remanded the case to the district court to determine whether al-Timimi had been improperly convicted on the basis of evidence obtained through the National Security Agency's warrantless surveillance program. *See* Eric Lichtblau, *Cleric Wins Appeal Ruling Over Wiretaps,* N.Y. Times, Apr. 26, 2006, at A17.

48. *See, e.g.,* The War on Our Freedoms (Richard C. Leone & Greg Anrig, Jr., eds., 2003); David Cole, *The Grand Inquisitors,* N.Y. Rev. of Books, July 19, 2007, at 53.

49. Dana Priest, *CIA Holds Terror Suspects in Secret Prisons,* Wash. Post, Nov. 2, 2005, at A1; James Risen & Eric Lichtblau, *Bush Lets U.S. Spy on Callers Without Courts,* N.Y. Times, Dec. 16, 2005, at A1; James Rainey, *2 Gulf Coast Papers Share Top Pulitzer,* L.A. Times, April 18, 2006, at A10; Leslie Cauley, *NSA Has Massive Database of Americans' Phone Calls,* USA Today, May 11, 2006, at 1A; Eric Lichtblau & James Risen, *Bank Data Sifted in Secret by U.S. to Block Terror,* N.Y. Times, June 23, 2006, at A1; Josh Meyer & Greg Miller, *U.S. Secretly Tracks Global Bank Data,* L.A. Times, June 23, 2006, at A1; Glenn R. Simpson, *Treasury Tracks Financial Data in Search Effort,* Wall St. J., June 23, 2006, at A1; Barton Gellman, Paul Blustein & Dafna Linzer, *Bank Records Secretly Tapped,* Wash. Post, June 23, 2006, at A1.

50. *See, e.g.,* Chris Cillizza, *Gore Says Bush Broke the Law with Spying,* Wash. Post, Jan. 17, 2006, at A3; Eric Lichtblau & James Risen, *Legal Rationale by Justice Dept. on Spying Effort,* N.Y. Times, Jan. 20, 2006, at A1; Michael Kranish, *Bush Calls Leak of Spy Program "Shameful,"* Boston Globe, Dec. 20, 2005, at A19; Peter Baker, *Surveillance Disclosure Denounced,* Wash. Post, June 27, 2006, at A1; H. Res. 895, 109th Cong., 2d Sess. (adopted June 29, 2006); Frank Rich, *Can't Win the War? Bomb the Press!,* N.Y. Times, July 2, 2006, § 4, at 10; Adam Liptak, *Gonzales Says Prosecutions of Journalists Are Possible,* N.Y. Times, May 22, 2006, at A14; U.S. Senate Judiciary Comm. Hearing on Dept. of Justice's Investigation of Journalists Who Publish Classified Information, 109th Cong., June 6, 2006, *available at* Lexis, News, All [hereinafter Senate Hearing] (testimony of Dep. Asst. Atty. Gen. Matthew Friedrich).

51. The attorney general's remarks are quoted in Liptak, *supra* note 50. For the Justice Department's explanation of its position, see the testimony of Matthew Friedrich, cited in note 50 above. For other defenses of this position, see John C. Eastman, *Listening to the Enemy: The President's Power to Conduct Surveillance of Enemy Communications During Time of War,* ILSA J. Int'l & Comp. L. (forthcoming); Gabriel Schoenfeld, *Has the New York Times Violated the Espionage Act?,* Commentary, March 2006.

52. For a comprehensive exploration of these laws, see Harold Edgar & Benno C. Schmidt, Jr., *The Espionage Statutes and Publication of Defense Information,* 73 Colum. L. Rev. 929 (1973). Important recent discussions include Stephen I. Vladeck, *Inchoate Liability and the Espionage Act: The Statutory Framework and the Freedom of the Press,* 1 Harv. L. & Pol'y Rev. 219 (2007), and Mary-Rose Papandrea, *Lapdogs, Watchdogs, and Scapegoats: The Press and National Security Information* (Boston C. Law Sch. Res. Paper 133, 2007), *available at* http://ssrn.com.

53. *See* New York Times Co. v. United States, 403 U.S. 713, 720–22 (1971) (Douglas, J., concurring); *id.* at 746 (Marshall, J., concurring); Statement for the Record of Geoffrey R. Stone to H. Perm. Select Comm. on Intelligence, May 19, 2006, *available at* http://intelligence.house.gov [hereinafter Stone Statement]. The history is recounted in Stone, Perilous Times, *supra* note 1, at 146–49.

The Supreme Court has long held that ambiguous statutes should be interpreted in a way that avoids "serious constitutional problems, . . . unless such a construction is plainly contrary to the intent of Congress." Edward J. DeBartolo Corp. v. Fla. Gulf Coast Bldg. & Constr. Trades Council, 485 U.S. 568, 575 (1988). This "cardinal principle" of statutory construction, *id.,* provides another strong reason to hold that § 793(e) does not apply to the press.

54. 18 U.S.C. § 798 (emphasis added); Senate Hearing, *supra* note 50 (remarks of Dean Rodney Smolla).

55. *See* Papandrea, *supra* note 52, at 11.

56. *See* Locke, Government, *supra* note 21, bk. II, §§ 88, 107, 145–48.

57. Stone draws a similar distinction. *See* Stone Statement, *supra* note 53, at 2–3.

58. New York Times Co. v. United States, 403 U.S. 713, 719 (1971) (Black, J., concurring).

59. *Id.* at 732 (White, J., concurring) (quoting the government's position in the Supreme Court); *id.* at 762–63 (Blackmun, J., dissenting) (quoting the opinion of Wilkey, J., in the D.C. Circuit); *id.* at 714 (per curiam) (internal quotation marks and citation omitted).

60. *Id.* at 730 (Stewart, J., concurring); *id.* at 726–27 (Brennan, J., concurring); *id.* at 731 (White, J., concurring). Two other members of the majority asserted that, under the First Amendment, "the publication of news may [never] be enjoined." *Id.* at 715 (Black, J., joined by Douglas, J., concurring).

61. *See id.* at 730 (Stewart, J., concurring); *id.* at 733–40 (White, J., concurring); *id.* at 752 (Burger, C.J., dissenting); *id.* at 759 (Blackmun, J., dissenting).

62. For a variety of proposals along the same lines, see Geoffrey R. Stone, *Government Secrecy vs. Freedom of the Press,* 1 Harv. L. & Pol'y Rev. 185, 204 (2007) [hereinafter Stone, *Secrecy*]; Heidi Kitrosser, *Classified Information Leaks and Free Speech,* 2008 U. Ill. L. Rev. (forthcoming); Papandrea, *supra* note 52, at 59–63.

63. The use of selective leaks has long been a common practice, *see* Papandrea, *supra* note 52, at 12–18, and has become especially troubling in recent years, *see* Ron Suskind, The One Percent Doctrine 169, 191, 341 (2006).

64. *See, e.g.,* David Cole & Jules Lobel, Less Safe, Less Free (2007). In August 2007, Congress authorized continuation of the NSA program on at least a temporary basis, while insisting on some degree of judicial oversight. *See* Protect America Act, Pub. L. No. 110–55, 121 Stat. 552 (2007).

65. *See* Priest, *supra* note 49.

66. *See* Alexander M. Bickel, The Morality of Consent 79–82 (1975); Rodney A. Smolla, *Information as Contraband: The First Amendment and Liability for Trafficking in Speech,* 96 Nw. U. L. Rev. 1099, 1167–69 (2002); Stone, *Secrecy, supra* note 62, at 186–97.

67. *See* Stone, *Secrecy, supra* note 62, at 195–97. For an argument in favor of a broader First Amendment privilege for employees, see Kitrosser, *supra* note 62.

68. *See* Papandrea, *supra* note 52, at 63–65. Nor should the government be permitted to make an end run around the First Amendment by calling reporters before a grand jury to testify about allegedly unlawful leaks by employees and then seeking contempt sanctions against reporters who refuse to reveal their sources. *See, e.g.,* Statement for the Record of Prof. Jonathan Turley Before H. Perm. Select Comm. on Intelligence 12, 16 (May 26, 2006), *available at* http://intelligence.house.gov (urging Congress to enact a reporters' shield law to prevent such abuses).

69. Texas v. Johnson, 491 U.S. 397, 399–400 (1989). For an excellent collection of materials on the flag-burning cases, see 2 The Constitution and the Flag (Michael Kent Curtis ed., 1993).

70. 491 U.S. at 414; *id.* at 422 (Rehnquist, C.J., dissenting); *see also id.* at 436 (Stevens, J., dissenting).

71. 496 U.S. 310, 315–18 (1990).

72. *See* Carl Hulse, *Flag Amendment Narrowly Fails in Senate Vote,* N.Y. Times, June 28, 2006, at A1.

73. *Johnson,* 491 U.S. at 429 (Rehnquist, C.J., dissenting); *Eichman,* 496 U.S. at 321 (Stevens, J., dissenting); David T. Prosser, *Desecration of the American Flag,* 3 Ind. Legal F. 159, 222–27 (1969).

74. 496 U.S. at 318; *see also Johnson,* 491 U.S. at 418.

75. 319 U.S. 624, 640–42 (1943).

76. *See* Steven H. Shiffrin, Dissent, Injustice, and the Meanings of America 10 (1999) (arguing that the First Amendment should protect flag burning as "a quintessential act of dissent").

77. *Johnson,* 491 U.S. at 422 (Rehnquist, C.J., dissenting).

78. In classical language, this is the political community that is created through the social contract.

79. 491 U.S. at 431 (Rehnquist, C.J., dissenting).

80. Sedition Act, ch. 75, 40 Stat. 553 (1918) (amending Espionage Act § 3, ch. 30, 40 Stat. 219 (1917)) (emphasis added).

81. *See* pp. 104–16.

82. *See Eichman,* 496 U.S. at 320–21 (Stevens, J., dissenting).

83. 394 U.S. 576, 578–79 (1969). According to traditional constitutional theory, alle-

giance and protection are reciprocal: individuals owe loyalty to the state in return for the protection they receive for their fundamental rights. *See* Steven J. Heyman, *The First Duty of Government: Protection, Liberty and the Fourteenth Amendment*, 41 Duke L.J. 507 (1991). From this perspective, Street's act of burning the flag—a symbol of his allegiance to the United States—was a perfectly natural and indeed highly eloquent response to his perception that the nation had failed to protect citizens like himself against lawless violence.

84. 491 U.S. at 431 (Rehnquist, C.J., dissenting) (quoting Chaplinsky v. New Hampshire, 315 U.S. 568, 572 (1942)).

85. In *Johnson*, Justice Brennan fails to appreciate this point when he characterizes the state's position as a claim that mistreatment of the flag may be prohibited because it "tend[s] to cast doubt on . . . the idea that nationhood and national unity are the flag's referents or that national unity actually exists." *Id.* at 413.

86. *See, e.g.*, Howard M. Wasserman, *Symbolic Counter-Speech*, 12 Wm. & Mary Bill Rts. J. 367 (2004).

87. This point accords with Robert Post's theory of public discourse. *See* Robert C. Post, Constitutional Domains 137–39, 187–88, 299–303 (1995).

88. *Johnson*, 491 U.S. at 403 n.3, 415 n.10, 418; *Eichman*, 496 U.S. at 315 n.4, 316 n.5.

Chapter 8. Speech and Violence

1. *See* pp. 104–16.

2. 395 U.S. 444, 447 (1969) (per curiam).

3. C. Edwin Baker, *Harm, Liberty, and Free Speech*, 70 S. Cal. L. Rev. 979, 989–92 (1997). For similar views, see Franklyn S. Haiman, Speech and Law in a Free Society 276–83 (1981); David R. Dow & R. Scott Shieldes, *Rethinking the Clear and Present Danger Test*, 73 Ind. L.J. 1217 (1998); Thomas Scanlon, *A Theory of Freedom of Expression*, 1 Phil. & Pub. Aff. 204, 212–13 (1972). In a later article, Scanlon retreats from this position on the ground that it places too much emphasis on the value of the listener's autonomy. T. M. Scanlon, Jr., *Freedom of Expression and Categories of Expression*, 40 U. Pitt. L. Rev. 519, 521–22, 533–34 (1979).

4. The following account is based on G. W. F. Hegel, Elements of the Philosophy of Right §§ 109–28 (Allen W. Wood ed., H. B. Nisbet trans., Cambridge Univ. Press 1991) (1820) [hereinafter Hegel, Philosophy of Right].

5. In some situations, the actor's responsibility should extend more broadly to include the consequences she could reasonably foresee would result from her act. For example, tort law generally holds individuals liable for reasonably foreseeable physical harms that are caused by their negligence.

6. Baker, *supra* note 3, at 992.

7. *See* Thomas Hobbes, Leviathan ch. XXV, at 176–78 (Richard Tuck ed., Cambridge Univ. Press 1991) (1651).

8. For a different analysis that reaches the same conclusion, see Joel Feinberg, *Limits to the Free Expression of Opinion* (1975), *in* Freedom and Fulfillment 124, 141–44 (1992).

9. Max Weber defines "social action" as action that is oriented toward the past,

present, or future action of others. *See* Max Weber, The Theory of Social and Economic Organization 112–15 (Talcott Parsons ed., A. M. Henderson & Talcott Parsons trans., 1947). This concept accurately describes both the speaker's act of incitement (which seeks to bring about unlawful action by the audience) and the listeners' ensuing conduct (which realizes the ends and intentions that were expressed by the speaker).

The point that incitement cannot be understood purely in terms of individual action may be illustrated by a *Doonesbury* cartoon from 1980. In the cartoon, the Gang of Four are on trial for inciting the murders of thousands of people during the Chinese Cultural Revolution; they defend themselves on the ground that the deaths resulted from "34,375 unrelated acts of passion." G. B. Trudeau, *Doonesbury,* Dec. 1, 1980, *in* Doonesbury Flashbacks CD-ROM (Mindscape 1995).

10. *See* Wayne R. LaFave, Criminal Law § 13.2 (4th ed. 2003); Model Penal Code § 2.06(a)(3) (Official Draft and Revised Commentaries 1980); 18 U.S.C. § 2(a) (2005). It is unclear how much impact the speech must have on those who actually commit the crime. *Compare, e.g.,* Model Penal Code, *supra,* § 2.06, cmt. 6(c), at 314 (stating that it is unnecessary "to inquire into the precise extent of influence exerted on the ultimate commission of the crime"), *with* LaFave, *supra,* at 674 n.51 (citing two cases that require some showing of actual influence). For theoretical discussions of this problem, see Kent Greenawalt, Speech, Crime, and the Uses of Language 262 (1989) (proposing that the speech must be "potentially influential"); Sanford N. Kadish, *Complicity, Cause and Blame: A Study in the Interpretation of Doctrine,* 73 Cal. L. Rev. 323, 355–64 (1985) (suggesting that it should be enough that the encouragement "*could have* contributed to the criminal action of the principal," so long as the contribution was "substantial").

11. *See* United States v. Peoni, 100 F.2d 401, 402 (2d Cir. 1938) (Learned Hand, J.); Kadish, *supra* note 10, at 354–55.

12. *See* Restatement (Second) of Torts §§ 876(b), 877(a) (1965).

13. Under the Model Penal Code, "[a] person is guilty of solicitation to commit a crime if with the purpose of promoting or facilitating its commission he commands, encourages or requests another person to engage in specific conduct that would constitute such crime." Model Penal Code, *supra* note 10, § 5.02(1). This provision, which accords with the common law, has been followed by a number of states. *See id.* § 5.02, cmt. 2, at 366–67; *id.* cmt. 3, at 370. Incitement may also be covered by more specific laws. For example, "statutes prohibiting incitement to riot are ubiquitous at the state and local levels," and a federal law (18 U.S.C. §§ 2101–02) makes it a crime to travel across state lines with intent to incite a riot. Haiman, *supra* note 3, at 263. *See also* 18 U.S.C. §§ 1091(c), 1093 (outlawing imminent incitement to genocide); *id.* § 2192 (banning solicitation or incitement to mutiny); *id.* § 2383 (prohibiting incitement to rebellion or insurrection).

14. *See* pp. 108–16.

15. The district court issued several opinions in the case, which are reported at 945 F. Supp. 1355 (D. Or. 1996) [hereinafter *ACLA I*]; 23 F. Supp. 2d 1182 (D. Or. 1998) [*ACLA II*]; and 41 F. Supp. 2d 1130 (D. Or. 1999) [*ACLA III*]. As I explain below, the court's decision in favor of the plaintiffs was reversed by a panel of the court of appeals, 244 F.3d 1007 (9th Cir. 2001) [*ACLA IV*], but the full court overturned the panel opinion and reinstated the district court decision, 290 F.3d 1058 (9th Cir. 2002) (en banc) [*ACLA V*]. The Supreme Court declined to review the case. 539 U.S. 958 (2003). Finally, the

district court issued an opinion reaffirming an award of punitive damages. 300 F. Supp. 2d 1055 (D. Or. 2004) [*ACLA VI*]. The facts in this section are drawn from these opinions, especially *ACLA III*, 41 F. Supp. 2d at 1131–53, and *ACLA V*, 290 F.3d at 1063–66.

16. 18 U.S.C. § 248(a)(1).

17. See *ACLA VI*, 300 F. Supp. 2d at 1057–58.

18. *ACLA V*, 290 F.3d at 1088 (characterizing the Nuremberg Files as a "hit list"). Some of the defendants described their movement as an "army" that was literally engaged in a "war" against their opponents — further evidence that they did not recognize a condition of peace to exist between themselves and their targets. See *ACLA III*, 41 F. Supp. 2d at 1139, 1144, 1146–47.

19. *ACLA V*, 290 F.3d at 1089–92 (Kozinski, J., dissenting) (emphasis added). In making this argument, Kozinski drew on an interesting and provocative article by Steven G. Gey entitled *The Nuremberg Files and the First Amendment Value of Threats*, 78 Tex. L. Rev. 541 (2000).

20. Kozinski got off on the wrong foot when he suggested that speech that causes fear can be banned only when it constitutes a threat: "[I]t is not illegal — and cannot be made so — merely to say things that would frighten or intimidate the listener. For example, when a doctor says, 'You have cancer and will die within six months,' it is not a threat, even though you almost certainly will be frightened. Similarly, 'Get out of the way of that bus' is not a threat, even though it is said in order to scare you into changing your behavior. By contrast, 'If you don't stop performing abortions, I'll kill you' is a true threat and surely illegal." *ACLA V*, 290 F.3d at 1089 (Kozinski, J., dissenting).

It is true that the speakers in Kozinski's first two cases would not be liable. By contrast, a person who falsely shouts to another, "You're about to be hit by a bus!" is liable for the tort of assault because she has intentionally and unjustifiably invaded the other's right to personal security. As the *Second Restatement of Torts* explains, an individual "may be equally frightened and alarmed, and the harm to his peace of mind may be equally great," when the actor makes him believe he is about to be injured by a third person or even by a natural force, as when he believes that the injury will come from the actor herself. *Restatement, supra* note 12, § 25, cmt. a. Likewise, a doctor who, knowing that the statement is false, tells a patient, "You have cancer and will die within six months" would surely be liable for intentional infliction of emotional distress. *Cf.* Wilkinson v. Downton, [1897] 2 Q.B. 57, 60–61. Kozinski is mistaken, then, when he implies that a speaker can be held liable for causing fear only when she issues a threat. Instead, statements that intentionally cause fear are wrongful whenever they seriously and unjustifiably infringe another person's right to personal security or emotional tranquillity.

21. Moreover, Kozinski greatly overstated the extent to which the *ACLA* defendants and the violent actors were "unrelated" to one another. One of the defendants, Michael Bray, had "served time in federal prison for conspiring to bomb ten clinics." *ACLA V*, 290 F.3d at 1064. Many of the *ACLA* defendants had close ties with an activist named Paul Hill and had worked with him on several occasions. See *ACLA III*, at 1134, 1139, 1146, 1148–50. After David Gunn was murdered, Hill helped to prepare a poster targeting Gunn's successor, John Britton, and later murdered Britton himself. *Id.* at 1135. The *ACLA* defendants publicly praised Hill and circulated a petition defending his conduct as

justifiable homicide. *Id.* Similarly, the defendants were "close friend[s] and associate[s]" of Shelley Shannon, who shot Dr. George Tiller in both arms and who "also later pleaded guilty to arson and butyric acid attacks on eight abortion facilities," including the Portland Feminist Women Health's Center, one of the plaintiffs in *ACLA*. *Id.* The defendants publicly endorsed Shannon's conduct, raised money for her defense, and declared that they "were very proud to be associated with" her. *Id.* at 1132, 1149–50. Of course, none of this shows that the *ACLA* defendants were legally responsible for the crimes committed by Bray, Hill, and Shannon. But it does belie the notion that the defendants merely encouraged violence by "third parties" who were unknown to them.

22. *See* p. 50.

23. *ACLA III,* 41 F. Supp. 2d at 1154.

24. *ACLA V,* 290 F.3d at 1101–02 (Berzon, J., dissenting) (quoting New York Times Co. v. Sullivan, 376 U.S. 254, 271 (1964)).

25. Of course, this conclusion is not limited to antiabortion protesters; it applies to anyone who makes statements that are clearly intended to threaten the personal security of others. For example, an animal rights group and six of its members were recently convicted of violating the Animal Enterprise Protection Act, 18 U.S.C. § 43, by maintaining a Web site that posted personal information about animal researchers and implicitly threatened violence against them. *See* David Kocieniewski, *Six Animal Rights Advocates Are Convicted of Terrorism,* N.Y. Times, Mar. 3, 2006, at B3.

26. *Cf.* Jürgen Habermas, Between Facts and Norms: Contributions to a Discourse Theory of Law and Democracy 147–48, 151 (William Rehg trans., 1996) (arguing that legitimate law derives from processes of "noncoercive communication").

27. *ACLA V,* 290 F.3d at 1104, 1107–09 (Berzon, J., dissenting); Virginia v. Black, 538 U.S. 343, 359–60 (2003).

28. For a somewhat different explanation, see *ACLA V,* 290 F.3d at 1106–07 (Berzon, J., dissenting).

29. For a similar argument, see O. Lee Reed, *The State Is Strong but I Am Weak: Why the "Imminent Lawless Action" Standard Should Not Apply to Targeted Speech That Threatens Individuals with Violence,* 38 Am. Bus. L.J. 177 (2000).

30. *See, e.g.,* John J. Kircher & Christine M. Wiseman, Punitive Damages § 5.1 (2d ed. 2000).

31. *Cf.* Gertz v. Robert Welch, Inc., 418 U.S. 323 (1974) (holding that punitive damages may be awarded in defamation cases only when the defendant knowingly or recklessly violated the plaintiff's right to reputation).

32. Rice v. Paladin Enters., 128 F.3d 233, 239 (4th Cir. 1997), *cert. denied,* 523 U.S. 1074 (1998).

33. One of the plaintiffs' lead attorneys was Rodney A. Smolla, a prominent civil libertarian scholar of the First Amendment. For an inside account of the case, see Rod Smolla, Deliberate Intent (1999).

34. Rice v. Paladin Enters., 940 F. Supp. 836 (D. Md. 1996), *rev'd,* 128 F.3d 233 (4th Cir. 1997), *cert. denied,* 523 U.S. 1074 (1998); Rodney A. Smolla, *Should the* Brandenburg v. Ohio *Incitement Test Apply in Media Violence Tort Cases?,* 27 N. Ky. L. Rev. 1, 8 (2000) [hereinafter Smolla, *Media Violence*].

35. *Restatement, supra* note 12, § 876(b) & cmt. d.

36. *Rice,* 128 F.3d at 247–48, 265–66; *see also* Eugene Volokh, *Crime-Facilitating Speech,* 57 Stan. L. Rev. 1095, 1174–79 (2005).

37. 128 F.3d at 239–41; Smolla, Deliberate Intent, *supra* note 33, at 25–27, 41, 65–67.

38. 128 F.3d at 241 n.2 (Joint Statement of Facts ¶¶ 4.a, 4.b, 7).

39. *Id.* at 253–55.

40. *See* Volokh, *supra* note 36, at 1182–83.

41. *See, e.g.,* Adam Smith, An Inquiry into the Nature and Causes of the Wealth of Nations bk. I, ch. II (R.H. Campbell et al. eds., Oxford Univ. Press 1976) (1776); Hegel, Philosophy of Right, *supra* note 4, § 182.

42. *See* Volokh, *supra* note 36, at 1182–83.

43. In some states, an individual can be prosecuted for aiding and abetting a crime when he knowingly assists in the commission of the crime. *See id.* at 1174 n.295. Other jurisdictions follow an intent standard, *id.,* which can be understood to mean either an intent to assist another in committing a crime or an intent that the crime come about. The Model Penal Code is ambiguous on this point. Under the Code, a person is subject to accomplice liability if he acts "with the purpose of promoting or facilitating the commission of the offense." Model Penal Code, *supra* note 10, § 2.06(3)(a). Under a literal reading of this provision, a purpose to facilitate is sufficient. According to the official commentaries, however, the defendant must have "a true purpose to advance the criminal end." *Id.* cmt. 6(c), at 315; *see also id.* cmt. 6(b), at 310 (the defendant must "have as his conscious objective the bringing about of [criminal] conduct").

44. *See* p. 137.

45. Any other rule would have perverse results. For example, the federal courts have generally held tax protesters guilty of aiding and abetting income tax evasion when they instruct others on how to file false returns, and have rejected the protesters' free speech defense. *See Rice,* 128 F.2d at 245–46 (discussing cases). From a First Amendment perspective, it would be bizarre to hold that these ideological speakers may constitutionally be punished (because they intend to bring about the crime of tax evasion), while at the same time holding that individuals who give the same advice for profit are entitled to protection (because once they have been paid, they are indifferent to whether their clients or customers go on to commit the crime). For a recent case that holds the promotion of tax fraud unprotected in a primarily commercial rather than political setting, see United States v. Bell, 414 F.3d 474 (3d Cir. 2005).

46. 395 U.S. 444, 447 (1969) (per curiam).

47. *Rice,* 128 F.3d at 255–65; Smolla, *Media Violence, supra* note 34, at 43.

48. *See, e.g.,* Baker, *supra* note 3, at 991 (asserting that "when speech plays merely the role of an instrument, free speech principles seldom offer protection").

49. *See, e.g.,* Pittsburgh Press Co. v. Pittsburgh Comm'n on Human Relations, 413 U.S. 376, 388–89 (1973) (holding sex-specific "help wanted" advertisements unprotected because they were instrumental to illegal discrimination).

50. *See* 128 F.3d at 241 n.2 (Joint Statement of Facts ¶ 5.a); *id.* at 255.

51. *See* Volokh, *supra* note 36, at 1161–62 & n.251 (describing the book's message as "a rejection of morality, and a sort of bargain basement Nietzschean praise for the 'man

of action' . . . 'who faces death as a challenge and . . . walks away the winner,' " (quoting *Hit Man*), but suggesting that the book's "crime-facilitating details" were unnecessary "to convey the political message").

52. *Id.* at 1208–09 (footnote omitted).

53. The problem of crime-facilitating speech raises many other complex and fascinating issues which I cannot do justice to here. Although I disagree with Volokh's position on *Rice,* his article provides an indispensable starting point for exploring the subject. The leading work on the relation between speech and crime in general is Greenawalt, *supra* note 10.

54. 315 U.S. 568, 569, 571–72 (1942).

55. *See* chapter 2. In formulating the problem this way, the Court followed Chafee. *See* 315 U.S. at 572 (citing Zechariah Chafee, Jr., Free Speech in the United States 149–50 (1941)).

56. *See, e.g.,* Haiman, *supra* note 3, at 252–60; Burton Caine, *The Trouble with "Fighting Words": Chaplinsky v. New Hampshire Is a Threat to First Amendment Values and Should Be Overruled,* 88 Marq. L. Rev. 441 (2004); Stephen W. Gard, *Fighting Words as Free Speech,* 58 Wash. U.L.Q. 531 (1980); Mark C. Rutzick, *Offensive Language and the Evolution of First Amendment Protection,* 9 Harv. C.R.-C.L. L. Rev. 1 (1974); Nadine Strossen, *Regulating Racist Speech on Campus: A Modest Proposal?,* 1990 Duke L.J. 484, 508–14.

57. On civility, see Hadley Arkes, *Civility and the Restriction of Speech: Rediscovering the Defamation of Groups,* 1974 Sup. Ct. Rev. 281, 305–17; on equality, see Richard Delgado, *Words That Wound: A Tort Action for Racial Insults, Epithets, and Name-Calling,* 17 Harv. C.R.-C.L. L. Rev. 133, 173–74 (1982); Charles Lawrence, *If He Hollers Let Him Go: Regulating Racist Speech on Campus,* 1990 Duke L.J. 431, 449–57 (1990).

58. For the view that free speech problems often involve "tragic choices" of this kind, see Susan H. Williams, *Feminist Jurisprudence and Free Speech Theory,* 68 Tul. L. Rev. 1563, 1579 (1994).

59. *See* Haiman, *supra* note 3, at 258.

60. *See* Feiner v. New York, 340 U.S. 315, 326–27 (1951) (Black, J., dissenting); Chafee, *supra* note 55, at 151–52.

61. Alexander M. Bickel, The Morality of Consent 72 (1975).

62. 645 P.2d 916, 918 (Kan. Ct. App. 1982). Many of the examples I use in this part of the book contain profoundly offensive language, for which I apologize. Unfortunately, discussions of the First Amendment often take place on an abstract level, without considering the exact nature of the speech at issue — something that I believe we must do to reach thoughtful judgments about whether it should receive constitutional protection.

63. Challenging this notion, Stephen Gard asserts that "it is fallacious to believe that personally abusive epithets, even if addressed face-to-face to the object of the speaker's criticism, are likely to arouse the ordinary law-abiding person beyond mere anger to uncontrollable, reflexive violence." Gard, *supra* note 56, at 572–75, 580. As I explain below, the fighting words doctrine does not suppose that a violent response is inevitable or uncontrollable. It is enough that the words provoke a strong desire to fight back and thus give rise to a substantial likelihood of violence. This clearly can be true of language

like that in *Gomez,* particularly if used in certain settings, such as a bar room confrontation. In the next section, I discuss how insults should be treated in cases where the victim is unlikely to fight back.

64. 645 P.2d at 918. For similar facts, see Bailey v. Binyon, 583 F. Supp. 923, 925 (N.D. Ill. 1984). The plaintiff's employer allegedly called him a "nigger" several times and told him that "all you niggers are alike." When the plaintiff responded that he did not appreciate the racial slurs and that he "wanted to be treated 'like a human being,'" the employer replied, "You're not a human being, you're a nigger." As the employee began to leave, the employer called him a "sissy" and said that if he were a man he would stay. The court denied a defense motion to dismiss the employee's claims for civil rights and Title VII violations.

65. *See* pp. 50–51.

66. Hobbes, *supra* note 7, ch. X, at 63–64; ch. XIII, at 88; ch. XV, at 107; ch. XXVII, at 206–07; *see also id.* ch. XXVI, at 185 (explaining that, within civil society, the laws of nature gain the force of positive law).

67. For a news story that suggests that this tendency is widespread if not universal, see *Thai Buddhist Monks Defrocked After Street Brawl,* Reuters, May 31, 2005. The article reports that five monks were defrocked and fined after a fight that "was the culmination of years of antagonism between monks from . . . two [neighboring] temples who had often exchanged curses, insults and rude gestures as they collected alms on different sides of a road." One of the monks was quoted as saying, "When an ordinary person is given a middle-finger sign, he will be mad. So am I."

68. *See, e.g.,* LaFave, *supra* note 10, §§ 10.4–10.7.

69. 315 U.S. 568, 572 (1942).

70. *See, e.g.,* Gooding v. Wilson, 405 U.S. 518, 525 (1972); Cohen v. California, 403 U.S. 15, 20 (1971).

71. 505 U.S. 377, 381 (1992). For a discussion of *R.A.V.,* see pp. 166–69.

72. *See* sources cited in note 56 above.

73. *See, e.g.,* Kent Greenawalt, Fighting Words: Individuals, Communities, and Liberties of Speech 52–53 (1995); Steven H. Shiffrin, Dissent, Injustice, and the Meanings of America 74–75 (1999); Lawrence, *supra* note 57, at 453–54.

74. Gomez v. Hug, 645 P.2d 916, 922 (Kan. Ct. App. 1982).

75. *See* Restatement, *supra* note 12, § 46 & cmt. j (limiting recovery to cases in which "the distress inflicted is so severe that no reasonable man could be expected to endure it").

76. *See* pp. 55–57.

77. Samuel Warren & Louis D. Brandeis, *The Right to Privacy,* 4 Harv. L. Rev. 193, 205 (1890).

78. Adam Smith, Lectures on Jurisprudence 105, 122–24, 480–81 (R. L. Meek et al. eds., 1978); Immanuel Kant, The Metaphysics of Morals *236–37, *332–33, *462–64 (Mary Gregor trans., Cambridge Univ. Press 1991) (1797); Hegel, Philosophy of Right, *supra* note 4, § 319R; Georg Wilhelm Friedrich Hegel, Lectures on Natural Right and Political Science 62, 97 (J. Michael Stewart & Peter C. Hodgson trans., 1995).

79. Some other legal systems afford protection against such insults. Under English law, for example, a person "is guilty of an offense if he . . . uses threatening, abusive or insulting words or behaviour, . . . within the hearing or sight of a person likely to be

caused harassment, alarm or distress thereby." Public Order Act, 1986, c. 64, § 5(1) (Eng.). It is a defense if the "conduct was reasonable." *Id.* § 5(3)(c). *See also* James Q. Whitman, *Enforcing Civility and Respect: Three Societies,* 109 Yale L.J. 1279, 1295–1312, 1344–60 (2000) (discussing German and French law).

80. *See* p. 55.

81. Restatement, *supra* note 12, §§ 652B, 652D(a). If this standard is considered too low, we might look instead to the *Restatement*'s definition of intentional infliction of emotional distress and require that the attack amount to "extreme and outrageous conduct." *Id.* § 46.

82. *See, e.g.,* Martin H. Redish, Freedom of Expression 55–56 (1984).

83. *See* pp. 70–71.

84. Gard, *supra* note 56, at 540, 547–48, 569.

85. Kant, Metaphysics of Morals, *supra* note 78, at *462.

86. As Charles Lawrence argues, the freedom to engage in reasoned discussion is enhanced rather than diminished by restrictions on abusive speech. *See* Lawrence, *supra* note 57, at 452–56. This view is consistent with Meiklejohn's notion that rules of order make free discussion possible. *See* p. 63.

87. State v. Chaplinsky, 18 A.2d 754, 758 (N.H. 1941). In fact, Chaplinsky claimed that the marshal and other officers had also insulted him, had condoned the crowd's violence against him, and had even participated in that violence. *See* Brief for Appellant at 2–6, Chaplinsky v. New Hampshire, 315 U.S. 568 (1942) (No. 255). For a critique of *Chaplinsky* that focuses on these facts, see Caine, *supra* note 56 .

88. *See* Rutzick, *supra* note 56, at 10.

89. 315 U.S. at 571–72.

90. New York Times Co. v. Sullivan, 376 U.S. 254, 270 (1964); City of Houston v. Hill, 482 U.S. 451, 462–63 (1987).

91. Lewis v. City of New Orleans, 415 U.S. 130, 135 & n.* (1974) (Powell, J., concurring in result).

92. The Model Penal Code takes a similar position. *See* Model Penal Code, *supra* note 10, § 250.4, cmt. 3, at 366. However, this protection should not necessarily extend to speech or conduct that actually threatens an officer with violence. *See, e.g.,* State v. Barth, 2005 ND 134.

93. *See, e.g.,* Caine, *supra* note 56, at 547–50; Gard, *supra* note 56, at 556–57, 565–69; Rutzick, *supra* note 56, at 10–11.

94. John Locke, Two Treatises of Government bk. II, §§ 1, 6 (Peter Laslett ed., Cambridge Univ. Press 1988) (1690).

95. Whitney v. California, 274 U.S. 357, 375–76 (1927) (Brandeis, J., concurring).

Chapter 9. Speech and Privacy

1. Samuel Warren & Louis D. Brandeis, *The Right to Privacy,* 4 Harv. L. Rev. 193, 205 (1890).

2. *See* pp. 57–59, 73–77 (defamation); pp. 144–46 (personal dignity).

3. On these two facets of the right to privacy, see pp. 56–57.

4. 530 U.S. 703 (2000). On the defamation cases, see pp. 73–77.

5. 530 U.S. at 707–10. *ACLA* is discussed in chapter 8 at pp. 131–36.

6. 530 U.S. at 708, 714–18, 724–28.

7. *Id.* at 741, 748–49, 750–51 (Scalia, J., joined by Thomas, J., dissenting).

8. Rowan v. U.S. Post Office Dep't, 397 U.S. 728, 736 (1970); Frisby v. Schultz, 487 U.S. 474, 484–85 (1988) (internal quotation marks and citation omitted).

9. Hague v. CIO, 307 U.S. 496, 515 (1939) (opinion of Roberts, J.); Perry Educ. Ass'n v. Perry Local Educators' Ass'n, 460 U.S. 37, 45 (1983) (summarizing the rules governing traditional public forums).

10. Schenck v. Pro-Choice Network, 519 U.S. 357, 373 (1977) (internal quotation marks and citation omitted).

11. *See* 530 U.S. at 741–42, 750–53 (Scalia, J., dissenting) (internal quotation marks and citation omitted).

12. *Id.* at 757.

13. 505 U.S. 833, 851 (1992).

14. *See* 530 U.S. at 757 (Scalia, J., dissenting); *id.* at 788–90, 792 (Kennedy, J., dissenting).

15. 403 U.S. 15, 21 (1971).

16. *See* 530 U.S. at 742–49 (Scalia, J., dissenting); *id.* at 765–70 (Kennedy, J., dissenting). For a stimulating debate on *Hill,* see *Colloquium,* 28 Pepp. L. Rev. 747, 747–54 (2001) (remarks of Akhil Amar, Erwin Chemerinsky, Douglas Kmiec, Michael W. McConnell, Kathleen Sullivan, and Laurence H. Tribe).

17. 530 U.S. at 736–37 (Souter, J., joined by O'Connor, Ginsburg & Breyer, JJ., concurring).

18. Paul Duggan, *"God Blew Up the Troops,"* Wash. Post, April 7, 2006, at B4; Lizette Alvarez, *Outrage at Funeral Protests Pushes Lawmakers to Act,* N.Y. Times, April 17, 2006, at A14; Eric Herman, *Funeral Protesters Coming Here,* Chi. Sun-Times, April 17, 2006, at 8; Respect for America's Fallen Heroes Act, Pub. L. No. 109–228, § 2, 120 Stat. 387 (2006) (codified at 38 U.S.C. § 2413).

19. The intrusion and distress that such protests cause are likely to be far greater than in some other cases in which the Supreme Court has upheld restrictions on speech. *See, e.g.,* Florida Bar v. Went for It, Inc., 515 U.S. 618, 625 (1995) (holding that a state rule barring lawyers from soliciting business from accident victims or their survivors for a thirty-day period was justified to prevent "intrusion upon the special vulnerability and private grief of victims or their families") (internal quotation marks and citation omitted); Frisby v. Schultz, 487 U.S. 474, 484 (1988) (holding that a ban on targeted residential picketing was justified to protect the "tranquillity . . . and privacy of the home").

20. The balance of rights should come out differently in a small category of cases, such as the funerals of former Presidents. Ceremonies of this sort are major public events which highlight the individual's public life. A demonstration outside such an event is likely to cause much less pain and intrusion, while the occasion provides a much more important forum for ideological expression. But considerations of this sort do not justify protecting demonstrations at other funerals, especially those of private figures such as soldiers killed in war.

21. However, I do not mean to suggest that such laws should be upheld only if they are content neutral in the strong sense that they have nothing to do with the communicative

impact of expression. The injuries that flow from funeral demonstrations result not only from the noise and distraction they involve, but also from the profound offense they cause to mourners. As I argued in chapter 6, however, regulations based on communicative impact should not be held to violate the First Amendment if they are justified to protect the rights of others. *See* pp. 91–95.

22. Judicial decisions on the constitutionality of funeral protest laws include Phelps-Roper v. Taft, No. 1:06 CV 2038, 2007 U.S. Dist. LEXIS 20831 (N.D. Ohio, Mar. 23, 2007); Phelps-Roper v. Nixon, No. 06-4156-CV-C-FJG, 2007 U.S. Dist. LEXIS 5783 (W.D. Mo., Jan. 26, 2007); McQueary v. Stumbo, 453 F. Supp. 2d 975 (E.D. Ky. 2006). In each case, the court held that the state law was content-neutral and was intended to serve significant government interests such as privacy. The courts then reached differing conclusions on whether the particular laws at issue — all of which were more restrictive than the federal statute — burdened substantially more speech than necessary to protect those interests. These cases suggest that the courts will uphold funeral protest laws if they are narrowly tailored. In another case, a federal judge denied Phelps's motion to dismiss a civil suit for invasion of privacy, defamation, and intentional infliction of emotional distress arising out of a demonstration he led at the funeral of a Marine corporal killed in Iraq. Snyder v. Phelps, No. RDB-06-1389, 2006 U.S. Dist. LEXIS 79020 (D. Md., Oct. 30, 2006). For an insightful discussion of the values involved in the funeral protest cases, see Njeri Mathis Rutledge, *A Time to Mourn: Balancing the Right of Free Speech Against the Right of Privacy in Funeral Picketing*, 67 Md. L. Rev. (forthcoming 2008).

In this section, I have focused on the demonstrations' impact on mourners. But one can also view the protests as a violation of the respect due to the dead. Some philosophers hold that a person's right to dignity extends beyond his death. *See, e.g.*, Immanuel Kant, The Metaphysics of Morals *295 (Mary Gregor trans., Cambridge Univ. Press 1991) (1797). Some contemporary legal systems take the same position. *See* Mephisto, 30 BverfGE 173 (F.R.G. 1971). Whether or not one accepts this view, I believe the community should have the power to prohibit certain forms of disrespect. As I explain in chapters 10 and 11, the community is founded on mutual recognition and respect. *See* pp. 170–72, 198. Of course, funerals are among the most profound ways that community members show respect for the lives of others. Conduct that intentionally disrupts or interferes with a funeral, like conduct that mistreats a corpse or desecrates a cemetery, violates communal standards of human dignity and respect. In this way, the demonstrations violate the rights of the community as well as those of the mourners themselves.

23. Florida Star v. B.J.F., 491 U.S. 524, 533 (1989) (internal quotation marks and citation omitted).

24. *See, e.g., id.;* Bartnicki v. Vopper, 532 U.S. 514 (2001) (holding that the media have a First Amendment right to publish an illegally intercepted conversation on a matter of public concern); Globe Newspaper Co. v. Superior Court, 457 U.S. 596 (1982) (striking down a statute excluding the public and press from a sex-offense trial during the testimony of an underage victim); Smith v. Daily Mail Publ'g Co., 443 U.S. 97 (1979) (holding that a state may not punish truthful publication of the name of an alleged juvenile offender lawfully obtained by a newspaper); Okla. Publ'g Co. v. Dist. Court, 430 U.S. 308 (1977) (overturning a pretrial order enjoining publication of the name of a juvenile defendant obtained during proceedings that in fact were open to the public); Cox Broad.

Corp. v. Cohn, 420 U.S. 469 (1975) (holding that a state may not punish accurate publication of the name of a rape victim obtained from judicial records open to public inspection).

25. 491 U.S. at 526–29; *id.* at 546 (White, J., dissenting).

26. *Id.* at 533 (quoting Smith v. Daily Mail, 443 U.S. at 103).

27. *See id.* at 537–38, 540–41; *see also id.* at 541–42 (Scalia, J., concurring in part and in judgment).

28. *Id.* at 533; *id.* at 542 (White, J., dissenting) (citation and internal quotation marks omitted). For an exploration of the devastating impact of sexual violence, see Susan J. Brison, Aftermath: Violence and the Remaking of a Self (2002).

29. 491 U.S. at 536–37.

30. *See* p. 162.

31. *See* Richmond Newspapers, Inc. v. Virginia, 448 U.S. 555 (1980) (holding that the public and press generally have a First Amendment right of access to criminal trials).

32. *See* Cox Broad. Corp. v. Cohn, 420 U.S. 469 (1975) (holding that the press has a First Amendment right to publish the name of a rape victim obtained from public judicial records).

33. Another argument for First Amendment protection holds that the media are justified in publishing the names of rape victims because this tends to eradicate the unjust stigma that society has traditionally imposed on them. But stigma is not the only harm victims suffer when their names are published. Rape inflicts deeper indignity, humiliation, and emotional distress than virtually any other crime, and these injuries may well be compounded when the rape is made public against the victim's will. These injuries are immediate and powerful, while any effect of publication in reducing stigma is likely to be long-run and incremental. Moreover, victims might well be discouraged from reporting the crime to the authorities if they knew that they thereby surrendered their right to anonymity. Under these circumstances, the benefit that would flow from a constitutional right to publish the names of rape victims does not seem to outweigh the injury to privacy. Instead, in a case like *Florida Star,* the individual should be free to choose for herself whether to allow her name to be published. This rule is likely to empower women and to promote gender equality more than a rule that allows the media to reveal a victim's identity without her consent.

34. Some other nations protect the privacy of victims in this situation. For example, the Canadian Supreme Court has upheld a law similar to Florida's on the ground that it was reasonably designed "to foster complaints by victims of sexual assault by protecting them from the trauma of wide-spread publication resulting in embarrassment and humiliation." Canadian Newspapers v. Canada, [1988] 2 S.C.R. 122, 130 (Can.). *See also* Eric Barendt, Freedom of Speech 235 (2d ed., paperback ed. 2007) (citing the laws of France and the United Kingdom).

35. 532 U.S. 514, 517–20, 533–34 (2001).

36. 491 U.S. at 534–36, 538–39; *see Bartnicki,* 532 U.S. at 546–48 (Rehnquist, C.J., dissenting).

37. *See Bartnicki,* 532 U.S. at 553–55 (Rehnquist, C.J., dissenting); *see also* p. 57.

38. *See, e.g.,* NAACP v. Alabama ex rel. Patterson, 357 U.S. 449, 462 (1958).

39. *See* 532 U.S. at 529, 533.

40. *Id.* at 536–37 (Breyer, J., concurring) (quoting Olmstead v. United States, 277 U.S. 438, 478 (1928) (Brandeis, J., dissenting)). For a caveat regarding Breyer's description of rights like privacy as "competing constitutional concerns," see p. 252 n.74.

41. 532 U.S. at 535–41 (Breyer, J., concurring) (internal quotation marks and citations omitted); *id.* at 553–56 (Rehnquist, C.J., dissenting).

42. For a discussion of this tort, see pp. 56–57.

43. *See, e.g.,* Eugene Volokh, *Freedom of Speech and Information Privacy: The Troubling Implications of a Right to Stop People from Speaking About You,* 52 Stan. L. Rev. 1049 (2000); Diane L. Zimmerman, *Requiem for a Heavyweight: A Farewell to Warren and Brandeis's Privacy Tort,* 68 Cornell L. Rev. 291 (1983). Harry Kalven, Jr., argued that the common law tort should be abolished, although he did not explicitly address the First Amendment issue. Harry Kalven, Jr., *Privacy in Tort Law — Were Warren and Brandeis Wrong?,* 31 Law & Contemp. Probs. 326 (1966).

44. *See, e.g.,* Kalven, *supra* note 43, at 329, 337; Zimmerman, *supra* note 43, at 335–36.

45. *See* pp. 56–57, 156–58. Eugene Volokh argues that, although the state should not be allowed to enforce a general right to privacy, it can afford some protection through contract law. "This," he says, "explains much of why it's proper for the government to impose confidentiality requirements on lawyers, doctors, psychotherapists, and others": when they agree to be your advisor, they implicitly promise to maintain confidentiality. Volokh, *supra* note 43, at 1057–58. By contrast, the state should have no power to suppress "[s]peech by people who have never promised to remain quiet about something." *Id.* at 1072.

In my view, it is a mistake to say that professional duties of confidentiality arise solely from contract. When you confide your personal affairs to a lawyer, doctor, or psychotherapist, you waive your right to privacy with regard to those matters, but only to the extent necessary for the provision of professional services. Thus, the professional's duty of confidentiality derives in part from the fact that you did not waive your right to privacy beyond those bounds. In addition, the professional undertakes to keep your secrets even beyond the scope of your common law right to privacy. Thus, the fact that professionals are bound by duties of confidentiality does not suggest that other people are free to reveal intimate information about your life so long as they never promised to remain silent. (To make this point even clearer, suppose that a patient tells her psychotherapist highly personal information about her ex-husband that she has improperly discovered during a bitter divorce. The patient does not care about protecting her ex-husband's privacy, and the therapist later publishes the information in a sensationalistic book. On Volokh's view, the therapist would not be liable to the ex-husband because she has never promised to respect his confidentiality. It seems clear, however, that she has violated his right to privacy in this situation by publishing personal information about him without his consent.)

The idea of contract is also relevant to privacy in another way. Volokh acknowledges that he might prefer to give up the right to speak about other people's private affairs in exchange for an assurance that they would not speak about his. *Id.* at 1051. Moreover, he seems to believe that this preference is widely shared, for he says that rules to protect privacy are likely to be "quite popular." *Id.* at 1100. If that is true, then if people had the ability to do so, they would enter into contracts in which each person promised to respect the privacy of others. As Volokh recognizes, people often do make such explicit or implicit contracts when they can, not only with professionals but also with businesses that collect data about them. It appears that people do not enter into such contracts more broadly only because it is impractical to do so. If that is the case, then one can argue that the law is justified in adopting the same rule that individuals would voluntarily agree to if they could. *See, e.g.,* Richard A. Posner, *Epstein's Tort Theory: A Critique,* 8 J. Legal. Stud. 457, 460 (1979) (sketching a similar argument for a general duty to rescue). Arguments of this sort are generally made in economic terms, but one can also make them from the standpoint of human liberty: if people in fact would make such a choice, then they should be free to use the political process to achieve collectively what they are unable to attain through their own separate, individual efforts, so long as the rule they adopt does not violate rights that are entitled to constitutional protection.

46. Zimmerman, *supra* note 43, at 293, 311–16.

47. *See* p. 59.

48. Volokh, *supra* note 43, at 1089–95; Zimmerman, *supra* note 43, at 351.

49. Volokh, *supra* note 43, at 1056; Zimmerman, *supra* note 43, at 323.

50. Robert Post reaches a similar conclusion from a sociological perspective. *See* Robert C. Post, Constitutional Domains 174–77 (1995).

51. Thomas I. Emerson, *The Right of Privacy and Freedom of the Press,* 14 Harv. C.R.-C.L. L. Rev. 329, 342–43 (1979).

52. Gertz v. Robert Welch, Inc., 418 U.S. 323, 340 (1974).

53. Of course, individuals are free to reveal personal information about themselves if they so choose. This suggests that we should consider informational privacy rules to be based more on the *source* than on the *content* of the expression. These rules are not predicated on the notion that it is inherently improper to communicate information about an individual's private life. Instead, they hold that the right to control this information properly belongs to the individual herself, and that she should have the power to decide whether it is communicated to others.

54. Rosenblatt v. Baer, 383 U.S. 75, 92 (1966) (Stewart, J., concurring).

Chapter 10. Hate Speech

1. For collections of writings on this problem, see Henry Louis Gates et al., Speaking of Race, Speaking of Sex (1994); Hate Speech and the Constitution (Steven J. Heyman ed., 1996); Mari J. Matsuda et al., Words that Wound (1993). On the history of the issue, see Samuel Walker, Hate Speech: The History of an American Controversy (1994).

2. 505 U.S. 377 (1992).

3. Virginia v. Black, 538 U.S. 343, 365 (2003) (holding that public ideological cross burning falls in this category); *see also* Collin v. Smith, 578 F.2d 1197 (7th Cir.) (holding that Nazis have a right to march in Skokie), *cert. denied,* 439 U.S. 916 (1978).

4. *See* Larry Rohter, *Brooklyn Man Tells a Florida Jury About Being Kidnapped and Set Ablaze,* N.Y. Times, Sept. 4, 1993, § 1, at 7.

5. *See, e.g.,* State v. Wyant, No. 90-CA-2, 1990 Ohio App. LEXIS 5589, at *3 (Ohio Ct. App., Dec. 6, 1990), *aff'd after remand,* 68 Ohio St. 3d 162 (1994); Restatement (Second) of Torts § 46, illus. 20 (1965).

6. *See* p. 143 (discussing Gomez v. Hug, 645 P.2d 916 (Kan. Ct. App. 1982)).

7. *See, e.g.,* Wisconsin v. Mitchell, 508 U.S. 476, 479–80 (1993), *discussed at* p. 168.

8. An incident at Arizona State University in 1989 provides a dramatic example of all of these offenses. A fight started between a black student, Toby Wright, and a white fraternity member, Sean Hedgecock, after Hedgecock allegedly said, "Fuck you, nigger." Two dozen fraternity members then emerged from their house and surrounded Wright and two other blacks, chanting racial slurs. The fight was broken up by police, who alleged that Hedgecock continued to shout epithets and threatened to "get those niggers and kill them." Later that night, Hedgecock saw two other black students and shouted, "Those are the niggers! They're back!" Several hundred people then flooded out of nearby fraternity houses, surrounded the blacks, and watched while a group of white fraternity members beat them up. The incident is recounted in Jon Wiener, *Words That Wound: Free Speech for Campus Bigots?,* 250 The Nation 272, 272–73 (Feb. 26, 1990).

9. *See* p. 145.

10. For an example, see United States v. McAninch, 994 F.2d 1380 (9th Cir. 1993).

11. For a powerful account of the injuries caused by hate speech, see Matsuda et al., *supra* note 1.

12. *See, e.g.,* Cotton v. Duncan, No. 93 C 3875, 1993 U.S. Dist. LEXIS 16161 (N.D. Ill., Nov. 12, 1993) (holding that cross burning may violate 42 U.S.C. § 1982 and the Fair Housing Act).

13. *See* pp. 70–71.

14. *See* pp. 177–79, 279 n.67.

15. 505 U.S. 377 (1992).

16. *Id.* at 379–80.

17. *See, e.g.,* Terminiello v. Chicago, 337 U.S. 1, 4 (1949).

18. In re Welfare of R.A.V., 464 N.W.2d 507, 510–11 (Minn. 1991); Chaplinsky v. New Hampshire, 315 U.S. 568, 572 (1942). The state court also held that the ordinance was constitutional insofar as it applied to expression that met the incitement test of *Brandenburg v. Ohio,* 395 U.S. 444 (1969).

19. *R.A.V.,* 505 U.S. at 381, 391, 393–94. Four Justices rejected the majority's reasoning but would have held the ordinance invalid on overbreadth grounds. *See id.* at 397 (White, J., joined by Blackmun, O'Connor & Stevens, JJ., concurring in judgment).

20. *Id.* at 388–89.

21. As I explain in the following section, group-based insults do not merely violate rights like bodily security and personal dignity; they also violate the right to recognition, which is the most fundamental right people have.

22. *See* 505 U.S. at 408–09 (White, J., concurring in judgment) (contending that the "overriding message of personal injury and violence" conveyed by fighting words "is at its ugliest when directed against groups that have long been the targets of discrimination").

23. In response to the contention that the "harms caused by racial, religious, and gender-based invective are qualitatively different from that caused by other fighting words," *id.* at 424 (Stevens, J., concurring in judgment), Scalia replied that, if this is true, it is due entirely to the fact that such harms are "caused by a distinctive idea. . . . It is obvious that the symbols which will arouse 'anger, alarm or resentment in others on the

basis of race, color, creed, religion or gender' are those symbols that communicate a message of hostility based on one of these characteristics." *Id.* at 392–93. But that would be just as true of the hate-based insults that Scalia assumed would be proscribable under a general fighting words statute. Indeed, the harm caused by *all* fighting words stems from the "message of hostility" they convey, whether that hostility is directed against the targets personally or against the groups to which they belong. *See id.* at 408–09 (White, J., concurring in judgment). Thus, the fact that the harms caused by racial, religious, and gender-based insults result from the expression of "a distinctive idea" does not mean that they are not more serious than the harms caused by other insults or that they do not justify greater regulation. For a similar argument, see Steven H. Shiffrin, Dissent, Injustice, and the Meanings of America 59 (1999).

24. 508 U.S. 476, 479–80, 487–88 (1993). For the state court decision, see State v. Mitchell, 485 N.W.2d 807, 815 (Wis. 1992).

25. 538 U.S. 343, 348, 352–57, 360–63 (2003). The state court decision is reported at 553 S.E.2d 738 (Va. 2001).

26. *R.A.V.* should be rejected not only because of its holding on hate speech, but also because of its dramatic expansion of the content discrimination doctrine. Under this doctrine, which I explored in chapter 6, the government may discriminate between different forms of expression only if it is able to meet the requirements of strict scrutiny. Prior to *R.A.V.*, the Justices applied this rule only to discrimination between different forms of constitutionally protected speech (such as the political and labor picketing at issue in *Police Department v. Mosley*, 408 U.S. 92 (1972)). In *R.A.V.*, the Court for the first time held that the rule also bars the state from drawing distinctions within *unprotected categories of speech* such as fighting words. This extension of the rule was ill-advised. The neutrality doctrine is predicated on the view that the government rarely if ever has a legitimate reason to regulate the content of speech that is protected by the First Amendment. The Court has therefore established a strong presumption against the validity of such regulation—a presumption that can be overcome only by a convincing demonstration that a particular regulation is necessary to achieve a compelling government interest. By contrast, the state generally does have authority to regulate speech that is unprotected by the First Amendment. For this reason, courts should uphold distinctions within unprotected categories of speech so long as the legislature has a substantial basis for drawing those distinctions. In *R.A.V.*, for example, it clearly would be reasonable for the St. Paul City Council to believe that insults based on group hatred cause greater harm to the targets and the community than other types of fighting words. Under these circumstances, a court should not substitute its judgment for that of the legislative body. For a more extensive critique of *R.A.V.*, see Steven J. Heyman, *Spheres of Autonomy: Reforming the Content Neutrality Doctrine in First Amendment Jurisprudence*, 10 Wm. & Mary Bill Rts. J. 647, 689–98, 710–14 (2002). For other explorations of the case, see Shiffrin, *supra* note 23, ch. III; Akhil Reed Amar, *The Case of the Missing Amendments:* R.A.V. v. City of St. Paul, 106 Harv. L. Rev. 124 (1992); Heidi Kitrosser, *Containing Unprotected Speech*, 57 Fla. L. Rev. 843 (2005); Cass R. Sunstein, *Words, Conduct, Caste*, 60 U. Chi. L. Rev. 795, 822–29 (1993).

27. For the Skokie litigation, see Collin v. Smith, 578 F.2d 1197 (7th Cir.), *cert. denied*, 439 U.S. 916 (1978); Vill. of Skokie v. Nat'l Socialist Party of Am., 373 N.E.2d 21

(Ill. 1978). The controversy generated a rich and extensive literature. *See, e.g.,* Lee C. Bollinger, The Tolerant Society (1986); Donald Downs, Nazis in Skokie (1985); Aryeh Neier, Defending My Enemy (1979); Raphael Cohen-Almagor, *Harm Principle, Offense Principle, and the Skokie Affair,* 41 Pol. Stud. 453 (1993); Daniel A. Farber, *Civilizing Public Discourse: An Essay on Professor Bickel, Justice Harlan, and the Enduring Significance of* Cohen v. California, 1980 Duke L.J. 283.

28. *See* pp. 57–59, 73–77 (defamation); pp. 127–30 (incitement); pp. 49–51, 131–36 (threats).

29. On the right to personal dignity, see pp. 144–46. For the reasons explained in chapter 11, hate speech also violates the right of target-group members to their image. *See* pp. 188–89.

30. *See Collin,* 578 F.2d at 1207.

31. 403 U.S. 15, 21 (1971) (internal quotation marks and citation omitted).

32. Harlan acknowledges this point to some extent when he observes that restrictions on speech may be justified where "substantial privacy interests are being invaded in an essentially intolerable manner." *Id.* Although he speaks of "privacy," it seems reasonable to extend his statement to other personality rights as well, such as personal dignity and emotional well-being.

33. This idea is clear not only in the natural rights tradition, but also in the rhetoric of racism itself. A classic statement appears in the *Dred Scott* case. In holding that the descendants of African slaves could never become citizens of the United States, Chief Justice Roger Taney asserted that, at the time the Constitution was adopted, blacks were universally "regarded as beings of an inferior order, and altogether unfit to associate with the white race, either in social or political relations; and so far inferior, that they had no rights which the white man was bound to respect; and that the negro might justly and lawfully be reduced to slavery for his benefit." Scott v. Sandford, 60 U.S. (13 How.) 393, 407 (1857). Of course, during the 1930s and 1940s, the Nazis regarded Jews and other groups as subhuman. For a more recent example, see Nicholas D. Kristof, *The Face of Genocide,* N.Y. Times, Nov. 19, 2006, § 4, at 13 (reporting that Arab militiamen in Darfur (a region of Sudan) have justified the rape and extermination of black Africans by telling them, "You blacks are not human. . . . We can do anything we want to you.").

34. Thomas Hobbes, Leviathan ch. XIV, at 91–92; ch. XV, at 107 (Richard Tuck ed., Cambridge Univ. Press 1991) (1651). Although he argues in the alternative here, Hobbes's own view is that "all men are equall" by nature. *Id.* ch. XV, at 107; *see also id.* ch. XIII, at 86–87.

35. *Id.* ch. XV, at 107–08; ch. XIII, at 88.

36. See John Locke, Of the Conduct of the Understanding § 6 (1706), *in* Some Thoughts Concerning Education and Of the Conduct of the Understanding 178 (Ruth W. Grant & Nathan Tarcov eds., Hackett 1996); John Locke, Two Treatises of Government bk. II, §§ 6, 63, 91, 163 (Peter Laslett ed., Cambridge Univ. Press 1988) (1690) [hereinafter Locke, Government].

37. *See* Locke, Government, *supra* note 36, bk. II, §§ 4, 6, 100, 102, 123, 172.

38. *See* p. 8.

39. *See* John Locke, A Letter Concerning Toleration 26–27, 33, 49–50 (James Tully ed., Hackett 1983) (William Popple trans., 1689). Similar language appears in Spinoza's

classic defense of freedom of speech and thought. Spinoza maintains that the true end of government is "to enable [individuals] to develope [sic] their minds and bodies in security, and to employ their reason unshackled," and he formulates many of the basic civil libertarian objections to censorship. Benedict de Spinoza, A Theologico-Political Treatise ch. XX (R. H. M. Elwes trans., Dover 1951) (1670) (quotation on page 259). At the same time, however, he argues that the law may restrict the expression of opinions that "by their very nature nullify the [social] compact." *Id.* at 260.

40. 3 G. W. F. Hegel, Philosophy of Subjective Spirit §§ 430–39 (M. J. Petry ed. & trans., D. Reidel 1978) (1830, 1845) (quotations from § 432A); Georg Wilhelm Friedrich Hegel, Lectures on Natural Right and Political Science § 124 (J. Michael Stewart & Peter C. Hodgson trans., 1995); G. W. F. Hegel, Elements of the Philosophy of Right §§ 36, 57R (Allen W. Wood ed., H. B. Nisbet trans., Cambridge Univ. Press 1991) (1820). For a comprehensive discussion of Hegel's view, see Robert R. Williams, Hegel's Ethics of Recognition (1997). For other recent works on the concept of recognition, see Axel Honneth, Disrespect (2007); Axel Honneth, The Struggle for Recognition (Joel Anderson trans., 1996) [hereinafter Honneth, Struggle]; Paul Ricoeur, The Course of Recognition (David Pellauer trans., 2005); and the essays by Charles Taylor, Jürgen Habermas, and others in Multiculturalism (Amy Gutmann ed., 1994).

41. *Cf.* Immanuel Kant, The Metaphysics of Morals *236 (Mary Gregor trans., Cambridge Univ. Press 1991) (1797) (explaining that the most basic right and duty one has is to "assert[] one's worth as a man in relation to others," by insisting that others treat one not as a mere means but also as an end). In recent decades, this form of speech has been exemplified by the civil rights movement, the women's movement, and the gay rights movement. On the fight for recognition as a social and political struggle, see Drucilla Cornell, The Imaginary Domain: Abortion, Pornography and Sexual Harassment ch. 3 (1995); Honneth, Struggle, *supra* note 40; Multiculturalism, *supra* note 40.

42. Abrams v. United States, 250 U.S. 616, 630 (1919) (Holmes, J., dissenting).

43. *Cf.* Gitlow v. New York, 268 U.S. 652, 673 (1925) (Holmes, J., dissenting) ("If in the long run the beliefs expressed in proletarian dictatorship are destined to be accepted by the dominant forces of the community, the only meaning of free speech is that they should be given their chance and have their way.").

44. *See* Alexander M. Bickel, The Morality of Consent 70–72, 76–77 (1975).

45. Robert C. Post, Constitutional Domains 1–2, 187–88, 299, 300, 302, 330 (1995); Robert C. Post, *Community and the First Amendment,* 29 Ariz. St. L.J. 473, 481 (1997) [hereinafter Post, *Community*]. The quotation is taken from Jean Piaget, The Moral Judgment of the Child 366 (Marjorie Gabain trans., 1948).

46. Post, Constitutional Domains, *supra* note 45, at 330.

47. *Id.* at 311–12, 323–29 (emphasis added).

48. *Id.* at 304, 327 (quoting John Rawls, *Justice as Fairness: Political Not Metaphysical,* 14 Phil. & Pub. Aff. 223, 230 (1985)); *see also* Robert Post, *Equality and Autonomy in First Amendment Jurisprudence,* 95 Mich. L. Rev. 1517, 1530–32, 1534 (1997) (book review) (asserting that "the state's obligation to treat ideas as if they were equal derives from the equal respect that the state owes to speakers as participants in the process of democratic self-governance").

49. Post, Constitutional Domains, *supra* note 45, at 303.

50. *Id.* at 330.

51. In response to the argument that the law can restrict hate speech because it conflicts with equality, Post draws a distinction between formal and substantive equality. According to Post, the principle that all persons must be allowed to participate in public discourse is a "formal" one. This principle is "the fundamental precondition of the possibility of self-government" and collective self-determination. By contrast, "[t]he norm of equality violated by racist speech . . . is substantive; it reflects a particular understanding of how we ought to live. It is the kind of norm that ought to emerge from processes of public deliberation." *Id.* at 313. However effective this response may be with regard to some forms of the egalitarian argument for hate speech regulation, it does not adequately respond to the argument I am making here. This argument is not based on the notion that hate speech may lead to political decisions that violate substantive norms of equality. Instead, my claim (elaborated below) is that the duty to recognize the equality of others is inherent in the concept of public discourse itself.

52. *Id.* at 300–01. Post defends this view most fully in his essay on *Hustler Magazine v. Falwell,* 485 U.S. 46 (1988), an essay which appears in *id.* at 119–78.

53. For a similar argument, see Lawrence Lessig, *Post Constitutionalism,* 94 Mich. L. Rev. 1422, 1462–65 (1996) (reviewing Constitutional Domains).

54. Post, Constitutional Domains, *supra* note 45, at 301; *see also id.* at 144–48.

55. *Id.* at 177, 311–12, 322–23, 443 n.112, 447 n.149; Post, *Community, supra* note 45, at 483.

56. This critique of Post's theory also sheds light on another central issue considered in this book: whether the state should be allowed to regulate speech in order to protect personality rights such as privacy, reputation, personal dignity, and emotional tranquillity. As I have indicated, although Post would allow the law to protect these values in ordinary community life, he holds that, under the First Amendment, "individuals must be free within public discourse from the enforcement of all civility rules, so as to be able to advocate and to exemplify the creation of new forms of communal life in their speech." Post, Constitutional Domains, *supra* note 45, at 151.

By contrast, I have argued in this section that participants in public discourse are not exempt from the duty to respect the rights of others. This point is clearest in the case of hate speech, which disrespects others at the most fundamental level by denying them recognition as human beings and citizens. But the duty also extends to other rights of personality. Although these rights may take different forms in different societies, they are not merely conventional. Instead, at their core is the basic principle of respect for human beings. The personality rights that are accepted within a particular social order reflect that society's best understanding of what such respect requires. Because the right to free speech is founded on the same principle, speakers have no blanket privilege to infringe the dignity and autonomy of others.

It follows that personality rights should not be denied all protection within public discourse. Instead, when free speech and other rights come into conflict, we should resolve the issue by assessing the value of the competing rights. For example, as I argued in connection with *Florida Star,* the First Amendment should not permit the media to publish the name of a rape victim without her consent and before anyone has been charged with the crime, for this act constitutes a serious invasion of privacy and does little to promote the legitimate interests of the public. *See* pp. 156–58. Undoubtedly, speakers should be free (in Post's words) "to advocate" that the law should afford no protection to privacy in this situation — say, on the ground that secrecy only increases the shame associated with rape and reinforces the myths that surround it. But speakers should not be free "to exemplify" this perspective by outing rape victims against their will, in violation of rights that the society deems essential to protect their privacy and dignity.

Recognizing that free speech should not always override other values, Post introduces the notion of boundary drawing. According to Post, we mark the boundary between the sphere of public discourse and other domains at the point where our commitment to the values underlying freedom of expression gives way to "other competing commitments, such as those entailed in the dignity of the socially situated self, in the importance of group identity, or in the necessary exercise of community authority." Post, Constitutional Domains, *supra* note 45, at 174 (footnotes omitted). Thus, while Post holds that civility rules generally may not be enforced within public discourse, that is not his last word on the subject. In cases like *Florida Star,* he would not rule out the possibility of finding that the newspaper's conduct exceeded the bounds of public discourse, and that this conduct should be governed by the civility rules that apply within the realm of community. *See id.* at 174, 397 n.311.

For several reasons, however, the idea of boundary drawing does not provide an adequate solution to the problem of conflicting values. First, it seems rather odd, both semantically and conceptually, to describe the publication of information in a newspaper as being outside the domain of public discourse. This is especially true in a case like *Florida Star,* in which most of the statements contained in the article (such as the fact that a rape had been committed at a certain time and place) were undoubtedly within public discourse. Second, Post views the imposition of such boundaries as a form of "ideological regulation of speech" for the sake of other values, as opposed to the ideological "neutrality" that characterizes the realm of public discourse itself. *Id.* at 174–78. For this reason, he describes such boundary drawing as "deeply distasteful" and contends that it should be confined within narrow limits. *Id.* at 177. By contrast, I have argued that free speech and personality rights rest on the same normative foundation. On this view, we do not achieve neutrality by allowing free speech to broadly trump other rights. Instead, the proper approach is to assess the competing values in an evenhanded manner in light of their relative importance to human freedom and dignity.

Finally, however useful the concept of boundary drawing may be in protecting values like privacy, which are defined in contradistinction to the public realm, there are other areas of law in which the boundary-drawing metaphor does not seem helpful. Suppose, for example, that a prolife activist sincerely believes that abortion not only results in the murder of unborn children, but also seriously endangers women who undergo the procedure. To advocate and exemplify this view, she publicly accuses a particular doctor of causing the death of two women in his care. Under the Supreme Court's decision in *Gertz v. Robert Welch, Inc.,* 418 U.S. 323 (1974), the state may award the doctor damages for defamation if he can prove that the statement was false and was made without reasonable care. In this situation, First Amendment jurisprudence upholds the application of a civility rule to a statement that is clearly within the domain of public discourse. As I argued in chapter 5, this is the correct result. *See* pp. 75–77. In this way, decisions like *Gertz* provide support for the view that personality rights are entitled to some protection within the realm of public discourse.

57. Alexander Meiklejohn, Political Freedom 24–25 (1960).

58. *Id.* at 25, 68–70. In an illuminating intellectual biography, the historian Lance Banning attributes a similar conception to Madison. As "a *revolutionary* statesman," Banning writes, Madison was "genuinely dedicated to a special concept of how decisions should be made in a republic. He believed that a republic ultimately rests on mutual respect among its citizens and on a recognition on the part of all that they are the constituents of a community of mutually regarding equals, participators in a polity that asks them to be conscious that they are, at once, the rulers and the ruled." Lance Banning, The Sacred Fire of Liberty: James Madison and the Founding of the Federal Republic 287 (1995).

59. Jürgen Habermas, Between Facts and Norms: Contributions to a Discourse Theory of Law and Democracy 496–97 (William Rehg trans., 1996). Michael Walzer also emphasizes the relationship between recognition and citizenship. "The experience of citizenship," he writes, "requires the prior acknowledgment that everyone is a citizen — a public form of simple recognition. . . . What is necessary is that the idea of citizenship be shared among some group of people who recognize one another's title and provide some social space within which the title can be acted out." Michael Walzer, Spheres of Justice 277 (1983).

60. Habermas, *supra* note 59, at 88, 107, 110, 119, 122–23, 125–27, 409.

61. *Id.* at 147–48, 151, 409. In discussing "violence-free" relations, Habermas draws on the work of Hannah Arendt. *See id.* at 147–48. For a valuable effort to work out the implications of Habermas's views for First Amendment theory, see Lawrence Byard Solum, *Freedom of Communicative Action: A Theory of the First Amendment Freedom of Speech,* 83 Nw. U.L. Rev. 54 (1989).

62. The law-and-literature scholar James Boyd White expresses this view in eloquent terms: "To imagine people as speaking is to imagine them in some deep sense as equals, for it is to recognize that each person has her own place in the world, her own mind and her own experience, her own right to express the meanings she finds in existence, from her own perspective. It is to create a polity based upon communication across difference, committing us to the acknowledgment of the reality of the experience of others." James Boyd White, Living Speech 42 (2006). White adds that racist speech is an "especially destructive form" of discourse because it denies its targets "their inherent right to grow and develop as unique and uniquely valuable human beings. In this way racism has kinship with the language and motives of war, . . . which reduces whole nations, with all their people, . . . to objects of fear and hate." *Id.* at 209.

63. This point, which is axiomatic in the natural rights tradition, is stressed by Habermas as well. *See* Habermas, *supra* note 59, at 174, 457.

64. Virginia v. Black, 538 U.S. 343, 365 (2003); Habermas, *supra* note 59, at 496. Following Kant, Habermas holds that although the law can regulate external conduct, it cannot compel individuals to act from good motives or to hold particular attitudes. *Id.* at 83–84, 130, 499; *see* Kant, Metaphysics of Morals, *supra* note 41, at *214, *218–19, *230, *239. It follows that the "law cannot oblige its addressees to use individual rights [such as freedom of speech] in ways oriented to reaching understanding," even though it is only by using their political rights in this way that they can achieve the ends of communicative freedom. Habermas, *supra* note 59, at 130, 461.

In my view, a ban on public hate speech would not violate these strictures against coercion. Such a law would not compel individuals to hold any attitude or to act from any motive. Instead, it would simply prohibit a particular form of external conduct, namely, the act of speaking in a way that violates the rights of others. In this sense, laws against hate speech do not coerce belief any more than do laws against any other kind of wrongful speech. Insofar as hate speech laws are justified to protect the rights of others, they also should not be regarded as inconsistent with Habermas's view that democratic deliberation should involve "noncoercive communication." *Id.* at 147. On the contrary, hate speech laws promote such communication by excluding the "violence" that consists in invading the rights of others. *Id.* at 148. In this way, such laws can help us to move toward the "structures of undamaged intersubjectivity" that Habermas regards as essential for "unleash[ing] the generative force of communicative freedom." *Id.* at 148, 151.

65. *See* p. 63. This discussion lends support to an argument that many scholars have made: that hate speech tends to silence its targets and undermine their right to free expression. Because political discourse involves interaction with others, an individual cannot fully engage in such discourse unless other citizens are willing to interact with her and take her views seriously. By refusing to engage in discourse with their targets and by dissuading other citizens from doing so, hate speakers curtail the ability of target-group members to take part in democratic deliberation. Hate speech can also silence its targets by diminishing their sense of personal security and by attacking their dignity in ways that discourage them from full participation in the life of the community. These considerations suggest that hate speech regulation is justified not only to secure other rights but also to protect freedom of expression itself.

66. For the leading statement of this view, see Collin v. Smith, 578 F.2d 1197, 1206 (7th Cir.), *cert. denied,* 439 U.S. 916 (1978).

67. Similar considerations lead to the conclusion that public hate speech should not be protected because of its contribution to the pursuit of truth. As I argued in chapter 4, the search for truth requires that people recognize one another as reasonable beings who are capable of participating in a common enterprise. *See* p. 67. By denying recognition to others, hate speech tends to defeat rather than promote the search for truth.

68. International Covenant on Civil and Political Rights art. 20(2); *see also, e.g.,* International Convention on the Elimination of All Forms of Racial Discrimination art. 4 (similar provision); S. Afr. Const. 1996, § 16(2) (stating that freedom of expression does not extend to "advocacy of hatred that is based on race, ethnicity, gender or religion, and that constitutes incitement to cause harm"); Jersild v. Denmark, 19 Eur. Ct. H.R. 1 (1994) (indicating that some restrictions on racist speech are compatible with European Convention on Human Rights); R. v. Keegstra, [1990] 3 S.C.R. 697 (Can.) (upholding a ban on willful promotion of hatred against racial, ethnic, and religious groups); Holocaust Denial Case, 90 BverfGE 241 (F.R.G. 1994), *in* Donald P. Kommers, The Constitutional Jurisprudence of the Federal Republic of Germany 382 (2d ed. 1997). For an overview of the legal approaches taken by the United States and other Western democracies, see Michel Rosenfeld, *Hate Speech in Constitutional Jurisprudence: A Comparative Analysis,* 24 Cardozo L. Rev. 1523 (2003).

69. It must be acknowledged, however, that the idea of "the community" recognizing a

particular right is not a straightforward one. This is especially true in the United States, where most regulation of speech takes place on the state and local levels. When a municipality such as the Village of Skokie adopts a law restricting public hate speech, it limits rights that individuals enjoy under the Federal Constitution. For this reason, it might be argued that such a law should be upheld only if it protects a fundamental right that is recognized not merely by the state or local community but by the nation as a whole. The difficulty with this argument is that the Supreme Court has held that, in the American constitutional system, the power to protect individual rights against private actors is largely committed to the states. *See, e.g.,* United States v. Morrison, 529 U.S. 598 (2000). Thus, individuals must generally look to state and local governments for protection, not only against hate speech but also against any other form of speech or conduct by private persons that infringes their rights. It follows that the issue of whether to recognize a particular right and grant it legal protection will usually be debated and decided on the state and local levels. It would be difficult for the national community to effectively address this issue when the federal government has no general authority to decide it. Moreover, if the courts were to strike down a law that was designed to protect a right that was justified in principle, on the ground that this right was not (yet) recognized by the national community, the effect would be to freeze our constitutional development by preventing our conception of free speech and other rights from evolving in the direction that it should. For these reasons, I believe that when American courts review a state or local law, they should not reject a right that is justified in principle and that is recognized by the jurisdiction that adopted the law. At the same time, under the rights-based approach, the courts retain authority to invalidate the law if they find that it unduly interferes with a proper understanding of the First Amendment right to freedom of expression. Moreover, if Congress believes that state or local measures interfere with First Amendment rights, it can pass legislation to enforce those rights under section 5 of the Fourteenth Amendment, and in my view such legislation should play an important role in resolving the issue.

70. *See, e.g.,* Shiffrin, *supra* note 23, at 80–86.

71. *See* p. 166.

72. For a fascinating discussion of this controversy, see Robert Post, *Religion and Freedom of Speech: Portraits of Muhammad,* 14 Constellations 72 (2007).

73. *See id.* at 81.

74. Similar considerations apply to the controversy over Salman Rushdie's novel *The Satanic Verses*—a controversy which was rekindled by the British government's recent decision to grant him a knighthood. *See, e.g., Iran Assails Britain for Honoring Novelist,* N.Y. Times, June 18, 2007, at A10.

75. Courts in Denmark and France have recently rejected lawsuits claiming that it was unlawful to publish the Muhammad cartoons. *See* Jan M. Olsen, *Danish Court Rejects Suit Against Paper That Printed Prophet Cartoons,* Wash. Post, Oct. 27, 2006, at A17; *Prophet Cartoons Ruled Not Offensive,* Weekend Australian, Mar. 24, 2007, at 14.

76. *Cf.* Habermas, *supra* note 59, at 151. For this reason, scientific inquiry should also receive the broadest constitutional protection, even when it reaches conclusions that some consider derogatory. For a similar view, see Mari J. Matsuda, *Public Response to Racist Speech: Considering the Victim's Story,* in Matsuda et al., *supra* note 1, at 17, 40–41.

77. *See* p. 168.

78. See Post, Constitutional Domains, *supra* note 45, at 329.

Chapter 11. Pornography

1. Miller v. California, 413 U.S. 15 (1973); Paris Adult Theatre I v. Slaton, 413 U.S. 49, 61, 69 (1973) (internal quotation marks and citations omitted). For a sophisticated defense of the conservative view, see Harry M. Clor, Obscenity and Public Morality (1969) [hereinafter Clor, Obscenity]; Harry M. Clor, Public Morality and Liberal Society (1996) [hereinafter Clor, Liberal Society].

2. *See, e.g., Paris,* 413 U.S. at 107–13 (Brennan, J., dissenting); Ronald Dworkin, *Do We Have A Right to Pornography?, in* A Matter of Principle 335 (1985); 2 Joel Feinberg, The Moral Limits of the Criminal Law chs. 10–12 (1985); David A. J. Richards, *Free Speech and Obscenity Law: Toward a Moral Theory of the First Amendment,* 123 U. Pa. L. Rev. 45 (1974).

3. *See, e.g.,* Thomas I. Emerson, The System of Freedom of Expression 496 (1970) (arguing that exposing a person to erotic material against his wishes may cause "direct [and] immediate" emotional harm and also "constitutes an invasion of his privacy"); 2 Feinberg, *supra* note 2, at 189 (suggesting that pornography may be regulated only for "prevention of the corruption of children, protection of captive audiences from offense, and the preservation of neighborhoods from aesthetic decay"); Laurence H. Tribe, American Constitutional Law § 12–16, at 909–10 (2d ed. 1988) (stating that "obscene speech . . . is subject — as is all speech — to regulation in the interests of unwilling viewers, captive audiences, young children, and beleaguered neighborhoods") (footnotes omitted); *Paris,* 413 U.S. at 106 (Brennan, J., dissenting) (suggesting agreement with Emerson and with the "view that the state interests in protecting children and . . . unconsenting adults may stand on a different footing from the other asserted state interests").

4. *See, e.g.,* Andrea Dworkin, Pornography (1979); Catharine A. MacKinnon, Feminism Unmodified chs. 11–16 (1987); Catharine A. MacKinnon, Only Words (1993); Pornography (Catherine Itzin ed., 1992); The Price We Pay (Laura Lederer & Richard Delgado eds., 1995); Rae Langton, *Speech Acts and Unspeakable Acts,* 22 Phil. & Pub. Aff. 293 (1993).

5. *See* Model Anti-Pornography Law, *in* Andrea Dworkin, *Against the Male Flood: Censorship, Pornography, and Equality,* 8 Harv. Women's L.J. 1, 24–28 (1985). The model ordinance defines pornography as

the graphic sexually explicit subordination of women through pictures and/or words that also includes one or more of the following: (i) women are presented dehumanized as sexual objects, things, or commodities; or (ii) women are presented as sexual objects who enjoy pain or humiliation; or (iii) women are presented as sexual objects who experience sexual pleasure in being raped; or (iv) women are presented as sexual objects tied up or cut up or mutilated or bruised or physically hurt; or (v) women are presented in postures or positions of sexual submission, servility, or display; (vi) women's body parts — including but not limited to vaginas, breasts, or buttocks — are exhibited such that women are reduced to those parts; or (vii) women are presented as whores by nature; or (viii) women are presented as being penetrated by objects or animals; or (ix) women are presented in scenarios of degradation, injury, torture, shown as filthy or inferior, bleeding, bruised, or hurt in a context that makes these conditions sexual.

Id. at 25. A version of this ordinance was enacted by the Indianapolis City Council but was struck down under the First Amendment in *American Booksellers Association v. Hudnut,* 771 F.2d 323 (7th Cir. 1985), *aff'd mem.,* 475 U.S. 1001 (1986), *discussed at* pp. 195–96.

For some liberal critiques of the antipornography feminist position, see Ronald Dworkin, Freedom's Law chs. 9–10 (1996); 2 Feinberg, *supra* note 2, at 143–64. For a thoughtful exploration of the conflict between the liberal individualist approach to the First Amendment and a feminist approach that focuses on harm to groups, see Robert C. Post, Constitutional Domains ch. 3 (1995).

6. *See, e.g.,* E. R. Shipp, *A Feminist Offensive Against Exploitation,* N.Y. Times, June 10, 1984, § 4, at 2 (describing an alliance between radical feminists and conservatives that led to enactment of the Indianapolis ordinance). For criticisms of this alliance, see Nadine Strossen, Defending Pornography 77–79 (1995); Robin West, *The Feminist–Conservative Anti-Pornography Alliance and the 1986 Attorney General's Commission on Pornography Report,* 1987 Am. B. Found. Res. J. 681.

7. *See, e.g.,* Nan D. Hunter & Sylvia A. Law, Brief Amici Curiae of Feminist Anti-Censorship Taskforce et al., in Am. Booksellers Ass'n v. Hudnut, 475 U.S. 1001 (1986), *reprinted in* 21 U. Mich. J.L. Reform 69 (1987–88); Strossen, Defending Pornography, *supra* note 6; Carlin Meyer, *Sex, Sin, and Women's Liberation: Against Porn-Suppression,* 72 Tex. L. Rev. 1097 (1994). For an excellent collection of writings from all sides of the feminist debate, see Feminism and Pornography (Drucilla Cornell ed., 2000).

8. For a communitarian view, see Michael Sandel, Democracy's Discontent 89 (1996) (maintaining that "self-governing communities" should be permitted to restrict pornography to protect "the good of communal respect"). For neorepublican views, see Frank I. Michelman, *Conceptions of Democracy in American Constitutional Argument: The Case of Pornography Regulation,* 56 Tenn. L. Rev. 291, 295–96, 304 (1989) (suggesting that pornography "silences women" and that regulation may be justified to allow full participation in democratic deliberation); Cass R. Sunstein, *Pornography and the First Amendment,* 1986 Duke L.J. 589, 603 *et passim* (arguing that pornography should be unprotected because it causes serious social harm, especially to women, and because it constitutes "low-value" speech which is remote from "the central concern of the first amendment, which, broadly speaking, is effective popular control of public affairs").

9. 354 U.S. 476, 484, 485, 487 & n.20 (1957) (quoting Chaplinsky v. New Hampshire, 315 U.S. 568, 572 (1942)) (emphasis added by *Roth* omitted).

10. Hurley v. Irish-Am. Gay, Lesbian and Bisexual Group of Boston, Inc., 515 U.S. 557, 573–74 (1995); Stanley v. Georgia, 394 U.S. 557, 565 (1969); Police Dep't v. Mosley, 408 U.S. 92, 95–96 (1972).

11. That is not necessarily to say that the self-fulfillment derived from pornography has great value. Although an individual may derive pleasure from pornography, this experience does little to satisfy what may be the deepest aspect of sexual desire—the desire to enter into relations with another person. *See* p. 191. For present purposes, however, the quality of this fulfillment is beside the point. As Mill observes, freedom consists

in the right to pursue one's own good in one's own way, so long as one refrains from injuring others. John Stuart Mill, On Liberty 14 (David Spitz ed., W. W. Norton 1975) (1859). If one does injure others, however, the value of the activity is relevant to determining whether it should nevertheless be privileged under the First Amendment. *See* pp. 190–94.

12. *See, e.g.,* C. Edwin Baker, Human Liberty and Freedom of Speech 121 (1989) (suggesting that protection of unconventional forms of speech and conduct may contribute to the process of social change).

13. *See, e.g.,* Jeffrey G. Sherman, *Love Speech: The Social Utility of Pornography,* 47 Stan. L. Rev. 661 (1995). Some scholars have argued, more broadly, that pornography may be understood as a genre that attempts to express "the truth of 'sex.'" Linda Williams, Hard Core 267, 276 (expanded paperback ed. 1999). For example, film studies professor Linda Williams maintains that "cinematic hard core can be read as a theoretical speculation on and analysis of the mythically concrete pleasures that it purports to display so directly and naturally." *Id.* at 275. In my view, this statement confuses pornography with the scholarly study of pornography: although the latter may involve a theoretical exploration of the cultural meaning of sex and gender, the former is a practical form of expression that is directed toward the stimulation of sexual desire. *Cf. id.* at 29–30 (defining film pornography as a "representation of living, moving bodies engaged in explicit . . . sexual acts with a primary intent of arousing viewers"). For this reason, I do not believe that most pornography should be regarded as making a serious contribution to society's search for truth about sexuality. Nevertheless, some works of pornography may have serious value in this regard. For a discussion of how such works should be treated under the First Amendment, see pp. 192–94.

14. *See* pp. 170–72.

15. *See, e.g.,* MacKinnon, Feminism Unmodified, *supra* note 4, at 158–61 (discussing the ways in which pornography dehumanizes women); Dworkin, *Against the Male Flood, supra* note 5, at 15–16 (same).

16. The MacKinnon–Dworkin ordinance can reasonably be interpreted in this way. That is especially true of the provision that defines pornography to include material that simply shows women in "postures . . . of sexual . . . display." *See supra* note 5.

17. Some of the arguments I make in this chapter also have a bearing on the category of nonviolent but degrading pornography. For discussions of this category, see Butler v. R., [1992] 1 S.C.R. 452, 484–85 (Can.); 1 The Attorney General's Commission on Pornography, Final Report 329–35 (1986) [hereinafter AG Report]. However, this category is more controversial and more difficult to define than is violent pornography. *See, e.g.,* West, *supra* note 6, at 705–06 (criticizing the way this category is defined in the AG Report). For purposes of clarity, my discussion will focus on violent pornography.

18. *See* United States v. Alkhabaz, 104 F.3d 1492 (6th Cir. 1997).

19. *See, e.g.,* MacKinnon, Only Words, *supra* note 4, at 3–5, 10–12, 15.

20. A deeper understanding of the problem of pornography can be derived from Hegel's account of the development of self-consciousness. *See, e.g.,* 3 G. W. F. Hegel, Philosophy of Subjective Spirit §§ 424–37 (M. J. Petry ed., 1978). For Hegel, this development begins with desire. The subject asserts himself in relation to external objects by possessing and consuming them and thereby making them his own. *See id.* §§ 427–28.

Thus, desire "is generally *destructive* in its satisfaction, just as it is generally *self-seeking* in respect of its content." *Id.* § 428. When the subject encounters another self, he finds his own selfhood threatened. *See id.* § 430. This leads to a struggle for recognition, which can be overcome only through mutual recognition. *See id.* §§ 431–36.

This account throws considerable light on the phenomenon of pornography as well as on that of hate speech. As we saw in chapter 10, hate speech corresponds to the stage in which the subject, threatened by the selfhood of others, denies them recognition and seeks to annihilate them. *See* p. 172. Pornography, on the other hand, corresponds to the stage of desire: it represents those it portrays as objects for the satisfaction of the viewer's sexual desires, that is, as sex objects. As I have suggested, to represent someone as a sex object is not necessarily to view her solely in this light. But violent pornography represents others solely as objects to be consumed and even destroyed. In this way, it denies them recognition as human beings.

21. *See* p. 68.

22. *See* pp. 58–59.

23. The following view of personality as a unity of the general and the particular is drawn in part from Hegel's account of the will. *See* G. W. F. Hegel, Elements of the Philosophy of Right §§ 5–7 (Allen W. Wood ed., H. B. Nisbet trans., 1991) (1820) [hereinafter Hegel, Philosophy of Right].

24. On the multifaceted nature of individual identity, see Amartya Sen, Identity and Violence (2006).

25. Again, this wrong can be understood in two somewhat different ways. One is to say that violent pornography infringes the right of each individual woman to her own image — an image that includes, as one of its constituent elements, the image of women in general. Alternatively, we can say that because the specific right at issue — the right to that part of one's image that constitutes the image of women in general — is one that is held in common by all members of the group, the right is best understood as a group right, that is, as a right that is held by the group itself. (For some theorists who take this view of collective rights, see Joseph Raz, The Morality of Freedom 207–09 (1986); Denise Réaume, *Individuals, Groups, and Rights to Public Goods,* 38 U. Toronto L.J. 1 (1988); Jeremy Waldron, *Can Communal Goods Be Human Rights?, in* Liberal Rights (1993); for a critique of this view, see James Morauta, *Rights and Participatory Goods,* 22 Oxford J. Legal Stud. 91 (2002).) The first formulation is more consistent with an individualist view, the second with a view that focuses on group identity. Whichever formulation one prefers, the basic point is the same — violent pornography portrays women in a way that is inconsistent with human dignity and in this way violates their right to their image.

26. *See, e.g.,* Drucilla Cornell, The Imaginary Domain: Abortion, Pornography and Sexual Harassment 103–05, 147–58 (1995). Although Cornell would generally protect pornography, she would allow the state to restrict public display on the ground that forced viewing of pornography assaults one's self-respect by showing one's gender as an "object of violation" that is "unworthy of personhood." *Id.* at 147–49.

27. *See, e.g.,* MacKinnon, Feminism Unmodified, *supra* note 4, at 184–89.

28. *See, e.g.,* Michelle Chernikoff Anderson, *Speaking Freely About Reducing Violence Against Women: A Harm Reduction Strategy from the Law and Social Science of Por-*

nography, 10 U. Fla. J.L. & Pub. Pol'y 173, 187 (1998) (citing studies suggesting that "nonviolent and nondegrading sexually explicit materials appear unrelated to violence against women").

29. Edward Donnerstein et al., The Question of Pornography xi (1987). As the authors explain, "[T]here are good theoretical reasons to assume that exposure to violent pornography will increase aggression against women," and "the research has borne out these assumptions." *Id.* They summarize these reasons as follows: "First, the antisocial effects — for example, the imitation of aggressive behavior and desensitization to violence — that researchers have found for individuals who observe mass media violence on television are expected to occur when this violence is presented within a sexual context. But aggressive pornography may be more potent than televised violence because it pairs both sex and violence. Coupling of sex and aggression in violent pornography may result in a conditioning process. Aggressive acts become associated with sexual acts in the viewers' minds. The result of this conditioning process would be that viewers become sexually aroused by violence. Several researchers already believe that this conditioning process is responsible for rapist behavior." *Id.* at 92 (citing several works by Neil Malamuth and others). In addition, frequent exposure to violent pornography may increase male viewers' acceptance of "the myth that women enjoy rape," and encourage men to believe that they will not be caught if they commit rape. *Id.* (citations omitted). For some summaries of the research that tends to support these hypotheses, see *id.* at 91–107; Anderson, *supra* note 28, at 183–91; Diana E. H. Russell, *Pornography and Rape: A Causal Model, in* Feminism and Pornography, *supra* note 7, at 48. As Donnerstein et al. make clear, the negative effects of depictions of sexual violence are not limited to violent pornography, but also result from materials that are violent but not sexually explicit, such as "slasher" movies. *See* Donnerstein et al., *supra,* at 108–36.

30. In particular, researchers do not yet "know if repeated exposure to violent pornography has a cumulative effect in producing aggression, or if such effects are only temporary." Donnerstein et al., *supra* note 29, at 100. Even more important, while many studies have found that male subjects who are exposed to violent pornography show increased levels of aggression in laboratory settings, it is controversial whether the same holds true in the real world. *See id.* at 174.

31. *See* pp. 49–50. In the liberal tradition, this sense of security is essential to liberty. As Montesquieu puts it, "Political liberty in a citizen is that tranquillity of spirit which comes from the opinion that each one has of his security, and in order for him to have this liberty the government must be such that one citizen cannot fear another citizen." Montesquieu, The Spirit of the Laws pt. 2, bk. 11, ch. 6, at 157 (Anne M. Cohler et al. trans. & eds., Cambridge Univ. Press 1989) (1748).

32. I am grateful to Susan Williams for suggesting this line of argument.

33. *See* pp. 171–72 (discussing Hobbes and Locke).

34. The quotations are taken from John Locke, Two Treatises of Government bk. II, § 6 (Peter Laslett ed., Cambridge Univ. Press 1988) (1690) [hereinafter Locke, Government].

35. *See* p. 186.

36. *See* pp. 70–71.

37. *See* p. 189.

38. Mill, *supra* note 11, at 60.

39. *See* p. 63.

40. The concept of relational rights also allows one to respond to another argument for protecting violent pornography. As we have seen, one reason for holding that pornography generally falls within the fundamental right to free expression is that it influences the society and its culture. *See* p. 186. But the right to participate in and contribute to the culture is a relational right, which must be exercised with due regard for the rights of other citizens. *See* p. 64. Because violent pornography infringes those rights, it has no general claim to protection on this ground.

41. *See, e.g.,* MacKinnon, Feminism Unmodified, *supra* note 4, at 176 (construing the model ordinance in a similar way).

42. *See* Clor, Obscenity, *supra* note 1, at 231–32, 236–38.

43. MacKinnon takes a similar position based on the overriding importance of equality. *See* MacKinnon, Feminism Unmodified, *supra* note 4, at 152–53 ("[I]f a woman is subjected, why should it matter that the work has other value?").

44. *See* pp. 67, 279 n.67. For a fuller discussion, see Steven J. Heyman, *Hate Speech and the Theory of Free Expression, in* Hate Speech and the Constitution lxii–lxiii (Steven J. Heyman ed., 1996).

45. *See* Mill, *supra* note 11, at 34–44.

46. *See* Cornell, *supra* note 26, ch. 3.

47. [1992] 1 S.C.R. 452, 478–83, 484–85, 488–89, 492–501, 505–06, 509 (Can).

48. Miller v. California, 413 U.S. 15 (1973); Paris Adult Theatre I v. Slaton, 413 U.S. 49 (1973).

49. 771 F.2d 323, 329 (7th Cir. 1985), *aff'd mem.,* 475 U.S. 1001 (1986) (quoting Indianapolis Code § 16–1(a)(2)).

50. *Id.* at 327–30.

51. *Id.* at 324, 328, 329 & n.2, 332.

52. *See* chapter 6.

53. *See* pp. 45–46.

54. In addition to raising substantial vagueness problems, *see* Am. Booksellers Ass'n v. Hudnut, 598 F. Supp. 1316, 1337–39 (S.D. Ind. 1984), the ordinance made no exception for works of serious value and thus might well have extended to material that should be constitutionally protected both under the traditional doctrine and under the rights-based approach.

55. Indeed, many civil libertarians doubt whether it is possible to regulate pornography in a way that does not violate the vagueness and overbreadth doctrines. *See, e.g.,* Paris Adult Theatre I v. Slaton, 413 U.S. 49, 84 (1973) (Brennan, J., dissenting); Nadine Strossen, *A Feminist Critique of "The" Feminist Critique of Pornography,* 79 Va. L. Rev. 1099, 1103–04 (1993).

56. 413 U.S. 15, 24 (1973) (internal quotation marks and citations omitted).

57. A law of this sort should not be struck down under the doctrine of *R.A.V. v. City of St. Paul,* 505 U.S. 377 (1992). Although *R.A.V.* held that the state is generally not allowed to ban a subset of an unprotected category of speech, Justice Scalia recognized that selective regulation is permissible "[w]hen the basis for the content discrimination consists entirely of the very reason the entire class of speech at issue is proscribable." *Id.* at 388. For example, "[a] State might choose to prohibit only that obscenity which is the

most patently offensive in its *prurience.*" *Id.* Similarly, it would seem that a state could reasonably decide to prohibit only obscenity that depicts sexual violence, on the ground that, in contemporary society, such portrayals are the most patently offensive to community standards. *Cf.* Virginia v. Black, 538 U.S. 343, 363 (2003) (upholding a ban on cross burning with the intent to intimidate others on the ground that such conduct is "a particularly virulent form of intimidation"). For criticism of the *R.A.V.* doctrine, see p. 273 n.26.

58. *See, e.g.,* MacKinnon, Feminism Unmodified, *supra* note 4, at 147 (insisting that the traditional concept of obscenity and the feminist concept of pornography "represent two entirely different things"). By contrast, it was by reinterpreting a traditional anti-obscenity law to focus on harm to women that the Canadian Supreme Court was able to reach the result that it did in *Butler.*

Although my argument has focused on the impact that violent pornography has on women's rights, the argument is not necessarily limited to those rights. Thus, if there are genres of violent pornography that deny recognition to men or other groups of people (or that violate their rights in other ways), such material should be regarded as wrongful for the same reasons.

59. R. v. Hicklin, 3 L.R.Q.B. 360, 371 (1868) (judgment of Cockburn, J.); *see also Paris,* 413 U.S. at 63 (holding that states may ban obscenity on the ground that it has "a tendency to exert a corrupting and debasing impact leading to antisocial behavior").

60. *See* p. 185.

61. John Locke, A Letter Concerning Toleration 49 (James Tully ed., Hackett 1983) (William Popple trans., 1689).

62. *See* pp. 40–41, 50–51; Hegel, Philosophy of Right, *supra* note 23, §§ 95, 98–99, 218.

63. *See* p. 86.

64. I should stress that, in saying this, I do not mean to imply that a bright line can be drawn between the public and private realms. The difficulty is not merely a practical one, but inheres in the very notions of public and private. The community is composed of individuals, and their interests make up the common good. As I explained in chapter 4, an important function of public discourse is to bring the concerns of individuals and groups to the attention of the community at large and to thereby transform matters once regarded as private (such as domestic violence or workplace safety) into matters of public concern. *See* p. 66. Indeed, even the most personal matters can be made into subjects of common interest, especially through art and literature. *See* Clor, Obscenity, *supra* note 1, at 230. For this to take place, however, the individual must transform her thoughts, feelings, and experiences into a form that is not purely personal, but that is understandable by and of interest to others.

65. 394 U.S. 557, 564–65 (1969). Of course, this right should not apply if the possession or use of the material would itself cause or perpetuate wrongful injury to another, as the Court has held in the context of child pornography. *See* Osborne v. Ohio, 495 U.S. 103, 108–11 (1990).

66. *See supra* note 3 (citing views of Emerson and Justice Brennan to this effect).

67. *See, e.g.,* Robinson v. Jacksonville Shipyards, Inc., 760 F. Supp. 1486 (M.D. Fla. 1991).

68. Hill v. Colorado, 530 U.S. 703, 716 (2000). For a discussion of *Hill,* see pp. 149–54.

69. 403 U.S. 15, 21 (1971) (internal quotation marks and citation omitted).

70. To be sure, individuals can sometimes avoid such material by averting their eyes. *See* Erznoznik v. City of Jacksonville, 422 U.S. 205, 210–11 (1975). But people who are in public places should have a right to enjoy the public environment and to participate in the life of the community without being forced to avert their eyes from intensely personal materials they do not wish to see.

71. *See* p. 184.

72. *See, e.g.*, Berman v. Parker, 348 U.S. 26, 33 (1954); Alexander M. Bickel, The Morality of Consent 74 (1975).

73. *See, e.g.*, Police Dep't v. Mosley, 408 U.S. 92 (1972).

74. *Cf.* pp. 152–54 (discussing *Hill v. Colorado*).

75. *See* Mill, *supra* note 11, at 91.

76. This position is consistent with the law of a number of countries. *See, e.g.*, Eric Barendt, Freedom of Speech 387 (2d ed., paperback ed. 2007) (describing the laws of Denmark, France, Germany, and the United Kingdom).

77. *See, e.g.*, Clor, Obscenity, *supra* note 1; Clor, Liberal Society, *supra* note 1; *see also* Bickel, *supra* note 72, at 73–76 (suggesting that the law can impose some restrictions on obscenity to protect the community's "environment" and "quality of life").

78. Paris Adult Theatre I v. Slaton, 413 U.S. 49, 59–60 (1973) (internal quotation marks and citations omitted).

79. *See, e.g.*, Locke, Government, *supra* note 34, bk. II, §§ 55–67; Mill, *supra* note 11, at 11, 97.

80. Pierce v. Soc'y of Sisters, 268 U.S. 510, 534–35 (1925).

81. *See* Kevin W. Saunders, Saving Our Children from the First Amendment (2003).

82. To put the point in traditional social contract terms, although the responsibility for educating children naturally belongs to the parents, *see* Locke, Government, *supra* note 34, bk. II, § 56, it is reasonable for them to delegate some of this power to the community.

83. *See, e.g.*, Reno v. ACLU, 521 U.S. 844, 895 (1997) (O'Connor, J., concurring in judgment in part and dissenting in part).

84. *See, e.g.*, Marjorie Heins, Not in Front of the Children (2001); Catherine J. Ross, *Anything Goes: Examining the State's Interest in Protecting Children from Controversial Speech,* 53 Vand. L. Rev. 427, 501–06 (2000).

85. *See* Daniel A. Farber & Philip P. Frickey, *Practical Reason and the First Amendment,* 34 UCLA L. Rev. 1615, 1642–43 (1987).

86. 390 U.S. 629, 639–43 (1968) (internal quotation marks and citation omitted). Under the statute, material was deemed "harmful to minors" if it predominantly appealed to the prurient interest of minors, was "patently offensive to prevailing standards in the adult community as a whole with respect to what is suitable material for minors," and lacked "redeeming social importance for minors." *Id.* at 633.

87. Sable Commc'ns of Cal., Inc. v. FCC, 492 U.S. 115, 126 (1989) (citations omitted); *Reno,* 521 U.S. at 875. In recent years, several federal courts have held that when the state seeks to restrict nonsexual material (such as graphic depictions of violence) on the ground that it is harmful to children, the state must meet the requirements of strict scrutiny. *See, e.g.,* Am. Amusement Mach. Ass'n v. Kendrick, 244 F.3d 572 (7th Cir.) (Posner, J.), *cert. denied,* 534 U.S. 994 (2001); Video Software Dealers Ass'n v. Webster, 968 F.2d 684 (8th

Cir. 1992). This standard is too demanding, however, for parents and the state should have a substantial amount of authority to shield children from material that is harmful to them. *See* Saunders, *supra* note 81, at 64–66, 162–63, 257–58. It does not follow, however, that such restrictions should merely be subject to the rubber stamp of rational basis review. Instead, the most appropriate standard would be a form of intermediate scrutiny, which would uphold the restriction if the state had a substantial basis for believing that the material impaired the moral or psychological development of children.

88. *See Reno*, 521 U.S. at 887, 889 (O'Connor, J., concurring in judgment and dissenting) (citation omitted); *id.* at 856–57 (opinion of Court).

89. *See, e.g.,* Ashcroft v. ACLU, 542 U.S. 656 (2004); United States v. Playboy Entm't Group, 529 U.S. 803 (2000); *Reno*, 521 U.S. 844. In *Playboy*, the Court invalidated a provision of the Telecommunications Act of 1996 that required sexually explicit cable television channels to fully scramble or block their signals or to limit transmission to late-night hours when children were unlikely to be viewing. In *Reno* and *Ashcroft*, which I discuss below, the Court struck down congressional efforts to regulate Internet pornography.

90. *Reno*, 521 U.S. at 868.

91. *See* pp. 69–73.

92. 521 U.S. 844 (1997). For example, the statute's prohibitions were not limited to material that was "harmful to minors" under *Ginsberg v. New York, see supra* note 86, and it made no exception for material with serious value. *See Reno*, 521 U.S. at 865, 877.

93. *Ashcroft*, 542 U.S. 656; COPA, 47 U.S.C. § 231.

94. 542 U.S. at 666–70.

95. *Id.* at 677–89 (Breyer, J., dissenting). For example, the record showed that Web sites could store credit card numbers or passwords at a cost of fifteen to twenty cents per number and that verification services were available to adults for less than twenty dollars per year. *See id.* at 682.

96. After upholding the preliminary injunction, the Supreme Court remanded the *Ashcroft* case for proceedings on the merits of the constitutional question. In 2007, a federal district court declared COPA facially unconstitutional and granted a permanent injunction against its enforcement. ACLU v. Gonzales, 478 F. Supp. 2d 775 (E.D. Pa. 2007).

Conclusion

1. For the view that "the Constitution is a charter of negative rather than positive liberties," see DeShaney v. Winnebago County Dep't of Soc. Servs., 812 F.2d 298, 301 (7th Cir. 1987) (Posner, J.), *aff'd*, 489 U.S. 189 (1989). For criticisms of this view, see Susan Bandes, *The Negative Constitution: A Critique*, 88 Mich. L. Rev. 2271 (1990); Steven J. Heyman, *The First Duty of Government: Protection, Liberty and the Fourteenth Amendment*, 41 Duke L.J. 507 (1991); Aviam Soifer, *Moral Ambition, Formalism, and the "Free World" of* DeShaney, 57 Geo. Wash. L. Rev. 1513 (1989); Robin West, *Reconstructing Liberty*, 59 Tenn. L. Rev. 441 (1992).

2. *See, e.g.,* Mari J. Matsuda et al., Words That Wound: Critical Race Theory, Assaultive Speech, and the First Amendment (1993).

3. Police Dep't v. Mosley, 408 U.S. 92, 95–96 (1972).

Index

abolitionists, 21, 24, 26, 217n63
abortion, 42, 61, 103, 127; information on availability of, 140; killing of abortion providers, 116; Nuremberg Files case, 131–36; sidewalk counseling outside clinics, 4, 149–54
Abrams v. United States, 26, 44, 65, 105, 173, 220n27, 231n52
advertising, regulation of, 46, 96, 243n4, 247n8
Advocates for Life Ministries (ALM), 131
affirmative action, 188, 227–28n25
Afghanistan, war in, 154, 256n47
African Americans, 165, 166, 167, 169, 180, 181
aiding and abetting, 106, 130, 139, 263n43
Alito, Justice Samuel A., Jr., 43
American Booksellers Association v. Hudnut, 82, 93, 195, 196
American Civil Liberties Union (ACLU), 30, 132, 137, 203–04, 223n47

American Coalition of Life Activists (ACLA), 131
American Constitutional Law (Tribe), 89
American Revolution, 11, 14, 110, 111, 230n51
anarchism/anarchists, 105, 112
animal rights activists, 262n25
antidiscrimination laws. *See* civil rights
Antifederalists, 12, 15, 18, 20
Aristotle, 228n27, 248n13
Arizona State University, 272n8
Ashcroft v. ACLU, 204, 289n96
assaults, 49–50, 51, 234n13; "assaultive speech," 4, 143, 207; free speech and, 54
assembly, freedom of, 14
Atkins v. Virginia, 227n24
Austen, Jane, 241n102
autonomy, 4, 37, 43, 47, 71, 78, 149; abortion and, 152; children and, 201, 202; content neutrality doctrine and, 83, 87, 92; freedom of communication